MISGOVERNMENT

When lawful authority prevents justice and prosperity

Mark Lipse

authorHOUSE®

AuthorHouse™ UK
1663 Liberty Drive
Bloomington, IN 47403 USA
www.authorhouse.co.uk
Phone: 0800.197.4150

Published by AuthorHouse 05/16/2017

ISBN: 978-1-5246-7673-5 (sc)
ISBN: 978-1-5246-7674-2 (hc)
ISBN: 978-1-5246-7672-8 (e)

Print information available on the last page.

This book is printed on acid-free paper.

To my father, grandfather, and mother – all great storytellers.

Contents

The question of questions for the politician should ever be – "What type of social structure am I tending to produce?" But this is a question he never entertains.

—Herbert Spencer, *The Man versus the State*

Chapter 1

On Lawful Authority

The worst evils which mankind has ever had to endure were inflicted by bad governments. The state can be and has often been in the course of history the main source of mischief and disaster.

—Ludwig von Mises

At the start of the twentieth century, for the first time in history, all the essential ingredients for elevating and improving the human condition on a global scale had been invented or created. Mankind had reached a summit in the quantity and quality of its existence unparalleled in height by any preceding age. All sciences, all arts, all trades, all industries – indeed, every field of economic, social, and organizational life – had reached an elevation that ushered in, for the first time, the prospect of plenitude in every aspect and at every level of human life. As a result, it was possible to achieve universal prosperity through economic development. The twentieth century is also the age when, across the globe, promoting economic growth and development and securing the prosperity of the general population became a conscious, explicit, formal policy objective and the avowed mission of every government. Growth and prosperity became the campaign promise of every politician, the incumbent as well as the opposition, the left and the right. In assuming this responsibility, governments formally and publicly committed themselves to economic interventionism. Economic interventionism is the belief that "wise and well-directed government action can abolish poverty, prevent severe unemployment, raise the standard of living of the nation and bring

1

about rapid social development."[1] Correspondingly, governments have demanded and got the powers necessary to direct all economic activities of its citizens. Prior to the twentieth century, a generalized sense or notion of a government responsible for economic development or for the prosperity of the general population had not been part of the political consciousness for most people. In a momentous revolution of popular expectations, it was during the twentieth century that the general population learned to desire and expect governments to promote economic development and universal prosperity.

Yet at the end of that same century, six out of every seven people on earth lived in countries that were variously described as poor, backward, underdeveloped, developing, third-world, formerly communist, non-advanced, emerging, or transitional – in other words, anything but rich and advanced. After a century of economic interventionism, not even 40 out of 190 countries had achieved the status of a developed country.[2] (For the sake of ease, we will call the other 150 countries non-advanced economies.) The twentieth century was, in fact, an age of ignominy, an age when the vast majority of the countries in our world had failed to advance and develop to a level equal to the full splendour of the arts and sciences. The age of promise was left unfulfilled. As a result of this state of affairs, for almost a century, billions of people in the greater part of the world (spanning generations) continued to live in the grip of oppression, wretched poverty, and ignorance. This is the horror of grandparents being born into poverty, ignorance, and servitude and not uplifted and enlightened. These people were made to live a miserable, brief life and then pass on that wretched condition to their children (who are subjected to the same degree of desolation and made to pass on their condition virtually unchanged to their grandchildren and later generations). Today, after a century of having placed our faith in economic interventionism, nearly three billion people, almost 40 per cent of the total world population, subsists on fewer than two dollars per day. Of these three billion, almost half live on fewer than one dollar per day. Almost a billion people do not have enough to eat. One billion do not have safe water. Nearly one billion people are illiterate. If we reflect on the fact that economic development has been a core mission of governments and politics for over a century and then take note of the fact that 80 per cent of all countries, comprising 85 per cent of the world population, have failed to achieve advanced-economy status, we are faced with a vast contradiction. At face value, governments across the globe claim to have laboured to promote economic development and prosperity, yet the results speak to failure on a global scale. To make matters worse, at the current pace of development, it is now a distinct possibility that most of the other 150 countries will, in the next decades, fail to achieve advanced-economy status and the accoutrements of universal prosperity and social development. This is tantamount to a near-permanent division of the world into a minority of successful economies and a majority of second-rate economies. This is a disquieting prospect.

The historical circumstances of development in non-advanced economies

How did a globally championed political objective – economic development – fail on a global scale? There are a number of very good explanations for this failure, and the obvious ones will be addressed briefly. Part of the explanation may be that there are circumstances under which economic development and prosperity are not possible. Mass violence is one obvious condition. Note that, over the length of the twentieth century, many countries suffered long spells of war (including civil war), extreme political violence, and social and political breakdown. Think of China, Vietnam, Cambodia, Afghanistan, East Timor, Colombia, Liberia, Ethiopia, Mozambique, Angola, Uganda, and Somalia.

There were also cases where economic development for the benefit of the people – in spite of the most strenuous and sanctimonious assertions to that effect – was, in terms of fundamental objectives, not the primary mission. Twentieth-century politics was to a large extent dominated by hatred and delusion. During that century, the greater part of heartfelt thinking with respect to the mission and uses of government was invested in pursuits contrary to the advancement of the interest of the people. From the start of the First World War until the fall of the Berlin Wall, the core objective of the dominant political movements was to use government for the promotion of horrendously vicious projects such as the glorification of war and conquest, world domination, racial supremacy, totalitarianism, collectivization, class warfare, mass murder, genocide, and personality cults. One of the greatest political developments of the twentieth century, the breakup of empires and subsequent decolonization – a cause in the interest of banishing oppression and exploitation and promoting freedom and dignity – was almost completely subverted and hijacked by tyrants, collectivist ideologues, and mass murderers. Not least, in many countries the true organizing principle of the state (contrary to stated policy) was not to generate economic growth and development for the benefit of the public; rather, the organizing principle entailed exploiting and plundering economies for the benefit of political elites and their cronies. This is a case of extreme corruption and kleptocracy, the rule of thieves. The archetypes of kleptocratic states are Nigeria, Mobuto's Zaire, the Philippines under Marcos, and Suharto's Indonesia. Long spells of war, political lunacy, massive corruption, and rule by thieves have robbed many countries of decades of time to develop.

Still, it is not the case that all non-advanced economies suffered mass violence, delusional politics, or kleptocracy. There are some countries where the mission of economic development was pursued seriously. Yet the general approach to economic development itself turned out to be seriously problematic. Ideology – foremost, the many varieties of communism and socialism – played a crucial role in wrong-footing societies in their pursuit of economic development. Countries such as Russia, Romania, Egypt, India, and China come to mind. For the greater part of the twentieth century, in a large part of the world, collectivist ideology or statist economics drove capitalism (free enterprise and free market economics) from the stage as the premier strategy for economic development. From the end of the nineteenth century onward, intellectuals across the globe for a period spanning a century adopted socialism as their dominant ideology. As a matter of fact, the most striking distinction with advanced economies is the degree to which, and the length of time over which, collectivist ideology and economics prevailed in non-advanced economies. Starting with the Bolshevik Revolution, virtually every non-advanced economy fell under the sway of some type of socialism and communism for one or more generations.

It is beyond the scope of this book to explain the nature of collectivist economics and what is so terribly wrong with it. Suffice to say, over the long run, collectivist economics has proven to be a failure. Never before has any system been so zealously and enthusiastically promoted as the high road to social and economic salvation and universal prosperity. In the end, it proved to be the worst possible system for achieving economic development and universal prosperity. It has distorted, retarded, or stopped – and in a number of instances even reversed – economic and social progress and development in many parts of the world. A coercive, tyrannical implementation of communist and socialist economic models almost invariably inflicted extreme suffering on large portions of the subject populations (including famine, starvation, and murder) on a massive scale in countries such as the Soviet Union, China, and Cambodia. Even a partial and less-than-brutal imposition of socialism was usually enough to stop development and growth as evinced by the infamous Hindu rate of growth of India from the 1950s to the 1980s. Notably, in the poorest, least-developed countries – especially in Africa – collectivist economics was actually transformed into a vehicle for enriching kleptocrats while serving to legitimize their rule. Socialist and communist economies within a few decades became moribund and then imploded over the course of the 1970s and1980s. In terms of immediate causes, collectivist economics is probably the single most important reason why six out of seven people find themselves living in non-advanced economies.

Economic liberalization and disillusion

This state of affairs ended with the onset of the Latin American debt crisis and, following that, the demise of the Soviet system. The aftermath brought the retreat of dictatorship, the end of ideological conflict, the discredit of collectivist economics, and the rise of democracy and market economics. The end of the Cold War decreased the level of war and political violence across the globe. The embarrassment of collectivist economics and totalitarianism was massive economic failure and unspeakable misery across the greater part of the world. Democracy and a retreat by government from collectivist economics were being actively promoted around the globe as the way to a better future.

From the 1980s onward, governments across the globe adopted a new, recognizably liberal template for economic reform that promoted growth and prosperity. State-sponsored economic development has been transformed; its markers became balanced budgets, free prices, free trade, foreign investment, stable currencies, deregulation, and institution building. The deal was that these prescriptions would set reforming countries – after an initial stage of pain and sacrifice endured by the public on account of economic retrenchment or dislocation – on the road to economic recovery and durable, prosperity-generating growth. Yet in view of the initial suffering caused by these reforms, the results proved bitterly disappointing. Although some of the economic fundamentals of the reforming countries are improved, in most countries, strong, stable, durable growth did not materialize. Whatever progress and growth was achieved proved anaemic and haphazard, and the benefits were distributed unevenly, often leaving out large portions of the populace. The question of faltering growth and the uneven distribution of its benefits is a real worry. Another way of demonstrating this is to note that, over the past three decades, not a single developing nation has managed to join the ranks of the rich world, which includes countries that have faithfully applied these recipes. In effect, the example and success of the four Asian Tigers (Hong Kong, Singapore, South Korea, and Taiwan) during the 1970s and 1980s has not been replicated in the two decades following the fall of the Berlin Wall. Worryingly, it does not seem as if this situation is about to change significantly in the next few decades. Except for two or three countries (China, Chile, and Malaysia, perhaps), it is unlikely that any other non-advanced economy will be joining the ranks of the advanced economies over the coming decades. Rapid and sustained economic growth is critical to transforming the fortunes of developing nations for the better. To achieve rich-country levels of development, we must see consistent annual growth rates averaging 7 per cent or more, sustained over at least three or four decades. Observe that, in most developing countries, this is not happening. Whereas a lower rate of growth will result in a measure of growth and progress, it is at best beneficial to only a portion of the population, and it is characterized by rising inequality and the exclusion of the rest of the population from the blessings of growth and development. People in many non-advanced economies sense this. They sense that they or their children will again be missing out on Western-style prosperity over the next few decades, and this fact causes despair and rage. Therefore, a profound sense of malaise, uneasiness, frustration, and disappointment sets in. Apparently, abandoning collectivist economics, decline in the number of dictatorships, advancing democracy, freeing trade, freeing prices, taming inflation, balancing budgets, allowing foreign investment, and stabilizing currencies are not sufficient in themselves for the advancement of the nations.

The twentieth century was the age when governments across the globe formally and publicly committed themselves to economic development and promoting universal prosperity through government interventionism. Interventionism presupposes wise and well-directed government action.

Yet observe that the twentieth century was also an age of massive, constant *misgovernment*. This massive and persistent misgovernment is one of the common denominators shared by virtually all non-advanced economies. Misgovernment has been the constant accompanying every ill of the twentieth century, including collectivist economics, dictatorship, and kleptocracy. One could have supposed that the demise of collectivism and dictatorship – and the decrease in the number of blatantly kleptocratic regimes and broad economic reform – would fit together with an increased sense of good governance. Yet a generalized sense of being badly misgoverned appears to persist in spite of the abandonment of these evils and the introduction of economic and political reforms. Governments today continue to claim responsibility for promoting economic development, stability, and prosperity. In the past three decades, however, governments have continued to exhibit an inability to head off financial crises and crashes and episodes of wholesale devastation of people's standards of living. The perennial problems of high unemployment, weak growth, and uneven distribution of development, income, and wealth appear intractable. Until recently, these problems were associated largely with poor governance due to collectivism, dictatorship, and kleptocracy. Observe that the cause of democracy and market economics is now suffering from the acute embarrassment that blatant, chronic, and systemic misgovernment have not been banished; many countries continue to face extreme corruption, bloated bureaucracy, overregulation, grossly mismanaged public finances, inflation, depreciating currencies, and a lack of progress on the rule of law. For democracy and market economics, this is very nearly an acute loss of innocence!

Misgovernment on a day-to-day level

If problems persist, either the underlying causes are unreformed or the reforms are inadequate or inappropriate. Clearly, the current set of reforms is leaving the condition of many people unimproved. This situation is bad for the morale of the people. This becomes clear when we start listening to ordinary people and what they are still complaining about. At this level, we sense continuity, not change. Observe that people are still frustrated and angered by aloof, corrupt, dishonest, and incompetent rulers. Businesspeople and economists chafe at many of the same issues (and obstructive bureaucracy and flawed economic policies). The failures on the front of social policies continue to dismay and engage humanitarians. Observe that all these complaints are about how *day-to-day* government operates. Corruption, red tape, flawed economic policies, and failing social policies – in other words, the way day-to-day government operates – can and do destroy the prospects for economic growth. It is at the level of day-to-day government that we can see an abundance of evidence showing that governments continue to apply their powers in ways that we can only describe as chronic, systemic *misgovernment*. Observe also that the day-to-day operations of government have proven to be virtually impervious to reform. Corruption and red tape seem virtually ineradicable. Governments persist in repeating the same flawed, destructive policies over and over again. Virtually without exception, obstructive, remote, wasteful bureaucracies survive every major crisis without meaningful reform. Growth-stopping regulatory regimes consistently resist thorough reform even in times of deep crisis. The many economic crises from Latin America to the Greek financial crisis do not appear to inspire a yearning for fundamental change in the way legal and administrative systems are structured and how these operate. Today, broadly speaking, not war, not ideological experiment, not imperialism, not rule by thieves, but misgovernment in its day-to-day operations is the single most important obstacle to development. In looking at this question, we are referring to the situation of countries mostly at peace, by and large reconciled with mainstream conceptions about free-market economics and having evolved beyond the most blatant manifestations of kleptocracy. In other words, to explain disappointing development, we are looking not at catastrophic failure – namely, war, extreme political violence, social collapse, and outright thuggery. For the majority of the nations, this is not the main issue anymore. Disappointing development is now mainly the result of a humdrum kind of misgovernment, the sort that is symptomatically manifest as bureaucracy, overregulation, inflation, corruption, and weak public finances. The question therefore is what is making misgovernment at the day-to-day level possible.

Manifestations of misgovernment

When we look at the manifestations of misgovernment, we are confronted by facts that are overwhelmingly clear in their significance. Let us for example name, item by item, the symptoms of economic weakness, malaise, or crisis: inflation, currency crises, banking crises, debt default, stagnating economic growth, unemployment, and massive informal sector activity. Observe that each symptom mentioned represents evidence of economic mismanagement *by government*: uncontrolled printing of money (monetary policy); overspending; runaway budget deficits and overborrowing (fiscal policy); bloated, wasteful, inaccessible, corrupt bureaucracy (public administration); and excessive business regulation (microeconomic policy). All of these ills are the consequence of government in action or *policymaking*. Observe that these *policy* powers essentially stand for political and administrative control of economic activity *through government*. In other words, misgovernment or economic mismanagement is, to put it in mathematical terms, a function of political and administrative authority and action. Policymaking, pure and simple, is the primary source of crisis, economic weakness, social deprivation, and underdevelopment. Note also that these policy powers flow from mandates to practise economic intervention. As noted earlier, economic interventionism stands for the belief in wise and well-directed government action. Yet the manifestations of misgovernment point to *imprudent and harmful* government action. Let us stop underrating the importance of government policy failure. Government policies that end in debt defaults, banking crises, and inflation impoverish very large groups overnight. Government policies that throttle growth and cause massive unemployment, make the urban poor view life as hopeless, which makes them desperate and wild and prone to riot and inclined to follow demagogues.

What does this mean? To understand certain forms of misgovernment, we may have to examine government as a system of power and mandates for action. One angle in our attempt to grasp the problem of misgovernment is to look at how governments apply this system of power to these mandates. Promoting economic growth and development is an explicit, formal policy objective of every government. Governments everywhere have claimed or been granted the powers necessary to direct all economic activities of its citizens. As a rule, we can say that governments across the globe have enormous powers and exercise them in a very wide range of functions. They regulate, direct, or control on various levels all sorts of economic activities. Formal recognition of property rights and the protection of property and contracts and formal approval for the establishment of a business (or for its operation) are, in effect, government services. Governments have unbridled tax-and-spend powers, can raise vast amounts of money through taxation, and control the supply of money and credit. Governments regulate employment practices, prices, and wages; they also regulate many business processes and practices. Undeniably, modern governments have powers of a magnitude that can make or break an economy. Governments can start and promote – but also stop – economic growth and development. This is not to say that the latter is necessarily the declared goal of any government, but that is the kind of power it possesses. Shouldn't this kind of power be examined?

Misgovernment is government

The examination of the dynamics of misgovernment requires special appreciation of a basic fact: misgovernment is fundamentally a form of government rule. It is government rule in the sense of policymakers *applying and exercising the art of government* (i.e., the political, legal, and administrative instruments, practices, techniques, and strategies by means of which rulers exercise power over people). It may not be government rule for the benefit of the citizenry, but it is unmistakably and in every respect government rule. Crucially, misgovernment cannot occur unless some form and degree of a *functioning* government exists. A functioning government in this sense entails a government able to perform its regular functions. Overregulation, overborrowing, and government-induced inflation (as forms of misgovernment) of necessity require the existence of a functioning government. Note that failed states – where a functioning government ceases to exist as happened in Somalia and Liberia – do not suffer from any of these ills. Misgovernment requires many of the instruments, structures, practices, and techniques of a functioning government; it requires policymaking by heads of state, ministers, senior bureaucrats, and legislators. The resulting policies are then implemented by a state with a functioning bureaucracy, including the civil service, central bank, or state enterprises. This implies some form of capability for *effective* government action. It is precisely the *effectiveness* with which government policies are implemented that makes possible overborrowing, debt default, overregulation, government-induced inflation, and banking crises, for example. Effectiveness in this sense should not be conflated with achieving socially desirable outcomes in accordance with commonly accepted or popular expectations, such as economic growth, increased prosperity, and improved public health. The meaning of *effectiveness* in this context should be narrowed down in the most literal sense, with no reference to the desirability of the outcome, to the *capability,* or to the ability of government to execute and enforce its policies. In other words, it is able to put into effect its will (i.e., impose policies of its choosing and, if necessary, to ignore and overcome resistance to such policies). Misgovernment requires the paraphernalia of effective government rule. The same structures, considerations, and concepts that underpin government rule also underpin misgovernment. The value of understanding that misgovernment is a form of government rule lies in a clear realization that misgovernment requires a functioning government and that a functioning government is not necessarily the same as good government. In short, a functioning government may well be instrumental in producing public ills.³

The point of this book is to explain the causes of misgovernment at the level of government systems and in terms of the structural issues with these systems. Put differently, the object of study is government at the level of law, administrative institutions, jurisdiction, authority, power, and policymaking.

Predatory jurisdiction

We are therefore confronted by a vast contradiction: the powers demanded for the pursuit of policies deemed necessary for economic interventionism (i.e., to promote economic growth and development) are the same ones as those that cause misgovernment or economic mismanagement. To explore one example, the power to pursue monetary policies is fundamentally the same as the one that causes monetary inflation. As we become conscious of the dangers of the powers of government, this awareness should cause us to ask ourselves: *By what right does government possess these powers?* Think about it: even though the application of these powers has frequently been the cause of a great deal of misery, we continue to consider it – almost without giving it any thought – normal or natural that governments possess these powers. What is more, to the extent that we are knowledgeable or aware of these things, we persist in believing that it is right that government should have these powers unchanged and unexamined. How must we understand and resolve this paradox?

What we first need is a conceptual framework for understanding the place of these powers in government. A crucial concept for understanding government powers is *jurisdiction.* One definition of *government* is the jurisdiction exercised over the people.[4] Jurisdiction in turn can be defined as the lawful right to exercise authority, whether executive, legislative, or judicial (or those things over which such authority may be exercised).[5] In short, policymaking and economic intervention generally presuppose jurisdiction. Jurisdiction is the appropriate concept for defining the powers that sanction policymaking and, therefore, misgovernment. It should be noted that the concept of jurisdiction makes sense only to the extent that government action has been subjected to formal and explicit rules and laws. Jurisdiction is the expression used by the legal profession, the judiciary, *and* governments for substantiating *valid* authority for government policy or action. As an expression of valid authority, the term *jurisdiction* denotes not only the powers that may be exercised, but also the bounds and limits within which government action is legal. We can now frame the matter of the dangers of the powers of government in terms of how jurisdiction relates to the problem of misgovernment.

Before going on to explore the relevance of the concept of jurisdiction as it relates to the issue of misgovernment, let us briefly visit the current views on misgovernment. The commonplace or classic perception of misgovernment is to view it as a manifestation of *bad politics* and *maladministration*. With respect to bad politics, we usually think of corruption, patronage, cronyism, favouritism, rent seeking, abuse of power, oppression, exploitation, political exclusion, political pandering, vote buying, fraud, theft, dishonest politics, and irresponsible power politics. We get bad politics when people perceive and exploit government power as a means to private gain. Bad politics symptomizes an absence of public spiritedness in government and politics: people seek power not for the good of the community, but for their own, narrow, mean-spirited personal benefit. In bad politics, government power is not intended to promote the public welfare. It is a means for extracting wealth or seeking personal glory – if necessary, by misleading, defrauding, manipulating, exploiting, or oppressing the people.

With regard to maladministration, we usually think in terms of poor management, failing leadership, and inadequate organization. It includes such ills as incompetence at various levels, lack of skills and know-how, wastefulness, flawed policy design, erratic policymaking, and absent and weak institutions. Maladministration usually occurs when the state lacks a cadre of skilled, competent rulers, managers, and public employees (and well-established institutions), or when skill, know-how, and organization are not valued. The first cause is frequently a mark of underdevelopment. This condition used to be an affliction common to many former colonies. This can only be solved, over time, by investment in education and institution building. The second cause, however, is the result of the same absence of public spiritedness referred to earlier. In fact, maladministration is frequently closely tied to the problem of bad politics.

These factors certainly explain a great deal of misgovernment; it is also an incomplete explanation of misgovernment. It is, as it were, a two-dimensional view of the causes of misgovernment, with bad politics and maladministration representing the two dimensions. Still, we can view the problem of misgovernment from a three-dimensional perspective. This is the point at which we should take note of jurisdiction as a factor relevant to the problem of misgovernment (i.e., the third dimension). What is never considered is the extent to which misgovernment could equally be the end product of jurisdiction (i.e., the lawful right to exercise authority). What we are referring to here are "commonplace" government powers, such as the power to regulate business, fiscal powers, and monetary powers. Ask yourself these questions: Why do we not consciously grasp excessive regulation, wasteful bureaucracy, inflation, excessive tax burden, and runaway budget deficits as the consequence of "lawfully exercised authority"? Why do we not conceive of or experience jurisdiction itself as a *source* of abuse? Please understand this well: the object of study is not abuse as the outcome of violating the limits of legal powers or authority (i.e., governments or rulers breaking laws or breaching constitutional, legal, or administrative procedures); instead, the object of study is the perfectly legal act of government itself causing injury to the interests of the public.

It is within the legal powers and authority of the executive branch to budget runaway deficits and parliaments to approve such budgets. Governments have the legal authority to borrow more money than they could ever repay. There are no limits to the number of rules and regulations a government could legally impose on trade and industry, and the courts can, will, and do enforce them. This is all within the scope of government jurisdiction, and if the result is disaster, the making of it was not less legal because of the result. In conclusion, this "lawful right to exercise authority" might be the sanction that hallows a form of abusive power over citizens. Let us call this form of lawful authority *predatory jurisdiction*. The choice of the term *predatory* reflects the degree to which lawful authority is amenable to evil, unfair, and unwise uses. It is introduced to enable us to mark off any scope of lawful authority that sanctions harmful government action from lawful authority that sanctions beneficial government action. The concept of predatory jurisdiction introduces a third dimension to the problem of misgovernment. Bringing the role of jurisdiction within the scope of our conception of misgovernment allows us to understand problems that cannot be resolved by limiting the explanation of misgovernment to bad politics and maladministration. Indeed, the introduction of the concept of predatory jurisdiction makes possible a more sophisticated view of the way governments operate and how they injure the public interest.

Since the last decades of the twentieth century, societies and governments in many developing countries and former-communist countries have been becoming increasingly settled and sophisticated. In such countries, government action is becoming increasingly subject to formal and explicit rules and laws. The question and role of jurisdiction, in other words, will become increasingly relevant. The more sophisticated and structured a government becomes, the more the question of jurisdiction will matter. The fact that governments become more sophisticated and more structured does not mean that they will also automatically govern more justly. Instead, it could mean that governments will now shift and resort to different, more sophisticated methodologies and means to disempower, exploit, oppress, and manipulate its subjects – the people. Unless people develop a three-dimensional view of misgovernment that includes a grasp of predatory jurisdiction, it will become increasingly hard to fathom the causes of misgovernment. Where once the two-dimensional view may have been practical and sufficient, it will become an increasingly crude, superficial, stale, and unsatisfactory way of understanding the reality of misgovernment.

To show the superiority of a three-dimensional perspective, let us take the case of overborrowing. A two-dimensional perspective would seek to explain overborrowing as the result of the irresponsible politics of overspending and weak government finances with the solution being greater prudence, integrity, and competence in the management of government finances. A three-dimensional view would additionally seek to examine and explain overborrowing in terms of predatory jurisdiction. It would seek to assess the scope of government jurisdiction in the matter of borrowing by exposing the absence of legal constraints on borrowing power, by evaluating the degree to which the lack of constraints contributed to the problem of overborrowing, by examining the impact of this lack of restraint on society, by coming to terms with the moral implications of unrestricted borrowing powers, and by considering whether or not such powers need restraining and by which means.

Jurisdiction is the keystone of policymaking and public administration. Think of government as an *administrative machine.* If instances of misgovernment and economic crisis are to have any meaning at all, it is essential that people start thinking of and understanding misgovernment and crisis as the outcome – or at least the by-product – of policymaking and administrative processes orchestrated by goal-oriented people authorized to operate the levers of this administration machine in accordance with legally defined powers. In other words, a sovereign debt crisis is not merely the result of some strange loss of confidence on the part of foreign creditors, it is also the final outcome of borrowing too much precisely because policymakers had the lawful authority to do so without restraint. Thus, the following question must be raised: Is it right that governments should have such broad powers that they can legally harm the interests of the people? To put the question differently: Is a system of government legitimate if, as a matter of jurisdiction, it readily allows the routine and unchecked exercise of powers that result in overregulation, wasteful bureaucracy, hyperinflation, overtaxation, runaway budget deficits, excessive borrowing, corruption, and the perpetuation of poverty? I think not.

The origins and sources of predatory jurisdiction

Predatory jurisdiction did not appear out of thin air. It is not a recent evolution in the way we are governed that has snuck up on us unnoticed. Predatory jurisdiction has, in fact, quite a pedigree and – as much as we may, at this stage, not be aware of its existence – a basis in our own frame of mind towards the mission of government. The single most immediate source of predatory jurisdiction is a widespread faith in economic interventionism. People across the globe have embraced the idea that wise and well-directed government action can abolish poverty, prevent severe unemployment, raise the standard of living of the nation, and bring about rapid social development. The general public has learned to desire and expect from government the promotion of economic development and universal prosperity. Accordingly, on the basis of this expectation (and at a basic level), people perceive government to be their primary benefactor. Correspondingly, they consider it natural that government should have the power to intervene. The very belief that government should be responsible for economic development provides a *prima facie* validation for the expansion of government powers.

Another basis for predatory jurisdiction is an unexamined legacy of unrestrained government authority and power. Essentially, present-day governments – and that includes most newly democratic countries – have inherited unrestrained powers with respect to policymaking from past regimes. The historic sources of these powers are often of an ancient and problematic nature. Such sources include despotism, autocracy, absolutist monarchy, and colonial rule. The essence of these forms of authoritarianism is that there are no restraints on the powers of the ruler. The ruler, at least formally, is above the law and exercises arbitrary or unconditional authority. In this framework, the lives and property of the people – and consequently, economic activity – were unconditionally at the disposal of the ruler. Most legal and political institutions were originally designed to deliberately achieve the subordination of major portions of the population to the will of the rulers. The institutions are part of a heritage that precedes popular representation and public accountability. The outer shape of the state was irrelevant. The rulers could be exploitative as were colonial acquisitions such as Belgian Congo or autocracies such as tsarist Russia and Mughal India. In all instances, the open and declared goal was to reduce the people to a resource for generating wealth at the disposal of the ruling regime. It was a reversal of the ends and means. The people are the means to the aggrandizement of the regime. Creating these systems of oppression virtually always required a great deal of bloodshed. The opening scenes in the creation of every legacy system in the developing world or former-communist world are the horrors varying from the conquest of Mexico to Stalinist collectivization and Leopoldian despoliation.

We need to grasp that most non-advanced economies have never known a system of limited government; most non-advanced economies have hardly known any respite from oppression and unjust government. The one constant in the political history of this collection of countries has been unrelenting tyranny. Historically, most countries categorized as non-advanced economies have been stacking one form of unlimited state power upon another. Most non-advanced economies have a heritage of either colonial government systems or some form of indigenous despotism ... or both. Despotic governments and colonial rule are, in effect, systems of unlimited government authority with the objective of crushing economic freedom – though class-based or racist in its application – for the purpose of making economic exploitation and exclusion possible. In these countries – except for the replacement of the colonial masters or aristocrats by a small and often kleptocratic elite – revolution or independence did not change the basic operational mode of government. As noted earlier, virtually every non-advanced economy at some point fell under the sway of one form or another of communism or socialism. This had deep and lasting influence on the political, legal, and administrative institutions of these states. There was in fact a brief moment in time when, for example, decolonization became almost synonymous with the introduction of socialist rule. In other words, in the non-advanced economies, collectivist ideas about the organization of the state reinforced the heritage of unrestrained authority. The effect of this was especially problematic.

Both the older autocratic traditions and the collectivist ideologies are by now discredited and abandoned. The institutional legacy, however, has been catastrophic. The central fact is that the vast powers of the state and a bureaucracy to match that power are still with us. And there is an even deeper problem: in the minds of people in general, the validity of these vast, unrestrained powers of the state remains unchallenged. Though the ancient autocracies and colonial empires have disappeared and collectivist ideologies have been discredited, the policy instruments and their logic inherited from these regimes and ideologies are mostly still there with the same reflexes as a basis for government action. The previous order may have disintegrated, but that does not mean that people have thereby automatically understood all the ramifications. The most important, and yet least understood, ramification is as follows: throughout history, our rulers have had unlimited power to intervene in the economy. It should be understood that, in order to plunder or exploit an economy, one must impose a regime of unrestrained authority. Collectivist ideologies lent new cachet to this ancient thirst for unlimited power while extinguishing the typically nineteenth-century instinct for limiting government power. After its discredit and collapse, that power (as vested in the state) remains unexamined, unreformed, and, therefore, undiminished in the economic lives of its citizens. The powers of the state in pre-communist, communist and post-communist Russia, colonial Dutch East Indies, Suharto's

Indonesia (and democratic Indonesia), the British Raj, India of Nehru (and today's India) are almost exactly the same!

In this socio-political framework, the rulers and the ruled have no awareness of private interests as a priori legitimate. Consequently, people do not pursue their interests as a matter of right. Instead, they pursue their interests much like clueless, frightened minors habituated to being required to seek permission for all their actions from and under the supervision of heartless, capricious adults. Observe that autocracies and totalitarian regimes have frequently idealized the ruler as a father caring for his children – the ruled – the father possessing unlimited and unconditional power over his children, and the children owing uncritical obedience to their father. Within this way of life, people think of their economic interests in terms of privilege – that all is a benefit to be granted down to us from those on high. The telltale mark is the ubiquity of patronage and cronyism in the developing world. We take for granted that all economic actions are unreservedly objects of state review or state control. The state can still, and we anticipate with not a single principled objection, that it will do so, assert licensing authority, give directives, set prices, prohibit or monopolize commercial activities, grant monopolies, set quotas, confiscate, nationalize, protect industries, grant concessions, and much more. None of these instruments are new. Public policy has been democratized in the sense that access to its levers is no longer formally the prerogative of a predefined group such as an aristocracy or a nomenklatura or European settlers. On the contrary, in quite a large number of countries, the old elites have lost power and the members of the new elites replacing them are often former members of the popular classes! Modern government is now openly accessible to every conceivable grouping of privilege seekers, which can exert pressure on the policymakers. Nevertheless, the mechanism is the same. The unrestrained authority inherited from past regimes is the bedrock of today's predatory jurisdiction. For non-advanced economies, the greatest of all revolutions – a break with this tradition of unlimited authority, the honest introduction of genuine limited government, a government for the benefit of the people – is yet to be achieved.

Another important cause of predatory jurisdiction is the sheer ignorance of the general populace (and that includes the larger part of the middle classes and the intelligentsia) regarding the "deep structure" of administrative and legal principles, concepts, systems, and practices. Generally, most people are acutely aware of politics and government in its outer appearances (e.g., the cop on the beat, the campaigning politician, the president making a speech, the civil servant behind the counter, and the subsidized bread and fuel). This deep structure is invisible to the public, yet it shapes and influences the way governments and its agents operate (including its outward manifestations). This almost-complete ignorance allows dysfunctional legal and administrative systems and the nefarious doctrines, principles, and practices that underpin this dysfunction to persist and fester unexamined, unchallenged, and, therefore, unreformed.

Consider how difficult it is to cope with the unknown. Can we realistically formulate correct and articulate demands for reforms when we fail to perceive that many of the problems of misgovernment originate in the deep structure of the state and government? Very few people see misgovernment or an economic crisis as the logical outcome of deliberate political and administrative processes made possible by governmental jurisdiction. This leaves the public totally defenceless against the depredations by a class of politicians, bureaucrats, and assorted insiders and cronies that have no compunction about ruthlessly exploiting this deep structure to pursue policies that bring them advantage – even if that, in the end, causes the devastation of the economy and, thus, society. Even more painfully, it disarms us – especially in cases where well-meaning policymakers propose policies that sound wonderful but are actually unsound and worthless. However, there is no stopping the thugs and the deluded unless we first have a standard by which to measure their deeds. It is almost beyond belief to see that pervasive misgovernment and a chronic recurrence of crises seem never to have inspired political thinkers to examine in moral terms this deep structure of principles, rules, and practices. Thus, faith in economic interventionism, the debris of history embedded in the system, and ignorance conspire to keep us in a perpetual state of misgovernment.

Benchmarking misgovernment

For what other reason should government need jurisdiction other than to do good? To the extent that we seek meaningful and lasting change, misgovernment, particularly when sanctioned by predatory jurisdiction, must become our focus. Misgovernment is an issue that people around the world are keenly aware of and vocal about. On the other hand, the kind or scope of jurisdiction that makes possible misgovernment is almost never in itself an object of moral evaluation or, more appropriately, given the amount of harm almost routinely inflicted, reassessment. The good or evil inherent to a certain kind or scope of government jurisdiction is almost never the object of study or investigation.

This is not to imply that government systems escape moral evaluation. Intriguingly, such moral evaluations often produce extreme results such as wholesale rejection of social, political, and economic systems (as do Marxists and anarchists). The other extreme is anti-corruption, anti-incumbent, or anti-establishment crusading; the advocacy of strongman rule; or less extreme, technocratic rule. The ideal in this instance is not to reform the structure of government or the state, but to purify it of immoral agents (i.e., the corrupt or weak or self-serving rulers and administrators). The common denominator of both approaches is that the legal and administrative doctrines, principles, structures, instruments, practices, or techniques – and ultimately the resulting jurisdiction – are never the objects of moral evaluation. Our objective, however, is not to overthrow whole systems; also, our focus is not on solving the problem of immoral agents. Instead, our purpose will be to uncover the considerations for reforming government jurisdiction.

Because we are not in the habit of critiquing government jurisdiction from a moral perspective, we have not consciously sought, defined, or set ethical standards by which to evaluate it. However, if we desire to uncover whether a certain kind or scope of jurisdiction is good or evil – meaning just or unjust, and, therefore, legitimate or illegitimate – we must establish a standard for its evaluation. The public, in other words, is in dire need of a standard – *a standard of justice* by which one can measure economic mismanagement. How many people are capable of telling you what the standard of justice is in the instance of government-induced inflation or a debt default resulting in a banking crisis, for example? If there is no standard of justice by which to measure economic mismanagement, what is the measure of good government? Is it then still reasonable to expect good government? Without a standard of justice, what will protect the citizen from economic mismanagement? The solemn words and promises of the politician?

This book will show that the appropriate standard of justice consists of the rights of the individual. It will present individual rights as the standard of justice fully applicable to economic mismanagement. Economic mismanagement, one way or another, involves the violation of these rights.

Without a conception of rights, the public has no means of understanding that government action is subject to ethical standards. Correspondingly, it would not be able to hold the actions of government to a standard of justice. This is obvious with regard to political and civil rights. To the degree that we believe in a free press – the result of the right of free speech – we find government behaviour, such as jailing journalists for what they write, reprehensible. To the extent that we believe in a fair trial for all – the result of habeas corpus – we find incarceration without trial unacceptable. It should become evident that violations of individual rights in the economic sphere (e.g., deprivation of property rights) are just as serious.

To raise the rights of the individual as the standard of justice, one must next define the concept of individual rights in order to establish a firm basis for its application as a contrast to the condition of predatory jurisdiction. The definition best suited for this purpose was provided by a philosopher, Ayn Rand, and it reads as follows: "A 'right' is a moral principle defining and sanctioning a man's *freedom of action* in a social context."[6] The value of this definition is that it serves as the perfect opposite to the concept of predatory jurisdiction. The essence of misgovernment as a result of predatory jurisdiction is that government applies its authority in ways that destroy or obstruct the ability of citizens to act in accordance with their own rightful interests. Predatory jurisdiction overwhelms and destroys the freedoms of the citizen, the security of his or her interests, or his or her welfare through the unwarranted assertion of political and administrative control over society and its members (or in a somewhat narrower context, the economy and its participants).

Note that Rand formulated this definition of rights in her essay *Man's Rights*, in which she examines the moral and practical implications of unlimited state authority in addition to its philosophical roots, and she rejects it as a destructive force in a human's life. The key concept in her definition is freedom. In the final analysis, the concept of rights is a conceptual instrument for the protection or preservation of individual liberty in the context of human relationships (i.e., society). Let us remember that government is ultimately nothing but the formal organization of human relationships or society. The question, then, is which standards rule this formal organization? We will not be discussing the merits of Rand's definition of rights. Further assessment thereof belongs to the province of philosophical enquiry. The concept of the rights of the individual originates in one branch of philosophical enquiry, namely, the theory of natural rights. For our purposes, the relevance of the concept of rights is strictly a matter of applied ethics. We will further explore this throughout this book by examining the concrete evidence of misgovernment.

The sweepstakes of virtue

The implication is not that the public has no relevant standards. After all, who hasn't complained about the greed, corruption, lust for power, dishonesty, or lack of integrity and incompetence of politicians? What of the heartlessness, corruption, incompetence, and inaccessibility of the bureaucrat? Do we not hanker after clean, honest, competent politicians and bureaucrats? Indeed, the public does set standards in terms of integrity, honesty, competence, responsibility, for example. Nevertheless, and important as they are, these are reflections on the *character* of politicians. As such these are not standards of justice, but standards of *virtue*. Though rectitude in any politician or policymaker should be deeply appreciated, it is not a sufficient basis for good government. People of virtue are absolutely necessary, but that is not enough. People of virtue come and go, and they are regularly succeeded by dishonest people. A system of unlimited authority puts the entire burden of good government on a person's integrity, and that is precisely what landed the five billion inhabitants of developing nations and formerly communist countries in hot water. Betting all our chips on the integrity of rulers and their minions is not going to solve the problem of misgovernment.

Before we go on, there is one piece of irony that deserves acknowledgement. In the end, only bona fide reformers can resolve the problems of misgovernment. A bona fide reformer is a person of virtue. In discussing the problem of misgovernment, we will give precedence to the topic of justice over the issue of virtue. Yet, at the end of the day, no justice is possible without some degree of virtue in play. Nothing can ever be achieved if the people cannot find virtuous leaders. However, the problem of finding a person of virtue to lead us out of the darkness is immense. We have no way of judging the inner quality of people as rulers before they have ruled; we can only go by their words or the pronouncements and promises that they make. And so, in this respect, we are, to a very large degree, at the mercy of fortune to give us a good leader. Fortunately, many countries have, from time to time, seen people of virtue rise to power. Every so often, dishonest people get their just deserts and reformers replace them. A major problem, however, is that such people of virtue seem to fail often. Note how often these people of virtue and reformers seem to lose momentum, squander opportunities, and fail to make headway against corruption and maladministration. It seems as if the success of reform is too often as predictable as the sweepstakes. Thus, the rule of virtuous people often ends in dashed hopes. Our theory of predatory jurisdiction is certainly meant to offer these people of virtue and their followers conceptual tools for understanding the problem of misgovernment better, to make reform a bit less of a trial-and-error effort.

In those sweepstakes of reform, some people have succeeded in bringing their countries out of the vale of tears. A few countries – namely, Korea, Taiwan, Singapore, and Hong Kong – have been extraordinarily fortunate to have outstanding and dedicated leaders or administrators such as Park Chun Hee, Kwoh-Ting Li, and Sun Yun-suan, Lee Kuan Yew, and Sir John Cowperthwaite.[7] These leaders have, via their efforts and accomplishments, compressed economic and social development in a timeframe of three decades on average. Though impressive, their examples do not reassure us completely. Each of these people had exceptional traits: character, vision, intelligence, and drive. But such people are rare. Also, all these people were authoritarians. Most authoritarian rulers are neither wise nor virtuous. For every Park Chun Hee, there are two dozen thugs like Ferdinand Marcos.

Same powers, different results

There seems to be a pattern to success and failure in reform. Compare two well-known reformers: Lee Kuan Yew and Jawaharlal Nehru. Both are westernized, Cambridge-educated lawyers and socialists. As prime ministers of formerly British possessions, they could have swapped offices and found the scope of their authority to be virtually the same. And yet the latter destroyed India's prospects for eradicating poverty by using this authority to create a monstrous bureaucracy, the notorious License Raj, and to socialize India's economy. Lee, the icon of many proponents of industrial policy, is regrettably never honoured for what was his greatest forte: restraint and prudence. Preserving and then improving the legacy of British legal and administrative systems is his greatest achievement.[8] In doing so, Singapore nurtured economic freedom, a liberal market system – in contrast, India stifled it. It is with good reason that the Index of Economic Freedom ranks Singapore as the second freest economy on Earth. The comparison of India with Singapore could be extended to countries such as Sri Lanka versus Hong Kong or Ghana versus Malaysia. Similar systems, same powers, very different results.

When we compare the performance of leaders such as Lee and Nehru, we usually note the differences in their actions and achievements. I have yet to find a study comparing their powers or the scope of their authority. It seems most likely that one would find that most governments possess similar or equally broad powers with regard to controlling, supervising or regulating economic activity. The man of achievements and his failing colleagues had the same powers; the one applied them sparingly and judiciously, the other used his powers without restraint or consideration. In other words, the Singapore and Indian governments have the same level of predatory jurisdiction at their disposal even though the former exercised restraint and the latter did not. Had Lee Kuan Yew, the socialist, wanted to follow Nehru's prescriptions for economic management, nothing *as a matter of jurisdiction* could have stopped his government from implementing them. All that stood between Singapore and the usual tale of developing-nation failure was the good judgement and virtue of a few men and women.

There are at least five billion people living in countries that have known no such luck. Apparently, the rate of recurrence of brilliance and virtue in political leadership is quite unsatisfactory. That and the clearly unchanging record of misgovernment and economic disaster should have served as an incentive for the public to worry more about the harm that a lesser or nastier breed of politicians and administrators with too much authority can inflict. If one cannot hope to live in a country so blessed with talented leadership – and five billion face that reality – it might be better for reform movements to concentrate on the protection of society and the economy against predatory jurisdiction. In fact, this thought is not new. Three hundred years ago, John Locke, writing in *The Second Treatise of Government,* already warned us by using the following quote:[9]

'The reigns of good princes have been always most dangerous to the liberties of their people.' For when their successors, managing the government with different thoughts, would draw the actions of those good rulers into precedent, and make them the standard of their prerogative, as if what had been done only for the good of the people, was a right in them to do, for the harm of the people, if they so pleased; it has often occasioned contest, and sometimes public disorders, before the people could recover their original right, and get that to be declared not to be prerogative, which truly was never so: since it is impossible, that anybody in the society should ever have a right to do the people harm … For prerogative is nothing but the power of doing public good without a rule.

Clearly, Locke warns us that unregulated powers – his prerogatives, our predatory jurisdiction – that seem safe and beneficial in the hands of good governments, are too dangerous to leave in the hands of weak and ill governments. Locke warns that, in the face of misgovernment, people may have to "recover their original right, and get that to be declared not to be prerogative." In other words, to remedy the problem of misgovernment, assert your rights and reduce or regulate the scope of government jurisdiction. He clearly states that "it is impossible, that anybody in the society should ever have a right to do the people harm." He is, in effect, spelling out the fundamentals of good government, and it will be a sorry day when modern government and economic policy may not be held to such a simple and basic standard. It might, therefore, be more sensible to shift the emphasis from demanding good leadership to imposing restraints (i.e., asserting individual rights, limiting jurisdiction, and instituting rule of law). We must not put the entire burden of good government on the moral disposition of this or that individual – that is a bad gamble. Lord Acton stated, "Power corrupts and absolute power corrupts absolutely." Unlimited authority or predatory jurisdiction is a temptation; should we not shield our leaders from its enticements for our sakes as well as theirs?

Advocating a new political awareness

As a brief exploration of history, political philosophy, and current political and economic circumstances have shown thus far, it is necessary to advocate for a new form of political awareness with respect to misgovernment (i.e., one that is based on a clear and lasting consciousness of the problem of predatory jurisdiction). We must move beyond narrowly typecasting misgovernment as purely a manifestation of bad politics and maladministration. Without a conception of jurisdiction and individual rights, our understanding of our political environment is incomplete. These two concepts – jurisdiction and rights – set the parameters within which government can lawfully exercise its authority. Without a conception of jurisdiction and rights, we rob society of the intellectual tools for managing, controlling, and directing government for the benefit of the people. Jurisdiction, like any other government responsibility, is something that must be designed and managed. Without a conception of jurisdiction, its scope will, by default, continue to be set by a class of politicians, bureaucrats, and rent-seekers that has, in many countries, abundantly demonstrated contempt for common sense, common good, and public interest.

Let us take misgovernment and economic crises as the point of departure and trace these back to predatory jurisdiction. After that, we can examine how that involves the rights of the individual. By taking such common concerns as inflation, sovereign debt defaults, corruption, and the size of the informal sector, we should be able to work out the scope of predatory jurisdiction. Moreover, sociologically, states and governments are always power structures. A conception of jurisdiction, therefore, requires an understanding of the dynamics of power and authority. These, then, are the subject matters of subsequent chapters.

Misgovernment *never* escapes the awareness of the public; on the contrary, people tend to be painfully aware that it affects them. In every poor country of the world, there is some form of chronic and systemic misgovernment in evidence (almost on a daily basis), which directly and palpably worries and aggravates a major segment of the population. Even for groups or individuals who are not the immediate victims, it is a constant backdrop against which their lives play out. Misgovernment subverts and frustrates the goals and ambitions of countless individuals. For this reason, it is almost unbelievable that there is hardly any intellectual or philosopher or politician in any developing nation that has seen fit to tap into this daily experience of the people to transform this raw material into a movement that promotes rational, rights-based reform of the institutions of government. After all, the record of government action is such a constant source of disaster and vexation that simply struggling against misgovernment should provide the aspiring reformer with a calling to satisfy a lifetime. No cause is more urgent because misgovernment is the single most important source of human tragedy. The ways in which governments harm society are not difficult to understand at all. The combination of the concepts of jurisdiction and individual rights provides just the perfect lens through which to clearly view the issue of misgovernment. The argument from predatory jurisdiction exposes a previously underexposed cause of misgovernment. It makes it much easier for the layperson to grasp the problem of misgovernment. It renders the task of reform much clearer. By extension, the concept of rights provides a vehicle for structuring and articulating popular grievances in a constructive manner; too often, popular grievance has been the catalyst for yet more mayhem as populist demagogues ride to power on the waves of rage.

I urge and encourage all who are unhappy with the current situation to use these concepts to transform the politics of reform. This should include politically minded voter-citizens, reformers, social activists, etc. The current political elite will not do this for us; it is really up to the concerned citizen, the aspiring reformist politician, the social activist, and the aggrieved victims to set this transformation into motion. In the past thirty years, most reform programmes have been elitist undertakings initiated by policymakers. To this degree, reforms tend to be technocratic and top-down processes. An example of this is economic reform as practiced during the past three decades: balanced budgets, free prices, free trade, foreign investment, stable currencies, the improvement of weak institutions, and the establishment of new institutions. These programmes were concocted by highbrow economists, international institutions, top-level bureaucrats, and crafty insider politicians jumping ship as old regimes collapsed. Ultimately, reforms are always technocratic processes because the actual implementation is an organizational and managerial matter. The problem is that misgovernment has, for too long, been treated exclusively as a technocratic subject intelligible to and soluble only by an elite group of professionals and insiders. The initiation and pursuit of reform does not have to depend entirely on the whims of the insiders. Also, our input on government failure does not have to be inarticulate rage only. The concepts of rights and predatory jurisdiction allow outsiders to transform the struggle for government reform at least in part into a bottom-up political process. Our aim should be to empower ordinary citizens, laypeople, by providing them with a heightened consciousness of their predicament and the concepts and language to express their concerns, demands, and arguments in an articulate and compelling fashion.

A specific note on the topic of economic interventionism: It is probably inevitable that critics will view a theory of predatory jurisdiction as advocating a government deprived of the means to pursue economic development. In our modern world, we take it for granted that it takes far-reaching government interference to abolish poverty, prevent severe unemployment, raise the standard of living of the nation, and bring about rapid social development. As a matter of practice, in most countries, people can no longer conceive of a world where governments are not directly responsible for these functions. It should be pointed out that ending government interventionism is not the objective of a theory of predatory jurisdiction. Nevertheless, it is reasonable to expect that the elimination of predatory jurisdiction will result in a decreased scope for government intervention. This last position raises the question of whether economic development is at all possible without governments possessing sweeping interventionist powers. Fortunately, modern history has provided a fairly recent example showing that economic development without government interventionism is possible. Pointed out by Milton Friedman, such an event occurred in Hong Kong during the second half of the twentieth century, precisely during the glory days of interventionism. At the end of this book (in Appendix A), an account is provided that showcases economic conditions in Hong Kong by the end of the twentieth century. The case of Hong Kong proves that economic development does not depend upon sweeping interventionist designs. It is also an excellent aid to the cause of promoting a new form of awareness regarding misgovernment.

In any case, economic interventionism itself will not be the subject of study in this book. The objective is not to critique economic interventionism on its merits per se; rather, the objective is to discover the causes of misgovernment insofar as these are the outcomes of the underlying structures of power and authority. It is not the objective to prove that misgovernment is an outcome of economic interventionism as such. The subject of study is the meaning of power and authority in the lives of people. We should meditate on how the lives of people are affected when government action is contemplated. There is an air of the unreal about debating what we want from government, without considering the means applied – in this instance, the required scope of power and authority, jurisdiction, and discretionary power – and the appropriateness of such means. Otherwise, we will (perhaps unwittingly and by default) lapse into applying the doctrine that the ends justify the means. Presently, in the pursuit of good causes, the destructive potential of government authority is not so much underestimated as it is ignored. The most important reason for this is that most people are extremely naive about and utterly ignorant of the terms of power, and for this reason, they leave it out of the equation when formulating their schemes. As a consequence, the expectation of the results of government intervention are inevitably rosier than they would have been if the blood and guts of power and authority, and the misery of life at the receiving end thereof, had been included in the equation in the first place.

Summary

The dividing line between rich and poor nations is, by and large, the same as it was one hundred years ago. Notably, the developed world is still predominantly white. At the end of the twentieth century, the rich, developed countries are largely the same Western nations that dominated the world at the start of the same century. The most important exception, Japan, is also an old, industrialized nation. Beyond these, there is a thin scattering of newcomers such as Spain, Greece, Ireland, Israel, Korea, Taiwan, Hong Kong, Singapore – and specific categories like tax havens, such as Cayman Islands and Bermuda, or oil states with smaller populations, such as Qatar and Kuwait.[10] Underdevelopment and poverty in most of the developing world dates from a period when imperial powers subjected great swathes of the world to oppression, exploitation, and discriminatory practices. After two generations of self-government, one is faced by the fact that a certifiably native breed of politicians and intellectuals have perpetuated this poverty and oppression. If the division of rich and poor, developed and underdeveloped, capitalist and non-capitalist, free and oppressed, once had the overtones of a colour bar imposed by foreign aggressors, it is now mostly self-inflicted. This is an intolerable situation. The question deserving an answer is: When will the day break heralding a new "Japan" – perhaps Brazil or Mexico, Egypt or Nigeria, Indonesia or India? Or are most developing nations destined to remain poverty-ridden, disease-ridden, debt-ridden, crisis-ridden, aid-dependent, folkloristic ghettos south of the Rio Grande and the Mediterranean? Are political leaders, the ruling political classes, and the intelligentsias in the poor countries serious about economic growth and universal prosperity for their fellow citizens? Do they really mean to raise the level of their people to the same height of dignity currently enjoyed in rich, white nations? Do political leaders in poor countries sincerely wish to rid their nations of banana republic and Bantustan reputations? Or is the limit of imagination and ambition of our political leadership material being the cock that conquered the top of a dunghill?

Korea, Taiwan, Hong Kong, and Singapore all proved that general prosperity can be achieved in three decades. Capitalism has raised the standard of living in these polities to a level unmatched in the rest of the developing world. In these countries, capitalism brings out the best of human beings: it enabled one generation of parents to secure a better life for their immediate offspring. Given technology, science, education, freedom, and capitalism, no child born today in poverty needs to reach old age never having known any measure of prosperity. On the record of Hong Kong or Taiwan, the year 2050 should go down in history as the year widespread poverty, deprivation, and backwardness were ended. At least four generations of people since the start of the twentieth century have pointlessly missed out on freedom, justice, and prosperity. From the current prevalence of misgovernment, it looks as if more generations will never know the good life. It is time to sharpen our minds, to reject falsehoods about capitalism (which originate in ideologies such as socialism and communism) that promised to end misery but magnified it greatly instead. The alternative is more generations wasting away in poverty and ignorance, living stunted lives. The evidence is overwhelming. From now on, every politician, every intellectual, every philosopher, every humanitarian, every reformer, every political activist who cannot accept the evidence is nothing less than a hater of truth and, to use some good, old-fashioned communist jargon, an enemy of the people. Anti-capitalists and anti-globalists call themselves the true friends of the poor. I implore the reader to disassociate himself or herself from idiocy and to seek knowledge. With such friends, I am obliged to quote Immanuel Kant: "May God protect us from our friends. From our enemies, we can try to protect ourselves."[11]

Chapter 2

Overregulation and Underdevelopment

I sit on a man's back choking him and making him carry me, and yet assure myself and others that I am sorry for him and wish to lighten his load by all possible means – except by getting off his back.

—Leo Tolstoy

In its treatment of constitutional law, the Encyclopaedia Britannica declares that the "currently dominant democratic ideal" is a "system in which the equality and the non-economic freedoms of persons are recognized and the state possesses all the means necessary to regulate the economy."[1] The notion that the state should possess all the means necessary to regulate the economy is extraordinarily vague. It seems to cover almost any degree or level of policymaking power. In fact, it does. Even in the most developed countries where traditions of good governance are relatively well established and highly regarded, it covers levels of policymaking power that have proven to be seriously injurious to the economy. In this instance, traditions of good governance do matter in an incremental sense. In advanced countries, these traditions serve – however incompletely – to impose at least a real process of deliberation on the adoption of economic policies. In the absence of such well-established traditions, the situation in non-advanced economies is out of control. Regardless of the existence or absence of a tradition of good governance, in most countries the current meaning of a state possessing all the means necessary to regulate the economy is that there are no limits to the number and kind of rules and regulations government can legally impose on trade and industry. This wide scope of authority is the essential prerequisite for overregulation. Properly understood, overregulation – or bureaucracy and red tape as it is also called – is possible only because of this scope of jurisdiction. Overregulation regardless of its harmful effects on the economy, is lawfully exercised authority. To say that the state should have all the means necessary to regulate the economy is to subject all economic activity to political control. This ideal is a profession in favour of unlimited political power and authority.[2]

Overregulation

It is our duty to understand that, when we speak of the economy, economic activity, and development, we are not discussing some abstraction beyond and above us. Basically, all of us together are the economy. That includes you, me, our children, our parents, our neighbours, and all the people on Earth. Economic activity is what we people, physically or mentally, do to make a living; it is our labour and the fruits of our labour; it is us working, trading, producing, doing business, building homes and places to work, farming, consuming, etc. Economic development is us doing more of this in better ways and doing so in ways that increase our wealth. We should never forget that any discussion about the economy is a discussion about ourselves; in economics, we the people at work are the subject material.

Likewise, the power to regulate the economy should concern us; it is about the power of government to decide the terms and conditions under which we the people will have to make a living. This is not necessarily wrong. At its best, the point of regulation is to ensure public order and proper business conduct to the extent that this cannot be achieved without institutional oversight (yes, government). The problem with regulatory authority starts at the point at which rules and regulations actually become obstructions to making a living. Overregulation is about rules and regulations (i.e., government) making it more difficult for us, or even stopping us, from making a living or improving our condition. Overregulation reduces economic growth by reducing the level of our activities, obstructing trading, production, and building – and because this reduces the level of employment, it makes it harder for people to find jobs. Given enough power, governments can regulate economic activity to a standstill. The consequence is a stagnant economy, high levels of corruption and cronyism, capital flight, unemployment, poverty, black market activity, etc.

To survive, people must build, produce, and trade. This is not an option; it is an imperative for the survival of the human race. To build, produce, and trade are legitimate pursuits precisely because they are right and necessary to the lives of people. As a matter of fact, people will build, produce, and trade regardless of their level of civilization, know-how, development, or the manner in which they are governed. People will do these things within the law if possible, but if pushed, they will break the law to survive – necessity knows no law.

Imagine a system of government where the rules and regulations are so numerous and so complex that it becomes it too difficult for the great majority of its citizens, especially those who are poor and lacking in education, to follow them and stay within the law while making a living or finding a place to make a home. Economies everywhere – those of rich and poor countries – are hampered to varying degrees by overregulation. In most poor countries, however, overregulation is so bad that the consequences are catastrophic in ways unheard of in rich countries. In poor countries, overregulation is a legal and administrative framework that prevents economies from developing and perpetuates backwardness, deprivation, poverty, and gross inequality as a result.

Mr De Soto's planet

The sheer impact of overregulation in terms of its role in and contribution to the problems of underdevelopment was first fully and properly uncovered by studies done by the Peruvian development economist Hernando De Soto and his Institute for Liberty and Democracy (ILD), headquartered in Lima, Peru. We are all indebted to Hernando De Soto for researching and exposing the scale of the effects of overregulation namely, exclusion and extralegality.

The term *exclusion* can be defined as the effective barring of people from formal economic systems and processes. When political, legal, and administrative systems and processes become obstacles to essentially legitimate objectives, such as producing and trading normal goods and services, the result for large numbers of people is exclusion. Again, necessity knows no law: when governments impose excessive regulations, necessity pushes people without the means to overcome such obstacles into the *extralegal sector* (often called the *informal sector*). Extralegality – or informality – is economic activity taking place outside the scope of formal legal and administrative systems and controls. The people making their livelihoods in the extralegal sector are unusually called *extralegals* or *informals*. These terms will be used interchangeably in the remainder of this text.

Mr De Soto and the ILD performed fundamental research into the causes of extralegality and uncovered a vast amount of evidence confirming a strong relationship between overregulation and extralegality. His findings have since redefined the terms of debate on public administration and policymaking. Many more researchers have since followed his approach and their conclusions have generally confirmed or added to his findings. The crux of De Soto's argument is that overregulation is a key factor contributing to underdevelopment. One researcher, Lennart Erickson, provides the most concise synopsis of what he calls the De Soto hypothesis:[3]

> De Soto argued that a key factor contributing to poverty in the developing world were the barriers placed by governments in the path of small-scale entrepreneurs. His story was straightforward: bureaucrats, either through needless licensing requirements or outright corruption, make setting up a legal business very costly. Not surprisingly, many would-be entrepreneurs are dissuaded from starting legal businesses in such conditions. Instead, they set up "informal" firms. These firms do not have the required permits and operate largely outside the reach of the government. However, they do so at a cost of productivity, lacking access to infrastructure, credit markets and legal institutions. It is important to note that the activity these firms engage in is not intrinsically criminal, e.g., drug dealing, but rather they are producing legal goods and services outside of regulatory norms.

There is probably no better way to provide an instant overview of the extent and impact of overregulation than by quoting the first two paragraphs of ILD history on its website:[4]

> In 1980, ILD's founder Hernando de Soto, then 38, returned to his native Peru after living in Europe since

the age of seven. De Soto, whose father worked in an international organization, was educated in Switzerland and had run one of the largest engineering firms in Europe. As soon as he began doing business in Peru, he realized that it took a kind of persistence, ingenuity, and bureaucratic savvy unheard of in Europe and the US. Wondering why this was so, he hired two recent law graduates to count the number of laws and regulations enacted in Peru since World War II. The results were astonishing: Peruvian governments had passed about 28,000 laws and regulations per year regarding how citizens produced and distributed wealth more than 100 laws each working day. Even more disconcerting was that further research indicated that this huge and ever-growing legal morass did not seem to address even remotely the needs of most of the nation's people. To confirm this disconnection between the law and the poor, De Soto decided to set up a two-sewing-machine garment factory in a Lima shantytown, and attempt to get it licensed. With the help of five university students who spent several hours a day wending their way through Peruvian bureaucracy, he discovered that to obtain a legal license to operate even such a small business took 289 days and cost 31 times the average monthly minimum wage. Here was incontrovertible evidence that the nation's laws were divorced from reality, generating more costs than benefits. Laws were difficult to understand and expensive to follow. Not surprisingly, Peru's majority opted for extralegality.

By way of comparison, a similar procedure would have taken three and a half hours in Florida and four hours in New York.[5] Furthermore, the student team discovered that it took eleven procedures to register this workshop in Lima, Peru at the cost of USD 1.231 (representing thirty-one times the monthly minimum wage).[6] This figure includes a loss of net profits equivalent to USD 1.037 as a consequence of the almost ten-month wait to begin business.

Let us convert these statistics at the federal minimum wage rate prevailing in the United States at the time of ILD's research work, as if registration there of such an uncomplicated business could cost thirty-one times the monthly minimum wage. At the minimum wage rate prevailing during the 1980s of USD 3.35 per hour, the cost of registering the aforementioned workplace would have been USD 18,000.[7] Actually, an entrepreneur in the United States could complete the process of registering a business for less than USD 300 – with little or no loss of earnings as a consequence of delays. Making a living within *and* complying with the law in some Western nations is apparently comparatively inexpensive.

The costs of remaining formal were also unreasonably high. In a survey of thirty-seven legally operating companies in sectors with singularly high levels of informality, such as foodstuffs, wooden furniture, textiles and garment manufacturing, chemicals and plastics, printing, basic metalworking, and mechanics and toys, ILD found that administrative personnel spent 40 per cent of their time on fulfilling regulatory requirements.[8] For the sake of comparison, a bank established in the Netherlands will be hard pressed to spend more than 5 per cent of its administrative talent on regulatory requirements.

> Peru, in fact, had become two nations one where the legal system bestowed privileges on a select few, and another where the majority of the Peruvian people lived and worked outside the law, according to their own local arrangements. How large was this extralegal sector? No one in the government seemed to have a precise idea. Once again, De Soto decided to find out for himself. From 1981 to 1984, he and a small group of associates the original ILD research team began walking the streets and shantytowns of Peru during late afternoons and weekends, talking to all sorts of people about their work and counting their businesses and enterprises. De Soto and his team discovered a new set of statistics about life in Peru, and their data were astounding: 90 percent of all small industrial enterprises, 85 percent of urban transport, 60 percent of Peru's fishing fleet (one of the biggest in the world), and 60 percent of the distribution of groceries emerged from the city's extralegal sector. Far from being the pests that the government and elites saw them as,

Lima's poor, in fact, were carrying the economy on their backs. The more people the ILD researchers talked to in the shantytowns and rural byways of Peru, the more they realized that it was not so much that the poor were breaking the law as that the law was breaking them. Even those who had tried to get into the system by applying for titles for their houses and other real estate or licenses to legalize their businesses complained that it was impossible to succeed; wending their way through the bureaucratic obstacles simply took too much time and cost too much money.

The stereotypical informal in the minds of the public is the street vendor or handyman. The reading above demonstrates that the scope of informal activity is far wider than these stereotypes. Researchers have found that it includes industrial activities such as foodstuff processing; furniture, textiles, and garment manufacturing; chemicals and plastics; printing; basic metalworking; and assembling toys and key, non-industrial activities such as domestic transportation, fishing, and grocery selling.

The scope of the informal sector is only limited by the degree to which formal procedure is indispensable. Personal lending and money transfers do not require formal procedure, and that results in a great deal of informal activity. International money transfers (e.g., via the halawa network of money changers) is one example where informal activity goes global. But mortgage banking and property insurance are so tied up with the formal legal procedure that informal activity in these trades is non-existent. In the same manner, large-scale industry, such as oil refining, is by its visibility – no hiding from official detection is possible – necessarily a formal sector activity.

Mr De Soto's findings have contributed to a growing awareness that one of the greatest obstacles to economic development in the developing world is the difficulty of official business formation, especially by members of the humble classes. It was Mr De Soto's finding that the legal requirements for starting a business (including the expense and the time it takes to meet them) are so onerous in most developing nations that small entrepreneurs are often effectively barred from setting up or doing business legally. Consequently, many start-ups take place illegally (i.e., they become part of what is called the extralegal or informal sector). This single difficulty forces the majority of entrepreneurial talent, and consequently their workforce, in the developing world to scratch a living in the informal sector.

There are other significant drivers causing extralegality. The size of the informal sector is also positively correlated to the tax burden and labour market restrictions, and it is negatively correlated to the quality of government institutions.[9] This means that, the higher the rates of taxation and the heavier the burden of complying with labour regulations, the larger the relative size of the informal sector will be. The quality of government institutions relates to the degree that government is clean, honest, fair, efficient, and effective. This is especially relevant in the case of enforcement efficiency (i.e., the ability to collect revenues and enforce regulations – the lower enforcement efficiency, the larger the relative size of the informal sector). In other words, the reasons for informality vary from hardship (due to a lack of access to government services, excessive taxation, and the cost of complying with regulations) to the existence of opportunities for evading enforcement.

The aforementioned ILD findings pertain to Peru. Analogies, however, can be found throughout the developing world. According to the World Bank:[10]

> The informal sector is a pervasive and persistent economic feature of most developing economies, contributing significantly to employment creation, production, and income generation. Recent estimates of the size of the informal sector in developing countries in terms of its share of non-agricultural employment range roughly between one-fifth and four-fifths. In terms of its contribution to GDP, the informal sector accounts for between 25% and 40% of annual output in developing countries in Asia and Africa.

The statistics for Mexico, for example – a much larger country than Peru – are dramatic. According to the OECD, the Mexican informal economy accounted for 44 per cent of urban jobs in Mexico and moved as much as 146 billion dollars per year, 12.3 per cent more than exports (USD 130 billion).[11] The National Statistical Office of Thailand – Thailand being one of the most successful emerging economies – found that, of the total employed persons in Thailand in 1994 (32.1 million), just 23.2 per cent were employed in the formal sector. That means that 76.8 per cent were employed in the informal sector![12]

Statistical evidence also shows that the size of the informal sector is strongly and *negatively* related to per capita income. Table 1 portrays the relationship between black market activity scores according to the *2001 Index of Economic Freedom* and per capita GDP for 155 countries. Correspondingly, the average per capita income for economies scoring 'Very low' on black market activity according to the *2001 Index* were almost *twelve* times the average for economies scoring 'Very high.' According to the explanatory notes of the *Index*, a 'Very high' level of black market activity also means that countries have black markets that are larger than their formal economies. In other words, about 2.1 billion people live in 44 countries where the greater part of national income must be earned outside the law – and they are desperately poor because of this predicament.

Table 1. Level of black market activity and per capita income

Level of black market activity	Number of countries	Population	Population figures as percentages	Per capita GDP at PPP In USD	Richest category X times richer than
Very low	22	762.952.804	12.8	28.348	1.0
Low	20	322.597.692	5.4	13.522	2.1
Moderate	31	594.327.490	10.0	5.817	4.9
High	38	2.170.841.899	36.3	4.052	7.0
Very High	44	2.119.909.037	35.5	2.462	11.5
Totals	155	5.970.628.922	100.0		

Data source: my own calculations based on *The CIA: The World Factbook*, 2001. The black market score was extracted from the *2001 Index of Economic Freedom published* by Heritage Foundation and *The Wall Street Journal*

For lovers of statistical analysis, correlation analysis also confirms the relationship between informality and poverty. To quote a World Bank policy research working paper written by Norman A. Loayza: "The correlation of the size of the informal sector with real per capita GDP in 1990 is -0.70, and its correlation with the share of urban population in the same year is -0.53. This suggests that the size of the informal sector is related to the development level of the country."[13] This assertion is confirmed by an analysis of the "Black market activity" scores for the 155 countries included in the *2001 Index of Economic Freedom.* The correlation of the black market activity scores for the *2001 Index* with the per capita GDP was −0.82, a figure indicating a very strong and negative relationship indeed.[14]

The informal sector, state sanction, and legal protection

Why are the consequences of inaccessible bureaucracy and the attempt to bypass the legal system so dismal? Because extralegality puts people at a real disadvantage: it limits them in their opportunities to transact. Essentially, extralegality is a source of vulnerability to state sanction. "Informal activities are subject to stiff penalties in the form of fines or capital confiscation."[15] Penalties and capital confiscation are frequently averted through the payment of bribes and commissions, but the threat of persecution itself must not be discounted as insignificant. In the case that informal agents are not the objects of corruption, the consequences are actually worse: the foundation of public power is the use of physical force and coercion. Law enforcement agencies in developing countries are hardly known for their tenderness and due process. On numerous occasions, in many countries, illegal markets, workshops, and squatter settlements have been cleared by the use of excessive force and the summary destruction of property (with no regard whatsoever for the needs, interests, and circumstances of the victims). In the final analysis, brute force is the foundation on which exclusion stands. Correspondingly, informals have every incentive to try evading the vicious business of extortion and official persecution:[16]

> In order to avoid being caught, firms scale down the size of their informal operations. In the case of purely informal firms, the efforts to avoid detection prevent them from achieving economies of scale and from choosing an optimal capital-labor mix; this is so because larger and more physical capital-intensive firms are easier to detect.

Therefore, extralegality, in itself, represents a perverse incentive that discourages economic growth as informal agents keep down the size of their operations. Surveying informal firms, De Soto found that informals "limit their operations or, if they need to grow, do so by dispersing their workers so that there are never more than ten in one establishment."[17] The National Statistical Office of Thailand confirmed a divergence in the respective sizes of formal and informal firms reporting that "most workers in the informal sector were in small businesses size employing not more than 5 persons, whereas most in the formal sector were in large businesses with 100 persons and over."[18] Undoubtedly, the vast majority of operations currently within the informal sector would remain small even if they could join the formal sector, but one still wonders at the potential, foregone growth.

Nevertheless, efforts to avoid detection are hardly keeping corrupt officials from exploiting the opportunity presented by extralegality. This is hardly surprising as in the final analysis it is precisely the size of the informal sector that makes detection of many of its agents unavoidable. Correspondingly, the cost of avoidance and bribery has been found significant. In *The Other Path*, Mr De Soto writes, "While the informal business owners interviewed said they paid out between 10 and 15 per cent of their gross income in bribes and commissions, the owners of formal small businesses said they paid no more than 1 percent."[19] These estimates apply to the situation of Peru, but let us nevertheless – and just for the sake of argument – apply them to the aforementioned OECD estimates for the Mexican informal economy. Doing so would mean that the servants of the law would be extorting something like fifteen to twenty-two billion dollars per year. By comparison, in 2000, the Mexican government spent twenty billion dollars on education. In that same year, foreign direct investment flowing into Mexico amounted to thirteen billion dollars. Please note that those bribes and commissions are not being paid by the rich; rather, they are being extorted from the poor. This is not a form of capitalist exploitation; this is an illegal racket organized by state officials. Also, such high costs do not aid the cause of capital accumulation, which is a necessary condition for economic growth.

Informality poses further obstacles to economic growth beyond the dangers of persecution and the costs of avoiding penalization. Because of their illegal status:[20]

> Informal agents do not fully enjoy public services, particularly those that allow them full, enforceable property

rights over their capital and output. This has a number of negative consequences: First, informal producers are poorly protected by the police and the judicial courts from crimes committed against their property. Second, since they lack the capacity to enter into legally binding contractual obligations, their access to capital markets, for financial, insurance, and corporative purposes, is seriously impaired.

Informal producers are hardly in a position to require protection by the police and judiciary from crimes committed against their property because any such requests would expose the illegality of their activities and properties – matters they seek to hide in the first place from these same branches of government. Accordingly, there is no sense or profit in investing in capital goods that are, under conditions of extralegality, particularly vulnerable to crimes, seizure, and confiscation.

Correspondingly, informal activities are typically limited to types of production that are, by and large, self-protected, namely, activities that do not require the protection of the law and "may be advantageously undertaken even in environments in which there are no individual rights to property or to contract enforcement."[21] As a matter of fact, only labour-intensive types of production such as the cottage industry, handicrafts, and personal services fall under this category, effectively excluding the informal producer from the benefits of capital-intensive production.

The same is true for trading activities. In the absence of legal protection or state sanction, informals themselves will mostly be limited to trades that are self-enforcing. In the words of Mancur Olson, another economist concerned with the question of underdevelopment, parties to such transactions "largely eliminate the danger that the other *will not reciprocate* by making both parts of the transaction simultaneous, by making trades only within families or other close social groups where the aggrieved individual can bring social sanctions to bear, by restricting trades to those who have invested too much to obtain a reputation for honouring deals to profit from failing to do so, and so on."[22]

Consider, then, all the types of production and transactions that informals cannot engage in. These comprise all types of production and transactions that require a legal right to property, freedom to commence and operate businesses, formal registration and enforceability, as well as the various secondary advantages of legality, freedom, and protection. Thus, without the right or license to start and operate a business, its owner cannot borrow money from banks for working capital. One of De Soto's findings was that informals also had massive amounts of informal properties or land, houses, and other buildings to which they hold no title or a defective title. Such properties cannot be mortgaged.

The great motor of economic growth is credit. In the West, business start-ups and expansion are intimately bound up with bank finance. This is why governments are so keen on the lower interest rates. Cheap credit fuels borrowing, and borrowing expands both consumer demand and business investment, which boosts economic growth. However, without proper credentials, such as property titles and proof of registration of (or licenses to) operate a business, bank credit is mostly unavailable.

This is also true in the developing world. Credit institutions will not deal with informals, and informals, in turn, often cannot finance sales beyond a certain point and therefore forego sales revenues. An informal in need of credit will, most of the time, face shut doors. Correspondingly, in the absence of formal title to properties and businesses, informals face extremely high capital costs. To quote Loayza: "Huq and Sultan (1991) report that in Bangladesh, in 1988, firms which depended on non-institutional sources to meet their financial needs paid rates between 48 to 100 per cent annually, whereas the borrowing rate from commercial banks was around 12 per cent."[23] Informal borrowing is four to eight times as expensive as formal borrowing. At these rates, it is hardly surprising that informal businesses cannot expand. Informality is a poverty trap.

Also consider that an informal, on account of his need to avoid detection, cannot easily advertise his goods and services. According to De Soto:[24]

> This helps them to remain unnoticed by the authorities, but it also prevents them from building their businesses. According to the U.S. Small Business Administration, two-thirds of all customers are brought in by the signs displayed outside shops or factories. Advertising can also help to offset the disadvantages of a poor location, compensating for the lack of visibility with effective communication. Informals cannot exploit this advantage, either.

Extralegality and underinvestment

The negative ramifications of extralegality are severe. The constraints related to extralegality help explain why developing countries suffer so much unemployment and underemployment and such low levels of productivity and capital investment. A cursory comparison of the size of the informal sector and informal employment statistics supports the hypothesis that extralegality depresses productivity. A comparison of the percentages of eleven countries (see Table 2) for which there were both informal sector size and informal employment statistics using data found in a Center for International Private Enterprise working paper by Catherine Kuchta-Helbling[25] shows that the average informal sector employment for these countries amounted to 64 per cent of non-agricultural employment. The average informal sector GDP was 31 per cent of non-agricultural GDP. In other words, two-thirds of the labour force appears to contribute a mere one third of the GDP. This suggests that the average formal sector participant might be four times as productive as his or her counterpart in the informal sector.

Table 2. Comparison of informal sector and labour force size		
Countries	Informal sector employment as per cent of non-agricultural employment	Informal sector GDP as per cent of non-agricultural GDP
Algeria	43	26
Benin	93	43
Chad	74	45
Colombia	38	25
India	83	45
Indonesia	78	31
Kenya	72	25
Mexico	55	13
Morocco	45	31
Philippines	72	32
Tunisia	50	23
Average of these eleven countries	64	31

Source of data: Tables 2 and 5 (in *Barriers to Participation: The Informal Sector in Developing and Transition Countries* by Catherine Kuchta-Helbling) The Center for International Private Enterprise, Washington.

Authors of informal sector and labour force-size statistics usually warn of the inexactness of their findings on account of the extreme difficulty of finding and uncovering reliable data. Indeed, perusing and comparing various studies yields substantial variations for many countries in the outcomes calculated. Nonetheless, their value is indicative. These estimates tell us that there is a substantial gap between the productivity of the formal sector and the informal sector with the latter being at a disadvantage vis-à-vis the former. Not all of this gap can be blamed on informality; one may assume that a significant portion of the variation will be accounted for by differing levels of education between informals and formals (with the latter likely to be better educated). Informals are generally people with humble, working-class backgrounds who tend to be rural migrants with an arrears in education.

Nevertheless, without credit and legal protection, people cannot or will not invest. There is an analogy in informal housing that shows the dramatically adverse impact of extralegality on investment. In the same way that overregulation dissuades informal agents from starting legal businesses, so an excess of regulatory and bureaucratic procedures prevents squatters from legalizing their real estate possessions. In his research on the question of informal housing, de Soto found that a majority of all real estate holdings in the developing world were held informally (i.e., without full and proper title). In the case of Peru, his research revealed that informal dwellings represented 53 per cent of all urban housing.[26] This is a common pattern throughout the developing. De Soto found – for Peru – that obtaining "legal authorization to build a house on state-owned land took six years and eleven months, requiring 207 administrative steps in fifty-two government offices. To obtain a legal title for that piece of land took 728 steps."[27] With government posing such obstacles to legal home ownership it is no wonder that informal housing is so common in the developing world. His research also uncovered that informal possession adversely affected both the value of the land and the dwellings and the ability and willingness of informals to invest. Indeed, why should they invest? Informal possessors often risk eviction and forcible relocation. Additionally, they cannot legally sell or rent out their housing, nor can they mortgage their real estate to gain the means for their improvement. Correspondingly, an ILD survey of the values of houses and buildings in thirty-seven neighbourhoods in Lima uncovered that people invested at least nine times more "when they are given some measure of protection by the formal legal system."[28] This, then, is the scale of underinvestment resulting from overregulation and extralegality.

The domestic mother lode of investment capital, the extralegal sector, remains unexploited; industrial development remains largely hidden in back alleys and arrested at the cottage industry and handicraft stage. But for access to credit, combining with one's own effort and the chance to transact freely and without fear of prosecution, many hundreds of millions of people should never have been poor in the first place. Trillions of dollars of investment opportunities are wasted and turnover revenues foregone.

The state that knew no citizens

It cannot be overstated that in many countries the informal sector is the only means to a livelihood for large groups of people. The totality of informal sector or black market activity is the sum of all troubles that people encounter when doing business legally. It is vital that we realize that the informal sector is a popular response to attempts to submit economic activity to political and administrative controls. Informal sector and black market activity are *always* a measure of how some part of the citizenry interacts with legal and administrative systems and controls. Properly understood, the informal sector is the consequence of governmental behaviour, (i.e., the outcome of a regulatory environment imposed by the government). Where government respects the legitimate objectives of its citizens, there can be no informal sector. To the extent that people feel no need or desire to evade laws, rules, or regulations there is no informal sector. Apparently, there is relatively little need to evade regulations in rich countries; whereas, in many poor countries there is clearly a widespread desire or need to do so. Therefore, the issue of informality boils down to a case of *The People vs. The State*. The "case" here is about the state criminalizing and marginalizing a significant part of the citizenry; it is about a state, a political elite, and its intellectual fellow travellers whose awareness of, feeling for, and approach to the interests of a large portion of the citizenry ranges from ignorance to indifference to hostility to hypocrisy to criminal opportunism.

The denunciation of overregulation and bureaucracy is not a call for the dismantlement of government. It is actually a call for access to and improved provision of state services such as property and business registration and recognition, police protection, enforcement of contracts, and the rule of law. These are vital and legitimate government functions that have been neglected, corrupted, and buried in bureaucracy. Formal business and property representation and providing legal protection are government functions deserving of improvement, expansion, and investment of tax money. Yet, after a century of neglect and distraction, creating and implementing an equitable and efficient system of formal property representation and protection accessible to all citizens and enterprises is bound to be a hard slog on every level. In this sense, we should therefore call for more and not less government! In this context, *more* entails a *greater quality* of government, one geared to improving the lives of the underserved, not just *more* in the sense of a *bigger government* without any clear and specific purpose. But the increased access to state services and relevance to the informals of any improvement of these services are, to a great extent, contingent upon deregulation and the rationalization of bureaucracy. In this respect, we must demand less government.

Summary

This chapter provided a brief sketch of the problem of the informal sector insofar as its existence is the consequence of excessive regulation and bureaucracy. The purpose of this chapter was to demonstrate the severity of the consequences of overregulation by providing insights, facts and figures. Overregulation and bureaucracy are manifestations of lawfully exercised authority unrestrained by any consideration of the true interests of the larger part of the citizenry, which includes the need for practical and formal recognition of property rights and the right of free enterprise.

In this chapter, we demonstrated the consequences of overregulation. In the next chapter, we will deal with the question of how we should rid ourselves of overregulation. On account of overregulation being a wide topic, we will limit ourselves to the subject matter of the regulation of business start-ups or *entry regulation*. The regulation of business start-ups is a matter directly related to the issue of individual rights. Governments in the developing world have done such a nasty job of raising barriers to access to the formal sector that there is a compelling case for a principled stand against entry regulation, which we will cover in the next two chapters. In these chapters, we will examine how overregulation relates to individual rights, demonstrating that there are comprehensive, rights-based solutions to the problem of overregulation.

Chapter 3

Entry Regulation

Old laws and rights, inherited
From age to age, drag on and on
Like some hereditary disease,
Stealthily widening, growing worse.
Wisdom turns to nonsense, good deeds prove a curse,
Your ancestors your doom!
The native right that's born with us,
For that, alas! No man makes room.
                           —Johann Wolfgang von Goethe, *Faust*

On the seventeenth of December in 2010, just before noon, a young man standing in the middle of traffic in front of the governor's office doused himself with gasoline and set himself on fire. Mohamed Bouazizi, an extralegal street vendor living in a Tunisian town called Sidi Bouzid, immolated himself to protest the confiscation of his wares and wheelbarrow (and the harassment and humiliation that had in the process been inflicted upon him by municipal officials).[1] Reportedly, local police officers had been targeting and abusing Bouazizi for years, repeatedly confiscating his produce and wheelbarrow. In the morning leading up to the incident, the police had attempted to extort money from him, allegedly because he did not have the required license to sell his produce. Bouazizi, a breadwinner in a family of eight, did not have the money to bribe police officials to allow his street vending to continue. The harassment was reported to be particularly humiliating; he had been slapped, spit at, and insulted by the police officers. It must have been the final straw for Bouazizi. He rushed to the governor's office to complain and demand redress. The governor refused to see or listen to him. In an interview with *Reuters,* one of his sisters stated, "What kind of repression do you imagine it takes for a young man to do this? A man who has to feed his family by buying goods on credit when they fine him ... and take his goods. In Sidi Bouzid, those with no connections and no money for bribes are humiliated and insulted and not allowed to live."[2] Observe that, at the other end of the same administrative apparatus that deprived Bouazizi of permission to pursue a livelihood, a corrupt President Zine El Abidine Ben Ali granted licenses and permits that made many of his cronies filthy rich. One extralegal, by setting himself on fire, sparked the Arab Spring of 2011, leading ultimately to the downfall of no fewer than four dictators in the Middle East.

The death of Bouazizi unleashed a wave of public rage, riots, and popular uprisings across the Middle East against corrupt, tyrannical rulers. Yet, worryingly, revolt in the Arab world seems to leave the rotten core of corrupt and obstructive legal and administrative systems untouched and unreformed. Bouazizi's humiliation and the consequent act of desperation generated an enormous amount of sympathy, anger, and publicity. Yet the oppressive system of licenses and permits (i.e., entry regulation, which Bouazizi struggled against) has remained virtually unexamined to this day. A man killed himself because he was not allowed to pursue a livelihood with any degree of freedom and dignity. Bouazizi was posthumously included in the award of the Sakharov Prize of 2011 in recognition of the "struggle for dignity, basic freedoms and political change in the Arab world."[3] Such words are premature and pretentious when one realizes that Bouazizi's act of desperation has inspired not one soul – not a single public figure, aspiring political reformer, or social activist – in the world to denounce and demand reform of a vile and tyrannical system of permits and licenses.

Defining entry regulation

The permit or license, which Bouazizi allegedly needed to pursue his trade, is part of a set of administrative instruments collectively called entry regulation. Entry regulation comprises those requirements that a business start-up must bear before it can operate legally.[4] Licensing, registration, filing, and certification requirements are the better-known forms of entry regulation. The term entry regulation is a rather more precise and comprehensive concept covering the regulatory requirements surrounding business start-ups than the usual concepts such as licensing, registration, or certification. Entry regulation is usually the first hurdle that must be taken when starting a business, frequently even in the case of the simplest, the most commonplace, or the humblest of occupations and enterprises. The essence of entry regulation is that all business is rendered illegal until permission, authorization, recognition, or submission of documents has been secured. With respect to entry regulation, the key concept is *permission*. The concept of permission is operative in two ways. One must either actively seek permission – as in licensing requirements – or one must meet certain requirements before one is allowed to operate a business – as in registration, certification, and filing requirements. In other words, by means of a set of requirements, the government determines whether or not one will be permitted to operate a business. The administrative and legal procedures surrounding ILD's attempt to establish a two-sewing-machine factory are an example of entry regulation. In rich, developed countries, entry regulation is generally seen as a benign, relatively non-intrusive, and legitimate form of business regulation. In most non-advanced economies, entry regulation is just about as non-intrusive as an anaconda wrapped around its prey.

Justice

The key to understanding the proposition of entry regulation as predatory jurisdiction is to contrast two concepts: *permission* and *rights*. Recall that, in the first chapter, we applied Rand's definition of the concept of rights: a moral principle defining and sanctioning a man's freedom of action in a social context. From this definition, a Rand scholar, Peikoff, derived the following argument: "A right is a sanction to independent action; the opposite of acting by right is acting by *permission*."[5] By this line of reasoning, the practice of entry regulation is in exact opposition to the concept of rights – entry regulation imposes a legal requirement to act by permission. Does this opposition also signify the violation of rights?

The relevance of this question is first and foremost a question of justice: If the informal sector is the consequence of an adverse regulatory environment imposed by governments, is it not reasonable to question the legitimacy of its means (in this case, the power of entry regulation)?

Exclusion and extralegality are largely the consequence of the denial of freedom caused by a legal requirement to act by permission, the fulfilment of which is demonstrably beyond the means and capabilities of hundreds of millions of informals.

Not every requirement to act by permission is a violation of rights. Property rights would be meaningless if possessions could be taken from their owners without their permission. In free nations, adult relationships are consensual (i.e., associations by grace of mutual permission). But *permission,* in this sense, flows from the possession of rights. Precisely because the individual has a right – meaning that the individual is free – any initiation of a relationship or transaction must be voluntary and therefore take place by mutual consent. Within the context of the exercise of rights the requirement to act by permission sustains the freedom of each and every individual.

However, the power of entry regulation does not derive from any demonstrable right; states or governments in themselves do not, as a matter of principle, possess rights. The power to regulate is a form of public power, its stated purpose being the protection and maintenance of the health, safety, or welfare of the citizens. In US constitutional law, it would fall within the scope of the legal concept of police power.[6] Naturally, the aim – the protection and maintenance of the health, safety, and welfare of the public – is not an issue. The question relates to the legitimacy of the *means* (i.e., the instruments of public power). Is it right that – as a matter of routine practice, which is currently almost everywhere the case – public power should include the unrestrained authority to impose a legal requirement to act by permission?

In this chapter we will start off by examining the question on an abstract level. We will subsequently investigate a number of practical concerns, including the economic arguments for entry regulation. We will also take a look at the question of its efficacy in achieving the objective of entry regulation (namely, the protection of the public interest).

The Fundamentals

The answer to the question – is the power of entry regulation a legitimate instrument of public power and policy – is articulated in Rand's definition of the right to life:

There is only one fundamental right (all the others are its consequences or corollaries): a man's right to his own life. Life is a process of self-sustaining and self-generated action; the right to life means the right to engage in self-sustaining action, which means: the freedom to take all the actions required by the nature of a rational being for the support, the furtherance, the fulfillment and the enjoyment of his own life. (Such is the meaning of the right to life, liberty and the pursuit of happiness.)[7]

People (and the informal, no less) need and have the right to engage in self-sustaining action. To that extent, the requirement to act by permission flouts the very definition of life itself. If "the freedom to take all the actions required by the nature of a rational being for the support, the furtherance, the fulfilment and the enjoyment of his own life" is the proper right of man, the requirement to act by permission presents an unwarranted attack on human nature. To take the argument to its logical conclusion: entry regulation *as a matter of principle* violates the rights of the individual, starting with the right to life.

Peikoff also provided the following elaboration on this right to life:[8]

The right to life means the right to sustain and protect one's life. It means the right to take all the actions required by the nature of a rational being for the preservation of his life. To sustain his life, man needs a method of survival – he must use his rational faculty to gain knowledge and choose values, then act to achieve his values. The right to liberty is the right to this method; it is the right to think and choose, then to act in accordance with one's judgment. To sustain his life, man needs to create the material means of his survival.

The requirement to act by permission encroaches upon the right to think and choose, then to act in accordance with one's judgement – the right to liberty or individual freedom. Informals, as much as anyone else, think and choose, and then they act in accordance with their judgement. So the right to liberty comes natural to them, and if informals have not so far presented an articulate and spirited argument in favour of their right to liberty, necessity and hardship have already compelled them to act accordingly – outside the formal system in many cases. Informality is a rational choice made out of necessity in the face of an unnatural or irrational system of political controls over the economy.

From life to economy to rights

If the rights to life and liberty matter, we have an obligation to face its meaning in the context of economic action. The process of self-sustaining action is the ultimate rationale for economic activity. The most important modes of self-sustaining action are production and trade. Production is a creative effort; it is about combining mental and physical effort to rearranging matter to craft an object with the capacity to meet a need. Trade is the voluntary exchange of value for value, each resulting from productive effort, to the benefit of both parties.[9] Production and trade are essential or necessary to human life; without production and trade, mankind would face mass starvation. Reality is quite final about this. If there are any doubts about production and trade being essential, consider the consequence of ceasing *all* productive effort and trade, from the paddy fields in Java to the factories in Detroit. The result is only too obvious to any rational person. Because humans – especially modern humans in their densely populated world – have no meaningful, alternative modes for self-sustaining action but production and trade, these are *necessary* and therefore *right*.[10] The value of this argument is that economic activity (formal and informal) is for the greatest part production and trade; conversely, economic regulations also pertain to productive effort and trade.

As a consequence, the proper corollaries of the rights to life and liberty are the *right to produce* and the *right to trade*. A person's objectives, dreams, ambitions, actions, and interests – in terms of productive effort and trade – are legitimate because they are necessary and right for sustaining that person's life. The existence of an informal sector is therefore evidence of the failure to acknowledge these rights and of injustice perpetrated by government. In other words, the informal sector's existence provides proof of predatory jurisdiction with entry regulation as a smoking gun.

Market failure

Our discussion up to this point has been philosophical in nature and sought to demonstrate that, as a matter of principle and for the sake of one's life, one should not have to act by permission – such a requirement is invalid. This line of reasoning does not by itself invalidate the need for government regulation ... and frankly, it never can.

The rationale behind regulatory authority is that market failure might necessitate government intervention. Market failure is an umbrella concept within economic theory for a wide range of scenarios and events in which unregulated markets result in outcomes that are suboptimal or less than satisfactory from a societal point of view. Essentially, the concept of market failure implies that there is room for improving the operation of a market, with such improvements yielding increased benefits for society. One example of market failure is the damage done by industrial pollution to people and their properties. Another example is the failure to assign property rights, which may limit the ability of markets to form or to operate properly. Intervention by government to use these examples can take the form of penalizing polluters through fines and creating effective property titles, respectively. The scope of market failure as a topic is so broad and varied, however, that it precludes further elaboration of this diverse topic. Strictly in the abstract (and without going into the specifics), government intervention might be justified when market failure occurs.[11]

Even so, the case of market failure never invalidates the necessity and rightness of self-sustaining action; market failure does not somehow diminish the necessity of productive effort and trade. The simple fact of necessity – which is a given derived from our existence as living creatures or our human nature – makes it right to engage in productive effort and trade. The rights to life, to engage in self-sustaining action, and to produce and trade are inalienable rights. The definition of *inalienable* is something "that cannot be rightfully taken away."[12] To put it simply, what is necessary for life cannot be wrong and should not be forbidden; there can be no requirement to act by permission because that would be contrary to nature. In other words, we are *not* making a case against regulation in its entirety – nor are we questioning the concept of market failure. We are simply questioning the legitimacy and the necessity of one form of regulation – namely, entry regulation.

Principles versus practical experience

Having examined the ethicality of entry regulation, there is still the issue of practical experience. Are there real and demonstrable benefits to entry regulation to the public, which on balance compensate for injuries arising from the infringement of rights?

There is a risk here that this question may be taken as suggesting the possibility that principle, as represented here by rights and practice or the workaday experience that governments encounter in dealing with market failures, may not be reconcilable. This is a variation on the common fallacy that there is some kind of dichotomy between principle and practice. Properly arrived at, a principle is not divorced from reality but derived from it. The term *principle* is, after all, defined as "a general truth or law, basic to other truths."[13] And a truth is "a statement or belief that corresponds to the reality."[14] In investigating the issue of entry regulation, we did reduce the matter to the essence of life. The right to life is a practical issue … but so is market failure.

A study, the results of which are presented in a Kennedy School of Government working paper, *The Regulation of Entry*, provides new and useful information for addressing the question at hand.[15] The Kennedy School paper also provides a synopsis of the standard theory and argument in favour of entry regulation, which reads as follows:[16]

> Pigou's (1938) now standard theory of regulation has been recently called the *helping hand* view (Shleifer and Vishny 1998). It holds that unregulated markets exhibit frequent failures, ranging from monopoly power to externalities. A government that pursues social efficiency counters these failures and protects the public through regulation. As applied to entry, this view holds that the government screens new entrants so as to make sure that consumers buy high quality products from "desirable" sellers. Such regulation reduces market failures such as low quality products from fly-by-night operators and externalities such as pollution. It is "done to ensure that new companies meet minimum standards to provide a good or service.

By being registered, new companies acquire a type of official approval, which makes them reputable enough to engage in transactions with the general public and other businesses." (SRI 1999 p. 14) The helping hand theory predicts that stricter regulation of entry, as measured by a higher number of procedures in particular, should be associated with socially superior outcomes.

The argument should be familiar because it is common currency in public discourse. The objective of the Kennedy School work group was to establish whether statistical analysis would validate or falsify the prediction. The abstract to the paper provides the answer:[17]

The official costs of entry are extremely high in most countries. Countries with heavier regulation of entry have higher corruption and larger unofficial economies, but not better quality of public or private goods. Countries with more democratic and limited governments have fewer entry regulations. The evidence is inconsistent with Pigouvian (helping hand) theories of benevolent regulation, but support the (grabbing hand) view that entry regulation benefits politicians and bureaucrats.

Properly understood, the paper refutes the prediction "that stricter regulation of entry, as measured by a higher number of procedures in particular, should be associated with socially superior outcomes."

It is not the purpose of the paper to evaluate the usefulness of the procedures as such. Nevertheless, the data presents such a variation – from one country to another for companies with comparable characteristics[18] – in the number of procedures that a start-up has to comply with in order to obtain a legal status that one is forced to question the usefulness of entry regulation. The results of the study show that the "number of procedures required to start up a firm varies from the low of 2 in Canada to the high of 20 in Bolivia."[19] Imagine, in a vastly more complex economy, business start-ups are apparently subject to fewer regulatory constraints than in a comparatively rustic society. As a matter of fact, the authors simply state that "better governments regulate entry less."[20]

The authors identify and list a total of sixty-six procedures required to create a company in the seventy-five countries of the sample.[21] In the list of procedures, the authors remark that plain vanilla registration "always present as a step ... is arguably the only truly necessary step for start-up."[22] For good measure, the working paper does not suggest that the actions controlled by the other sixty-five procedures are all unnecessary. Some of the procedures are silly. One example provided is the permit to play music in public, which is obligatory for every firm in Colombia, regardless of whether it contemplates playing music.[23] Nevertheless, many of the actions involved – for example, the check for uniqueness of the proposed company name – are indeed quite necessary, but it does not have to be entry regulation.

Finally, on the effectiveness of entry regulations as administrative controls, the authors remark:[24]

> Since firms operating unofficially avoid nearly all regulations, a large size of the unofficial economy in countries with more regulations would contradict the prediction of the helping hand theory that regulation effectively protects consumers. ... The fact that countries with severe market failures have more abusive governments by itself limits the normative usefulness of the Pigouvian model.

Actually, the working paper leaves no doubt that there are practical uses for entry regulation. The working paper concludes by stating, "All the evidence is naturally consistent with the tollbooth version of the grabbing hand model. Entry appears to be regulated more heavily by the less attractive governments, and such regulation leads to unattractive outcomes. The principal beneficiaries, if any, are the politicians and the bureaucrats themselves."[25] What is this tollbooth version of the grabbing hand model? To quote the working paper:[26]

> The tollbooth view, holds that regulation is pursued for the benefit of politicians and bureaucrats (De Soto 1990). Politicians use regulation to favor friendly firms and other political constituencies, and thereby obtain campaign

contributions and votes. In addition, "an important reason why many of these permits and regulations exist is probably to give officials the power to deny them and to collect bribes in return for providing the permits." (Shleifer and Vishny 1993, p. 601). ... In this theory, the regulation of entry enables the regulators to collect bribes from the potential entrants and serves no social purpose. ... More extensive regulation should be associated with socially inferior outcomes, particularly corruption.

From the same working paper, we gather that not even the World Bank could resist putting the case in the strongest possible wording:[27]

"When someone has finally made the decision to invest, he then is subjected to some of the worst treatment imaginable [...] In a few cases this treatment consists of outright extortion: presenting the investor with insurmountable delays or repeated obstacles unless he makes a large payoff [...]"

The standard theory of regulation is derived, as the Kennedy School paper suggests, from Arthur C. Pigou's welfare theory.[28] Since Pigouvian welfare theory provides the standard non-ideological rationale for economic intervention qua externalities, it behoves us to heed Pigou's dicta on the subject of applying theory. The following is a quote from a paragraph Pigou devoted to the subject of public intervention in *The Economics of Welfare*:[29]

In any industry, where there is reason to believe that the free play of self-interest will cause an amount of resources to be invested different from the amount that is required in the best interest of the national dividend, there is a *prima facie* case for public intervention. The case, however, cannot become more than a *prima facie* one, until we have considered the qualifications, which governmental agencies may be expected to possess for intervening advantageously. It is not sufficient to contrast the imperfect adjustments of unfettered private enterprise with the best adjustment that economists in their studies can imagine. For we cannot expect that any public authority will attain, or will even whole-heartedly seek, that ideal. Such authorities are liable alike to ignorance, to sectional pressure and to personal corruption by private interest.

Pigou called this paragraph his "argument for non-interference by public authorities."[30] If, as Pigou argued, "the force of this argument ... is, clearly, not the same at all times and places,"[31] it definitely applies to the greater majority of governments in the developing world and not a few in the developed world besides.

A positive case for entry regulation fails on practical *and* ethical grounds. The enforcement of regulations of any kind is always a highly complex and exceedingly difficult matter. The organizational or institutional aspect should never be underestimated. It is therefore unconscionable that governments should waste financial and human resources on attempts to implement regulations that violate serious principles.

The case of the rich countries

In spite of the argumentation so far, there is the prima facie case of the rich countries with regard to entry regulation. Governments in rich countries, as much as those in poor countries, have the authority to issue regulations imposing requirements to act by permission. There are no rich countries that recognize a right to life or liberty following the Randian definition. Citizens in rich countries have no direct judicial recourse against entry regulation for violating rights so defined. Indeed, in this respect, rich countries do not appear to offer any real or visible distinction vis-à-vis poor countries. The essence of the prima facie argument will be that rich countries also impose entry regulation and seem none the worse for it. The example of rich countries is troubling because poor countries often emulate them. To shore up the legitimacy of entry regulation, proponents in poor countries in favour of entry regulation are quite likely to point out that rich countries also use entry regulation. The argument is obviously simplistic, but simplistic arguments are common currency in political discourse. It is for this reason that we must anticipate what is in fact a reactionary position. It is a certainty that this type of counterargument will be launched.

Consequently, a failure to address the issue would needlessly draw out the whole discussion to the cost of the poorest members of humanity.

One way to refute the prima facie case of the rich countries is to do a bit of number crunching. When we review the results published in the Kennedy School paper discussed earlier in this chapter, we discover that levels of entry regulation correlate strongly with a large variance in standards of living of European nations. One axis on which the variance can be analysed is the north–south divide in the European Union while limiting the analysis to members that had acceded to the Union by 1995.[32] This selection serves to include European countries commonly categorized as rich, while excluding formerly communist countries. If one applies language grouping – the criterion being an official Germanic or Romance language as the majority language in the selected countries[33] – as a proxy for the division between northern and southern nations, it turns out that northern nations have, on average, fewer entry procedures than southern nations and are richer (see Table 3).

Table 3. Entry regulation – Average statistics of EU countries by language grouping				
Classification	Number of Procedures	Time (business days)	Cost (as share of GDP per capita)	GDP (1997) in USD per capita
Germanic	6,56	51,11	0,11	24.679
Romance	12,60	84,40	0,27	15.742

These numbers stem from my own calculations, which are based on data derived from Table III, page 28, *The Regulation of Entry*, by Simeon Djankov, Rafael La Porta, Florencio Lopez de Silanes, and Andrei Shleifer; *Working Paper No. 1; Visions of Governance in the 21st Century Project*, Kennedy School of Government, Harvard University.

To be brutally honest, without joining the European Union, some of Europe's most bureaucratic nations (such as Greece, Portugal, and Spain) would probably have remained at non-advanced levels of development and prosperity.[34] On the other hand, Sweden and Finland, late entrants to the EU, already had levels of prosperity above EU averages. But Sweden and Finland have virtually laissez-faire levels of entry regulation. Entrepreneurs in Sweden can finish the process of certifying a business in roughly seventeen days by paying USD 654 in government fees and completing just four procedures. In Greece, it took roughly fifty-three days to complete thirteen procedures and costs USD 5.452 in government fees.

Greece is also a substantially more corrupt society than Sweden.[35] When "examining separately the relationship between entry regulations and corruption in countries with above and below world median income," the Kennedy School work group concluded the following: "The results show that regulations actually have a stronger effect on corruption in the subsample of richer countries." This simply means that data regarding rich countries are actually better material for determining the relationship between levels of corruption and entry regulation than poor country data. The reason for this is that rich countries, as a group, exhibit greater variation in levels of entry regulation and corruption than poor countries, which are, as a rule, both corrupt and overregulated.

Yet the prima facie argument also rests on a number of omissions. To start with, it ignores what we can call the *wealth effect*. Next, it ignores Western history. These factors are the topic of the next two sections.

The wealth effect

Essentially, the wealth effect refers to the immensity of the riches of the West – that is, the vastness of its capital resources, the wide distribution of capital among the population, the relative ease of access to capital, the prevalence of high incomes, and the immensity of the pool of expertise available to address every regulatory issue. All these factors contribute towards an ability by broad sections of the public to overcome burdensome regulation to a degree not possible in poor countries.

That there is a problem with regulatory burden – at this point, we are discussing the entire range of economic and social regulations – in the West is beyond doubt; the findings by economists are unambiguous on the issue. Indirect government spending via regulations and mandates is, according to one estimate, around 10 per cent of national income in the United States.[36] In other words, American business spent around one trillion dollars (2000 est.) on complying with regulations to stay legal. That represents an amount larger than the collective GDP of the fifty-eight poorest countries, which have a combined population of more than nine hundred million people.

The estimates for the cost of compliance can be the subject of dispute, but despite whatever the precise figures may be, businesses – and, indirectly, the public – in the West collectively spend amounts on regulatory compliance that the people in poor countries can only dream of. All the same, the simple truth is that the Western peoples can, up to a point, afford to do so because their wealth. Consider entry regulation from a transaction cost perspective. Entry regulation requires a capital outlay including the official cost of the various procedures, earnings foregone because of delays and time spent on the arrangements involved, and money outlays for professional assistance with the bureaucratic paperwork. One could argue – again, up to a point – that people planning to start a business in the West usually have the money, in effect, to "buy" permission.[37] People in the West are generally affluent enough to finance these "start-up costs" from their current incomes or personal savings (and failing that, with the proceeds from loans, which are frequently raised by issuing mortgages to lenders).

The aforementioned Kennedy School working paper seems to confirm this proposition. The authors found that, in developed countries, government fees for certifying a new business varied from USD 72 in New Zealand to a horrendous USD 11.612 in Austria. To the entrepreneur in New Zealand, the USD 72 represents out-of-pocket expenses. Yet even in the extreme case of Austria, government fees are, in the context of Western levels of affluence (GDP per capita was USD 25.549),[38] affordable: the fees fall within the price range of a new, small car, such as an Opel Corsa. Looked at from a strictly financial point of view, the cost of starting up a small business is usually within the means of a majority of the people in the West. Under the current circumstances and all else being equal, affluence makes entry regulation affordable. To that extent, entry regulation is not necessarily perceived as a menace to liberty; it is as if prosperity dulls the need to stand on tightly argued principles.

Though rich countries do not appear worse off as a consequence of applying entry regulation (because of the wealth effect), the same cannot be said about poor countries. Low standards of living and the lack of access to (and the extreme expense of) capital means that the majority of people in poor countries do not have the means to purchase permission. The Kennedy School working paper demonstrated that the official cost of certifying new businesses was (as a percentage of GDP per capita), on average, almost seven times higher for the poorest quartile of countries in the sample than for the richest quartile.[39] The poor are truly cursed; out of near-subsistence levels of income, they must pay a vastly higher proportion than the citizens of rich nations for the privilege of starting a business – and that doesn't take into account the cost of delays and corruption.

Let us make a portrayal of what we shall call a *model victim* of entry regulation. The bare essence of a model victim is a self-employed person without capital, formal skills, access to benefits, access to credit, earnings higher than minimum wage levels, or steady employment prospects (formal or informal). How is this person going to meet the transaction costs of entry regulation? The answer is obvious: he or she cannot. The two-sewing-machine garment factory experiment by the ILD should dispel any illusions to the contrary. In practice, the model victim of entry regulation is not an imaginary creature; there are hundreds of millions of such victims walking about in the developing world. Altogether, in developing countries, entry regulation is *not* affordable.

Actually, the wealth effect and the affordability of start-up costs depend upon a number of preconditions. One condition is the requirement of a reasonably clean, honest, and efficient administration. This requirement is essential for keeping the actual transaction costs of entry regulation predicable and as low as possible (or at least close to official levels). An inefficient administration can result in costly delays and raises business costs and uncertainty. Alternatively, a dishonest, corrupt administration would likely introduce "informal" costs of expediting procedures, such as bribes and intermediation, creating further uncertainty while elevating business costs. The other, more crucial condition is the requirement that entry regulations should not deliberately raise barriers to entry, which would be insurmountable for legitimate practitioners of a business or trade.[40] It should never be forgotten that the state possessing all the means necessary to regulate the economy has the authority and power to do that. When this authority is abused, all bets are off and the wealth effect counts for nothing.

All these conditions break down in the case of developing countries. Politics and public administration are frequently inefficient, dishonest, and corrupt. In many cases, entry regulations are designed to raise barriers to entry, and the intention is to exclude the greater part of the public from not just a few, but from many trades. To use the aforementioned working paper data, an entrepreneur in India can finish the registration process in sixty-one days. In practice, "obtaining a business license requires endless trips to government offices, and the process can take a year or more."[41] India is also acknowledged to be one of the most corrupt societies.

According to the Randian definition of life both the venture capitalist in Silicon Valley and the street vendor in Rio de Janeiro are engaged in self-sustaining action. That much they have in common. The concepts of the right to life and liberty, to produce and trade apply equally to the venture capitalist and the street vendor. It is only when the transaction costs of entry regulation become unbearable *and* when one runs out of alternative means of support that the importance of properly argued rights to life and liberty, to produce and trade become evident.

The common law tradition

Ignorance of Western legal history is the basis for failing to acknowledge the historic role of rights in mitigating the power of the state to impose entry regulation. There is a strange silence in mainstream literature on the subject of entry regulation, its relation to individual rights, and its history. It is true that Western governments have never relinquished entry regulation as a policy instrument. Nor has entry regulation, as a subject, been the object of deliberate, comprehensive, and principled criticism.

Nevertheless, certain Western nations have a strong, centuries-old tradition in favour of economic freedom that is virtually non-existent outside the Western world. This tradition has long been critical of economic interventionism and excessive regulation. Judicial activism in England and the United States from the seventeenth century to the beginning of the twentieth century represented one strand in this tradition of economic liberalism.[42] Just how important the role of this judicial activism was to introducing economic freedom becomes evident from an examination of the history of the *common law right to a lawful occupation* in England and the United States, which was the object of principled resistance for good reason. The value of this example lies in the grasp that a social system based on individual rights and the rule of law can serve to protect citizens against perverse regulatory practices.

For those unfamiliar with legal tradition, it should be interesting to learn that jurisprudence – and Anglo-Saxon jurisprudence even more so – is often in the habit of expressing the most commonplace ideas and concepts in the most charming and old-fashioned terms, which can cause confusion because, often, the public has a different understanding of the same terms. In this vein, the struggle against the *monopoly grant* became an important strand in the development of the common law right to a lawful occupation. Anglo-Saxon jurisprudence spoke of *monopoly* to describe any instance where the exercise of a trade (including the humblest livelihoods) was threatened by undue restrictions. Nowadays, the problem of monopolism is perceived almost purely in terms of illegal practices engaged in by private businesses. There is little or no regard for the role of government in sustaining monopoly power. Seventeenth-century jurists in England – substantial men born to power, close to power, and used to exercising power – were far more perceptive about the true nature of monopolism; these men recognized that such power could be derived from only one source: a government grant. To these early jurists in Britain, the term *monopoly* referred to companies supported and protected by the coercive power of the state. Also, today, the term monopolist calls up the image of a large rogue corporation cornering the supply of goods. During the Elizabethan age, and long after that, monopolism was not primarily a matter of large corporations seeking and gaining exclusive privileges; after all, in that age, there were very few big businesses – certainly nothing on the scale of today's General Motors or Royal Dutch Shell. Instead, monopolism was more of a widespread social phenomenon that affected humble occupations (e.g., the arts and the crafts of the time). Guilds, for example, often secured exclusive recognition for themselves as the only legitimate practitioners of a craft or a trade within a defined locality (a town or city) on the basis of town or Crown legislation. Likewise, factories often secured exclusive privileges for manufacturing. No profession was safe from such exclusive privileges. De Soto provides the example of residents of Pastrana, Spain, who enjoyed an exclusive privilege effective within a radius of twelve leagues to manufacture and trade ribbons! Up to the end of the eighteenth century, private, public, and guild monopolies had a tremendous impact on urban life and trade throughout the realms. Monopoly franchising was deeply resented by the common people who lived under the constant threat of being suddenly disqualified by law from practicing an occupation, which would deprive them of their means to survive and thrive. As with today's entry regulation, yesterday's monopoly franchising resulted in a great deal of exclusion and informal-sector activity. The monopoly grant, whatever its form, was entry regulation *avant la lettre*.

Monopoly grants were originally an ancient method and acknowledged prerogative of the Crown for raising revenues and rewarding loyal subjects. A royal prerogative is an exclusive and unquestionable right belonging to the Crown. Monopoly grants were a very important source of revenue. In England, during the reign of Elizabeth I of Tudor,[43] monopoly grants generated almost 50 per cent of revenue. An important reason for the English Crown to seek to preserve the grant of monopolies as a royal prerogative was the fact that raising taxes was subject to approval by Parliament. Therefore, gaining revenues by granting monopolies was also a ploy to evade Parliamentary supervision.

Monopoly franchising caused hardship for the practitioners of occupations affected as a consequence of being suddenly excluded from the exercise of what had been a formerly free and lawful occupation. The resulting antagonism was sharpened by the liberality with which Elizabeth granted patents of monopoly to favourites and servants. Furthermore, towards the end of Elizabeth's reign, the common opinion was no longer a factor that could be ignored. The sixteenth century was the scene of the rise of the landed classes, and by the end of it, "the Commons was replacing the Lords in importance because the social element it represented had become economically and politically more important than the nobility."[44] The long and short of the argument is that the landed classes were, by their relative wealth, now the premier class of tax payers represented in Parliament – a factor of no mean consequence to a royal administration and household chronically short of funds.[45]

The attack on the royal prerogative of monopoly franchising was first undertaken in Parliament. In regards to Elizabeth's response, the Encyclopaedia Britannica informs us that "Elizabeth had sense enough to avoid a showdown with the Commons, and she retreated under parliamentary attack on the issue of her prerogative rights to grant monopolies regulating and licensing the economic life of the kingdom."[46] Leading mercantilism historian Eli Heckscher provides more details:[47]

In the latter part of Elizabeth's reign a storm broke out against her unlimited grants of patents of monopoly as rewards to her favourites and servants. The old queen, however, understood how to quiet the minds of the people with such skill that parliament refrained from making any decision on the question. The queen referred the legality of the patents of monopoly to the decisions of the ordinary courts. The patent of her courtier, Darcy, for the production and import of playing-cards gave rise to the famous Case of Monopolies (Darcy v. Allen or Allin 1602/3). Without any qualification and without any attempt at prevarication, the decision declared the patent invalid.

What is the historical significance of *Darcy v Allen?* It is the first instance in which a sovereign monarch referred the issue of the royal prerogative to grant monopolies to a common-law court, submitting the matter to its examination; she accepted its verdict while personally declaring that such patents were contrary to common law.[48] This created a precedent that future monarchs could not escape from and failed to reverse. The precedent permanently reduced the scope of the royal prerogative and the revenue-raising powers of the Crown. But aside from the extraordinary precedent, the *Case of Monopolies* is equally important for what it says about monopolies. Heckscher argues as follows:[49]

The opponents of the privileges had also at their disposal certain *economic* arguments, and from the point of view of economic history these are obviously the most interesting. The judgment in the Case of Monopolies is particularly important, for arguments were employed which concerned not the interests of those excluded, but the common interests of all. It was stated first: 'The sole trade of any mechanical artifice, or any other monopoly, is not only a damage and prejudice to those who exercise the same trade, but also to all other subjects.' Then the disadvantages were specified in three points, first 'the price of the same commodity will be raised, for he who has the sole selling of any commodity may and will make the price as he pleases.' Secondly, 'the commodity is not so good and merchantable as it was before' – as counsel for the defendant, Fuller treated this point of view very exhaustively – and the following argument was relegated to the third place: 'It tends to the impoverishment of divers artificers and others who before, by the labour of their hands in their art or trade had maintained themselves and their families.'

Although Heckscher was less interested in the "interests of those excluded" and more in the "common interests of all," the third argument was not a lesser argument as evidenced by the ruling in the second question of the case: whether the grant was available or not in law. Again, the judge resolved that the grant represented:[50]

A monopoly against the common law, and against the end and scope of the Act itself; for this is not to maintain and increase the labours of the poor cardmakers within the realm, at whose petition the Act was made, but utterly to take away and destroy their trade and labours, and that without any reason of necessity, or inconveniency in respect of person, place, or time, and eo potius [sic], because it was granted in reversion for years, as hath been said, but only for the benefit of a private man, his executors and administrators, for his particular commodity, and in prejudice of the commonwealth.

So, there we have it: these quotes are precisely the case of today's informals. A seventeenth-century, common-law court – or, more accurately, the writer of this report of the ruling (the attorney general in the case, Sir Edward Coke) – had already identified that poverty and economic exclusion is, to a large degree, caused by oppressive legal or administrative systems. With this and subsequent cases (but also the Statute of Monopolies of 1624), English, common-law jurists and the parliamentarians were actively engaged in restricting the power of the executive branch of government to impose entry regulation. The ruling in the *Case of Monopolies* proved a landmark in providing the argumentation for formulating and buttressing a common-law right to pursue a lawful trade. After this, hundreds of cases in England and the United States reiterated the common-law right to pursue a lawful trade more often than not with reference to the *Case of Monopolies* for support. The gist of this account is that, for the length of three centuries, the Anglo-Saxon nations had a legal instrument: this common-law right – which is partially analogous to the Randian concept of the right to life and liberty – which contributed formidably towards cutting down regulatory restraints and increased the scope of economic freedom. Also, according to Heckscher, the struggle against monopoly franchising was instrumental in widening the concept of liberty – a development that contributed greatly to the evolution of laissez-faire doctrine.[51]

These factors merged most completely and explicitly in the United States. Its legal system is a common-law system, the Constitution is a document embodying the Enlightenment principles, and the rule of law is its premier principle (derived from the common-law system and the Constitution). The Supreme Court's treatment of the case of *Butchers' Union Co v. Crescent City Co.*, 111 US 746 (1884) is probably one of the finer examples of how these traditions coexisted and meshed.

Several parishes (counties) in eastern Louisiana desired to move all meat and butchering slaughterhouse activities to a location outside the city limits. In so doing, the state legislature granted the Crescent City Livestock Landing and Slaughter-House Company a twenty-five-year monopoly to supervise all slaughterhouse operations. This monopoly grant effectively threatened to put all butchers in these parishes out of business. To quote the ruling: "The act of Louisiana compelled more than a thousand persons to abandon their regular business, and to surrender it to a corporation to which was given an exclusive right to pursue it for 25 years." The Supreme Court found and ruled that the monopoly grant was unconstitutional. In its ruling, it stated that the monopoly grant violated common law, the right of property, the right to the pursuit of happiness, and equal protection. Seldom has any ruling been so liberal in terms of the number of rights considered infringed. Note in the following quote how Justice Field goes to great lengths to spell out both the common-law rights and the natural rights:

> In the grant of these exclusive privileges a monopoly of an ordinary employment and business was created. A monopoly is defined 'to be an institution or allowance from

the sovereign power of the state, by grant, commission, or otherwise, to any person or corporation, for the sole buying, selling, making, working, or using of anything whereby any person or persons, bodies politic or corporate, are sought to be restrained of any freedom or liberty they had before or hindered in their lawful trade,' *All grants of this kind are void at common law, because they destroy the freedom of trade, discourage labor and industry, restrain persons from getting an honest livelihood, and put it in the power of the grantees to enhance the price of commodities. They are void because they interfere with the liberty of the individual to pursue a lawful trade or employment* [italics added]. …

As in our intercourse with our fellow-men certain principles of morality are assumed to exist, without which society would be impossible, so certain inherent rights lie at the foundation of all action, and upon a recognition of them alone can free institutions be maintained. These inherent rights have never been more happily expressed than in the declaration of independence, that new evangel of liberty to the people: 'We hold these truths to be self-evident' - that is, so plain that their truth is recognized upon their mere statement - 'that all men are endowed' - not by edicts of emperors, or decrees of parliament, or acts of congress, but 'by their Creator with certain inalienable rights.' - that is, rights which cannot be bartered away, or given away, or taken away, except in punishment of crime - 'and that among these are life, liberty, and the pursuit of happiness; and to secure these' - not grant them, but secure them - 'governments are instituted among men, deriving their just powers from the consent of the governed.' *Among these inalienable rights, as proclaimed in that great document, is the right of men to pursue their happiness, by which is meant the right to pursue any lawful business or vocation, in any manner not inconsistent with the equal rights of others, which may increase their prosperity or develop their faculties, so as to give to them their highest enjoyment* [italics added]. The common business and callings of life, the ordinary trades and pursuits, which are innocuous in themselves, and have been followed in all communities from time immemorial, must therefore be free in this country to all alike upon the same conditions. The right to pursue them, without let or hindrance, except that which is applied to all persons of the same age, sex, and condition, is a distinguishing privilege of citizens of the United States, and an essential element of that freedom which they claim as their birthright. *It has been well said that 'the property which every man has in his own labor, as it is the original foundation of all other property, so it is the most sacred and inviolable. The patrimony of the poor man lies in the strength and dexterity of his own hands, and to hinder his employing this strength and dexterity in what manner he thinks proper, without injury to his neighbor, is a plain violation of this most sacred property* [italics added]. It is a manifest encroachment upon the just liberty both of the workman and of those who might be disposed to employ him. As it hinders the one from working at what he thinks proper, so it hinders the others from employing whom they think proper.'

To illustrate the continuity of the common-law tradition, read Justice Bradley's argument in the same ruling:

I hold it to be an incontrovertible proposition of both English and American public law, that all mere monopolies are odious, and against common right. The practice of granting them in the time of Elizabeth came near creating a revolution. But parliament, then the vindicator of the public liberties, intervened, and passed the act against monopolies. 21 Jas. I. c. 3. The courts had previously, in the last year of Elizabeth, in the great Case of Monopolies, 11 Rep. 84b, decided against the legality of royal grants of this kind. That was only the case of the sole privilege of making cards within the realm; but it was decided on the general principle that all monopoly patents were void, both at common law and by statute, unless granted to the

[111 U.S. 746, 762] introducer of a new trade or engine, and then for a reasonable time only; that all trades, as well mechanical as others, which prevent idleness, and enable men to maintain themselves and their families, are profitable to the commonwealth, and therefore the grant of the sole exercise thereof is against not only the common law, 'but the benefit and liberty of the subject.'

Note that when Chief Justice Popham [the judge presiding in the *Case of Monopolies*] resolved that the monopoly grant was against "the benefit and liberty of the subject" it was still 1603, prior to the Enlightenment era. That did not prevent post-Enlightenment jurists such as Bradley from bringing Popham's reference to liberty within the scope of the constitutional rights, which are, in fact, the Enlightenment's natural rights. Nevertheless, such action is perfectly legitimate because the kernel of meaning in the concept of liberty was always, even in medieval times, *freedom of action*. An improved understanding of the human condition or new facts and knowledge may require an extension or refinement of a concept's meaning beyond its original understanding by previous generations. This is how science operates, and why should it be any different for legal philosophy? If legal philosophy does not allow it, it should deserve no more respect than alchemy.

The case of *Butchers' Union Co v. Crescent City Co.* is a document showing how a legal system protected "more than a thousand" practitioners of the butchers' trade against monopoly franchising. Where the state of Peru saw fit to impose eleven permits, the law in England and America protected what Field calls the "common business and callings of life, the ordinary trades and pursuits, which are innocuous in themselves." Peikoff's definition of the right to liberty as the right to think and choose, and then to act in accordance with one's judgement resonates in Justice Field's argument concerning how the monopoly represented "a manifest encroachment upon the just liberty" of both the employer and the worker: "As it hinders the one from working at what he thinks proper, so it hinders the others from employing whom they think proper." This line of reasoning is doubly interesting because Field apparently understood that entry regulation, here in the form of monopoly franchising, destroys employment opportunities along with business opportunities.

The argument that rich countries also impose entry regulation and that they are none the worse for it is proven incorrect. Even if such an argument seems plausible today, litigants and the common-law courts in ages past clearly thought otherwise.[52] The English people *did* struggle to free themselves from the destructive force of regulatory power in the hands of the executive branch of the government – and one that was specifically a form of entry regulation (i.e., monopoly franchising). For three centuries, there was a legal standard for reviewing regulations. In American legal science, this type of judicial review is called economic substantive due process. To apply a definition taken from a fine article by a student of law: "Economic substantive due process was a means by which the real effect of a regulation of private contracts could be analysed to determine whether the regulation was really a legitimate exercise of police power or a protectionist or monopolistic scheme."[53] For a proper view of the use to which the Supreme Court put economic substantive due process, read this quote from the ruling in the case of *Adams v. Tanner*:[54]

> Because abuses may, and probably do, grow up in connection with this business, is adequate reason for hedging it about by proper regulations. But this is not enough to justify destruction of one's right to follow a distinctly useful calling in an upright way. Certainly there is no profession, possibly no business, which does not offer peculiar opportunities for reprehensible practices; and as to every one of them, no doubt, some can be found quite ready earnestly to maintain that its suppression would be in the public interest. [...] Happily for all, the fundamental guaranties of the Constitution cannot be freely submerged if and whenever some ostensible justification is advanced and the police power invoked.

Observe the analogy within the first three lines of the quote to the proposition: a case of market failure never invalidates the necessity and rightness of self-sustaining action. Clearly, the court was directly concerned with protecting the freedom of the individual to engage in self-sustaining action.

For a proper perspective of the history of economic substantive due process, it should be noted that this type of judicial review[55] disappeared during the New Deal[56] in the United States. A full and proper analysis of why is beyond the scope of the topic at hand. For the purposes of this chapter, it should suffice to note that the issues and events involved in and the causes of the demise of economic substantive due process go beyond the issue of direct entry regulation.

We have looked at just three rulings, but there are hundreds of cases, and they all form part of a system of jurisprudence and legal doctrine that set clear limits to the scope of regulatory power. This jurisprudence represented a conscious effort on the part of jurists to secure the protection and preservation of the freedom to pursue a lawful business. These then were the conditions under which Great Britain and the United States modernized and industrialized their economies and indeed for the last two and a half centuries it is the Anglo-Saxon group of nations that have dominated the world economy. As for these two nations, they have long – and loudly so – claimed that liberty was the foundation of their prosperity. Without the high sanction of principles – rights as part of the legal system – it would have been far more difficult to participate in the formal legal system, and many citizens in England and the United States would no doubt today have been mired in the same degrading circumstances of the extralegal sector. The restraint of entry regulation by the application of rights went a long way towards increasing economic freedom. One of the ideas behind our theory of predatory jurisdiction is as follows: freedom in the form of free enterprise, free trade, and free markets is fundamental to prosperity. Free enterprise was the key factor to industrial development in England and the United States. Never perfect or complete, the freedom gained was eventually sufficient to allow most economic pursuits within these countries to take place within the formal legal system.

Both from the *Case of Monopolies* and the case of *Butchers' Union Co v. Crescent City Co.,* it reads loud and clear how deeply the monopoly grant was abhorred and how acutely aware people in England and the United States were of how monopolization threatened even the common or humble professions such as making cards or slaughtering animals. Precisely because of this, it is even more surprising that entry regulation just as abusive does not seem to provoke the same loathing and instant association with oppression as monopoly franchising once did. This can only be the result of a conception of life in which the concept of rights as pertinent to economic pursuits is completely absent.

Surely, denouncing entry regulation as the instrument of disempowerment and humiliation for the many and the promise of freedom and the dignity of rights for the same should be highly rewarding campaign issues in many developing nations for anti-establishment politicians taking the stump. Just the controversy and invective from the establishment and the various vested interests, which is sure to follow, should bring the benefit of instant name recognition for the clever, resilient, and intrepid campaigner.

The logic of entry regulation

There is still the matter of the internal logic of entry regulation. The stated idea behind the regulation of entry is that the government should screen new entrants to ensure that new companies meet minimum standards for providing a good or service or for dealing with negative externalities. The stated purpose of the screening process is to weed out undesirable producers and sellers. The objective is laudable. Nevertheless, the means, entry screening, poses problems.

The essence of the argument in favour of entry regulation is that, because we usually do not know which entrant poses a risk, each and every entrant must be screened in order to discover the entrant posing the risk. To justify the screening of every entrant, each and every entrant must be presented as posing a risk until proven otherwise. Without this assumption, even if only implicit and unnamed, screening each and every entrant loses its rationale. The fact that a majority of the entrants are law-abiding or prudent or competent is irrelevant in this calculus for the reason that we do not know which entrants do not pose a risk. To translate this line of reasoning in emotional terms: because we do not know beforehand which entrants can or cannot be trusted with freedom of action, none should be trusted. This is a prima facie case in favour of government jurisdiction over business formation – that is, perceived risk becomes direct grounds for compelling all potential entrants to submit essentially legitimate objectives to screening before starting a business.

The problem is that this argument sets up government as the final arbiter of who is deserving of trust. This thought is utterly contrary to the conception of the rights of the individual being inalienable. The rights of the individual are not contingent upon the question of trust. A perception of risk, realistic or not, does not invalidate the necessity and rightness of self-sustaining action. That some entrants may eventually prove to be dishonest or incompetent, that some businesses entail a hazard (such as pollution), in no way detracts from the rightness and necessity of productive effort and trade. In other words, government cannot and should not be the final arbiter of who is deserving of entry. One produces and trades of necessity and by right, not by permission because government deems one fit to pursue a trade.

Yet what of the argument that the unfettered exercise of economic rights – that anathema to leftists, populists, and conservatives alike – poses problems for society that can be addressed only by restricting the scope of these rights. Surely we cannot set loose on society business entrants who will defraud the public, pollute, and put up for sale defective goods? This line of reasoning holds the implicit assumption that economic rights are somehow more problematic than the various other forms of freedom we take for granted. Consider the following question: are economic rights more problematic than political and civil rights? Does unfettered business formation pose problems far more serious than free speech, for example?

There are clear analogies between free speech and free enterprise. Free speech results in the expression of ideas and opinions that rile and anger significant portions of the public. Large portions of the public loathe free enterprise. Blasphemy, pornography, demagoguery, libel, public blacklisting, false accusation, incitement to violence, and sedition are abuses of free speech. Pollution, selling defective goods, and fraud are abuses of free enterprise.

In principle, one can make a case for censorship against any form of expression and speech that is intended for broadcasting or printing. Blasphemous speech on television and pornographic literature offend certain religious people. False accusations, innuendoes, and libel are injurious to decent political discourse and harmful to personal reputations. Yet, in liberal democracies, we do not force the press, publicists, political speechmakers, or anyone else to submit to censorship with the intent to discover and pre-empt these actions. Yet this is not to underrate the dangers inherent to the aforementioned practices. Libel and false accusation ruin political careers, surely a tribulation at least as harrowing as ruination by fraud. Public blacklisting by environmentalists can severely damage a company's bottom line. Demagoguery panders to prejudice. Consider this: in terms of fatal consequences, uncensored hate speech, demagoguery, and warmongering have been infinitely more injurious to humanity than industrial pollution. Uncensored incitement has frequently ignited pogroms, riots, rebellions, and even wars. Did not the demagogue Hitler avail himself of free speech in the Weimar Republic to promote his party to power? Uncensored ultranationalist demagoguery in Weimar Germany by politicians like Hitler helped prepare the ground for the destruction of Europe and the Holocaust.

In any case, the aforementioned abuses of free speech are, by and large, already illegal – but then again, so are pollution, fraud, and the sale of defective goods. Somehow, we are willing to risk the many bad things that can result from abusive speech without also imposing censure. When the use of speech is demonstrably injurious, we deal with it by a simple ban of identifiably abusive practices and prosecution. Yet is entry regulation and screening not the economic equivalent of censorship?

The sentiment that the exercise of economic rights is somehow more problematic than that of political and civil rights is a double standard. This becomes evident when one reads the line of reasoning applied in Justice Louis Brandeis's concurrence in the *Whitney v. California* case (1927). Frequently referred to as the greatest defence of freedom of speech ever written by a member of the high court, Justices Brandeis and Holmes provide latitude for exercising the right of speech to a degree almost unthinkable in the field of economics:[57]

> Fear of serious injury cannot alone justify suppression of free speech and assembly. Men feared witches and burnt women. It is the function of speech to free men from the bondage of irrational fears. To justify suppression of free speech there must be reasonable ground to fear that serious evil will result if free speech is practiced. There must be reasonable ground to believe that the danger apprehended is imminent. There must be reasonable ground to believe that the evil to be prevented is a serious one. Every denunciation of existing law tends in some measure to increase the probability that there will be violation of it. Condonation of a breach enhances the probability.

Expressions of approval add to the probability. Propagation of the criminal state of mind by teaching syndicalism increases it. Advocacy of lawbreaking heightens it still further. But even advocacy of violation, however reprehensible morally, is not a justification for denying free speech where the advocacy falls short of incitement and there is nothing to indicate that the advocacy would be immediately acted on. The wide difference between advocacy and incitement, between preparation and attempt, between assembling and conspiracy, must be borne in mind. In order to support a finding of clear and present danger it must be shown either that immediate serious violence was to be expected or was advocated, or that the past conduct furnished reason to believe that such advocacy was then contemplated.

Those who won our independence by revolution were not cowards. They did not fear political change. They did not exalt order at the cost of liberty. To courageous, self-reliant men, with confidence in the power of free and fearless reasoning applied through the processes of popular government, no danger flowing from speech can be deemed clear and present, unless the incidence of the evil apprehended is so imminent that it may befall before there is opportunity for full discussion. If there be time to expose through discussion the falsehood and fallacies, to avert the evil by the processes of education, the remedy to be applied is more speech, not enforced silence. Only an emergency can justify repression. Such must be the rule if authority is to be reconciled with freedom. Such, in my opinion, is the command of the Constitution. It is therefore always open to Americans to challenge a law abridging free speech and assembly by showing that there was no emergency justifying it.

Moreover, even imminent danger cannot justify resort to prohibition of these functions essential to effective democracy, unless the evil apprehended is relatively serious. Prohibition of free speech and assembly is a measure so stringent that it would be inappropriate as the means for averting a relatively trivial harm to society. A police measure may be unconstitutional merely because the remedy, although effective as means of protection, is unduly harsh or oppressive. Thus, a state might, in the exercise of its police power, make any trespass upon the land of another a crime, regardless of the results or of the intent or purpose of the trespasser. It might, also, punish an attempt, a conspiracy, or an incitement to commit the trespass. But it is hardly conceivable that this court would hold constitutional a statute which punished as a felony the mere voluntary assembly with a society formed to teach that pedestrians had the moral right to cross uninclosed [sic], unposted, waste lands and to advocate their doing so, even if there was imminent danger that advocacy would lead to a trespass. The fact that speech is likely to result in some violence or in destruction of property is not enough to justify its suppression. There must be the probability of serious injury to the State. Among free men, the deterrents ordinarily to be applied to prevent crime are education and punishment for violations of the law, not abridgment of the rights of free speech and assembly.

Few business start-ups – most certainly not a two-sewing-machine garment factory – pose a "clear and present danger" to apply one criterion for free speech restraint. The problems signalled in this opinion have been acknowledged as applying equally to the various other basic rights, though it seems that the logical conclusion is mostly evaded.[58] The argument in favour of unfettered business start-ups, as with free speech, is not a concession to wrongdoing; rather, it is an argument from principle and one that is – given the vastness of the informal sector in many countries as a consequence of the exclusionary effect of bureaucracy and overregulation – a most necessary one to make. Observe how well the inalienability of the right of free speech limits the encroachments on our freedom. Consider the concepts of rights as a controlling device for managing the scope of government authority in order to lessen the harm that proceeds from too much power in the hands of the many men with political ambitions but without the skills and virtues of statesmen such as Lee Kuan Yew.

The uses of entry regulation

By now, one might be loath to consider whether entry regulation can be effective at all. The main question that comes to mind is what kind of risk is amenable to screening. The uses and methods of entry screening, insofar as it is necessary, are technical issues, which are best left to the sciences of public administration, management, and accountancy. Where practical issues challenge the administrative sciences, one must expect a myriad of complexities and difficulties. For this reason, this treatment must, of necessity, be viewed as no more than the briefest sketch touching on the most important issues.

Screening is most amenable to those instances where reputations, competence, and negative externalities can be ascertained beforehand. Qua reputation, one considers the instance where there are records of past behaviour, such as police records. As to competence, one considers the availability of credentials, such as, for example, diplomas. Negative externalities, of which industrial pollution is an example, can be deduced from the nature of the business planned. In the first two instances, the argument is more abstract, the issues readily understandable; in the latter instance, the treatment is largely by illustration to shortcut the complexity of the subject matter.

Screening on reputation is a form of behavioural risk assessment. Although past behaviour is not proof positive that the person in question will repeat the offense, there are valid concerns in a number of instances. The idea of a convicted swindler launching a finance company or a convicted child molester setting up a day care centre is, obviously, deeply troubling. These are defensible cases of "clear and imminent danger." Here, we have cases where people, by their own wrongdoing, have compromised their reputations and the inviolability of their own rights (to liberty) because they would not desist from violating those of others. Given the often-substantial risk of recidivism, police records in such instances function as proxies for intentions and character to some degree. This is so especially when the offender seeks to enter or re-enter commerce in trades or areas of life where he or she committed the offense. In these cases, however, entry regulation by character should become a crime prevention remedy focused on convicted felons. One could conceive of legislation requiring that convicted offenders report or register their plans or activities with, for example, parole or probation boards. Regulation of entry focused on specific categories of citizens with demonstrable records of offensive behaviour would serve a valid purpose without subjecting the general populace to unwarranted scrutiny of lawful objectives.

In any case, beyond the existence of formal records of past behaviour, it is virtually useless to screen on intention and character. Intentions, honesty, (and by degrees) character and competence are – before the facts created by action – matters of the mind or soul. Consequently, they remain unfathomable and elusive. The fact of the matter is that the authenticity of stated intentions cannot be verified. The true will of each individual is a mystery until that person has acted out his or her intentions. Likewise, again barring verifiable records of past behaviour like police records, true character is inscrutable. Without verifiable records of past behaviour, the moral fibre of each man or woman is revealed only by his or her future actions.

It may be a circular argument, but dishonest traders are by definition neither open nor honest about their intentions, characters, or degrees of competence; in the deception, the true intentions and characters and competencies of mala fide entrants are concealed. The objective and principle of the villain is to deceive and abuse for gain. Frequently, the villain is actively engaged in both frustrating and avoiding prevention and detection.[59] Factually, most regulatory regimes do not seriously attempt entry screening on intentions and character where there is no record of past behaviour. On issues of intention and character, one is almost completely dependent upon criminal code and prosecution after the incident.

Competence is easily measured only in professions where formal credentials are the norm. Yet, where formal credentials are available, entry screening is a virtually redundant process. Formal credentials are usually issued by recognized bodies and parties, mostly educational establishments or professional associations. Concurrently, the point of credentials – for example, a diploma – is to declare a person competent. What value is entry screening by governments supposed to add to this process? One can only consider the question of the authenticity of the credentials, but here we run into the issue of our fears versus clear and present danger once again.

A simple prohibition against unqualified entrants should in specific instances be quite sufficient and is most likely already in place.[60] In the Netherlands, accountancy and law are legally protected professions, and the qualifications of which are administered by recognized professional organizations. There is no government-administered screening of entrants, and there are virtually no cases of bogus practitioners. Illegality, technical issues, and professional jealousy are, in these instances, the effective deterrents. Redundancies are rarely effective and mostly burdensome.

Finally, in many lines of business there are no formal qualifications. In such trades and industries, business start-ups in which the entrants have no previous business experience or record of service are a common occurrence. If inexperience is a total disqualifier, the greater part of the currently existing formal sector businesses should not exist, which is a ridiculous proposition. Moreover, in some occupations the question of competence is irrelevant given that little skill is required. Also, where no formal qualifications exist, simply getting on with the business is sometimes the only way to accumulate experience. If the right to engage in self-sustaining action is paramount, this avenue to a livelihood must not be denied.

There is also an excellent case in favour of entry screening when direct danger can be deduced from the nature of the business planned. The unlicensed manufacture and sale of arms, especially military hardware, is such an imminent and serious danger to society that there is no bona fide argument that can bring these trades within the scope of the right to life and liberty. Technically, these trades indisputably involve productive effort and voluntary exchange, but these are not activities unambiguously directed at self-sustaining action. Arms are as easily used in aggressive action as defensive action. The very existence of a weapon poses an immediate, grave, mortal threat. At the individual level, only hunting weapons provide a justifiable (but still ambiguous) case for self-sustaining action, as in hunting for food and sport. However, there is no positive reason why a civilian would need a battle tank or a nuclear weapon or an F-16. Of course, this line of reasoning is totally inapplicable in most lines of business. In few businesses is it possible to make a similar case of clear and present danger as well as to assert doubts in terms of the applicability of the premise of self-sustaining action. It is not even applicable in the case of – and brace for the howls that must rise from the ranks of the environmentalists – heavily polluting industries.[61] It is the exception that proves the rule. Virtually every other type of business is clearly directed at engaging in self-sustaining action. This is an exceedingly wide scope considering "all the actions required by the nature of a rational being for the support, the furtherance, the fulfilment and the enjoyment of his own life."

Qua externalities, the single most important issue that agitates the passions of our age is the environment. Strictly from a technical point of view, entry screening, by the nature of business, is a valid method for ascertaining, addressing, and even pre-empting externalities. But the problem with the advocacy of entry regulation is that method and the problem of externalities eclipses the issues of essentially legitimate objectives and principles. As noted earlier in this chapter, that some businesses entail a hazard (such as pollution) in no way detracts from the rightness and necessity of productive effort and trade. As for the technical side of the issue, the thing to remember is that there are alternatives to entry regulation. The proper response involves addressing directly the problems posed by negative externalities, not denying rights. Legislation and regulation directly focused on the externalities is, in principle, a legitimate course of action. Let us examine the example of a truly bad risk of toxic pollution: lead refining.

Lead refining is an example of a perfectly legitimate economic activity, and yet it is a highly toxic process. There is no justification for the prohibition of such a valuable and necessary activity, but building a lead refinery in a dense urban area may not be a very good idea. Pre-specifying standards about the distance from built-up areas with an eye for public health and safety concerns is a reasonable measure. Other reasonable requirements include imposing emission standards, effluent standards, solid-waste disposal, and residue disposal rules. Pollution and poisoning accidents could be dealt with through pre-specified liability stipulations insofar as general tort procedures prove inadequate. Also, even if such a project were started away from built-up areas, adjacent properties and businesses might still prove problematic. For these situations, an indemnification procedure could be instituted so that any significant loss of value of or damage to nearby properties or activities could be reimbursed.

In view of public health concerns, it would be reasonable to institute a notification procedure. A notification procedure would require that all manufacturers processing or producing hazardous substances report such projects to the authorities responsible for public health. The notification procedure could include a requirement that the developer quantify and disclose expected emissions, effluents, solid-waste, and residues. A notification procedure has the following advantage: authorities would still be adequately informed without stopping the developer from proceeding with business. A notification procedure would not be entry regulation as long as it did not constitute an approval procedure. As a matter of practice, this notification requirement is not likely to be a substantial burden since specifying expected emissions and effluents is an engineering issue inherent to industrial projects.

Observe that each and every suggestion here is respectful of information requirements, public health concerns, and property value concerns. Such an approach would be fair because it would allow a business to proceed legally and without hindrance. In fact, in many developed – and some developing – countries, most of these regulatory requirements suggested are already in place. In this respect, entry screening procedures are more often than not redundant.

There is no gainsaying the fact that lead refining is a toxic process. And precisely for this reason entry regulations can be viewed as all the more onerous. It is far too easy for politicians and environmental defence groups to use the licensing process for extortionate or obstructive purposes by using yellow press tactics to whip up fear and rage among the public. Let us be very clear: abolition of entry regulation of itself is hardly a diminution of regulatory powers with respect to negative externalities as such. Any concern with respect to negative externalities can be met with proper legislation, rulemaking, and appropriate judicial powers. If you are afraid of pollution, research the question and legislate or litigate. If you fear for worker safety, research and legislate or litigate. But do not rob people of their freedom to pursue a life; that is not a valid or legitimate option. Regardless of the good or bad intentions, entry regulation is about exercising power over the lives of people and, in the end, nothing good is ever achieved by that.

Note that environmental defence groups dearly value entry regulation for its potential to stop projects. Yet that power should be no source of optimism to the environmentalist or, for that matter, the public. The power to license raises, from an environmental perceptive, serious ethical and strategic concerns: licensing power represents governmental sanction. Consider the case where a licensing procedure ostensibly provides for an environmental assessment. Also consider the instance where the standards applied in the assessment are – often by design – inadequate or ambiguous. This is frequently a real concern. If the government finds in favour of the project and issues a license, that often entails virtual legal impunity for the polluter or developer. Note how large, government-sanctioned projects in the developing world, such as hydroelectric projects, often result in loss of land and livelihood of the occupants of the land affected ... not to mention the environmental damage. Frequently, these occupants are driven off their land without due process or just compensation, with the project developers cold-bloodedly waving government-issued licenses. The argument is now full circle: when a license is finally gained, it sanctions an assault by a private party on both property rights *and* the environment. Finally, a significant project stopped in one place may crop up in places where environmental concerns get short shrift. To concerned third parties such as the environmental movement, entry regulation is, in the long run, a zero-sum game with victory in one place cancelled out by losses elsewhere. No just cause truly benefits from power games. In the final analysis, the end does not justify the means, but if it is any consolation, the end is more important than any specific means. In any case, it should never be forgotten that most business start-ups are not nearly as frightful in their potential environmental impact as lead, zinc, nickel, petroleum, or copper refineries; nuclear power plants; or hydroelectric projects. The worst cases are the worst reasons for justifying entry regulation precisely because the problems involved are so grave, the issues so specific and complex and entirely out of touch with the infinitely more modest concerns of the greater number of entrants.[62]

However, after all the fury of argumentation and fever of theorizing, the examination of the day-to-day practice of entry regulation is one hell of an anti-climax: the majority of the procedures for starting up a company listed in the Kennedy School paper are not screening procedures at all. The largest group of non-screening procedures includes registration requirements (thirty out of sixty-six) for formally representing the company and tax-, industry-, and labour-related filings. This is twenty-nine procedures too many. The authors of the aforementioned Kennedy School working paper mention that in "the most efficient countries" company registries performed a variety of the same procedures "automatically, without involving the entrepreneur in any way."[63] Here we have a case of people around the world having to battle bureaucracy to meet redundant filing requirements because government fails to pull its act together and provide a single stop. It is a legitimate assumption that various government departments may need data on business start-ups for a variety of reasons. Yet the physical distribution of data among the departments is not necessarily a responsibility of the citizen; that is an organizational issue. This observation by itself is not an argument against the uses of entry regulation. Nevertheless, it does place the Pigouvian rationale for entry regulation in perspective. Even a simple reading of the procedures demonstrates that, for a majority, the rationale must be sought in pure bureaucratic waste and institutional decadence.

Line jumpers

There is one specific evil that must be addressed on the subject of entry regulation. In countries where entry regulation poses a serious problem, there are usually many people who pride themselves on being able to network around these obstacles, of having so-called connections. Many others admire or envy these networkers and connected people. Be that as it may, networking savvy, though certainly a talent of some sort, deserves no admiration. Networking is a perverse and unclean way of life. It is a glorified form of beggary, line jumping, manipulation, and toadying. Networking punishes integrity while requiring and rewarding its opposite. Shamelessness, cynicism, slyness, obsequiousness, deceitfulness and ruthlessness are the essential traits of the networker. Accordingly, networking goes against the grain of many people and when circumstances force us to try it, we feel soiled for the experience and humiliated when it did not work.

The sheer premium put on the skill of networking and exploiting connections versus the disdain felt for those unversed in these practices serves as an insidious source of complacency and conservatism by the "winners" and fatalism by the "losers" about bureaucracy. The glamour perceived in networking and admiration accorded to connected people distracts attention away from the unfairness of it all and reinforces the status quo. The question of guilt is diluted and transferred to the victim, who blames himself or herself for having scruples and lacking savvy. The responsibility for tackling maladministration or mitigating its consequences is transferred from governments to each and every supplicant.

The perversity of the networker and his or her admirers or enviers is also a failure of the intellect. Rather than making it his or her business to identify and claim his or her natural right – to pursue a lawful occupation – the networker makes a career out of acting by permission instead. The pride of the networker, in his or her savvy, is based on his or her flair at turning submission to an oppressive system into a personal advantage and exploiting his or her own extortion for material benefit. But it is not only the networker who disowns his or her birthright. The error of those who admire or envy the networker is greater because they, by their admiration and envy, prove themselves equally ignorant of their natural right – but in their case, without any profit to show for it. The practice of networking is admirable only in an environment where people are totally oblivious of their rights and where an all-pervasive requirement to act by permission is experienced as a natural state of affairs that must be cleverly exploited or else suffered in resignation.

Let us be blunt about the matter: businessmen or businesswomen consummate at exploiting connections are not heroes. Instead, they are the enemy of the people. The custom of the networker is the lifeblood of the corrupt systems that perpetuate the miserable condition of the majority. In a way, the networker could be thought of as the equivalent of a collaborationist – one who cooperates with the enemy, which is, in this instance, the almighty bureaucracy or patronage-dispensing politician. As with the collaborationist, he or she undermines the cause of the oppressed. In their turn, admirers and enviers resemble fellow travellers.[64] In any case, both the networker and his or her admirer and envier are conformists and philistines. These portrayals must be made and used by any reform movement. Naming and denunciation are necessary instruments for raising consciousness and clarifying positions in the run-up to purifying the system of these unclean practices. It is imperative for any social and political movement that wishes to take on overregulation to tear down the glamour of networking and connections. Networking must be exposed for being an unclean activity that bleeds society of virtue and corrupts the regard for skills by transferring admiration from productive effort to consummate glad-handing. Networking must be exposed for being a vile, pathetic, and vulgar substitute to standing up for and laying claim to one's natural right.

On another level, networking represents a political problem. When people fulminate against free enterprise, free markets, and the rise of individualism, they should take a good look at the human condition in a bureaucratized society. Free markets, liberalism, and secularization have jointly and separately been blamed for replacing "the web of mutual obligations which bound people together in ethnic, religious, or other communities with a society predicated on competition and atomistic individualism."[65] In the bureaucratized societies of the developing and formerly communist countries, webs of mutual obligations still bind people together in ethnic, religious, or other communities – or, more accurately, mafias. Networks and connections are the sinews of such webs of mutual obligations. But these webs or networks are spoils systems. Entry regulation is one of the various instruments for spreading favours within and cementing such a web of mutual obligations.[66] Although it may provide cohesion within the ruling group, it fuels murderous rage and hatred among the competing groups. Networking separates the citizenry into insiders and outsiders, the privileged and the excluded. It is the modus operandi of a divided society.

This is the tragedy of communal strife in ex-Yugoslavia, Lebanon, sub-Saharan Africa, the Middle East, and the Indian subcontinent. All of these societies would be less tense and unstable if economic freedom replaced spoils systems based on ethnic, tribal, or religious "webs of mutual obligation." The tragedy is that many of these peoples have a work ethic, grit, and entrepreneurial spirit that would shame many Americans and West Europeans. But for the constraints of bureaucratic society, the majority of the Lebanese, Indians, Nigerians, and other, would long since have bootstrapped themselves – almost purely on the strength of personal effort – out of poverty.

It is little known that the Netherlands was an intensely sectarian society not long ago.[67] The stability of Dutch society in view of this sectarianism owed much to religious toleration and political freedom. But in addition to those boons, economic freedom was an indispensable part of the equation because it allowed groups (or individuals from such groups) that could not share in political power the freedom to pursue, without hindrance, their own social and economic development. Economic freedom in this respect served as a pressure-release valve. One of the joys of life in rich countries such as the Netherlands, Great Britain, and the United States is that it is possible to pursue many ambitions without an obsessive concern about having to network with bureaucrats, politicians, and their cronies. It allows for clean living and efficient conduct of business. Suave and bland phrasings – "web of mutual obligations" – and the glamour of savvy networking deceive; it is merely a clever, pleasing way of describing the subordination of an individual or group to the will of another. The objective of webs of mutual obligations is to preserve the standing, privilege, or pecuniary interests of one specific group at the expense of outsiders – literally. The idea of liberty is to remove such shackles. Without coercion the final authority in all matters pertaining to the happiness of the individual is the will of that same individual, and then the webs of mutual obligations cease to matter and are replaced by voluntary relations.

Summary

It is a basic fact of life that, to sustain oneself, one needs to create the material means of one's survival. To survive, people must create, build, produce, and trade. This is not an option; it is an imperative. Entry regulation is a twisted type of government authority. It forces people to do something contradictory (namely, to seek permission for pursuing an inescapable necessity). From its nature as an imperative, the pursuit of self-sustaining action should have been recognized as an inalienable right. People should not be required to seek permission to sustain their lives. The idea of a government as the final arbiter of whether one is deserving of permission is an offense against human nature.

Entry regulation also depends upon a highly inconsistent and selective reading of people's rights and freedoms. We have come to accept the prohibition of free speech as a measure so stringent that it would be inappropriate as the means for averting anything but clear and present danger to society. And yet we are unable to conceive of entry regulation as a measure unduly harsh or oppressive – even though, in many countries, its practice is so obstructive that it sabotages the most innocent attempts by ordinary people to freely pursue essentially legitimate objectives within the formal sector. As in the case of free speech, the argument in favour of free enterprise is not a concession to wrongdoing; rather, it is an argument from principle that is necessary to make. If the right to life and liberty matters, we have an obligation to accept their relevance in the context of economic action. The existence of an informal sector will therefore constitute evidence of a failure to acknowledge these rights and of injustice perpetrated by government in many instances. Ironically, a large size of the informal sector in countries with burdensome regulations also contradicts the prediction of the helping hand theory that regulation effectively protects consumers.

Entry regulation is a government power of ancient standing. Often, the sheer antiquity of a government power acts as a legitimizing force. Yesterday's propaganda transmutes into today's popular beliefs and articles of faith as people over the ages grow utterly habituated to its practice. Eventually, memories of freedoms previously enjoyed are lost in the mists of time. It is this habituation and oblivion that has rendered people – including the actual victims – incapable of perceiving the unnaturalness of entry regulation. Note that, even in countries suffering the most extreme regulatory burdens, people rarely blame the system of entry regulation for their troubles. Instead, people tend to blame themselves for not being savvy at networking. They hate the bureaucrats for failing to be helpful and administering the regulations corruptly. We need to change this situation. The people must be taught that they do not need to be savvy at networking because they should not need permission in the first place. They must be taught that asserting inalienable rights trumps collaborating with bureaucracy. The objective should be to teach the people that the world would be better off without entry regulation.

Chapter 4

The Abolition of Entry Regulation

The only way to deal with an unfree world is to become so absolutely free that your very existence is an act of rebellion.

—Albert Camus

In the previous chapter, we concluded that the world would be a better place without entry regulation. We found that entry regulation does not have any redeeming features. For this reason, I propose total and complete abolition of entry regulation as a means to regulating the economy. This is not merely a proposal to deregulate or to simplify bureaucracy; rather, it is a move to extinguish one specific type of government power to the maximal degree. The move to abolish entry regulation should be thorough and methodical, and it should apply to all types of lawmaking and regulatory power that make possible entry regulation. In most nations, governments, policymakers, politicians, and bureaucrats have failed to demonstrate that they can handle the power to regulate the economy through entry regulation fairly and responsibly. So-called administrative reforms and anti-corruption efforts seldom diminish licensing requirements and other forms of entry regulation sufficiently to the point where normal people can do business with government on better terms. At the same time, the existence of huge informal sectors proves daily that the paper on which the entry regulations are written are fit only as kindling for bonfires.

Entry regulation is much easier to use as an instrument of collusion and corrupt practices and erecting barriers to entry than as an effective means for screening entrants. The uses for entry regulation are wider than its stated objective (i.e., weeding out undesirable producers and sellers). Take entry regulation and consider it literally in the context of a state possessing all the means to regulate the economy. What you get is power stripped of well-defined or objective standards (i.e., standards that are equally clear or predictable about duties as well as freedoms). It becomes power unrestrained by any consideration whatsoever for the rights of the individual (to engage in self-sustaining action, of earning a livelihood, or of pursuing his or her happiness). And there is no remedy to the logic underlying entry regulation. The authority to make people act by permission is arbitrary power. Entry regulation is the single most repressive legal instrument against private initiative in the hands of government.

Abolition of entry regulation should go a long way towards addressing the problems of disempowerment, corruption, exclusion, and informality. The ability to start and operate businesses without permission would mean instant and extensive empowerment of the individual, especially those now confined to the extralegal sector. In one stroke, the extralegal sector would become part of the legal business sector – to that extent, the problem of inaccessible public institutions, excessive regulation, and regulatory burden would be eliminated.

The move to abolish a specific type of government jurisdiction may come across as highly unusual. However, such a move is by no means unprecedented. The authority of government to practice censorship is an example of a type of government jurisdiction that has been abolished in many countries. Censorship was once universally practiced in one form or another in virtually all countries. In many countries, formally designated organs of the state were responsible for censorship. There have been many instances where censorship was in actual fact widely perceived to be a proper function of the state. This was usually the case where the state was seen to be and accepted as the guardian of religious faith or ideological doctrine. Yet, where people became aware of and claimed their right to free speech, the power of government to practice censorship was largely abolished. It is by means of this analogy that we should understand the appropriateness of the idea of abolishing entry regulation as a government power.

The benefits of abolishing entry regulation

The abolition of entry regulation eliminates a whole set of transaction costs constituting an enormous gain in efficiency. It would do away with all formal and informal expenses involved with the licensing process. No more fees, but especially no more bribes. The savings to informal business owners of not having to resort to bribery to avoid penalties would be considerable; recall Mr De Soto's finding that the informal business owners in Peru paid out between 10 and 15 per cent of their gross income in bribes and commissions, whereas the owners of formal, small businesses apparently paid no more than 1 per cent.[1]

Imagine, also, the relief of not being held up by or being spared the interminable waiting and the uncertain outcome of application efforts. Such time and cost savings would result in a considerable lowering of barriers to entry, especially for small business ventures.

Abolition of entry regulation would result in a tremendous release of entrepreneurial energy, a boost for business expansion, and economic growth. The higher economic growth of the 1990s enjoyed by India is almost entirely attributable to the partial dismantling of the License Raj. After enjoying a compound rate of growth from 1950 to 1992 of approximately 2 per cent, the infamous "Hindu" rate of growth, India's annual growth figures surged to 5 to 6 per cent. A more complete dismantlement of the still burdensome requirements could very well result in even higher growth figures.

Legalization would also result in an increase of employment opportunities. The six hundred thousand businesses legalized during the 1990s in Peru no longer need to keep down the size of their operations in order to avoid detection and penalties. If these businesses eventually employ, on average, one extra person, that would signify six hundred thousand extra jobs. If only one in every thousand of these newly legal businesses employs at least one hundred people, that would mean at least sixty thousand extra jobs.

Entry regulation is the basis for most monopolies and cartels in many trades and industries. Entry regulation is an opportunity for graft, patronage, and cronyism. Policymakers frequently raise barriers to entry at the prompting of special interests that wish to do away with the competition by restricting access to their line of business. Whole political networks in countries such as Thailand thrive on dispensing patronage to business cronies. In Marcos's Philippines and Suharto's Indonesia, crony capitalists flourished on monopoly grants.

Abolition of entry regulation would, in one stroke, eliminate all government-enforced monopolies, cartels, and anti-competitive arrangements. It would expose erstwhile crony capitalists to the full rigor of free markets and honest competition by a class of businessmen and businesswomen focused on consumers instead of profiting from glad-handing and sucking up to political patrons. The savings on monopoly profits would translate in a direct gain in purchasing power for consumers. Abolition of entry regulation is one powerful blow for the meritocratic ideal of a level playing field where ability is the supreme standard.

Abolition of entry regulation is a direct and significant advance for freedom of the individual, open society, justice, and equality. This advance in freedom does not favour only established business and foreign investors; it is of equal, direct, and immediate benefit to every private venture that is now confined to the extralegal sector. Imagine the relief simple folks would feel if they were spared the tragedy of completing impenetrable application forms and being bullied and fobbed off by rude bureaucrats with their perplexing explanations and requirements. The elimination of entry regulation would restore a measure of simplicity, honesty, and dignity to the pursuit of business. Simplicity, honesty, and dignity! These quietly delicious conditions, virtues, and qualities so absent in license-ridden societies where politicians and bureaucrats rob people of their innocence and force some into unclean and humiliating compromises and reduce the rest to impotent poverty. Abolition would empower honest, hardworking men and women, enabling them to compete on equal terms with networkers who would now have to earn an honest living without the advantage of government connections. Any way we look at it, abolishing entry regulation is a positive step for the people and the economy.

Politics and bureaucracy without entry regulation

Abolition of entry regulation changes the dynamics of politics, bureaucracy, and society. Abolition is one step in the direction of a separation of state and economy. Abolition is a declaration of independence for every man or woman capable of productive effort. Without entry regulation the individual is no longer dependent upon bureaucrats or politicians for starting and operating a business. This last effect has strategic value if one is interested in dismantling patronage networks with the purpose of weakening the grip of dishonest and corrupt politicians and bureaucrats on society. Corrupt politicians and bureaucrats would lose one very important lever for profiteering, nepotism, petty tyranny, extorting bribes, exacting favours and votes, and colluding with business cronies. Politics, politicians, bureaucrats, networking, and connections will suddenly become a lot less important to the welfare of the people.

Also, abolition would be a boon to multi-ethnic or multicultural societies. Abolition could help reduce tension by channelling the energies of many groups towards the pursuit of their own development in the economic sphere without having to resort to political competition and all its never-ending frustrations, grievances, obsessions, and dangers. Political and bureaucratic positions and appointments would depreciate in value as economic freedom expanded the scope of business, and as career opportunities opened to ambitious outsiders *and* insiders. Economic freedom contributes to making the dominance of the political system by this or that ethnic, tribal, religious, or language group – a situation that is often unavoidable given the multi-ethnic, multi-confessional, or multilingual composition of the majority of nations around the world – somewhat less of an issue. Crucially, for politically dominant groups or ruling political factions promoting economic freedom could be a way of compromising with and pacifying competing factions and groups. Finally, the developing world is full of ethnic and religious communities where hard work and entrepreneurship is highly valued. Abolition frees these groups to get on with building up the economy both for themselves and their fellow citizens.

The mechanics of abolition

Abolishing entry regulation as such does not require elaborate institution building; on the contrary, it requires abolishing, suspending, or amending laws and regulations. Of equal importance, it renders a whole category of bureaucrats useless. To that extent, it is an excellent reason for closing down those parts of the bureaucracy responsible for entry regulation and discharging redundant personnel. The savings potential is undoubtedly substantial.

Nevertheless, the rewards are far greater than the financial savings. We already noted that entry regulation is easier to use as an instrument of collusion, corrupt practices, and the erection of barriers to entry than as a bona fide measure to promote so-called social efficiency. But to reverse the logic, abolition of entry regulation has a bonus: the corresponding and automatic elimination of a whole category of corrupt practices. Within this context, no need for the hard, slow, and uncertain process of anti-corruption reforms and measures. One can dispense with the frustrations of criminal investigations and prosecutions that go nowhere. In this respect, abolition is the ultimate disinfectant.

Many politicians promise regulatory reform and anti-corruption measures. Once in office, most of their reform programmes usually end up as broken promises. One reason for this is that reform of entry regulation frequently rests on the implicit assumption that entry regulation is a legitimate government function. The point of reform is to try to make entry regulation work but without the corruption and inefficiency. The objectives are, in other words, to rationalize or simplify the procedures or to strengthen or restructure existing institutions, implement anti-corruption measures, prosecute corruption cases, for example – not to abolish them. The problem with this type of reform is that it requires cooperation by the very institution slated for reform. Additionally, one must often rely upon other bureaucracies such as the police and the judiciary, which are frequently just as corrupt. The response is usually opposition, resistance, and sabotage from within, and the record of failed reforms across the globe shows these forms of subversion to be highly effective. Abolition, on the other hand, does away with the need for cooperation with the bureaucrats in question. To rephrase that, the relevant bureaucracies and bureaucrats are out of the loop and under the axe. When you are about to be dispensed with, insider resistance and sabotage is no longer an issue. Outsiders can do the planning and execution of the abolition efforts; all that is necessary is a team of jurists, accountants, managers, some senior civil servants, and fresh support staff.

Abolition is also most useful in another respect: maintaining the integrity of the reform effort itself. Bureaucracies, as long as they exist, mean appointments for members of the reforming party. These offices are the slippery slope down which many a reforming administration has skidded to dishonour and ruination. Offices beckon the weaker members of the reform party with the prospect of prestige, and soon after with the profits of exploiting power for private gain. The reform party itself is compromised. Soon, business as usual reasserts itself. The expectation of a clean government is dashed again. Abolitionism, however, is a root-and-branch measure that leaves no offices. In effect, it shields the members of the reform administration from temptation. Abolition of entry regulation is a rather elegant and extremely efficient way of forcing a clean sweep while maintaining discipline and integrity within the reform movement. It yields quick but lasting results.

The legal aspects of abolition

The purpose of advocating abolition of entry regulation goes beyond the objectives of what is commonly called deregulation and simplification. The objective should be a permanent reduction of unwarranted political and administrative power and expansion of individual or economic freedom. In other words, we should seek the extinguishment of one form of predatory jurisdiction. Our aim, after all, is fundamental or constitutional reform.

The problem with deregulation and simplification is that they are usually limited reforms that leave political power and predatory jurisdiction intact. Any advance today can be undone again tomorrow, and that is exactly what happens time and again. Compare tax reform to the abolition of censure and the affirmation of the right of free speech (or the abolition of slavery!). The consequence of the adoption of an inalienable right of free speech and the abolition of slavery was an absolute and enduring expansion of individual freedom. Now look at tax reform.

The authority or jurisdiction to tax is, in its essence, a form of unlimited authority inherently unconstrained by property rights. This conflict between rights and authority can never be resolved because taxation is such a necessity to the existence of government that the lawful exercise of this authority must be tolerated. The complications of rulemaking are therefore unavoidable and, after every tax reform, the complexity immediately starts to grow again. But though the power to tax is fundamental to government, entry regulation is not.

It is beyond the scope of this book to write at length on how to abolish entry regulation. It should be sufficient to provide a brief sketch of the steps involved. Abolition of entry regulation includes three steps: simplification, deregulation, and constitutional reform. Here, simplification means that bureaucracy would be limited to a single point of service for and a single procedure for business registration and the issuance of registration certificates. Deregulation includes inventorying laws and codes specifying entry regulations with the objective of abolishing, suspending, or amending them. Concurrently, abolition requires amending or reforming constitutions. In the context of the proposal to abolish entry regulation, deregulation and simplification may be seen as the regulatory equivalent of a spring-cleaning. Constitutional reform, on the other hand – at least in the bona fide form – is the means by which the gains achieved by deregulation are preserved for the long term.

Abolition requires that constitutions be amended with the object of removing or changing all articles, which would allow governments to make laws that limit the freedom to establish a business. Moreover, using an analogy to the first amendment of the US Constitution, an article should be adopted with the purpose of creating an enumerated right that government "shall make no law abridging the right to pursue a trade, occupation or work." This wording is a serious matter because there are constitutions in which the right to pursue a trade, occupation, or work are ostensibly enumerated. Article 22 in the South African constitution comes to mind.[2] However, in these cases – see also the aforementioned article in the South African constitution – there is usually a provision effectively stating that government may regulate the practice of these trades and so forth. Such provisions almost always provide governments with near-unlimited authority to regulate entry, thus rendering the constitutional protection of rights virtually meaningless.

Finally, the constitution in question should be amended to provide for judicial review in case this is not possible under the existing regime. It must also provide for the independence of the courts from the other branches of government. Without these two amendments, there is little chance that any reform will stick, and justice for all will remain elusive.

Business registration

Abolition, though legalizing the extralegal sector, would not formalize it. For that, one more step is required: proper representation of a business (i.e., formal recognition of its existence through business registration). The abolition of entry regulation should not be interpreted as the abolition of business registration. Business registration is a necessity not only in terms of formal representation, but also for public administration and law and order. Governments must raise taxes, and businesses should contribute their share; formal representation through registration facilitates law enforcement. When all enterprises and properties are properly registered, it is much harder to avoid detection of criminal activities or evade taxation. This is one reason why societies in developed countries are, as a rule, more orderly than those of developing nations where the greater part of society is underground. Observe that tax revenue as a share of national income is generally significantly higher in rich countries than in poor countries. Proper registration of enterprises and properties is an efficiency matter for law enforcement, public administration, and property recognition.

Nevertheless, we must prevent business registration from (again) becoming the Trojan Horse that will turn it into entry regulation. One avenue is reducing registration requirements to a single, straightforward notification procedure based on objective timing. The registration requirement should be a duty to notify, not an approval procedure. The concept of objective timing refers to the timing of the notification. Also, businesses should register within a pre-specified period *after* an objective pre-specified event. What is such an objective event? The commencement of a business is such an objective event. Specifying that notification may take place only after commencement of business has the extra benefit of presenting government with a fait accompli.

Nevertheless, in the interest of public health and safety, there are other objective events. Significant industrial or urban development projects are almost always conceived, documented, and formally adopted beforehand. In such a case, the finishing of – or the formal and definitive adoption of – the business plan or the building/development plan presents an alternative objective event before the commencement of business. A registration law could specify that, when a business plan or building plan or development plan has been drafted, the objective event for specifying the term within which a business must be registered will be the moment of its completion or adoption. Such a registration would not prejudice the right of the entrant to proceed with business; rather, it would allow authorities to monitor and inspect in a timely fashion the plans, proceedings, and activities for infractions of, for example, public health and safety regulations.

Abolition, a panacea?

Abolition of entry regulation is not a cure-all. It is just one big step in the right direction. It does not solve problems or forms of corruption that do not involve entry regulation. Consider police corruption, patronage with regards to public employment, corruption of the judiciary, favouritism with respect to supplies procurement, or rigging public tenders. It would not put an end to waste in bureaucracy. Lack of education presents a serious constraint on the pursuit of opportunities that abolition of entry regulation does not address. Social ills such as racial or gender discrimination would still pose a problem.[3]

Many informals will not be able to turn abolition into business or social success. As in the formal sector, not everyone in the informal sector is a true entrepreneurial talent; lack of jobs is a factor just as important in pushing people to self-employment in the informal sector as frustrated commercial talent. But even for those who cannot turn abolition into a personal success story, there are consolations. Abolition is a tremendous advance in dignity for the humble classes. This is not an exaggeration because the humiliations to which informals are subjected are often severe. The police force in Bombay was at one time equipped with electric truncheons for driving off and dispersing street vendors.[4] This is contempt and sadism elevated to administrative practice. Also, that a class of people of few means should fork over 10 to 15 per cent of their gross income in bribes is a disgrace. Not only are people poor because of misgovernment, but we must also kick them when they are down and, with naked greed, snatch the last piece of bread from their very mouths. At the very least, legality will spare former informals official harassment and the considerable expense of bribes paid to avert punishment for what is essentially the pursuit of a bare subsistence. Even if a person would not be able to better his or her standard of living, surely we cannot argue that it is therefore preferable that this person should go about his or her business furtively instead of freely. To disparage abolition because not everyone will measurably prosper from it deprives informals of their humanity or their need for some measure of toleration and respect. The poor–but–proud theme has been an all-time favourite of socialists and populists; in this respect, abolition of entry regulation is putting the money where your mouth is.

Overregulation overall

Abolition of entry regulation would still leave open the issue of non-entry type regulation. Non-entry type regulation – at least formally – affects the operation rather than the start-up of businesses. Examples are labour legislation, worker and public health and safety legislation, and currency trading restraints. Many of these non-entry type regulations implicate so-called freedom-of-contract issues. Freedom of contract is the freedom of individuals or groups of individuals to choose which kind of contracts to make and with whom to make them. Abolishing entry regulation is not the same as promoting freedom of contract; yet, in practice, the issues are sometimes inseparable. In some cases, one cannot abolish entry regulation without next raising the issue of freedom of contract; to start a business, one must also have the freedom to do business. An entrepreneur who wishes to set up an import business would be free to do so after abolition of entry regulation, but the inability to get permission to buy foreign currencies would present an effective barrier to entry. Onerous labour laws present further obstacles by making labour more expensive for formal businesses than for informal operations. These are freedom of contract issues. Let us further elaborate these two examples.

Without freedom of contract as an enumerated right, non-entry type regulation that effectively sets barriers to entry would create a *substantive* test issue with respect to a freedom of entry provision. (The constitutional provision suggested earlier – that governments should make no law abridging the right to pursue a trade, occupation or work – would be that freedom of entry provision.) The substantive test issue is the question of whether a regulation would or would not materially (as opposed to formally) represent an infraction of a constitutional right. In the case of the import company, foreign currency licensing would not pass the formal infraction test; it is not a regulatory provision *formally* imposing requirements with respect to the start-up of a business. On the other hand, obstructive foreign exchange licensing would pass the material infraction test with flying colours; buying foreign exchange currencies is such an immediate and material necessity to the import business that, without the effective or substantial freedom to purchase foreign exchange, an import business is literally impossible.

Minimum wage or social security legislation is already much more difficult. It is not a formal requirement regarding the start-up of a business. Also, it does not formally prevent a business from hiring people. However, it does raise the cost of labour. In this respect, it is a material encumbrance on doing business. However, labour is not the only cost factor, and minimum wage and social security legislation also affect the competition. Then again, forced increases in labour costs do not affect businesses equally; capital-intensive operations will be less affected than labour-intensive operations. Also, farming out work or outsourcing is a way to manage rising labour costs. As this line of argumentation shows, in the case of minimum wage and social security legislation, it is very difficult to arrive at a solid case of direct or material entry regulation. A freedom of contract doctrine is likely to be better at dealing with issues such as labour legislation than a freedom-of-entry doctrine.

In the absence of freedom of contract as an enumerated right, some form of substantive testing will always be necessary to squash the most obvious or flagrant attempts at legislative trickery. At the same time, there are limits beyond which substantive tests become counterproductive and controversial. The essence of the controversy of substantive testing is trying to smuggle in unenumerated rights – in this instance, freedom of contract. This is deeply problematic because it would set off the age-old controversy between legal positivists and natural law proponents.[5] Freedom of contract and freedom of entry are best dealt with as discrete topics.

Beyond the informal sector

A freedom of entry doctrine is bound to raise controversy on a wide range of issues beyond extralegality. Abolition of entry regulation would clash with protectionist designs or economic nationalism. Abolition would mean that foreign businesses, including multinationals, would be able to freely commence business; it would demolish most legal restrictions on direct foreign investment. It would also bring free trade; it would, on substantive testing, result in the cancellation, suspension, or scaling down of many unduly harsh import restrictions, including currency trading, import licensing, import quotas, and excessive import tariffs.[6] Abolishing entry regulation would, on principle, make it difficult to protect domestic industries. Is this a problem? Not if you value individual freedom and economic wisdom. Free foreign investment brings capital, know-how, and better-paying jobs. Free trade raises the standard of living while forcing domestic industries to do better. Accepting free foreign investment and free trade is part of the deal if one wishes to address the problem of entry regulation and the informal sector. Individual rights cannot be dealt out in small, measured doses.

Nevertheless, anti-globalists, anti-capitalists, protectionist lobbies, industrial policy advocates, and xenophobes are bound to hate the very idea. But, in the long run, these groups should be at a disadvantage for the reason that abolition is a straightforward proposition easily understood by the victims of entry regulation (of which there are hundreds of millions). Still, at this point in time, foreign investment and international trade, as issues, could not be further from the minds of most informals. A large part of the informal sector concerns non-tradable products and services, such as domestic transportation, construction, grocery sales, and maintenance and repair services. On the other hand, to the degree that the issue of foreign investment and trade has any bearing on their business, informals are themselves likely to be victims of protectionist measures (and in competition with the same protected industries). The fact that the informal sector exists is already proof of its competitiveness – such is economics. Freedom and legality will only sharpen their competitiveness by eliminating the cost of penalties and improving access to capital. To this extent, foreign investors and informals could very well be natural allies. With freedom of entry, they would, from opposite directions, force protected sectors to shape up or squeeze them out of business.

The question of the impact of abolition and free trade on the agricultural sector is a far more sensitive issue. The primary issue here is the free import of subsidized produce from the rich countries. This is the problem of false competition and dumping. In principle, this would not worry a free trader: if foreign governments are willing to subsidize consumers abroad, thus raising their standards of living, so much the better. Still, there are hundreds of millions of people involved, mostly the peasantry, whose livelihoods could be instantly devastated. Economic dislocation and the consequent misery on that scale are impossible to gloss over. It cannot be the aim of any free trader to casually ignore the wholesale devastation of the countryside. Fortunately, legal systems have remedies for extraordinary circumstances, namely, the transitional provision.

A transitional provision allowing the regulation of imports of agricultural products for a specific number of years is a possible course of action. However, to prevent such a provision from turning into protectionism, such a provision must be worded as being legislation against false competition. A transitional provision should not provide carte blanche on the regulation of imports. Agriculture, including peasant farmers, should be subject to competitive forces just like any other economic sector. Countervailing duties and anti-dumping measures are, for a while, acceptable. Outright bans on importation or duties with protectionism in mind are unacceptable.

The public sector

Abolition of entry regulation also eliminates public monopolies – including those in education, health services, utilities, and broadcasting media – which is another theme not necessarily related to the issue of extralegality. These sectors are always the heaviest regulated enterprises in any given country, especially in terms of entry regulation. However, working out the anticipated effects of the freedom of entry doctrine for the various public sector services is an undertaking that is beyond the scope of this book. Nevertheless, the immense value of this observation impels us to explore the case of at least one public sector service. Therefore, let us look at the example of education, which is (along with healthcare) probably one of the most explosive issues within the context of entry regulation.

Strictly from a rational point of view, it is the height of perversity that people should be stopped from putting *their own money* – mind you, private capital or contributions, not tax money! – in sectors such as education and health services where there is a constant and pressing shortage of financial resources. This is even more relevant in developing countries where a continuing shortage of schools and teachers and clinics and doctors perpetuates illiteracy, ignorance, and poor health conditions. Also, on the question of quality public provision, it has been more of an affliction than a relief. It is a common opinion that private education and healthcare are frequently of superior quality than public education or health services. Entry regulation simply prevents the greatest number of people from enjoying the best possible education and healthcare that money can buy them.

"A common assumption about the private sector in education is that it caters only to the elite, and that its promotion only serves to exacerbate inequality."[7] This assumption is totally at odds with reality. Inequality is not a public-sector-versus-private-sector issue; it is, as a matter of fact, already rampant *within* the public system. Public schools in rich neighbourhoods (in cities such as São Paulo or Johannesburg) are immeasurably superior in quality to public schools in poor neighbourhoods in the same cities. Rich municipalities in the United States, as a rule, provide better public education than poor municipalities, not to mention the shameful state of inner city public schools. The children of members of the nomenklatura of the Soviet Union went to special state schools and most certainly did not mix with the children of the proletariat. Love and natural parental instincts drive the rich and powerful to arrange for their offspring the finest education that money can buy, regardless of whether this must be done via public or private systems. Because free public education is failing large portions of the general population in many countries, the poor are now driven by precisely the same parental instincts as the rich and powerful to seek better education in private schools.

Let us examine the case of private schools in India. The following is true according to the E.G. West Centre:[8]

> Recent research points to the growing presence of private schools serving low-income families, in India and elsewhere. Parents send their children to these schools because the public sector fails them. In India, the Probe Report found that in only 53 per cent of a random sample of government schools for the poor was there any teaching going on at all. By contrast, the same survey found in the private schools there was 'feverish' teaching activity, with teachers committed and accountable. ... This parlous state of affairs has created the huge market of 'budget' private education, serving the poor and low-income families.

It should be obvious that the private schools for low-income families are hardly going to be the posh, state-of-the-art establishments that the very term *private school* usually brings to mind. The prices charged for this "budget" private education should, at a glance, disabuse the reader of any such illusions. Fieldwork by James Tooley, professor of education policy, revealed that schools included in a federation of 500 private schools (from kindergarten to grade ten) serving poor communities in slums and villages in India charged fees ranging from USD 0.60 to USD 3.50 per month.[9] Concerning affordability, Tooley notes, "Fees of around USD 10 per year are not affordable by everyone, but they are to a large number of poor families."[10] Observe that these schools are "run on commercial principles, not dependent on hand-outs from state or philanthropy."[11] These schools, then, were fully funded by fees charged to low-income families.

It is almost inconceivable that schools could provide real value on such meagre fees. Without further information, one is inclined to suspect that dishonest operators might be scamming low-income families on a massive scale. And yet, prepare to be shocked: according to one study, "Children in unaided private schools had 70 per cent better scores in reading and 90 per cent better in mathematics."[12] More so, according to the same study, the cost per child was Rs 2008 a year in government schools and Rs 999 in unaided private schools.[13] Despite operating at half the expense, Indian private schools for the poor are better than public schools. The facts concerning teacher pay and quality are summed as follows by Claudia Hepburn:[14]

> Though the quality of their teachers is clearly superior, private schools are able to attract and keep their teachers while paying them less than half of what public schools pay. Whereas public schools pay roughly USD 95 to USD 200 per month, private schools pay from USD 9.50 to USD 119 depending on location and qualifications. They pay less because they have less.

The aforementioned unaided private schools are unrecognized institutions. The term *unaided* refers to the fact that these schools do not qualify for subsidies. According to the evidence, we are thus confronted by the odd circumstance of unqualified institutions outperforming recognized establishments. In any case, unaided private schools are the education sector equivalents of informal businesses. Also, as is the case with informal economic activity, so unaided private schools are not marginal phenomena at all. We have the following from *Businessweek*:[15]

> While no precise figures are available on the number of private schools, a recent study estimates 36% of school children in dirt-poor Uttar Pradesh, India's biggest state, attend them. The Akhil Bharti Vidya Bharti, a Hindu organization, operates some 15,000 affiliated private schools with around 2 million students. A.K. Shiva

Kumar, an economist from UNICEF, says the number of parents willing to pay tuition fees "completely disproves anyone who ever argued that these 'ignorant rural folk' are not interested in education."

Why are they outperforming recognized institutions? The reasons are summed as follows by Tooley:[16]

> Most parents would prefer to send their children to private schools if they could afford them. Private schools, they said, were successful because they were more accountable: "the teachers are accountable to the manager (who can fire them), and, through him or her, to the parents (who can withdraw their children)." Such accountability was not present in the government schools, and "this contrast is perceived with crystal clarity by the vast majority of parents."

For an idea how clear, examine this quote from *Businessweek*:[17]

> Farmer Girish Arya, who lives in a hamlet near Talaguar, sends his daughter to the government school: He can't afford the 50 cents monthly tuition at the private school. But he wishes he could. "In the private school, people can put pressure on the teachers to be sure they work," the weather-beaten farmer says wistfully. "In the government school, even if the teacher doesn't teach half the time, we can't say anything."

The issue here is that direct producer subsidies render public schools unaccountable to their clients, the parents of the children. For unsubsidized private schools, it is the parents that are the paymasters. To subsidized public schools, parents are nothing; withdrawing children does not necessarily result in a proportional loss of subsidies. The teachers in public schools are in no way dependent upon the pleasure of the parents; there is no financial incentive to provide good service.

Here, one must have a bit of understanding concerning the effect of marginal revenues on profits or losses. In an unaided private school, the withdrawal of each and every child results in an immediate loss of revenues without a corresponding reduction in fixed costs (including salaries). The withdrawal of even a minority of students can turn a profitable operation into a loss maker. Customer satisfaction is of the essence. In other words, teaching the children well makes for happy parents. Teachers in public schools, on the other hand, receive a government salary, and the schools' expenses are paid from an annual subsidy. The vital expense items (namely, salaries and premises of free public schools) do not depend upon direct revenues such as school fees paid by parents or pupils. The management or teaching staff at the public school suffers no instant financial penalties for failing to provide customer satisfaction.

Apparently, there is compassion in market forces. But this is not compassion handed down from on high; instead, it is the pride of empowerment and independent action. Market forces allow parents to secure a superior education for their beloved children from a clutch of rupees. Even so, these schools, which were "run on commercial principles, not dependent on hand-outs from state or philanthropy," were also found to be quite compassionate in one more respect: "The great majority of the schools offer a significant number of free places – up to 20 percent – for the poorest students, allocated on the basis of claims of need checked informally in the community."[18]

Providing free public education has, until now, been sold to the public as the epitome of compassionate government policy. To introduce some balance of perspectives, we must note some findings by the Indian, government-sponsored *Public Report on Basic Education in India* (PROBE) from 1999 as recapitulated by Ashok Desai:[19]

> It reported on a survey of 195 government and 41 private schools in 188 villages in Bimaru states. When the investigators visited them, usually late in the morning, there was no teaching going on in 111. In 79, the head teacher was absent.
>
> Teachers had kept some schools closed for months. In one, the teacher was drunk, and only a sixth of the children were present. In others, teachers got the children to provide liquor. One head teacher used the children as domestic servants. One did not know the name of a single child in his school.

Even in otherwise good schools, "Inactive teachers were found engaged in a variety of pastimes such as sipping tea, reading comics or eating peanuts, when they were not just sitting idle [...] And this pattern is not confined to a minority of irresponsible teachers – it has become a way of life in the profession."

The government monopoly of education and supervisory authority of private schooling derives its sanction from the claim of a need to prevent inequalities in education, to ensure proper standards of education, and to promote the development of society. And yet the ugly face of inequality in education in India is as follows: regulated, supervised, subsidized, and expensive but inferior public education versus unregulated, unsupervised, unaided, and cheap but superior private education. When the record proves that one is often substantially better off receiving education at an "unqualified" establishment than in a "proper" school, it is an absurdity to continue to pretend and insist that a state should have the power to license and supervise schools in the interest of public welfare. Entry regulation works just as bad for education as it does for business. One can only conclude, as does Claudia Hepburn, "that the public in general—and the poor in particular— would be better served by regulatory and investment climates conducive to the development of private schools than they are by government-run schools."[20] Save one child, save the world.

Almost every argument against free-sector education – or health services, for that matter – is made from fear and lack of trust of market forces and schools run on commercial principles. The fear of many is that the best teachers will use their freedom to sell their services to the highest bidders (i.e., the rich), leaving the poor with inferior teaching. In fact, many of the best universities in the world – mostly established in the United States precisely because that country allows this principle to operate in its universities – are also the most expensive. We found, however, that private education can benefit the poor as well as the rich. The better-paid teachers are not necessarily doing the best job as evidenced by the situation in India. In this case, the better-paid teachers failed the public and the lesser-paid teachers serving in unaided schools did the better job.

But this is argumentation by way of information. The final argument, however, is the moral argument. The moral argument is that people – the parents and the teachers – should have real and substantive freedom to act in accordance with their own judgement. Entry regulation of private schools diminishes this freedom and creates a captive market for a school system unaccountable as well as unresponsive to parents. The general principle here is that one should not have to live at the sufferance of the state. More specifically, the education of children or the pursuit of a career in education should not depend on a government's sufferance and indulgence.

Entry regulation of education goes contrary to the natural instinct of parents to nurture their children to the best of their ability. To interfere with the freedom of the parent to buy, on behalf of their children, the best education they can pay for is, in effect, to deprive the parents of the freedom to seek happiness and prosperity for their children. A public monopoly on education reduces rather than enhances a parent's ability to take care of his or her children. It also destroys parental authority by destroying the ability of parents to choose.

The right to pursue one's calling freely and in accordance with one's own vision falls within the scope of the freedom to take all the actions required for the fulfilment of one's own life. The essence of freedom is independent action. Teachers are not a special breed of slaves that should have no say or choice in the way they wish to pursue their profession, to be corralled and penned into the public system. Teachers are free beings with a right to pursue their own objectives of which government should not be the final arbiter. Private education should not exist at the sufferance of the state, to be allowed reluctantly and preferably in small doses to satisfy irresistible pressure groups such as religious denominations, the rich and powerful, and odd elements like expatriate business communities.

As a matter of principle, if any teacher wishes to sell his or her services to the highest bidder, that should be none of the business of the state or the public. The motives of teachers should not be suspect because they wish to start for themselves or seek employment outside the public system. Being a teacher does not make one less human or superhuman. One remains a human that must, in most cases, make a living to support oneself. The wish to support oneself should never be at the mercy of the state – not even when it concerns the teaching profession.

On the other hand, the teaching profession is one of those rare professions that is about more than just doing business or merely eking out a living. To many teachers, their profession is a *calling,* and they are often deeply imbued with a desire to lift humanity to a higher plane of existence – not just economically, but also intellectually, culturally, and morally. Often, the spread of education is the ideal all by itself. Abolition of entry regulation is that much more likely to allow teachers genuinely committed to such ideals to pursue their calling. Such educators often feel compelled to pursue their calling outside the public system, feeling repelled by its decrepitude or frustrated by its failure to service all communities. Alternatively, they may, on grounds of conscience, disagree with the curriculum provided in the public sector. Let us not make life more difficult than it already is for such idealists by imposing burdensome regulatory requirements.

The Formal Sector

Abolition of entry regulation is not a measure for addressing only informal-sector problems. Entry regulation adversely affects the formal sector as well as the informal sector. Formal businesses are similarly confronted with red tape and corruption. Many businesses cannot in any way be done informally. Small personal loans are possible in the informal sector; mortgage banking, security trading, and insurance are not. Nor is large-scale manufacturing or project development. In a way, one could say that one of the main problems in the developing world is that its formal sector – and, consequently, economic growth and development – is cramped by entry regulation. The symptoms vary from the size of the informal sector to low levels of direct foreign investment to incomplete industrialization to undersized, primitive, and weak financial sectors (and, equally, the lagging development of the education and health-service sectors). On a more tactical level, abolition of entry regulation is about not putting all of one's eggs in one basket. Freedom of entry allows all sectors or processes to develop at their proper pace and thereby contribute to economic growth and overall prosperity. Economic growth and development requires an open, all-embracing formal sector, one that readily soaks up every, but especially entrepreneurial, talent. Entry regulation is an extremely inefficient and abusive way to deal with perceived risk or fear or public interest concerns or market failures.

Rights lab

Have we covered the topic of entry regulation from every angle? Not by a long shot! What we have done in this chapter is cover the question of principle plus various areas of immediate concern. There are undoubtedly concerns with respect to abolition that have not been dealt with. Some of these are awfully simple, yet awkward questions. Would freedom of entry result in the abolition of driving licenses? Would it mean access for unskilled persons into the medical profession? These questions and others like these deserve serious consideration and, no, we are not advocating abolition of driving licenses or a free-for-all situation in the medical profession.

This is not the place to supply solutions for every possible contingency, nor is it necessary. What is being promoted here is a general principle. In daily practice, there are always borderline cases, and the exceptions to the rule. This is why we are not merely asserting a principle but also advocating constitutional reform. Whenever a principle is raised to constitutional law it is both inevitable and natural that its scope will be tested. This is the beauty of the practice of judicial review and constitutional jurisprudence. Judicial review is the "laboratory" where many practical, difficult, and often controversial issues are resolved. Constitutional rule raises a hurdle that can only be surmounted by applying one's intellect. This is certainly better than the current situation in which governments can mindlessly apply their powers, regardless of the consequences of its actions for the welfare of the citizens.

Judicial review forces parties with opposing views on a matter of principle to argue their point of view in a forum where questions of right and procedure must be considered. For an example of how this works, one merely has to look at the evolution of the right of free speech in US constitutional law and jurisprudence. This is the value of raising a principle to constitutional law: the principle will be argued time and time again, in the process educating the people about their rights and teaching their representatives, the legislators, some degree of prudence. Constitutionalism combined with judicial review is probably one important reason why Americans are so unusually conscious of their rights as compared to other nations. Indeed, observe how Supreme Court rulings have a degree of impact on popular consciousness in the United States that is unparalleled anywhere else.

Summary

The purpose of advocating a freedom of entry doctrine is to improve the human condition by advancing basic rights and free enterprise. Still, every principle has not only champions, but also dissenters. No doubt there will be critics who will find the abolition of entry regulation an absurd suggestion. Up to a point, this reaction is quite understandable. Let no one fail to grasp the order and depth of change that is being advocated. What is being called for here is the purging of a particular form of political and administrative control over social and economic conduct that meshes with much of social and economic life. Let us be generous and assume that the critics have no benefit in maintaining bureaucracy and patronage networks, and that these critics are not motivated by anti-business sentiments, and that they are purely inspired by a concern for the welfare of society.

There is no reason why the protection of the public interest requires the use of entry regulation of economic activity. Let us not quibble about the evident – namely, the criminal. If one activity or another is criminal, the only appropriate response is prohibition; licensing criminal activities is tantamount to legitimizing unlawful behaviour. If, on the other hand, an activity is not criminal but results in negative externalities, the proper response is to deal directly with these externalities. We must stop equating the advocacy of free enterprise with the propagation of mayhem, predation, pollution, immorality, or anarchy. The solution to market failure is not making the start-up of a business an obstacle course; rather it is thoughtful lawmaking and effective enforcement.

These are answers that the critics could have thought of themselves; all that is required is an enquiring and flexible mind. Abolition of entry regulation must be advocated because we must lift the heavy hand of an oppressive, dishonest, and corrupt state from economic activity. The principle is right and necessary – right because productive effort and trade require freedom, and necessary because the record of government on fair and reasonable exercise of regulatory power in most countries is so bad that nothing less than rigid principle can offer protection.

Chapter 5

Dead Capital

Our refuge is upon the soil, in all its freshness and fertility – our heritage is on the Public Domain, in all its boundless wealth and infinite variety. This heritage once secured to us, the evil we complain of will become our greatest good. Machinery from the formidable rival, will sink into the obedient instrument of our will – the master shall become our servant – the tyrant shall become our slave.

—George Henry Evans,
Workingman's Advocate. *July 6, 1844*

The term *dead capital* was coined by De Soto to illustrate the nature of and the problem with extralegal possessions. Dead capital represents the unrealizable capital value of possessions such as houses, crops, and businesses for which informals have no access to the legal processes for representing their property (i.e., titles, deeds, and statutes of incorporation). Consequently, informals are unable to use these possessions to create capital by engaging in legal and financial transactions in which formal procedure is indispensable (e.g., mortgaging property, issuing shares in equity, property insurance, and conveyance of property). Research by De Soto established that, worldwide, approximately 85 per cent of all urban parcels in developing and formerly communist countries turned out to be informal. In other words, in the developing world, the greater part of urban real estate represents dead capital. The severity of the problem with dead capital is probably best understood by trying to imagine what would happen if we destroyed the property rights on 85 per cent of all homes in rich countries.

What if: destroying property representation in rich countries

In many rich countries one half to three quarters of all household units own the homes and apartments they occupy. Suppose you woke up one morning, resident and homeowner in the United States, and learned from a morning news broadcast that property title records of 85 per cent of all homes in your country have vanished. The anchorperson continues to report that, without proper title, jurists and courts would no longer certify the legality of real estate transactions or recognize mortgages thereon as proper security. Meanwhile, the government seems strangely unresponsive to the crisis; the senior policymakers appearing in the newscast seem mildly surprised but somewhat blasé. Furthermore, they are unforthcoming in terms of solutions and blandly promise to refer the matter to some obscure congressional committee. A lowly and poker-faced government spokesman advises affected homeowners to pursue the "usual" adjudication procedures to restore their titles while sidestepping all questions from the journalists at the press conference about the nature of these procedures. A legal expert being interviewed by the newscaster warns that existing adjudication procedures are exceedingly complex and time-consuming affairs. According to his estimates, it would take at least eighty to ninety years to restore the proper title to a majority of the properties.

While watching the news, you realize that buyers will not be inclined to pay the same prices for houses lacking proper title as those with proper title. Without proper title the buying and selling of most homes will become an extralegal transaction (i.e., to a large extent, the activity is comparable to black market trading). Because bankers will not accept a mortgage without a secure title, you soon grasp that 85 per cent of the entire housing stock in the nation can no longer be mortgaged. Without mortgaging, finance homes bought and sold may have to be paid for out of the savings of the buyer. You grasp that most people do not possess savings balances equivalent to the house prices you have been accustomed to in your life. Average household savings are usually just a fraction of average home values. Thus, you would never be able to sell your house for the price you originally paid for it – nor would you buy another one for more that the savings you can muster. The horror would sink in as it dawned on you that house prices would start crashing across the country shortly after the broadcast.

With crashing house prices, the size of your debts will soon exceed the value of your home. Should you ever wish or need to sell your home, you will never be able to repay your debt in full from the proceeds of the sale. This fact matters in many ways. For example, if you were a middle-aged person or on the brink of retirement, it would occur to you that your home equity position (i.e., the difference between the price of your house and the remaining mortgage debt on it), which you had hoped to cash in at some point after your retirement, will have been wiped out. Your future pension happens to be of modest size, so you are probably staring at poverty in old age. Young, home-owning professionals desiring to move in pursuit of a career will suddenly find themselves unable to repay their present home loans from the proceeds of selling the old house and face a screaming shortage of legal property available at the point of destination. Moving and making a career will now be far more difficult and financially hazardous.

Suddenly, the very idea of having to repay your mortgage seems infuriating. At the same time, your terror will be mitigated somewhat by the realization that, in case you cease to pay, your banker will have a hard time seizing your home. Bankers watching the same news and drawing the same conclusion will realize that vast numbers of debtors will probably take advantage of the situation to cease payments of instalments on their home loans. Suddenly the most secure source of collateral a banker could wish for turns into an ocean of credit risk. A steady source of profit will turn into the largest source of losses ever in the financial world. Mortgage lending, now the single largest source of lending by type to consumers and businesses in rich countries, would practically cease.

If you were one of those many millions of small businessmen or businesswomen who uses his or her home or business property as collateral for business loans, you will also be dismayed by the realization that having lost his or her collateral, your banker will, in all likelihood, be cutting off your credit line in the next twenty-four hours. Without credit and strapped for cash, small- and medium-sized businesses would soon start to fail by the hundreds of thousands and start sacking millions upon millions of workers. Bankers will see their carefully husbanded small business loan portfolios turn into a wasteland of destroyed business relationships and a tidal wave of red ink. Also, many of the employees fired by cash-strapped or failing businesses would no longer be able to repay their home loans, thus accelerating the pace at which the gold in mortgages would turn into rivers of red ink.

In summary, trillions upon trillions of dollars' worth of business loans and mortgage-backed loans and securities – or many trillions of financial assets on the balance sheets of banks or held by institutional investors such as pension funds, insurers, and investment funds – would soon start to evaporate. Banks would start to fold. Pension funds, including your own, have traditionally been great investors in mortgage loans, mortgage-backed securities, and real estate. As their financial assets evaporate and their real estate portfolios melt down, so does your pension plan. The destruction of our real estate property system would result in the annihilation of the entire financial system as we know it; it would trigger an economic crisis of proportions far surpassing the Great Depression during the 1930s.

Most likely, you did not know before but now discover that something you and most of the citizens of rich countries have always – without the slightest doubt or even a passing thought – taken for granted (i.e., proper title to homes ... in other words, *acknowledged property rights*), represented one of the pillars supporting the prosperity of the nation as well as your own. It should be crystal clear to you that the so-called political leaders who failed to preserve the system for securing and protecting your property rights are either grossly incompetent or worse: saboteurs.

The unimaginable reality

Think of how utterly clueless we are about the potential destroyed when a majority of the population of a country such as Egypt, Peru, or Indonesia find themselves deprived of access to effective property rights! We are completely oblivious of the inadequacy or decrepitude of property systems in these countries and the dismal economics involved. That 85 per cent of all property titles in the United States or the Netherlands or France could possibly be destroyed, that policymakers in rich countries could be so incompetent and uncaring, is inconceivable. Of course, that is a good thing for people living in rich countries. Yet, in poor countries, this total indifference by policymakers is *common practice*. What is beyond belief in rich countries is day-to-day, real-life experience in poor countries. At the start of this chapter we already noted that, worldwide, approximately 85 per cent of all urban parcels in developing and formerly communist countries appear to be informal. Here, *informal* means that the title of ownership is non-existent or else seriously flawed because it is either invalid, incomplete, or in violation of some law or procedure. In Egypt, 92 per cent of urban real estate and 83 per cent of rural real estate is informal. In the Philippines, the figures are 57 and 67 per cent, respectively. These figures represent the efforts of billions of people possessing or building homes, stores, and workshops and managing farms without proper titles. Such properties vary in size and value from makeshift hovels to solid and valuable properties. For example, the value of urban informal houses in Port-au-Prince can vary from USD 500 for a shanty to USD 75.000 for a veritable villa.[1] The latter value may surprise the reader, but the fact of the matter is that, in many countries, even the affluent have serious trouble cutting through red tape and resort to a degree of informality. The ILD estimated that, in 1997, the value of urban and rural informal real estate worldwide approximated USD 9.3 trillion.[2] Please let the significance of this figure sink in; this figure represents the capital, the fruit of backbreaking labour, the blood and sweat and tears of billions of people for which governments either fail or refuse to provide proper titles.

Strictly symptomatically, the most important reason for this situation is dysfunctional legal and administrative systems. Essentially, that means that legal and bureaucratic requirements make it too burdensome for the greater majority of people to gain proper title to their possessions. Egyptian and Haitian public administrations are prototypes. Research shows that the procedure to gain access to unoccupied, unclaimed, and unused desert land for construction purposes (and to register these property rights in Egypt) took between six and fourteen years and required seventy-seven procedural steps involving no fewer than thirty-one government offices including, among others, the Prime Minister's Office, the Ministry of Defence, the Mining office, Social Affairs Ministry, and the Antiquities Department.[3] In Haiti, it took sixty-five bureaucratic steps and two years, on average, to obtain a five-year lease on government land. To buy this land required another 111 bureaucratic hurdles, including the involvement of the president, the prime minister, the council of ministers, the senate, the National Assembly, other unlikely offices, and twelve more years.[4] To wait so long for so many permissions is unbearable. Life is more urgent than that. This is the reason why people in the developing world squat by the billions.

Trying to legalize your possessions may actually be dangerous. If a squatter in Egypt, say, attempts to regularize the status of his properties, he risks eviction, demolition of his home, imprisonment for up to ten years, and a steep fine to boot[5]. This is a showstopper for almost all informal real estate owners, most of which are humble folks without the leverage to obtain justice. To resist evictions is to risk brute force at the hand of the authorities. In fact, on numerous occasions in many countries, squatters have been shot for resisting eviction. Are the majority of the Egyptians criminals? The opposite is true. In good old communist jargon, it is the state and all the defenders of the status quo that are the enemy of the people.

Finally, let us not forget that informality as such is hardly the issue sometimes. This is the case where outright hostility to property rights over land is official and deliberate policy. Ethiopia provides a revealing archetype. The Marxist notion that the state should own and allocate all the land is still official government policy. "Peasants' rights over the ground their families have tilled for generations are conditional on them living on or near it. Owners who have not cultivated their farm for two seasons risk having it confiscated. This ties them to a location and a way of life that offer little hope of advancement. Even the most ambitious think twice before seeking their fortune in the city, because if things do not work out they may have nowhere to return to."[6] Indeed, 88 per cent of its labour force is still employed in agriculture. Ethiopia, unsurprisingly, is one of the ten poorest countries in the world. This is what we mean when we call a country's rulers saboteurs.

Credit and proper title

Credit is the way to the land of opportunity. Credit allows people short on financial resources to realize their objectives with borrowed funds. It allows entrepreneurs to invest in more or better equipment for expanding production or raising productivity. Farmers can make their land more productive by investing in better seed, irrigation systems, or farm equipment. Families can buy, build, and furnish larger and more comfortable homes. In short, credit expands both business investment and consumer demand, which boosts economic growth. Life in a rich country (e.g., the United States or the Netherlands) without mortgage finance is unimaginable. In rich countries, real estate development and finance are primary catalysts of economic growth. In the West, home ownership, business start-ups, and economic expansion are intimately bound up with banking and insurance. Virtually all housing starts and project developers and two-thirds of business start-ups in rich countries are financed through mortgage-backed lending. Lending, however, is a risky business, and bankers will seek to mitigate that risk. Risk is reduced through various means, including establishing the identity of the borrower, confirming his or her formal domicile, gaining proof of business registration and licenses to operate a business, and requiring collateral, such as mortgages, pledges of assets, or leasing arrangements.

But without such formal credentials, credit and insurance is mostly unavailable. This is also true in the developing world. The problem for people in poor countries is that very few can prove that they own their land or their homes because they do not have title deeds. Businesses are frequently unregistered and unlicensed (i.e., informal). Usually, informal businesses do not have a formal domicile. Informal real estate properties are frequently unregistered. In other words, banks cannot register mortgages taken and debt collection agents have no formal domicile to visit, for example. An informal in need of credit will, most of the time, face shut doors. Credit institutions and insurers will not deal with informals. In turn, informals cannot finance sales beyond a certain point most of the time and, therefore, they must forego sales revenues. The aforementioned USD 9.3 trillion is not available as collateral. This means that a workshop cannot mortgage its real estate to finance better machinery and equipment, and farmers cannot mortgage their land to finance investments in improved irrigation systems. Trillions of dollars of investment opportunities are wasted and turnover revenues foregone. Save for access to credit and the people's own effort, many hundreds of millions of people should never have been poor in the first place. In the words of De Soto, the USD 9.3 trillion is *dead capital*.[7]

Special note must be taken of the charge that financial institutions impose biased credit policies upon the poor. Be that as it may, when countries such as Egypt and Indonesia have extralegal real estate in the 85–90 per cent range, practically all property in the land is unavailable for collateralization and thus inaccessible to bank finance. Without some common interest (i.e., a good reason why a banker should provide credit), informals and bankers might as well be regarded as living on different planets. The point is that proper titles and collateral are levellers in the sense that they provide both the banker and the applicant for credit with the appropriate means for communicating intelligibly and effectively about the degree of credit risk involved without prejudice as to the status or background of the latter. In the final analysis, the greatest foe of the poor is not the banker but the indifferent government that fails or refuses to provide the informals with proper titles and secure property rights.

Chapter 2 already demonstrated how the extralegality of informals' livelihoods puts them at a real disadvantage: their opportunities to transact are severely limited. Establishing a business and its derivative, employment opportunities, and making one's home becomes, on one hand, a source of vulnerability to state sanction and, on the other hand, a cause for denial of legal protection. The price of informality is the criminalization of a majority of citizens in many nations precisely because they pursue essentially legitimate objectives. Extralegality is also an opportunity for petty tyranny and corruption by officials such as police officers and inspectors of various government agencies. The cost of avoidance and bribery is significant. In short, the one and the same legal system is inaccessible, hostile, and corrupt.

Without legal protection and credit, people cannot or will not invest much. In the same way that overregulation dissuades informal agents from starting legal businesses, so an excess of regulatory and bureaucratic procedures prevents squatters from legalizing their real estate possessions. ILD research in Peru – where informal dwellings represented 53 per cent of all urban housing – uncovered that informal possession adversely affected the value of the land, the dwellings, and the ability and willingness of informals to invest. Correspondingly, an ILD survey of the values of houses and buildings in thirty-seven neighbourhoods in Lima uncovered that people invested at least nine times more "when they are given some measure of protection by the formal legal system."[8] Should we dare conclude that the scale of underinvestment resulting from overregulation, extralegality, and lack of credit must equal a quantity in the neighbourhood of nine times USD 9.3 trillion?

One way to grasp the severity of the problem is to compare the supply of property titles to the supply of credit. Economic growth, business investment, and the supply of credit are closely related. Increased credit extension stimulates business activity, and that activity increases economic growth. In large, sophisticated economies, central banks often combat a sluggish economy by instituting a so-called loose credit policy. In that case, the central bank buys large quantities of treasury securities in the open market, which gives banks additional money to lend at lower interest rates. This abundance, or looseness, of credit is intended to stimulate borrowing and invigorate the economy. Tight money is the opposite of loose credit. Tight money is the result of the central bank's decision to sell securities in the open market, which reduces bank reserves and makes borrowing more expensive. A tight money policy is designed to slow down a rapidly accelerating economy. Often, one of the salient characteristics of an economic recession or depression is the contraction of the supply of credit by the financial sector. Right or wrong, it is for this reason that governments all over the world pursue monetary policies during recessions with the objective of boosting credit extension in order to increase the rate of economic growth. By analogy, the effect of dead capital in poor countries on credit extension and economic growth is the equivalent of a perpetual and draconian tight money policy causing a deep and permanent depression. Restricting the supply of valid and effective title to property constricts the supply of credit. The chronic poverty and deprivation in non-advanced economies should, in part, be understood as symptoms of a perpetual depression caused by a structurally constrained supply of valid property titles.[9] Let us push the analogy in the most literal way: imagine what would happen to any economy if the supply of credit were reduced by 85 per cent. The suggestion probably sounds stranger than it is in reality, but this is exactly what happens during banking crises. Indeed, during banking crises, the supply of credit collapses, which triggers or intensifies deep economic depressions in the corresponding countries. Note that any government deciding to practice tight money in the middle of a recession or depression would have the business sector, trade unions, financial sector, economists, and voters up in arms against it.[10] Note that it is our own ignorance on this point that has rendered us completely incapable of effective and articulate opposition to misgovernment in this area.[11]

The wealth of the poor

The sheer size of the estimates uncovered by De Soto's research redefines the entire debate about the causes of underdevelopment. For one, those who are deemed poor are sitting on top of a vast mountain of wealth that they created via their own effort. Savour this moment. This is the fundamental and defining discovery implicit to all ILD research. Prior to Mr De Soto's breakthrough publications, policy specialists, politicians, the intelligentsia, publicists, and people across the entire spectrum of ideologies practically unanimously saw the poor as fundamentally incapable of creating significant wealth through productive effort. The massive amount, USD 9.3 trillion, should put paid to an unfounded belief.

Apparently, the poor are the world's most underrated self-help society. USD 9.3 trillion is almost one hundred times more than the total amount of development aid received by developing countries since 1970.[12] Informal real estate in the Philippines amounts to USD 132.9 billion.[13] That amount is five times the value of total mineral production (USD 23.6 billion) over a period of twenty years (1979–1998). If the "exploitation" of the natural resources of developing countries should be accepted as a concern, the problem of extralegality dwarfs it. Many of us are familiar with big business statistics, yet we marvel about the size of informal capital created in the face of adversity and obstruction by the government. Case in point: Peru's informal capital, estimated at USD 74.2 billion, is two times the total assets of its one thousand largest, private, formal enterprises.[14]

Without playing down the precariousness of their existence, the picture that emerges from ILD's findings is also that the poor are quite independent, industrious, and business-minded people. When there is no employment for them in the formal sector, they will get on with their lives by setting up on their own – and they survive doing so. Extralegality harbours a huge reservoir of productive talent.

Mr De Soto's objective is to demonstrate why capitalism works for the West and seems to fail in developing nations. He has provided us with a view of the problem of poverty through one set of missing or dysfunctional institutions: the systems and institutions necessary for the representation of property rights. In doing so, De Soto shows us that our understanding of the legal context of poverty and exclusion is deeply flawed. The poor are not bereft of property; they are able to create significant amounts of wealth by their own effort and have a massive amount of property in their keep. In short, they are bereft of access to property rights. Property rights are not inimical to the poor, but the absence of property rights is. The modern poor have material ambitions and needs that are surprisingly bourgeois. Indeed, extralegals have a need for systems of representation of ownership and credit that are essentially capitalistic.

The aforementioned figure (i.e., USD 9.3 trillion) should make us think very hard about the nature and quality of government and leadership of poor countries. To start, it goes to show that developing societies are basically ruled by people who are clueless about one of the most fundamental requirements of a modern economy – most likely because they are entirely uninterested in the facts. That last point should not surprise us. The vast majority of the power elites and the intelligentsia of the developing world are leftist in their ideological orientation. Private property and property rights have never been positive issues with the Left – and a large part of the Left is deeply hostile to property rights. And yet durable development is not possible without a working legal and administrative system that secures property rights. Accordingly, if the objective is to achieve genuine, durable development, then the greater part of the political classes of the developing world is, by dint of their ideological orientation, unfit for public office.

We need to start thinking about how to raise the nation to a higher standard of governance. This is a conscious task. It requires us to develop litmus tests and benchmarks with which we can measure the policies of our governments. One such benchmark is universal access to legal title to property. We must start to expose, resist, and oppose all leaders and policymakers who are insufficiently knowledgeable and caring about the need for adequate property representation systems. Because these are complex issues, we cannot directly rely on the general public to do this. Any movement forward on this issue will have to come from a new breed of social activists and advocates who will organize the informals into viable and effective constituencies that cannot be ignored. It is only via these activists and constituencies that the idea of property rights will achieve mainstream acceptance.

Lord of the land

Up until this point, this chapter has been, in part, a synopsis of some of the writings by Mr De Soto. The hope is to portray the severity of the problem of access to legal occupancy and ownership of land. It is, on one hand, a story of gross negligence by government and, on the other, of predatory jurisdiction. One can hardly find better proof of this than in the many and bizarre types of government offices that must be visited in Egypt and Haiti to obtain a property title to state land.

What must we do about it? What must we make of this predatory jurisdiction? The first question is the easier one to answer: we must reform, deregulate, and streamline the various administrative processes involved. Some of this is – at least from a technical viewpoint – fairly easy to carry out. Deregulation is the process of identifying and removing all excessive rules and involvements by irrelevant government offices. Streamlining administrative processes, however, is quite difficult. Streamlining administrative processes is about reforming dysfunctional bureaucracies – a delicate process involving the preservation of certain functions, offices, and institutions while reforming and improving their management, organization, and public relations. The importance of the process of deregulation and streamlining administrative processes cannot be underestimated. It is not possible to establish a well-functioning property system without creating a favourable regulatory environment and setting up clean and effective administrative systems. The world's most developed countries all have effective, reliable, well-managed property systems. Conversely, the world's poorest countries lack such property systems. In developing countries and former communist countries, messy regulatory systems and corrupt, mismanaged land registries and dysfunctional judiciaries undermine the process of developing effective property systems and disempower the people. Of course, this is not the place to deal with how to deregulate and streamline given the highly technical nature of the material involved.

When we look at the problem of informal property, we should ask what makes predatory jurisdiction possible. As in all cases of predatory jurisdiction, some fundamental right is being denied. In the case of informal property, it seems that the right to pursue and create property is being denied in some form. Yet this does not seem like a fully satisfactory definition of what is happening; after all, informal property often exists in countries where property rights are formally acknowledged and where there is also formal, titled property. Strictly speaking, there seems to be some kind of flaw or omission in this system that prevents a considerable number of people from legitimizing their property claims. Maybe we should start with the question of *how* property comes into existence. The next step is to determine the similarities and differences between formal and informal property.

In the most basic sense, all property originates in the act of occupying and using land. Someone must take a piece of land, use it, and in doing so lay claim to it as his or her own. Informal property and formal property share this quality. In both cases, people take possession of a piece of land, use it, and claim it as their own. The difference in quality, on the other hand, can be distilled from the definition of property: the *legal* right to the possession, use, enjoyment, and disposal of a thing. Thus, in essence, informal property is an acquisition and possession or an object of use and claim to ownership that failed to make the full and complete transition to the status of legally owned property.

Why is it that the majority of possessions in the developing world cannot make this transition? The cause again is predatory jurisdiction: it is entirely up to the government to decide the rules under which people can get legal title to land. Governments can make these rules as difficult as they like. There are, in practice, no restraints on the power of government in this matter. In other words, there does not seem to be any operative standard of justice that limits government in the accumulation and exercise of these regulatory powers. This is evident from the fact that the situation of the people – their factual, legitimate need for land – does not seem to play any substantial role in the making of these rules. The need for land and the rightness of the act of occupying land in view of this need do not seem to be primary considerations in terms of the legality of the deed of occupation, of taking possession, of making use of it, and of claiming it as one's own. What happens in the case of informal property is that the legal system does not give recognition to factual occupation, possession, and use of land as a logical and, therefore, bona fide source of a property right. The law does not recognize the act of occupation and taking possession as a valid cause for lawful possession and ownership. As a consequence, informals cannot, *as a matter of right,* through the act of occupation and making use of land, create a claim to lawful possession and ownership of their properties. Thus, already in the stage of occupying land, the informals encounter a problem with the legal system.

This situation is very strange; after all, what else besides its occupation and use could be the source of lawful possession and ownership of land? At this point it is necessary to remember that a formal title to property is in all nations a grant from the state. The hallmark of informal property is the absence of such a grant. Yet, when the act of occupation is not acknowledged as the source of a property right, the only source of lawful possession and ownership remaining is the will of the state to make a grant. When the grant of title is an act of state not rooted in the recognition of any right to create property by the act of occupation, then the title is almost like a gift from the state. The state and its agents are now purely the merciful patrons to the grantee, and the grantee becomes no more than a supplicant, a beggar. When there is no right acting as a constraint, the will of the state to accede becomes arbitrary policymaking power. In other words, it is entirely up to government to set the rules for issuing grants. What is wrong here? Pure discretionary policymaking power as the only source of legal property is a violation of the natural order.

The natural order

The natural order in the human cosmos involves people seeking land for productive purposes – and in the process establishing occupancy rights and claims of ownership. This is basically what humanity has done with land throughout history. Over the millennia, millions and millions of people took possession of millions upon millions of square kilometres of land in this manner and initiated its use for cultivation, trade, industry, and building homes. Peasants, dirt farmers, yeoman farmers, large landowners, townsfolk, industrialists, religious orders, squatters, speculators, and property developers – all had, at some stage, a hand in this process. Today, this process is still going on in much of the developing world. Each year, the people clear land for cultivation and cities expand at breakneck speed.

We tend to take these enormous stretches of cultivated land and built-up areas throughout the world for granted. We are rarely in the habit of reflecting upon the question of how it all came into existence. Yet let it sink in for a moment that all land cultivated and built-up today had, at some point in the past, no occupants or owners. These days, almost no one seems to realize that there was always a first person taking possession of virgin land, clearing it, and breaking the soil for the first time to cultivate it or to build a home or a workplace. While doing so, that person claimed the land as his or her own and desired that others should acknowledge that claim – not to please his or her fancy, but in recognition of the necessity and rightness of acting in the interest of his or her self-preservation.

Humans, by nature, are producers and builders. To sustain their lives and to create their comforts they *must* produce and build. To produce and build requires the use of land; the use of land is fundamental to the act of production and building. One cannot produce one bushel of grain without first clearing, ploughing, and sowing a piece of land; one cannot build a house without clearing a lot and sinking foundations into the ground. Human nature – biological and psychological necessity combined with an inborn drive to create – is the source of the urge that people have to take possession of land and apply it to the uses required for self-preservation and the enjoyment of life. Thus, humans cultivated land and built homes and workplaces on the land. This process of self-sustaining action (referred to in chapter 3) is the ultimate rationale for land occupancy, use, and ownership. This means that, ultimately, when all things are considered, humans cannot be denied land. Basic necessity validates his or her right to occupy land and claim its ownership. In this respect, he or she cannot even, on the point of principle, be required to act by permission (i.e., he or she takes land, uses it, and lives on it by right and on the basis of necessity).

Homo sapiens are also extraordinarily fertile, adaptive, and expansionary species. People overcome scarcity through the expansion of their habitats, and this categorically includes expanded land use. Accordingly, the growth of populations across the globe has meant and will mean the expanded use of land. We are not in the least ignoring the very real problems posed by an expanding global population; rather, we are merely stating a fact, one that cannot and should not be ignored. Ignoring certain facts about human nature does not solve the problems of global population growth.

The vast quantities of extralegal real estate held by billions of people across the developing world are essentially a manifestation of this natural order. It behoves us to understand that fundamental necessities – in other words, those that accrue from our very nature – are basically irrepressible. Land is a fundamental necessity. Even when the state fails to make proper legal and administration arrangements – and even when we fail to understand the dynamics of our natural order – life will go on and, driven by necessity, people will do what they have to do – including occupying land.

This report of the natural order is a rather high-level overview. To speak of the right to occupy land and that no one may be required to act by permission in taking land raises in sensible people questions that deserve answers. What is the scope of this right to occupy land? Does it sanction land theft? What does it mean to say that people cannot be required to seek land by permission? What is the role of the state? What does history tell us regarding this matter? What is the environmental perspective of this right? These are complex questions without simple answers. Nevertheless, in the following sections, we will explore some meaningful and useful answers that could work to the benefit of all.

The right to occupy land

Beyond the discovery of fundamental necessity, the scope of the right to occupy land is probably best clarified by explaining what it does not include. The right to occupy land is not intended to promote theft, robbery, and violence. Rather, the outcome of the right to occupy land is private property. For this same reason, it can hardly be the cause of its demise. The very concept of private property would become meaningless if the right to occupy land applied to private property. The right of each individual to engage in self-sustaining action is the basis of both property rights and the right to occupy land. The point of the right to occupy land is to ensure access to land as a means of production. Property rights, then, protect the ownership of the means of production acquired as well as the fruits of one's productive efforts. Without the security that one has control over the means of production or the fruits thereof, one becomes the prey of one's neighbour. How does one secure one's survival and comforts? What is the sense of investing one's labour in a piece of land – clearing a piece of land to plough it for cultivation or to build a home or factory on it – when others can simply take it all away from you? In this context, property rights are instrumental in keeping this right of *each* individual to engage in self-sustaining and non-conflicting action. Essentially, it is the rule of *live and let live*; occupy land if you must, but respect the right of your neighbour to secure his or her means of self-preservation. Consequently, the right to occupy land can only refer to unused, unoccupied, or *unappropriated* land. Land already occupied, used, or owned is not open to occupation by another.

History frequently offers an extremely messy and problematical view of this process: our natural order is an abstraction in that it ignores, for didactic reasons, the dark side of history and human nature. Historically, land has often been the object of robbery on a massive and bloody scale. We know of many horrific episodes that have played out in many different lands on countless occasions. Many times, the first occupants – and then, often in succession, the subsequent occupants – were evicted from their lands, slaughtered, or subjugated and reduced to serfdom and slavery on their own land. Nevertheless, no matter how complicated the view from history, when we strip away all the convolutions of history we are still reduced to that basic picture of a person taking possession of land out of necessity. No injustice or horror of history can cancel out fundamental necessity and thus destroy the principle of right. Bad things happening in the history of humanity cannot detract from the fact that humans need land to produce and make homes. Hitler's abusive application of his right of free speech during the Weimar republic does not destroy the right of Germans today to enjoy freedom of free speech. The only proper way to look at many injustices recorded in history is to perceive them for what they are: the best-known and most vicious cases of violating the inherent rights and freedoms of all human beings.

The eternal standing of rights

Why are we so keen on the question of unappropriated land? What makes the question of unappropriated land and the right to occupy it so important and relevant today? For the majority of people in the developing world, the problem is not access to virgin land in the present or the future; rather, it is the legal status of land that they have already occupied and used. Indeed, the overwhelming need is for the formalization of the enormous amount of extralegal property already in existence rather than the issuance of currently unappropriated lands. Access to presently unappropriated land seems, by comparison, a lesser issue.

The crux of the matter, however, is that *today's* extralegal property was *yesterday's* unappropriated land. This extralegal property represents a past that continues to haunt us in the present. It is a past in which the transformation of unappropriated land into property got off on the wrong foot. Essentially, up to this date, those past acts of taking possession of what was originally unappropriated land have not been acknowledged by any sovereign authority as a proper exercise of rights. The moment of de facto occupation may lie in the past, but the problem of its recognition is still with us today. Let us remember that a great deal of informal real estate cannot be traced in any land register; to that extent – to the land registries and the government – this is often still unappropriated land!

Throughout this chapter, the line of argumentation in advocating the right to occupy land is conducted mostly in the present or future tense. Because of this methodology, it may seem as if the emphasis lies with the taking of land in the present or the future. It should be understood, however, what we are aiming for. Though the line of reasoning may apply the present or future tense, natural rights are timeless in their application – it is the existence of the human species that calls forth natural rights. Thus, natural rights span all of human existence, including our past, present, and future. If the actions of the individual fall within the scope of freedoms sanctioned by his rights, it does not matter whether he acted in the past, present, or future; his actions are legitimate for all eternity. The right to occupy land, therefore, does not merely sanction free settlement of currently unappropriated land in the present and future, *but also* all previous occupations. We are not just advocating the right to occupy land with its current or future exercise. From a practical perspective, the spearhead issue entails securing a basis for the legitimacy of past occupations and, in view of the number of eligible individuals, the need already runs in the billions. The economic-interest angle would be improving the lot of those billions by transforming trillions of dollars of dead capital into live capital. Yet it is obvious that, because the occupation of unappropriated land will continue to be a mass phenomenon due to population growth, the right to occupy land provides for the present and future as well.

It should be noted that there is no way to limit the validity of a right to a specific period in time. Each human carries his or her right in himself or herself precisely because he or she is a member of the human species, regardless of the age he or she was born in. Therefore, when a right is rejected (because one does not wish it to be practiced now or in the future), all past actions sanctioned by that right are automatically deprived of their legitimacy. Indeed, take the example of slavery to demonstrate this logic. Historically, slavery was considered a natural state of affairs; slaveholding was considered a legitimate enterprise that was often a source of prestige. One must observe that, because these activities are now deemed morally wrong, unjust, or criminal – and certainly not a right – we now frequently consider past activities of this kind unjust. This is why many Americans and Europeans feel embarrassed about their nations' historic role in slavery: their views on past actions changed retroactively in accordance with their estimation of the legitimacy of these pursuits.

Government, unappropriated land, and public domain

Let us now contrast the right to occupy land against the modern practice. In the modern world, it is the rule that all unappropriated land is deemed government-owned land (also called public land or public domain). With regard to government ownership of land, public domain describes absolute and complete ownership by the state. The term *absolute,* in this instance, refers to the fullest and most superior right of property in terms of land – full discretionary power to sell or give away land. In the form of government ownership of land, this means that governments, as a matter of principle, have the final authority to decide whether such public lands may or may not be distributed to the public. Full discretionary authority means that the government can impose any number of rules and regulations, conditions, and restrictions on the process of alienating domain land. Currently, there are no governments that recognize without reservation the principle of an original right of the individual to occupy land. By extension, governments do not recognize any rights qualifying or limiting control of the public domain; governments across the world have, as a rule, the authority to compel the people to seek permission to use or possess public land. This, then, is the stark contrast between the rights of the citizen and the authority of the state.

Where did this system of public domain come from? The existing system is inherited from an ancient world of absolutist, despotic rule. It was a time when kings and emperors were the supreme owners of all land, and its distribution was their prerogative – a power used for rewarding the servants of the king. The royal domain was primarily an instrument for exercising and preserving the power of rulers pursuing their personal glory. In other words, the royal domain was never meant to serve the common good and was always established by the decree of kings seizing part or all the land in the realm without the slightest regard for the rights of the contemporaneous occupants, mostly the peasants dwelling on the land. To add insult to injury, such royal decrees usually entailed reducing the king's subjects to servitude. In fact, the distribution of the land to the servants of the king generally included its occupants as chattel. Fortunately, the condition of servitude has since been abolished in most nations. Yet the discredit and end of absolutist monarchical rule around the globe did not result in a corresponding discredit of the idea of domain as discretionary control by government of the land. In the absence of a public conscious of their rights and lacking a clear grasp of the proper role of the state, this absolute power defaulted the state. Presidents and ministers and bureaucracies have since replaced kings, and the adjective *royal* has been replaced by *public*. The motives and interests may have changed, but the common good gets lip service and the disposal of public land is still entirely at the discretion of the rulers and the vagaries of power politics. Thus, we face the consequences of a historic failure to grasp or accept the imperatives of human nature and the consequent rights of the individual and, following that, to think through the role the state. The legacy is exclusionary public land policies or the failure to provide institutionalized access to public land, official neglect, and criminalization in place of empowerment, massive extralegality, trillions of dollars of dead capital, and unbearably slow and unequal development in much of the developing world.

The role of the state: landlord or servant of the people?

By having this complete right of property, government can act in the likeness of a private owner. This is very odd when one considers the mission of government. Unlike individuals, states do not exist for their own sake, as ends in themselves. The state is – or if it's not, it should be – an entity instituted by the citizenry to serve the people; its sole purpose is to serve the public interest. As such, it cannot be the beneficiary of "rights." To pursue the argument to its logical conclusion, governments should not enjoy property rights – and certainly not in the likeness of a private citizen. It should not be the purpose of domain to create an enduring and exclusionary claim of ownership by government of land. For private property owners, the public interest is not the first or only concern; a "selfish" regard for their own interests with respect to the land owned by them is legitimate. Governments, on the other hand, do not have private interests because they exist only to serve the public interest. In the case of government, full and superior right of property becomes a source of predatory jurisdiction. Therefore, from the premise that it is the purpose of the state to serve the public interest, it follows that there is no point in allowing government so much discretionary power – in this instance by granting it absolute ownership rights of land – that it can arbitrarily refuse to release public land for distribution to or deny the grant of title to actual or aspirant occupants. On the contrary, good government means providing a legal framework that, in principle, acknowledges and facilitates the occupation of land wherever and whenever clear need presents itself. Beyond that, the only justification of government control over unappropriated land is to keep the peace in the interest of public order and to ensure its orderly distribution when demand manifests itself. Government ownership of unappropriated land can be viewed as a trust held by government in view of the absence of a formal land use or property claim by private parties. In a properly governed society, government is no more than a temporary custodian with a duty to distribute domain land and surrender title when people present their need for it. As soon as a user for the land steps forward, the rationale for its status as public domain ceases to apply.

The aforementioned argument states that absolute ownership of land by the state, *in principle,* means full discretionary control of unappropriated land by government. This, however, is not to say that, in current practice, control of public land by government is never qualified by other legal and administrative arrangements. The mere existence of procedures for applying for state land as such – even though complying with them is usually excessively difficult and time-consuming for ordinary citizens – illustrates the point. All the same, in no way do these procedures accede to the premise of a right of the individual to occupy land. Instead, the purpose of many of these procedures is to narrowly ease and formalize access by special interests or pressure groups to public domain. Here, the ruling principle is expedience and adhocracy. Only when moneyed or powerful interests that cannot be denied because of power politics need access to unappropriated land will policymakers act to provide effective and formal access. Still, many such procedures are formulated as notionally open to the wider public. Nevertheless, this must not be taken as proof that there is, on this matter, some awareness on the part of government, however residual or rudimentary, that there are circumstances where the state must serve and yield to the interests of the private citizen. Modern legal language and procedures habitually phrase procedures in terms of equal service to a general public. This is more a ritual nod to the principle of equality before the law – in many countries, these are meaningless words – than the recognition of the rights of the individual. If one wishes to introduce some measure of real sensitivity to the interests of the public into public land policy, the starting point is accepting the need to define the rights of the citizen in this respect.

The requirement to act by permission

The assertion that, in the matter of occupying land, people cannot or should not be compelled to act by permission requires further elaboration.

Again, as mentioned in chapter 3, not every requirement to act by permission is a violation of rights. Property rights would be meaningless if things could be taken from their owners without their permission. Therefore, the immunity from the requirement to act by permission can only apply to unappropriated land. It is only in the case of unappropriated land – today, that often means public land – that the requirement to act by permission is contrary to the natural right. To reverse the argument, if one needs permission to occupy unappropriated land, the very act of engaging in self-sustaining action or the pursuit of life itself becomes the object of the requirement to act by permission. By imposing this requirement, one raises over an individual an authority – which, in modern life, inevitably means government – with the power to ignore the legitimate interests of its citizens (in this case, his need for land).

This is not mere theorizing! This is the reason why the greater part of all real estate in the developing and formerly communist countries is extralegal. In other words, governments around the world ignore the needs of the majority of their citizens for proper title. In the cities and towns of the developing and formerly communist countries alone, out of 2 billion urban dwellers, at least 1.7 billion people now live in informal urban dwellings.[15] Ironically, this massive scale of informal activity also means that the vast majority of developing-world citizens do not seek permission. Perhaps the masses lack the intellectual sharpness, rhetorical skills, and media savvy to methodically and articulately formulate a repudiation of the requirement to act by permission but, in the meantime, sheer necessity has already forced most of them to act accordingly.

In the case of private property, the requirement to act by permission – in this case that of its owner – protects something of real significance: the control of the owner over his means of production or the fruits of his labour. But what does the requirement to act by permission from government, in the matter of unappropriated land, protect? The answer, in terms of property interests (possessory rights, user rights, and ownership claims), to the question is *nothing*. Unappropriated land, by definition, has no users, occupants, or owners. For that reason, there can be no injured parties. Also, states and governments do not have private interests. To that extent, the power of government to require permission to occupy the land is pure predatory jurisdiction. Here, without any benefit to society, government seeks to control the actions of its citizens and thereby limit them in their right to engage in essentially lawful pursuits. This is the essence of arbitrary power. This is one reason why so many people in the developing world cannot claim property: their government possesses the power to dream up any number of rules or regulations it sees fit to impose upon the people without the slightest consideration for whether it conflicts with the rights and interests of the citizens.

The case becomes slightly more complicated when one takes into account the fact that the development of previously unused, unoccupied land may result in negative externalities. Clearing and cultivating land can increase the rate of erosion of topsoil. Deforestation – especially in mountain areas – can, on account of more erosion and run-off, seriously increase the danger of flooding downriver. Residential use of land on the edge of water reservoirs increases the risk of pollution of public water supplies (due to sewage spills and road run-off), thereby posing a menace to the public health. Yet again, negative externalities never invalidate the necessity and rightness of self-sustaining action. The risk of increased erosion and run-off on account of agricultural use of land is not a sufficient reason to ban the practice of agriculture. Agriculture is a fundamental necessity for the sustenance of humankind. The challenge is to find ways to address our concerns with respect to externalities. There are many techniques, ancient and modern, for effectively preserving topsoil or reducing the rate at which erosion occurs.

The task of a government should not entail submitting the enterprise of a man or woman to arbitrary power or the whims of policymakers; rather, the task should be to regulate sensibly. We are not making a case against the regulation of negative externalities as such – only against the idea that government should have blanket powers to turn its citizens into beggars for a vital resource – namely, land. Also, if the occupation of some specific piece of land entailed unacceptable risk to the public safety and health, maybe its settlement should be forbidden. There is no point in granting permission to engage in activities that constitute unacceptable risks to public safety; doing so is the equivalent of sanctioning gross negligence or criminal behaviour. One can imagine that government should have the power to bar development or settlement of land adjacent to water reservoirs in the interest of public hygiene. Alternatively, governments may need the power to regulate the settlement of steep hillsides if there is going to be a massive erosion and run-off problem that seriously increases the danger of flooding downriver. But a great deal of land does not pose such risks to public safety. The settlement of the desert plains near Lima or Cairo, or the urbanization of prairie land near Buenos Aires or forestland close to Moscow, poses few extraordinary public safety or hygiene problems. Also, not all externalities are so serious or even objective that land use should be regulated or circumscribed. For example, people may wish to prevent development of the countryside in their neighbourhood because of its scenic beauty. Yet, in all fairness, do the aesthetic desires of one group of citizens really outweigh the basic housing needs of another group of citizens?

In calling the requirement to act by permission a violation of rights, we are not advocating a free-for-all situation where people may occupy land in a chaotic manner. It is the task of government to uphold the law and to provide for order and public safety. Also, government provides and plans for public amenities requiring space such as public roads, sidewalks, gutters, parking spaces, parks, public squares, market grounds, monuments, schools, government offices, water reservoirs, military bases. In other words, government may have to reserve public land for that purpose. Furthermore, it is the task of government to protect existing private property from unlawful occupation. To enable it to carry out its tasks in an efficient and orderly manner, it is necessary that government should have the authority to impose an application procedure preceding the actual and practical exercise of the right to occupy land. However, any such application procedure should be no more than a notification requirement prior to the act of occupation that enables government to perform its duties in view of its responsibilities to the public. Therefore, there is, in practice, an element of permission involved, but it is one that does not accrue from unlimited authority. Rather, it is derived from a narrowly defined mandate in which the grant is certain except in clearly defined cases as mentioned earlier. The only justification of any such procedure is to arrange for an orderly exercise of this right. A rejection of the requirement to act by permission is an abstract argument from natural right and against unlimited authority. One starts from abstract principle and concedes ground only to the extent that clear, practical necessity – supported by good reason – demands it.

Currently, the occupation without government permission of unappropriated land is, as a rule, either illegal or an act without the sanction or protection of the law. Without the counterbalance of clear, effective, acknowledged rights and freedoms – in this instance, the right to occupy land – the requirement to act by permission easily degenerates into inaccessible and unaccountable bureaucracy that often leads to the systematic criminalization of the legitimate objectives or interests of the people. To the degree that criminalization results, law enforcement without the effective counterbalance of rights is oppression and persecution. Now, oppressors masquerade as law enforcers. Procedure sanctions narrow-mindedness and petty tyranny by bureaucrats. The mechanical exercise of the bare principle of government control of public land passes for good government. Yet good government is not an unthinking exercise of power without the slightest regard for the needs of hundreds of millions of people actually living on public land or desiring to do so. As a matter of fact, the first proper question should have been: Why was the public domain not opened to settlement in the first place when an overwhelming need for this land – as if hundreds of millions of people already living on the land is not clear and convincing evidence – became obvious?

Status quo

The argument so far has been mostly about fundamentals. In practice, the majority of informal occupants will never be prosecuted by the state for illegal or extralegal occupancy of state land. Basically, there are two scenarios here: one where the occupation without notification is illegal and one where that is not necessarily the case. The first situation is more of an urban issue – in cities, informal settlements usually start out as illegal invasions of state land. The second is largely a rural phenomenon. In rural areas, land occupation without formally notifying the authorities is often based on customary practice preceding the modern state.

The problem in the first case is clear enough. Here, extralegal possession is no more than tacitly allowed occupation. Nevertheless, this tacit acquiescence must be understood properly: it is toleration in the absence of the will or the desire (or possibly the means) to enforce domain. As such, it does not represent a genuine step towards governments recognizing occupancy as a legitimate interest. This becomes evident as soon as governments and various, powerful special interests allied to it discover a use for the land; they then pursue its clearance, frequently without even the suggestion of any recompense. Examples of this include the building of dams or highways or nature reserves. As soon as a specific use is found, all bets are off. The rationale of tacit acquiescence is that most governments, democratic or authoritarian, have no desire to pursue a policy that is both unworkable and unpopular without any offsetting gain. Very few governments are eager to take on the task, for example, of clearing out 85 per cent of all urban dwellers. To pursue this last example to its logical conclusion would require military force on a horrendous scale, which brings to mind the forcible emptying of towns and cities in Cambodia under Khmer Rouge rule. On the other hand, projects such as building roads, which have the advantage of being quite popular with the general public, usually affect only a small percentage of the total number of informals. In a sense, societies under the sway of all-powerful governments are at war with themselves. It is only the lack of means and the unwillingness to consistently pursue mass eviction that gives them a semblance of peace. It is actually – to push the war analogy – more of a long-standing, indefinite, and uneasy truce that is occasionally punctuated by desultory skirmishes.

In the second case, some degree of government recognition may have been accorded to certain customary practices surrounding the use of unappropriated land. In many African and Asian countries, this happens to be the case. As such, informal occupants are not illegal occupants of the land. Yet the logic that these occupants live on their properties on the sufferance of government is ultimately the same. In many of these cases, the occupation, use, and possession of land under these customary practices can create possessory rights for the occupant that are adverse to claims of another individual. Still, they do not create any effective ownership claims adverse to the state, which – in spite of its status as custom land, for example, tribal land – often stays the superior landowner. Occupants of customary land are often as summarily pushed off their land, as in the case of the illegal occupant. Usually, there is little legal recourse and the same risk of rough treatment when resisting seizure when the aforementioned government and its allied interests find a use for the land that does not include its present occupants. This is evident in the case of Bihar, where tribal people are pushed off their land when mineral resources are found below their property; and one can observe comparable results in Mozambique, where some peasants are told that their region has been declared a nature reserve. Otherwise, governments are usually happy to leave the peasants with the illusion that their customary practices mean something. Similarly, politicians normally have no desire to disturb peasants practicing their customs because doing so will make them unpopular without any offsetting gain.

Right, law, and good government

The foregoing sections of this chapter have outlined why this status quo is not acceptable. Essentially, the status quo prevents people in many societies from exploiting the one instantly available capital resource. Also, exclusionary policies destroy the dignity of the people. Rules and regulations that make it virtually impossible for hundreds of millions of people to provide a legally secure home for their spouses and children are extraordinarily humiliating. Making a simple and reasonable request for land akin to running a gauntlet in a hostile bureaucracy or the favour of patronizing politicians is a crushing experience. And yet some people will still find the idea of the right to occupy land too radical. The main concern with those holding this position is that they fail to appreciate how abject the position of people without rights is. In all likelihood, most people do not fathom just how badly governed most societies are. Additionally, they do not appear to grasp that it is already extremely difficult to take on misgovernment (and the more serious it is, the more difficult it becomes).

To start from the premise that people should not have this right is to leave by default the legitimacy of extreme powers – the very source of misgovernment and, thus, miserable conditions – unchallenged. This means that we start the fight for good government, which is, in large part, a struggle for justice, with an unbelievably heavy handicap. Rights are standards or benchmarks against which the actions of the state or government can be measured. In effect, the rejection of a right is the rejection of an ethical standard. The absence of ethical standards, such as rights, affects our perception of government actions profoundly. Without the measure of some ethical standard, not one bad law or flawed procedure can be shown to be a wrong inflicted against the people in the sense of an injustice. The absence of a standard of justice, the right to occupy land, takes the pressure off governments to consider the proper interests of the people and to reform. This means that extralegal possession remains a wrong whenever positive law, government policy, or bureaucracy says it is. Without the identification of rights, legal systems can never see informal people for what they are: citizens pursuing essentially legitimate objectives. Instead, they are viewed only as lawbreakers. That is a very poor position from which to demand justice and good government. Consider the case of the right of free speech. Without a grasp of the right of free speech, how can citizens refute and challenge the authority of governments to censor their opinions? If the right of free speech were unfounded, the act of defying the censor would amount to lawbreaking – no more and no less. That makes prosecution of the offender the right thing to do (i.e., proper government authority and lawful action). In this way, the absence of a standard of justice turns virtue (i.e., upholding the law), into a destroyer. Formulating and advocating rights, on the other hand, is a way to give a voice to the people so they can articulate their interests and resist oppression and suffering. People conscious of their rights might revolt rather than beg and grovel for proper title or land in front of high and mighty bureaucrats or glad-handing politicians.

Of course, even without a right to appeal to, one is still capable of appreciating the humanitarian and practical aspects of the problem in cases of wrongdoing. Most people, including many policymakers, once fully awake to the scale of the problem, would scarcely see any virtue in driving billions of people off their current possessions. Yet this kind and scale of lawbreaking can only be put right through acts of toleration and charity by the state, such as a pardon. The extralegal, in other words, sinks to the level of a lawbreaker in search of mercy and toleration – hardly a dignified or honourable position in life. Yet mercy and toleration is not the same as fully and rationally acknowledging the legitimate interests of the people. This highlights a failure of fundamental thought. Frankly, it is unlikely that many extralegals think of themselves as wrongdoers and charity wards deserving little more than mercy and toleration – and if they do, they should not have to – but more as victims of exclusion, oppression, humiliation, official neglect, and corrupt and dishonest politics. In fact, real citizens do not depend upon the size of a social problem to achieve recognition of their needs and interests; rather, they insist on their rights. Observe also that, in general, people tend to be glad, happy, or relieved to receive pardons. Nevertheless, pardons do not inspire pride. To dismiss the right to occupy land is to spit on the dignity of the people. Finally, pardoning lawbreakers frequently clashes with the sense of justice held by law-abiding citizens who may perceive the pardon as a reward for lawbreaking. This is not good for the moral fibre of society. It is better, then, to take the high road of natural right that clearly addresses the question of right and wrong.

American history[16]

These days, the advocacy of the right to occupy land is completely foreign to modern political discourse. In nineteenth-century United States, however, it was a popular and controversial cause that culminated in a powerful grassroots movement: the Free Soil movement. American legal and political history provides an unparalleled example of this principle at work. The idea that there are lessons to be learned from the American experience relating to the process of integrating extralegal possessions into the formal property system was first proposed and elaborated upon by de Soto.[17] The application of this principle during the nineteenth century is one of the most important sources of America's tremendous economic wealth and power today.

When the British settled the American shores, they brought with them their legal traditions. English law presupposed the context and condition of a long-settled country under the sway of a sovereign king. Common to most Old-World legal traditions, English law presupposed that all unappropriated land belonged to the sovereign. Unauthorized occupation, *squatting,* as it was called, was illegal or at the least created no possessory rights that could be asserted against the sovereign. Yet, in the Americas, the sovereign was far away across the ocean, empty land extremely abundant, and the emergent colonial authorities overextended in their attempts to control these vast, sparsely populated lands. Therefore, movements of settlers were very difficult to control, making it virtually impossible to put a stop to squatting. Thus "with no initial resistance and many opportunities, squatting on available land quickly became a common practice."[18] This relative impunity, however, was not without problems for the settlers. The common-law system of the English did not provide ways for dealing effectively with issues typical of frontier society. It had no effective or positive procedures for dealing with squatting as a customary practice (i.e., for recognizing property rights where sovereign accession was absent or dubious). For example, without the court's approval, squatters had no clear title adverse to ownership claims by other individuals, such as claim jumpers.

Also, even if government control was overall ineffective, individual squatters or squatter communities could be and were the object of official opprobrium and harassment. Irate authorities used armed force to evict squatters from their lands and burn and destroy their dwellings and crops from time to time. Not least, governments saw unappropriated land as a source of revenue. The authorities would raise such revenue by issuing land grants, which had the benefit of creating taxable properties, and conducting land auctions. Such land grants and auctions frequently collided with prior occupation by squatters. The resulting conflicts were often bitter and violent and protracted when squatters refused to surrender their possessions or pay for the land.

This indeterminate legal condition persisted after the American Revolution. Nevertheless, the social and political makeup of this new country was one of vigorous representative institutions and traditions and a rights-conscious population consisting largely of migrants and relations and descendants thereof. It was perhaps inevitable that squatters were met with sympathizers among their representatives in government. In a country where people were deeply conscious of their rights and militant in defending them – and yet where a great part of the existing property could not find sanction in traditional sources of law and authority – an alternative source of legitimacy would be found. The essence of the problem and its resolution was that, under English law, squatters had no property claim on the value of improvements (land cleared, dwellings built, crops planted) made to land occupied illegally, even when only by mistake. In the absence of effective power to prevent squatting, and as a matter of equity, various colonial authorities came to consider such improvements as a valid source of property claims. Various states before independence, and the federal government after, enacted statutes and acts recognizing such claims, allowing the squatters to purchase the property they had improved. This ground-breaking policy, unique to US history, was called *pre-emption*. Through this process, vast quantities of unappropriated land in the United States became private property eventually. The Encyclopaedia Britannica provides a fine synopsis of this legal procedure:[19]

> Also called squatter's rights, in U.S. history, policy by which first settlers, or "squatters" on public lands could purchase the property they had improved. Squatters who settled on and improved unsurveyed land were at risk that when the land was surveyed and put up for auction speculators would capture it. Frontier settlers seldom had much cash, and, because they held no title to their land, they even risked losing their homes and farms to claim jumpers prior to the government auction.

143

Squatters pressured Congress to allow them to acquire permanent title to their land without bidding at auction. Congress responded by passing a series of temporary preemption laws in the 1830s. Bitterly opposed by Eastern business interests who feared that easy access to land would drain their labor supply, the preemption laws also failed to satisfy the settlers seeking a permanent solution to their problems.

In 1841 Henry Clay devised a compromise by providing squatters the right to buy 160 acres of surveyed land at a minimum price of USD 1.25 per acre before the land was sold at auction. Revenues from the preemption sales were to be distributed among the states to finance internal improvements.

The Pre-emption Act of 1841 remained in effect for 50 years, although its revenue-distribution provision was scrapped in 1842. The law led to a great deal of corruption – nonsettlers acquired great tracts of land illegally – but it also led to the passage of the Homestead Act of 1862 by making preemption an accepted part of U.S. land policy.

Although I have no evidence for this, the concept of *improvements* as a source of property rights was probably not a chance innovation entirely. The concept can be traced back to English philosophical tradition with which Americans, as descendants of British settlers, were fully familiar and which had considerable influence on the development of American legal and political traditions and institutions. For illumination, one should refer to the philosophical writings by John Locke:[20]

> Though the earth and all inferior creatures be common to all men, yet every man has a property in his own person. This nobody has any right to but himself. The labour of his body, and the work of his hands, we may say, are properly his. Whatsoever then he removes out of the state that nature hath provided, and left it in, he hath mixed his labour with it, and joined to it something that is his own, and thereby makes it his property.

Essentially, this is the basis for Locke's argument – sometimes called his labour theory of property – that improvements of land make the land the property of the improver:[21]

> As much land as a man tills, plants, *improves* [italics added], cultivates, and can use the product of, so much is his property. He by his labour does, as it were, enclose it from the common. Nor will it invalidate his right to say everybody else has an equal title to it, and therefore he cannot appropriate, he cannot enclose, without the consent of all his fellow-commoners, all mankind. God, when He gave the world in common to all mankind, commanded man also to labour, and the penury of his condition required it of him. God and his reason commanded him to subdue the earth – i.e., *improve* [italics added] it for the benefit of life and therein lay out something upon it that was his own, his labour. He that, in obedience to this command of God, subdued, tilled, and sowed any part of it, thereby annexed to it something that was his property, which another had no title to, nor could without injury take from him.

As a man of his time, Locke spoke of God as the provider of this bounty. One can, if one prefers, use the concept of *nature* as a substitute for the term *God* without prejudice to the significance of Locke's line of argument. It must be clear in any case that he basically and, *avant la lettre,* formulated a right to occupy land: "He [God] gave it [land] to the use of the industrious and rational, and labour was to be his title to it."[22] Not government fiat, then, but God or nature and a person's labour were the real sources of property.

The history behind pre-emption clearly has its analogy in the problems of the informals of the modern developing world. The problem of today's informal is precisely the same as that of the American squatters in that they have made improvements on their land that are on account of a hostile legal environment not recognized as a valid claim to property. In their time, American squatters faced the same problem, and pre-emption was invented by Americans to resolve it. Pre-emption was a popular cause in America during the nineteenth century. What was different between nineteenth century America and present-day developing-world society is the degree to which people are aware of their rights and conversely how little awareness of their rights there is among the populations of the developing world. It is this degree of rights consciousness that enables Americans to resolve seemingly intractable problems; it is the absence of any such consciousness in the developing world that allows the exact same type of problems to fester indefinitely.

The Free Soil movement

American political and legal history is a veritable gold mine in the matter of land rights. There was actually a political movement dedicated to the cause of free land. Also called the Homestead Movement, it "promoted the free ownership of land in the Midwest, Great Plains, and the West, by people willing to settle on and cultivate it. The movement culminated in the Homestead Act of 1862."[23] The movement had its origin in the desire of western farmers for free land in opposition to the dominant view of the federal government that public lands should be distributed through land sales and auctions in order to raise revenues. The catalyst for the rise of this movement to prominence was provided by eastern labour movements and reformers joining the farmers in their call for free land. The eastern labour movement and reformers viewed the issue of free land as a means of keeping wages high by providing excess labour an escape from unemployment and low-paying jobs with free farmland as the safety valve. Labour reformers sought to expand the options available to the working-class people of the east: those who looked at the conditions in the eastern cities and found them not to their liking would then be able to leave for greener pastures in the west. For the same reason, it was bitterly opposed by eastern employers and landowners. The former because they "did not want workers to have the option of leaving low-paying jobs for a farm in the West." The latter because they "feared the threat to land values posed by a huge public domain given away to anyone willing to settle on it."[24] Curiously, then, the Free Soil movement should to some extent be seen as more of a worker movement (i.e., it derived its power from the desire of the early American labour movements to strengthen the economic position of the workers).

Prior to 1830, there was no concerted drive for homestead legislation. However, from the start of the third decennium of the nineteenth century until 1862, the year of the adoption of the Homestead Act, the United States witnessed the spectacular growth of one of its most remarkable and influential movements. Originating in New York and starting with the foundation in 1829 by labour reformer and newspaper editor, George Henry Evans (1805–1856), of a newspaper, *The Working Man's Advocate,* the movement spread across the United States. By 1850, it embraced the support of at least six hundred of the over two thousand papers that were published in the United States.[25] "Believing that land policies could be changed through political action, Evans organized the National Reform Association [established in 1844]. Through its numerous state branches, the organization pressed for free homesteads in the West. The group's motto was 'Vote yourself a farm.'"[26]

This movement at one point even generated and gave its name to a political party, the Free Soil Party (1848–1854), which was later one of the founder factions of the Republican Party. The party's historic slogan called for "free soil, free speech, free labor, free men."[27] Never more than a minor party during its short existence, it nonetheless managed to garner at least 10 per cent of the vote during its first national run for election, demonstrating wide identification of its cause. Its influence was demonstrated by facts such as how its share of the votes caused the Democratic Party to lose the election and that, during its existence, it had a dozen congressmen who held the balance of power in the House of Representatives.[28] It must be noted that the Free Soil movement was also closely allied to the anti-slavery movement. As a consequence, the movement also had to contend with its opposition by southern slaveholders, who, for that reason, also blocked homestead legislation. Therefore, it was only when the southern participation in the federal government ceased in 1861 – the year that the southern states seceded, causing the American Civil War – that homestead legislation finally passed. The Homestead Act of 1862 enabled people to gain gratis ownership rights to 160 acres of public land.[29] By the end of the nineteenth century, over 80 million acres had been distributed to approximately six hundred thousand farmers. Interestingly, the same president, Abraham Lincoln, who signed the act into law also abolished slavery.

Essentially, any reading of the homestead movement – and the Internet is probably one of the best sources of information on the topic – reveals a picture of people battling to diminish the discretionary control of the federal government over the public domain. Discretionary control by the government was seen as an instrument of exclusion, exploitation, and oppression of the workers and the trough that fed an alliance of corrupt politicians, land speculators, and big business interests. The Free Soilers' cause entailed a call for justice, equality, and economic independence for workers. It is my fondest wish that the history of pre-emption and the homestead movement would one day become widely known in the developing world and inspire men and women there. It should serve as the model for how a working-class movement can overturn the slavish awe with which virtually all people in the world (especially in poor countries) regard the power of the state.

Politicians, reformers, and NGOs should take heed: The Americans distributed 80 million acres of land. Yet in the developing world and formerly communist countries, there are already more than 300 million informal urban dwellings and 1.8 billion hectares of informal rural lands awaiting formalization and billions of (potential) votes are involved.[30] If the vote is what you care about, then pre-emption could be the most salient issue.

The non-Western experience

The American experience is immensely valuable in terms of what we can learn from it. Nevertheless, it is also imperative that we grasp how different the non-Western experience is from the American experience. The non-Western experience poses an extraordinary challenge. Crucially, non-Western societies have no meaningful historical experience or memory of private property systems and property rights as beneficial to society as a whole. In this case, the concept of society includes the great mass of common people, not just the privileged classes. Many non-Western societies do not have indigenous traditions of widespread private property ownership by common people – in contrast to a privileged class – preceding the colonial era. In precolonial times, common property systems were frequently the default pattern. There was also a subset of non-Western societies where the common people largely subsisted as serfs and slaves on large estates owned or held by a small, privileged class. Property systems based on a modern conception of private property rights were usually first introduced as adjuncts to the system of colonial exploitation. This first encounter with modern private property systems was frequently a dreadful experience to large portions of the native populations. The experience with modern private property systems was especially marred by the manner in which the grant of private property rights was applied during the colonial era. Colonial authorities usually granted the right to occupy land selectively to white settlers – often at the expense of the natives. The natives were frequently driven off their land or denied access to choice land. To heap insult on injury, these natives were frequently forced to work for the settlers on the very same land they had been deprived of. The right to occupy land, which enriched a class of racist, white settlers, went hand in hand with the oppression of and impoverishment of the natives. Altogether, the right to occupy land, private land ownership, and capitalism have very negative connotations in many non-Western societies.

The issue facing the non-Western societies struggling to free themselves from colonialism and indigenous despots was how to deal with a legacy of inequality, oppression, exploitation, and exclusion. One should realize that different ideologies respond very differently to such problems. In dealing with these problems, the prevailing tendency in Western societies has been to solve such problems by seeking to extend freedom by granting equal rights, mostly in the sense that the rights, freedoms, and immunities enjoyed by the privileged groups become available on equal terms to members of groups formerly subjected to inequality, exclusion, oppression, and exploitation. The right to vote was originally limited only to the privileged classes, the aristocracy, and the rich. Later, gradually, it extended to all classes. The rights included in the Magna Carta – for example, the right to due process – were originally intended for freemen[31] only. It took some time before those rights were extended to all citizens.[32]

Yet the reverse is also possible. The unfairness of a system can be seen as proof that the system as a whole is illegitimate and beyond redemption. Crucially, during the twentieth century, the single most important contributor to this state of mind was Marxist ideology and its superficial identification of the privileged minority as the *capitalist class,* the majority as the *proletariat,* and the existing legal and administrative system as the *juridical and political superstructure* that legalized so-called class domination. That the privileged minority frequently enjoys the benefits of formal property rights (and the majority is routinely deprived of access to this right) seems to vindicate the Marxist position that property rights serve as an instrument of class domination. Altogether, this Marxist analysis must have seemed like such a clear-cut and satisfying explanation that it appears to have extinguished among its practitioners and advocates any desire to further examine the juridical and political superstructures. Marxism and its many offshoots was the dominant system of thought for most of the twentieth century; consequently, the desire to use the improvement of property systems as a means to improve the position of the poor was forestalled.

Evil systems that cannot be redeemed should be abolished. Therefore, the solution from a Marxist perspective is not to reform the system – to secure access for the poor to property systems and to secure their property rights – but to abolish property rights for all and to destroy property systems as part of the overthrow of the capitalist system. Note that the fact that the poor can accumulate vast amounts of property does not fit at all in a theoretical model where people are, quite neatly, divided into two identifiable classes: the propertied classes and a dispossessed proletariat. Also, the fact that the poor can benefit in meaningful ways from accumulating property cannot be reconciled with an anti-property stance.

The leftist orientation had a deep impact on how the question of property rights was approached in non-Western societies. It is the ill fortune of the non-Western world that, from the end of the nineteenth century onward in both the colonial states and the non-Western imperial states, newly emerging modern elites adopted socialism as their dominant ideology. For nearly a century, the vast majority of the modern elites and the intelligentsia of the non-Western societies were leftist in their ideological orientation. Leftist ideologies are usually deeply hostile towards property rights. For nearly a century, policymakers in the developing world saw private property rights as an evil that should be abolished or pushed back. In their contempt for property rights, these elites halted the development of or, in a number of instances, even abolished the institutional framework necessary for supporting private property systems. Instead, policymakers dreamed of and pursued to some degree the collectivization of the economies of their countries. Essentially, a century of leftist politics and policymaking stopped many states from building up a body of deep institutional knowledge of how to manage or develop private property systems.

The very absence in most developing nations of properly functioning private property systems constitutes a problem. This absence induces a state of ignorance both at the level of the ruling class and at the level of the ruled. Both the rulers and the ruled lack the experience of its benefits. Often, if people do not know about something, they do not consciously miss it. This ignorance of the benefits becomes self-perpetuating in that it robs people of a positive, practical experience with private property systems. Altogether, the leftist orientation, the colonial experience, and the ignorance of its benefits has left the developing world's political elites, intelligentsia, and populations suspicious of and indifferent to the task of developing private property systems.

However understandable these sentiments may be, the fact of the matter is that, in the post-colonial era, much of the world went through a multitude of developments: independence, revolution, modernization, population growth, increases in education, expansions of modern infrastructure, industrialization, urbanization, and migration from the countryside to the cities. These developments fundamentally reshaped the nature and structure of their societies and involved and resulted in an enormous expansion of economic activity that was fundamentally dependent upon a huge expansion of land use. The occupation of vast expanses of land was vital to this expansion. In effect, for the people in the developing world, the occupation of land changed from being an instrument of oppression, deprivation, and exploitation to becoming a fundamental necessity and source of wealth.

The task is to break free of this prejudice, ignorance, and indifference. We need to appreciate a number of facts. For one, we need to lift up our gaze, look at our surroundings, and take notice of the fact that the so-called poor have created through their own effort an enormous amount of wealth. Policy specialists, politicians, the intelligentsia, and people across the entire spectrum of ideologies practically unanimously saw the poor as fundamentally incapable of creating significant wealth through productive effort. We need to grasp that this is an unfounded belief. The modern poor have material ambitions and needs that are essentially bourgeois; what they need are systems of representation of ownership and credit that are essentially capitalistic. We need to abandon flawed ideological positions and notions; we need to overcome the flaws or omissions in systems of governance that prevent people from legitimizing their property claims.

Summary

Land is an elemental necessity for the survival of people. Basic necessity validates a natural right to occupy land and claim its ownership. One cannot produce or build without exploiting land. To build a home, one must first sink foundations in the ground. To raise a crop, one must till the soil. Minerals are mostly extracted from the earth. For the sake of one's well-being one should not be denied land. People's need for land must not be subordinate to the arbitrary dictates of the state. The proper mission of the state is to protect and serve its citizens. The state must respect and protect one's right to life – and that includes one's right to occupy land and to claim and establish property rights. In the matter of unappropriated land, the state is no more than a temporary custodian with a duty to distribute domain land and surrender title when people present their need for it. Any powers of government that go beyond these duties are surplus to requirements and have proven injurious to the well-being of the people. Indeed, the exercise by governments across the globe of their excessive powers to impose onerous rules with respect to the titling of land property is one of the most important sources of oppression, injustice, disempowerment, underdevelopment, poverty, and deprivation. In every respect, people deprived of proper title to their possessions suffer debilitating disadvantages in comparison to those enjoying clear title. The capital in their land is dead. A person selling real estate without proper title gets no more than a fraction of the price that the owner of property enjoying clear title would. He or she cannot insure his or her possession. He or she cannot use it as collateral for borrowing. These are serious obstacles to improving one's life, accumulating wealth, or doing business. Not least, without clear title, one's legal position is inferior to that of those with proper title. In many cases, occupation of land without proper title is viewed as squatting (i.e., lawbreaking). Without proper title, the occupant can suffer eviction from his or her possessions without any form of consideration of his or her personal circumstances or interests or compensation of his or her investments. Without proper title, one often has no recourse to legal protection in land disputes. It is difficult to believe that people suffer such disadvantages without any sense of being wronged. Yet the failure of the people to grasp their natural right and assert its precedence over the will of the state certainly makes it dreadfully easy for policymakers to neglect their duty to serve the people. If people do not fully understand the causes of their problems and cannot express their grievances in clear terms, one can hardly hope to see any improvement in their condition. The example of nineteenth-century America and the Free Soil movement demonstrates how rights consciousness and activism overcame opposition from various vested interests, conservative sentiment and unsympathetic government. These days, the advocacy of the right to occupy land is completely foreign to modern political discourse. Yet, if ever there is one issue as amenable to democratic, progressive, activist, and popular politics, it is certainly land rights. Land rights reform is the one issue that can tangibly and directly benefit the majority. We should wish that reformers and advocates would see the light and adopt the cause of land rights reform for the betterment of society.

Chapter 6

Free Land and Its Enemies

Good intentions will always be pleaded for every assumption of authority. It is hardly too strong to say that the Constitution was made to guard the people against the dangers of good intentions. There are men in all ages who mean to govern well, but they mean to govern. They promise to be good masters, but they mean to be masters.

—Daniel Webster

There is an enormous amount of ideological, political, and emotional capital invested in the predatory powers of government over access to land, land use, and land ownership. The notion that the occupation and exploitation of land by private citizens could serve as a sufficient and rightful claim to lawful possession and ownership is bound to be anathema (or at least deeply troubling) to many people. There are causes and interests with agendas for the use of land as a resource that cannot be reconciled with the right to occupy land. Two major examples of such causes referenced in this chapter are preservationism and anti-capitalism. The aim of preservationism is to protect the wilderness. The various anti-capitalist systems of thought seek to promote, for redistributionist purposes, public ownership of land and natural resources. However looked at, these are agendas that cannot coexist with the rights of individuals to appropriate land and effectively claim property rights. These agendas hinge on the power to deny access to land and property rights. The essence of rights is that the individual cannot be stopped from pursuing his or her objectives – in this instance, to take possession of land and establish property rights thereon. Rights would render these agendas unachievable. The common denominator for all such programmes is that their feasibility is wholly dependent on government power, policymaking, and intervention. Private initiative, voluntary action, and moral suasion are ineffective means of implementing preservationist and redistributionist agendas. Moreover, only the state can effectively deprive people of their rights and freedoms (and thereby achieve the subordination of the private interest to their agendas). Therefore, these programmes require the repudiation of rights and freedom. The groups and movements espousing these causes seek to increase government power at the expense of this freedom. Indeed, groups and movements espousing these causes are engaged in a virtually ceaseless propaganda campaign against the right of access by individuals and private enterprise to land and natural resources. Preservationism and the ideal of public ownership over unappropriated land and natural resources with a state that possesses full property rights are causes that have sunk incredibly deep roots into most societies. In the political discourse, these systems of thought go virtually unopposed. The discourse is currently a one-way street that leads to ever more government power. That this harms the legitimate goals of billions of people is almost completely ignored. Therefore, it is useful to pause and reflect on these causes and interests in light of the right to occupy land and the concept of predatory jurisdiction.

Preservationism versus rights

One of the biggest obstacles to the idea of an inalienable right to occupy land is preservationist ideology. The issue here is the significance of the right to occupy land from the view of the values and goals of preservationists. A major aim of the preservationist movement is to pursue the preservation of any remaining wilderness on unappropriated land. Preservationists take the view that nature has value in and of itself and should therefore be preserved for its own sake. The preservationist is usually already unhappy with the amount of wilderness that has already disappeared because of human settlement and economic activity. Any further development of public lands represents an unwarranted encroachment upon nature that must be resisted. Having no means of their own to enforce their views, preservationists usually see government power as the means to achieve their objectives. Full control for the state over public land affords governments the jurisdiction to keep undeveloped land from being developed. To conserve the wilderness in the United States, preservationists have, for over a century, systematically striven to expand and capture the power of the state to prevent further use or development of the public domain. The abolition of the Homestead Act in 1976 was largely driven by the growing influence of the preservationist view on government policy regarding the management of the public domain. Today's preservationists have the same in mind for the tropical wildernesses in developing nations. The objective of preservationist groups is to make governments put a complete and permanent end to the clearance and exploitation of tropical forests in places like Borneo.

The issue is not that preservationists would consciously and deliberately seek to deny the poor adequate housing or proper title to their possessions. In this respect, they will probably be little concerned with the retroactive regularization of existing informal possessions; this aspect of the right to occupy land is of little interest to them. Instead, their concern is its enduring operability, especially one directed at any part of the remaining wilderness. In this respect the right to occupy land entails a tremendous and permanent rollback of state power that makes it much harder for governments to prevent the lawful appropriation of government land by private citizens, thereby preserving the wilderness. This is exactly what preservationists oppose. Preservationists will fear that various forms of government control over land now considered normal and even legitimate will be curtailed or endangered. Many people will have apocalyptic visions of a free-for-all situation in which the masses overrun every last bit of pristine nature and rapacious loggers clear-cut the last virgin timber stand on the distant edge of a logged-out wasteland. One must place the significance of such fears and objections in context.

To start with, these visions of doom are based on the hidden or subconscious presumption that increasing the powers of government will result in the protection of the wilderness against destruction. This is a myth. In terms of formal powers, governments already have all the powers necessary to regulate land use. These formal powers are not actually translating into effective protection of the wilderness. In fact, the situation has long been *out of control* ... if we must use such terms. Vast numbers of people are already invading and settling unappropriated lands – that means cutting down forests, breaking the sod in savannas and grasslands, and settling on state land on the fringes of towns and cities – as they see fit and without permission from governments. Every year, satellites beam down pictures of burning tropical forests representing thousands upon thousands of square miles of land being cleared for farming and ranching – often actions for which the settlers cannot show permits or titles and governments cannot produce surveying records. The fact is that the wide powers of government are not protecting the environment at all *and* they are preventing people from regularizing their situation. This is a situation with no winners.

The preservationism is also at loggerheads with the reality of demography. To the extent that populations and economies continue to grow, humanity's need for land will prove unstoppable. This is a fact that must be recognized: subject to the exigencies of population growth and economic development, unused land will continue to be taken into development. To that extent, there is no way to stop the expansion of land use. In the long run, land will remain unused only to the extent that expanding populations and economies find no need or use for it. Our only choice is whether this will happen with the blessing of governments or not. Three or four billion informals have already and irreversibly occupied, taken into cultivation, and built over millions of square kilometres of land across the globe. The hope that people will leave alone presently unused land is nothing more than delusion. In fact, prepare yourselves for the fact that, within this century, another few million square kilometres will likely be taken into use. The juggernaut of population growth and economic development will roll over all opposition. The idea that governments should attempt – without considering demographic and economic trends and the needs of the citizenry – to prevent the use of undeveloped land is absurd. How are governments going to avoid the appropriation of unused land when at least two billion people will be joining us in the next thirty years?

Furthermore, the governments of the world may not have the means to provide housing for the billions of people now living and working on informal real estate, much less for the billions that will join us over the course of one lifetime. Even if government would get serious about preventing squatting and take upon itself the task of building homes for a growing population, how is it going to avoid using undeveloped land?

But the impact of population growth and economic development in terms of expanding land use must not be overstated. Across the developing world a vast population shift is taking place from the countryside to towns and cities. The greater part of the population growth will therefore end up in urbanized areas. Also, population growth is slowing throughout the developing world. Furthermore, technology is continuously increasing yields per acre and reducing the need for labour in agriculture. This means that the rate at which human habitat growth increases should lag substantially behind the rates of population and economic growth and tend to concentrate within and near already densely populated areas and around cities. Governments can substantially accelerate these developments. Improved government policy – promoting literacy and education, family planning and birth control, urban development, and spreading information and technology to the countryside – could result in a greater deceleration of population growth.

The irony of the preservationist movement is that, though it is intensely and romantically involved with nature, it is at once entirely blind to and deeply negative about one aspect of nature: humanity. To that extent, it is ill equipped to cope with reality. This all must sound horrifying and infuriating to preservationists. Nevertheless, let them consider the facts as they stand. To persist in promoting a philosophy to the point of ignoring the human condition is to be both indifferent to human necessity and in denial about human nature. If there is a shred of humanity and decency in the heart of the preservationist, let him or her realize that human nature and necessity makes right.

The problem with preservationism is that it is a single-issue movement. As such, it suffers from problems typical of single-issue movements. Such movements frequently pursue goals through direct action strategies. Yet, occasionally, these goals might be achieved with greater effectiveness in indirect ways. Essentially, if there is any central problem to be identified from the perspective of the preservationist cause, it is population growth. Population growth multiplies all the ills that trouble preservationists, (e.g., industrialization and the increased need for raw materials, farmland, and urbanization) – all of which encroach upon the wilderness. Perhaps, in terms of wilderness preserved, the outcome would have been vastly superior if, in the past four or five decades, the preservationists had invested more in supporting family planning or female education and done more to make life more difficult for morally conservative governments, especially the government of the United States and many African nations. Problems are not solved by ignoring the wider context of an issue and the problems that confront people in their pursuit of self-preservation.

The right to occupy land also poses a philosophical challenge to preservationism: How legitimate is a government that puts the preservation of forests and wetlands above the rights and needs of the people? The idea that government must value nature in and of itself is a huge step in the direction of raising a doctrine that government's highest mission is not to serve the people but to place nature above its citizens. Preservationism as a philosophy is anti-republican; it subverts the ideal that the state is instituted to serve the people. In this respect, preservationism resembles theocracy in which the interests of the people are made subordinate to higher gods and divine morality. Let us remember that, historically, religious authorities have been indifferent to the suffering of people. Christian churches refusing to sanction the use of condoms on moral grounds (in other words, ignoring human nature) has greatly contributed to the horror of the AIDS epidemic in Africa. Many theologians in the Islamic world point to sacred texts to deny equal rights and freedom to women and go as far as sanctioning the abject submission of women to men. Why is it wrong for bishops and imams to ignore the interests of the people but right for preservationists to do the same? Is not a distraction from and devaluation of the interests of the people caused by preservationist ideals just as wrong?

Maybe some critics will argue that this concern about preservationist ideology is overdone in the context of the developing world (i.e., in the developing world, it would not be the main argument against the right to occupy land). It is frequently observed that poor countries tend to give priority to economic development above preservation. Be that as it may, the problem with this line of argument is that governments in the developing world – despite the priority issue – have preservationist policies and objectives. It is not for nothing that several of the largest and most famous national parks – who has not heard of the Serengeti National Park? – are established in Africa, our planet's poorest continent. Also nowadays, political elites in many developing countries tend to be increasingly well-educated folks with westernized views who are keenly aware of and share the ideas and concerns of their Western peers – frequently with little regard for the domestic ramifications of such views. Additionally, political elites in the developing world who have a great appetite for government power will note and adopt any argument to its advantage. Government jurisdiction is generally based upon a heritage of powers supported by or defended on the basis of various legal doctrines and political ideologies. For those policymakers in the developing world keen on preserving the power of the state, it does not matter that preservation does not get the same priority as economic development. What matters to them is that the preservationist argument supports and secures the legitimacy of their power and authority, including that over public land. Finally, environmentalism, of which preservationism is only one branch, has become such an overarching theme in modern political discourse that criticism from that quarter cannot be ignored. Observe how themes such as globalization, international trade, and corporate governance have become intertwined with the environmentalist debate. All these considerations make a proper answer a must.

Still, what of the charge that the advocacy of the right to occupy land would rob government of its power to protect the wilderness, that its outcome would be the diminution of the power of governments to establish national parks, forest reserves, or wildlife reserves (and, on occasion, render existing preservationist laws null and void)? Is it not a terrible thing to deprive government of these powers? Is this what we are advocating? First of all, it seems likely that these critics will raise these questions, but not as an overture to reconciling the causes of preservation and the empowerment of people; rather, they will raise the questions to sow distress within the public. Therefore, there is a compelling reason for answering such questions. Frankly, the idea that governments would *not* have these powers is rather upsetting. There is great beauty in nature. The desire to see much of it preserved is a precious sentiment. There is no virtue or glory in the idea of a massive ecosystem, such as the Amazon rain forest, being clear-cut to extinction. The preservation of the wilderness also serves the cause of preserving many species of plants and animals from extinction. That animals and plants should go extinct because we did nothing to protect the wilderness is frankly horrific. There are even perfectly utilitarian justifications for protecting the wilderness. The wilderness is an immense reservoir of plants and animals with great economic, scientific, and medical value. Would it not be gross negligence to allow the extinction of an unknown species of plant that could cure a currently untreatable disease? Government can be a powerful instrument in the cause of preservation. Yet the first duty of government should be to serve the people, not to revere the wilderness above the interests of the citizenry. However fond we may be of our ideals, we must guard against these when these make us enemies – usually not deliberately, but mostly unintentionally – of the more vulnerable members of our species. The right to occupy land should still be superior to the power of government to put public land beyond the reach of the citizen.

Yet the assertion of such a principle is not quite the same as saying that the people would need every bit of public land to be at their immediate disposal. One can imagine government having the power to establish specific reserves subject to some form of constitutional or judicial review for determining the impact of the establishment of such a reserve on the interests of the general public (i.e., whether it materially diminishes the welfare of the people). If it does not materially affect the prospects for prosperity of the public or cause grievous and irremediable harm to individuals, there is no reason why a nature reserve cannot be established. In quite a few cases, its establishment may be a boon to the economy. Parks from the Serengeti to Yellowstone yield considerable tourist revenues. In any case, even if government should have the power to establish nature reserves, it must never have the power to bar all public land from the exercise of the right to occupy land. Preservation should be a very specific and circumscribed power applying only to specifically identifiable locations with definite boundaries that never comprise the entire public domain. As to how to achieve this goal in a balanced way is for legal thinkers to discover.

It should be possible to concede the validity of a principle while desiring leeway for competing interests that may be worth pursuing equally. This appears to be the case with the right to occupy land and the cause of preservation. Yet there is a risk in making the right to occupy land anything less than literal in its application. A literal application precludes predatory discretion on the part of the public authorities – a benefit to the public in countries where authorities abuse their powers without compunction. As soon as the application of a right is less than literal, one introduces discretion. It is precisely discretionary power that is the problem in the developing world where corrupt and dishonest politicians and bureaucrats exploit every bit of discretionary power. Also, note that this discretionary power has not served the cause of preservationism at all thus far. In Indonesia and Malaysia, corruption based on bureaucratic powers is directly responsible for the wholesale destruction of rainforests in Sumatra and Borneo. Frankly, one could make a case that preservationists and future advocates of the right to occupy land have a common interest: an end to misgovernment.

Paradoxically, only countries with a proven record of respect for the rights of individuals and laws of the land can establish legal systems where rights are both real and yet not always literal in their application. Note that, in the developed countries, property rights are well protected, yet the right is not absolute. Preservationists must understand that, unless developing countries adopt genuine rule of law, start practicing honesty in government, and come to terms with the needs of the informal masses, there is no point in discussing balanced legal systems. The first priority is going to have to be the precise and uncompromising articulation of the principle of the citizen's natural and inalienable right to life, liberty, and the pursuit of happiness – and that includes a right to land. You cannot honestly and in good faith expect people who, at every attempt to live a normal life, are deprived of their rights, ignored, despised, neglected, abused, impoverished, and forced to live in squalor (and persecuted for that) to care about the beauty of nature or the potentially beneficial uses of unknown species that may prove valuable in the future.

Anti-Capitalism

Preservationism is not the only source of ideological opposition to the right to occupy land. The various strands of anti-capitalism will probably prove to be a fertile source of arguments against the right to occupy land. The main accusation that anti-capitalists could level against the right to occupy land is that it would enable capitalists to grab public resources or public wealth for private profit. This critique is, among other things, based on the assertion that public land represents a common or collective property of the citizenry. Its transfer into the hands of capitalists deprives the people of its collective patrimony and its exploitation for private gain robs the people of the fruits of this collective property. This development eventually subjects the people to capitalist exploitation and contributes to their impoverishment.

Indeed, the level and scale on which business enterprises could make use of the right to occupy land are in a totally different category as compared to that of the average person. It would include the use of huge tracts of land for the exploitation of large-scale agricultural enterprises, mining operations, the building of factories, railroads, harbours, and airports, for example. For the pursuit of these activities, the capitalist could claim, free of charge, unappropriated land as a matter of right. The very idea is going to be scandalous or monstrous in the eyes of many people. Yet the application by the capitalists of their right to occupy land would be of tremendous value to society. The charge to the contrary by the anti-capitalist is pure slander. It may well be very difficult to persuade people that even rich capitalists or large capitalist corporations should have free access to land, but it is both a logical and valid application of the right to occupy land, and it is one that deserves open acknowledgement, encouragement, and proper defence. That requires, among other things, puncturing some of the false claims used in anti-capitalist rhetoric.

Let us start with the claim that unappropriated land represents a common or collective property of the citizenry. By what logic do the people or citizenry or public collectively own unappropriated land (i.e., land that is unused, unclaimed by anybody, and empty of people)? If we apply John Locke's theory of property rights – "as much land as a man tills, plants, improves, cultivates, and can use the product of, so much is his property" – we must soon conclude that the people do not deserve the crown of ownership.[1] Locke's theory has also been called for obvious reasons a *labour theory of property rights*. It is the labour of people and the improvements to the land or its produce that are the source of property ownership rights.

To pursue such a labour theory of property rights to its logical conclusion: the only entity or unit capable of labour is the individual. The fact that labour can only be performed at the individual level is basic and final. The argument that organizations, including governments, can also perform labour is false: organizations and governments contract individuals to perform their labour, and what benefit accrues to these organizations was first created by the labour of these individuals. To every effort, even when described as constituting a joint or collective effort, the fundamental and indispensable unit is the individual and his or her labour. Without that unit, nothing happens; the individual human being is the prime mover.

By the same logic, the *people* as an entity or unit are no more than an abstract concept; it is not a unit of labour. As an entity, it is, by its very quality of being only an abstraction, incapable of any productive effort. Concepts such as the people, the citizenry, and the public were originally coined to describe a collection of individuals who share the attribute of being members of a specific, usually national, community. These concepts are linguistic constructs that allow us to generalize and efficiently refer to the role of this collection of individuals as members of society in political processes. To inflate the meaning of such concepts beyond such usage is to pollute public discourse, or worse, to manipulate it. As a body, entity, or unit, the people have no basis for claiming and justifying any right of ownership to unappropriated land and, to that extent, the very concept of collective ownership should be deemed invalid.[2]

In the real world, the concept of collective ownership of unappropriated land is meaningless. To understand why, one must ask the following question: What does this collective ownership right of unappropriated land protect? In the case of private property rights, it is clear what is being protected: the control of the owner over his or her means of self-preservation (i.e., the freedom to produce and enjoy the fruits of his or her labour). But collective ownership rights by the public of unappropriated land – looked at in terms of the beneficial interests of the members of the public (in other words, the individual) – protects nothing; the state of land being unappropriated, unused, and undeveloped means that no one derives any value from it *precisely on account of its being unappropriated, unused, and undeveloped.* In other words, following Locke's labour theory of property rights: precisely the quality of being unappropriated land renders any claim of collective ownership – as an expression of the beneficial interests of the members of the public – meaningless. It is not as if the public, after the appropriation of something it did not use or derive benefit from at all in the first place, is suddenly, tangibly, measurably, and inevitably poorer off than before; people will not inevitably and, as a matter of cause and effect on account of its appropriation, suffer a loss of income, lose their homes, their livelihoods, or their workshops.[3] Without a clear, demonstrable loss of some sort of value, one cannot claim injury. Actually, the occupation of unappropriated land by productive, enterprising members of society, especially when done for profit, should be a boon to the public in that it increases the country's stock of capital assets, its productive capacity, and, by extension, its earning power, and the housing stock, thereby increasing the commerce and wealth of the nation. This is what we are being "protected" against by the ideal of collective ownership rights.

The fruits of the land versus the fruits of labour

But the collectivist will counter that the point of collective ownership is to ensure that the people will enjoy their so-called rightful share of the fruits of the land. The benefit to the public of the collective ownership lies not in mere ownership of unused land or undeveloped resources, but in the fact that the riches of the land will accrue to the public. Yet this is a swindle: what is or once was unappropriated land and undeveloped resources can only gain or yield value when improved or extracted by the labour of people – and not a moment sooner. The so-called fruits of the land are really the fruits of labour. The claim to the fruits of the land is really no more and no less than a looter's hunger for the fruits of the productive efforts of his or her fellow citizens. To better understand the dishonesty, consider the following quote by Locke:[4]

> Nor is it so strange, as perhaps before consideration it may appear, that the property of labour should be able to overbalance the community of land. For 'tis labour indeed that puts the difference of value on every thing [sic]; and let any one [sic] consider, what the difference is between an acre of land planted with tobacco, or sugar, sown with wheat or barley; and an acre of the same land lying in common, without any husbandry upon it, and he will find, that the improvement of labour makes the far greater part of the value. I think it will be but a modest computation to say, that of the products of the earth useful to the life of man nine tenths are the effects of labour: nay, if we will rightly estimate things as they come to our use, and cast up the several expenses about them, what in them is purely owing to nature, and what to labour, we shall find, that in most of them ninety-nine hundredths are wholly to be put on the account of labour.

Also, consider this comment by Locke: "For this labour being the unquestionable property of the labourer, *no man but he can have a right to what that is once joined to* [italics added]."[5] This is what collectivists want us to overlook by calling the fruits of labour, the fruits of the land. Thus, we have also answered the charge that, by giving free access to unappropriated land or undeveloped resources to the capitalist, one robs the people of their "rightful" share of the fruits of the land; in fact, it is the capitalist that is being defrauded and, to our shame, in the name of the people.

But that is not all: abstract entities – here, the public – being what they are, cannot directly or, as it were, personally assume control of this collective property. Thus, practical, day-to-day control must inevitably default to some small gang of alpha males,[6] usually collectively described as a government, supposedly, and we must pray that that is also the case, representing the "people." Also, any payback – financial or political – accruing from collective property will, as a rule, go first to the state and not the people. Therefore, to whom the benefits of this payback accrue and how these are applied is in the final analysis decided not by the people but by our political bosses who, as experience tells us, are not often very considerate of the interests of the public. In the end, to the public the ideal of collective ownership is really pie in the sky. On the other hand, our rulers, these honourable trustees and servants of the people, now possess (on account of this ideal) an instrument – legal control of access to resources – for extorting from any and all (but especially the hated entrepreneur) both servility and the fruits of productive effort.[7] Land and resources that should have been freely accessible become instruments of patronage and cronyism. The outcome of any type of collectivization – and that is what the collective ownership of unappropriated land amounts to – is to diminish the citizen (more specifically, the entrepreneur) and deprive him or her of free access to resources and the freedom to act in accordance with his or her own interests.

Moreover, such claims also represent a perversion of justice: by creating and popularizing the concept of popular ownership of unappropriated resources, anti-capitalists can now portray any such appropriation by private parties as an injury of the public interest. It is precisely this attitude of distrust and hostility that deprives private enterprise of optimal access to the riches of the land; suspicious and resentful to capitalist enterprise, governments grant access under such onerous conditions as to discourage private enterprise. Often, enormous amounts of resources are left undeveloped because giving access to these resources under more realistic terms would be political suicide. And so many poor nations sabotage their own economic development and rise to general prosperity. The paradox of the idea of undeveloped resources as collective property of the citizenry is that its final result is not increased wealth for the people but the prolongation of widespread poverty. The ideal of common ownership of public resources by the citizenry is nefarious in that it misleads the people on the question of what their real interests are. It substitutes the tangible value to real individuals of the right to occupy land for pipe dreams; it makes it more difficult for the public to recognize the far more real value of the right to occupy land and the difference that it could make in their lives in ways that the falsehood of common ownership never will.

The charge that the right to occupy land will open public lands to capitalist exploitation can also be answered on a more general note. The point of advocating the right to occupy land is the advancement of the rights of the individual. The very essence of this right is anti-statist: it seeks to limit the scope of government power and authority. Anti-capitalists are generally advocates of ever-greater power to the state. The right to occupy land so clearly limits the power of the state that it cannot be anything else but anathema to them. Yet it is precisely the rich, the powerful, and the corrupt that have captured, monopolized, and wielded the power of the state to their advantage on many occasions. In the current system, where no right to occupy land is acknowledged and state power is unlimited, powerful families, crony capitalists, and corrupt policymakers have time and again conspired with public enterprises and governments to transfer public lands into their hands with impunity, and those very unlimited powers were instrumental in this process. The exploits of logging companies in Indonesia would not have been possible without the collusion of government officials and political godfathers. Even today, in Brazil's interior, large land properties are regularly being carved out by hook and crook. The truly powerful do not need rights to advance their designs; they commonly do so without the slightest reference to rights. On the other hand, with the introduction of the right to occupy land, the state, by definition, would no longer be an instrument of privileged, exclusionary access to resources. Politicians and bureaucrats who have wielded state power over the public domain as instruments of patronage and cronyism would now find these powers drastically reduced. Currently, the poor are totally out of the picture vis-à-vis the rich and powerful. The profusion of procedures that the rich and powerful negotiate or cut through by means fair and foul hopelessly entangle the humble classes. The right to occupy land is not meant to stop the rich or powerful; rather, it is intended to level the playing field by giving the humble classes equal and real access and rights to land.

The issue is not whether some rich and mighty capitalist would gain the opportunity to amass a large amount of real estate property, but whether the working-class citizen desiring proper title to his or her possessions or applying for unappropriated land will get fair treatment. The whole point of a right is to secure equal and just treatment for all. When all's said and done, it is not only the rich who desire property, but also the humble classes – and for good reason. Essentially, the desire of informals for proper title to the land occupied by them is very much a bourgeois aspiration. In the heyday of socialism, collective ownership of land of one flavour or another was peddled as the way to uplift the poor and working-class citizens and to protect them against capitalist exploitation. Actually, collective ownership of land has proven to be as much an instrument of disempowerment as serfdom and no less a poverty trap. The Chinese peasant coming into focus in the fields of Mao's collective farm on the eve of Deng's reforms was a pitiful, cowed, terror-struck, starving scarecrow. In a new world that is essentially capitalistic, why not provide the people with rights corresponding to that system and their effective application and protection?

Finally, as for the horror of capitalists gaining free access to large amounts of land, I suggest that people should get over it. What are the real options? To make the capitalist pay a hefty price for unused land plus bribes to a corrupt government or bureaucracy? Would you not prefer to have the capitalist spend this very same money directly and free from interference by corrupt officials on job-generating capital investments? Any money that a capitalist must pay to the government and corrupt officials reduces the amount available for real capital investment. Also, such moneys paid for land will probably be wasted by spendthrift governments or stolen by corrupt officials. And God forbid that he or she might decide *not* to spend anything in the first place because the price and bribes demanded make him or her forgo the investment and take his or her money abroad! The problem of the poor countries can be summed up in a word: underinvestment. Corruption, overregulation. bureaucracy, and capital flight cause underinvestment. The predicament of poor countries is too little investment in agriculture, factories, housing, and infrastructure (such as roads, railroads, harbours, and airports). The more capitalists are free to invest their money in such enterprises, the greater the expansion of productive stock and infrastructure, the more economic growth will be realized, and the closer these countries will get to prosperity. Imagine a country with no shortage of harbours, airports, railroads, and roads that has thousands upon thousands of new factories, mining operations, and plantations – and many millions of new jobs soaking up unemployment, which is what capitalists can easily deliver if only they could get on with it. This is what abhorrence of the right to occupy land, of property rights, and of free enterprise and capitalism stops us from achieving.

Jurisdiction galore

I have treated the topic of discretionary control of public land as predatory jurisdiction in depth. Nevertheless, this is not to suggest that other forms of government jurisdiction such as zoning, building codes, and rental controls are somehow lesser issues. Without going to the same length as in the case of public land, let us take a look at how these powers involve predatory jurisdiction. As a matter of fact, it is probably more accurate to speak of various types of predatory jurisdiction. It is obvious that the outcome of flawed policymaking and administrative mismanagement is, in each instance, the same: a tremendous shortage of housing, dead capital, and stunted economic development. Nevertheless, the different types of authority involved require very different arguments for addressing the extent to which these various types of government authority are legitimate or predatory. One could think of predatory jurisdiction over real estate markets as a multilayered cake.

For most of our discussion of land rights, we implicitly assumed without further elaboration that, basically, the state allows private ownership of land. This assumption is problematic in its own right. In some countries, private ownership of land is not allowed. In many countries – even those that formally allow private ownership – hostility against private ownership of land is a serious obstacle to the property law and administrative reform. Though a prohibition against or far-reaching curtailment of private property rights by the state does implicate predatory power, this is, first and foremost, an issue to be resolved at the level of ideology or political philosophy.

Next, governments frequently regulate the uses of land – namely, zoning. Zoning policy is a critical determinant of formal housing and business expansion. In the case of zoning, the issue is the rationale of government authority in the matter of land use when that government may not even own the land in question: Why should governments have the power to control, restrict, or regulate the use of privately owned land?

Governments also control building activity through building permits and building codes. In most countries, one must apply for a permit to build a house, its issuance being conditional upon complying with a building code.

Finally, there is rental control and the issue of freedom of contract. In the case of rental controls, the question is as follows: By what right does government intervene in what are essentially voluntary trading relationships between tenants and landlords?

We can make general statements about the degree to which all these types of authority are legitimate or abusive: when restrictions result in dramatic housing shortages and impediments to business growth, the liberties of the citizens affected and their pursuit of happiness – or to be more specific, prosperity – are oppressed. Yet how this works out for each jurisdiction requires detailed answers for each specific type of government power. At this level, there is no single, all-embracing answer. The latter three instances of predatory jurisdiction are reviewed in the sections that follow, though not in the same order.

Stewart's account

It is almost an article of faith that the pursuit of profit must, by definition, be injurious to the interests of the poor. One of the most hated exponents of entrepreneurship is the landlord. The caricature of the miserly, greedy, and cold-hearted landlord is one of those classical archetypes of the capitalist exploiter of socialist and populist lore. It is practically received wisdom that free markets do not supply housing that is both affordable and of decent quality – very few people believe otherwise. By extension, it is a popular belief that rental controls and building codes represent legitimate interventions by government that benefit low-income households. Nothing can be further from the truth. In 1997, *The Wall Street Journal Forum* published a particularly fine article on the subject by a real estate developer, Mr Donald Stewart, Jr, and the nefarious consequences of political control of rental prices in Brazil.[8] The vast favelas around Rio de Janeiro (and most other metropolises in developing countries) so morbidly displayed in documentaries about poverty can thus be understood in a different light. Most people see the growth of slums in the developing world as a failure of capitalist economies to provide for the poor. According to Donald Stewart, Jr, however, the favelas are there because of misguided government policies and counterproductive administrative mechanisms. Two major government policy flaws contribute *directly* to the existence of the slums. First, forty-three different rent control laws since 1921 (many prohibiting rental increases and both real and inflation adjustments) have made the rental business a losing game, given the high and uncertain rate of Brazilian inflation over the years. Second, state housing regulation, which dictates a whole set of minimum requirements for dwelling sizes, windows, and doors, has pushed the cost of even the smallest units out of the reach of most Brazilians. The effect of these regulations and conditions has been to devastate the rental housing market in Brazil. Thirty years ago, over two-thirds of the housing construction was for rent; today, only about 3 per cent of total housing units are built for rental. Improvements in the rental laws since 1991 have not been sufficient to provide incentives for an increase in construction of rental properties. The so-called failure of the markets to provide cheap rental units turns out to be an efficient but unintended market response to government intervention: no opportunity for profit, no investment. In the words of Mr Stewart:

> Of course these regulations were intended to 'protect' poor people from the pernicious greed of unscrupulous landlords who otherwise would build only low quality houses, houses that bureaucrats and politicians would not consider acceptable. Policymakers think that the choice is between decent houses of differing standards. But in fact they have created a choice between an affordable house for low-income people or the favelas. Since the former is not possible, the latter is the only alternative.

Psychology may also be at work here. The measure of what constitutes decent (as opposed to substandard housing) is in part a function of one's own circumstances as well as one's values and prejudices. The thing with policymakers is that they almost always hold middle-class or upper-class values and prejudices. What is substandard housing in the mind of the policymaker, as a member of the middle or upper class, may well be an improvement in conditions to the tenant compared to what was left behind in the countryside. What is worthless and hideous to look at from a middle-class perspective may have value to its occupant. To translate the perspective of the affluent in economic terminology: the utility of a slum dwelling is zero. Because it would not suit his or her taste or circumstances; he or she would never think of buying such property; psychologically, the informal property does not represent wealth to the higher classes. Is it conceivable that this has blinded the policymaker to the value it has to the poor and makes him or her underestimate the value the poor can generate? The fact of the matter is that slum dwellers actually buy, rent, and sell these properties. Informal properties all over the developing world are traded for thousands of dollars. By the end of the 1990s, informal extensions on desert land near Cairo had an average value of USD 11.500.[9] Even a simple shanty in Port-au-Prince had a value of at least USD 500. This is one reason why squatters threatened by eviction often battle it out with the police. To the poor, eviction from and demolition of their properties may be the destruction of their life's savings, their only significant and valuable investment. The value of Egypt's informal real estate properties exceeded USD 240 billion, which is 6 times the value of total savings and time deposits in commercial banks in Egypt.[10] On the other hand, to the policymakers and their affluent constituencies, the same removal of squatters and the destruction of their dwellings represents a sanitary measure and the just desserts for illegal occupancy.

As with so many other economic activities, what cannot be done legally will move underground. We have it from Mr Stewart that the construction of rental properties has moved to the favelas:

> In a favela, where rent control law is not enforced, rents are paid in US dollars and tenants who don't pay are quickly kicked out. Considering the investment and the income, this is good business. The result is an abundance of favelas units to rent.

Apparently, the hated landlord is irrepressible, and the prospective tenants are not being over-particular with their customs. What is the appropriate response? Will it be more repressive laws and measures? The disaster of administrative interference in rental property development, the price of extralegality, the opportunity for improved living conditions, and the greater choice foregone become clear with the following argument by Mr Stewart:

> As a shopping center developer, I studied the low-income housing market as an investment. I found that we could profitably build and rent 225 square foot units (approx.: 25 square meters), for three persons, with low finishing standards and no interior walls but with water, sewage and electricity. These would contrast sharply with a typical favela unit, where six or seven people live in 100 square feet (approx.: 11 square meters) with no sewage facilities. If each of the three tenants paid a rent equivalent to 25 percent of the monthly legal minimum wage, our investment would be more profitable than building and renting shopping centers. (That's despite the fact that the minimum wage is so low that even a twelve-year-old boy selling chewing gum at a traffic light earns more.) Such profit potential means that there would be enough capital, know-how and entrepreneurial capacity to build millions of decent, affordable units. The market could create wider housing choices, greater supply and downward pressure on prices.

Stewart's account about the extremity of rent controls and building codes in Brazil that forces millions of people into favelas is another exposé of the unrestrained power of the state. In the case of rental controls, this power infringes upon freedom of contract. Freedom of contract is the idea that individuals should be free to bargain among themselves about the terms of their own contracts without government interference.[11] Rental controls destroy freedom of contract in that the landlord can no longer freely negotiate rental charges with the tenant. Instead, the state sets the maximum rents allowed. By extension, this results in a form of deprivation of property by the state in favour of the tenant. The fruits of the investment in the rental property are transferred from the landlord to the tenant: the landlord is deprived of income to favour the tenant. Often this deprivation of income is so extreme that the landlord can no longer recover his or her original investment. When this is the case, landlords cease to invest in legal sector housing with the consequences sketched earlier by Stewart.

Zoning and building codes

Much informal property, mostly in or near urban areas, violates zoning rules. Yet, when hundreds of millions of people must live in violation of them, one should eventually wonder whether these zoning regimes are bona fide. Are these people breaking the law or is the law tripping them up? Zoning is a policy instrument for gaining greater physical order in cities. The orderliness of cities in the Netherlands, Germany, or Sweden owes a great deal to zoning regulations that were put in place as early as the nineteenth century. Yet, in Peru, De Soto found that much zoning was originally adopted with the purpose of discouraging rural migration to the cities. For example: "In the 1930s, a ban was imposed on the construction of cheap apartments in Lima."[12] The authorities apparently expected that the scarcity of cheap apartments would discourage impecunious rural dwellers from settling in the cities. The city folk of those days – and many today – viewed rural migration with hostility. From this perspective, zoning is a form of discrimination against rural migrants or a perverse form of class warfare waged by urban dwellers against rural migrants.

In retrospect, the use of zoning as a means of controlling population flows failed miserably and spectacularly. In many developing countries, the majority of the people now live in towns and cities. Over the last forty years, Latin America went from 70 per cent of the population living on the land to 70 per cent living in urbanized areas. In various developing countries, 50–90 per cent of the urban population may now be living in violation of one zoning regime or another. In the meantime, many – probably most – cities in developing countries are severely congested, chaotic, unsafe, unsanitary, and unspeakably ugly. The point of zoning is to channel urban growth in orderly ways, not to prevent it. Apparently, the misuse of zoning as an instrument of population flow control undermined its proper use as a means of promoting orderly urban expansion. Where governments use zoning to exclude people from city life, the outcome is the opposite of what zoning is supposed to achieve: it forces migrants to settle and live in chaotic and unsanitary conditions.

The test of whether a zoning law constitutes a justifiable or predatory authority is whether it respects, without overstraining their personal resources, the right of people to relocate, acquire property, build homes, develop neighbourhoods, and pursue access to the amenities of modern life in the cities. These rights are the corollaries of the right to life, liberty, and the pursuit of happiness. Marking off areas to be occupied by public amenities such as roads, sidewalks, gutters, squares, public buildings, public parks, monuments, and recreation areas is a legitimate use of authority. On the other hand, imposing minimum purchasing prices on lots is an abuse of authority given its potential for systematically excluding (and thus discriminating against) lower-income buyers. Prohibiting settlement and other forms of land use near water reservoirs to minimize the danger of their pollution in the interest of public hygiene is a legitimate use of zoning authority. Using zoning laws to block urban expansion beyond the limits of presently built-up areas – for example, through defining rural zones, green belts, or buffer zones – is discriminatory and, as we can deduce from the slums that spread around them, counterproductive. Many city dwellers see urban expansion as a consequence of rural migration as a threat to the quality of the urban environment. Yet the other side of the story is that rural migrants come to the cities in order to seek a better life. There is no way to accommodate them except through the expansion of towns and cities. Why should the fears, fancies, and prejudices of folks in the city count for more than the rights, dreams, ambitions, and material needs of newcomers from the countryside? Developing country governments that seek to impose constraints on rural migration cannot be deemed liberal, representative or democratic – in actual fact or in spirit – because they have decided to act in favour of one portion of the populace, usually a privileged minority group, by denying another group, often the majority (including rural migrants) its liberty.

Building codes can be just as discriminatory. Frequently, we suffer from the illusion that a rule or regulation is unimpeachable when it reflects our ideals or because it is founded on good intentions. It may indeed seem pretty awful to argue against rules and regulations designed to ensure decent housing for the poor as well as the rich. Yet it seems as if high-mindedness robs its purveyors of their sense of irony. Is it not ironic to see how a rule meant for the benefit of the poor increases the plight of the poor? We already noted the example of Brazil earlier in this chapter. There, building codes, rental controls, and other measures are counterproductive in that they cause shortages of legal rental housing, driving people into favelas.

If building codes prevent landlords from building affordable housing for the poor, have we really achieved justice for the poor? Therefore, the majority of the poor are required to fend for themselves and build their own homes. And yet, unsurprisingly, the building codes would also apply to the building plans of the poor. It is unlikely that informals would live in fear of a visit from a building inspector. However, it is also nearly inconceivable that the impecunious homebuilder would do anything so daft as submitting his or her plans to any building inspector for approval. The informal homebuilder would know the outcome, and it is in this sense that building codes contribute to illegal construction. And that raises a few questions: what if large numbers of people cannot afford to comply with a rule on account of their poverty? Is it reasonable to both require the poor to comply *and* ignore their financial situation? Can we require a poor man to build his home in accordance with rules that are too burdensome for him to comply with? Is this not tantamount to making poverty a crime? How dare we make the necessity of the poor to manage with the means at his or her disposal an affront to decency? It appears that the rules that promote decent housing in practice cause exclusion and criminalization. Of course, some people will be undaunted by these arguments stating that the injustice is not in such building codes but in society failing to provide decent housing for the poor. These arguments fail the test of reality and reason: most poor people live in poor countries and poor countries *by definition* do not have the means to take care of their poor. In poor countries, the poor will, as a matter of practice, have to take care of themselves unaided. As such, one cannot expect the poor to live beyond their means. If the poor must manage by themselves, it behoves us not to weigh down their efforts with unaffordable building codes that prevent them from providing, however humble, a home for their families. Building codes more than any other form of predatory jurisdiction hits the poor in their weakest spot: the wallet. Again, the objective is not to advocate for the abolition of building codes; the point is to advocate for some test of their reasonability.

Elementary economics revisited

Let us apply elementary economics and financial theory to the problems raised by De Soto and Stewart. If anything drives up prices, it is scarcity. Red tape surrounding titling of land – in other words, misgovernment – should, in effect, create a scarcity of land within the legal sector. This scarcity should be reflected in relative land prices. Indeed, the World Bank confirms this fact for India: land prices relative to incomes are ten times higher in Delhi and Mumbai than in Tokyo.[13] Relatively high land prices drive up the price of housing units, which results in a higher break-even point for real estate development, less building activity of (and thus greater scarcity in) housing units. The same logic applies to the rental business as well. Stifling regulation of property development through building codes drives up the cost price of housing units. In the meantime, by driving down the rates of return on rental property, rental controls destroy the incentive to build housing units and contribute directly to a scarcity of housing within the legal sector.[14]

Next, combine scarcity and price controls and black markets will flourish. Recall how Prohibition in the United States resulted in a thriving black market for alcohol. It is no different in rental housing markets. According to De Soto: "In Cairo, the legal tenants of apartments whose rents were frozen in the early 1950s at sums now worth less than a dollar a year subdivide these properties into smaller apartments and lease them out at market prices."[15] This example is doubly ironic as well as instructive: the rent controls imposed during the 1950s were intended to protect the legal tenants from the greedy landlords. By the 1990s, these legal tenants turned into unique parasites: they pay their own landlords no more than a notional rent and act as slum landlords to illegal subtenants. What an astonishing and dismal combination: we have people who manage to have standard issue socialist law on their side when paying rent and, at the same time, they manage to earn rent at laissez-faire market rates!

So much government, so few markets

To pursue the issue of predatory jurisdiction to its logical conclusion means that the state, without liability to it or its agents, has the right to proscribe, override, or encumber essentially legitimate objectives at will. To test this proposition, let us assume that building a house, providing a service, or developing a business and making a profit are legitimate objectives. At the same time – and in line with the belief in wise and well-directed government action and that the state should have all the necessary means to regulate the economy (that is, untrammelled authority) – it is one of government's functions to provide for or encourage the supply of decent, affordable housing to the poor.

Thus, in accordance with their standards of affordable housing, governments have adopted rent control laws that legally destroy a landlord's livelihood and the capital value of his or her property by forcing him or her to rent his or her property at prices below cost. Also, governments, in the interest of decent housing, can and do adopt building codes that are prohibitive when it comes to low-cost housing. When landlords refuse to invest under these conditions, the rental business collapses, and a shortage of legal rental units will soon appear. Yet because decent and affordable housing is a public policy issue, there is no liability on the part of government to landlords for damages or to prospective tenants hard-pressed to find decent, affordable, and legal housing.

Also, consider the fact that governments are perpetually short of funds for extending the supply of public housing. Discretionary power provides government (again, without liability) with the scope for policymaking wherein it can subordinate public housing policies to budgetary considerations. In other words, when deficit reductions become the prime concern of government, it is perfectly free to opt for spending cuts in housing programmes regardless of the public need. At the same time, governments refuse to issue, sell, lease, or rent state land because policymakers do not trust the poor or working class to be able to adhere to legal standards of decent housing. Concurrently, their very notions of what is decent stops them from waiving building codes to allow people to build their own homes and thus alleviate the housing shortage created by its own policies. We have a dog chasing its own tail. In the meantime, the need of a sizable portion of the citizenry for some alternative is ignored without any form of redress. Hardship is not even a mitigating circumstance for extralegal behaviour: in the public interest, government has anti-squatter statutes on its books. Note that, by now, both rights and markets are completely out of the picture.

This is the situation in most countries. Large portions of the urban population in many developing nations continue to live *unnecessarily* in difficult conditions. Policies that are detrimental to the economy carry no liability for the government and its agents. The costs or damages are entirely and with total impunity socialized (i.e., the burden is, by default, shifted to society). Wise and well-directed government appears to be an elusive quality, even while the state possesses all the necessary means to regulate the economy. This is a palpable and destructive reality. The daily experience of people is life in a world where their public benefactor has and insists on having terrifying power. But then, to quote Laurent Tailhade, "Qu'importe les victimes si le geste est beau?"[16]

Rights for the poor ... a silver bullet?

The day that individual rights or natural rights will be recognized as valid ways to protect and empower the people will mark a huge step forward in history. Nevertheless, by itself, the recognition of rights is not a cure-all for the problems facing informals. Fighting for rights is not quite the same as building the institutions so essential to the business of translating property rights and economic freedom into the live capital of De Soto. Gaining the recognition of rights, however important, does not of itself resolve the issue of formal property representation. The business of combating predatory jurisdiction in public domain, zoning, rent control, and building codes would legalize a great deal of informal real estate. However, by itself, that would not result in its absorption into the formal sector where the real economic and social advantages of proper title and economic freedom are achieved. Once the fight for rights is won, there is still the battle of reforming and improving the performance and management of land registries, land laws, civil courts, surveying offices, public domain offices, and sundry bureaucracies involved in the land business. These critical and legitimate government functions have often been neglected, demoralized, and corrupted. To organize effective property representation, we need reliable land registers, a competent and ready supply of surveyors, jurists that will understand the intricacies of land laws, and responsive public domain bureaus, for example. To get these will require substantial investment of financial, technical, and human resources, and this is probably even more difficult than the part of crusading against predatory jurisdiction. Yet the advocacy of rights is of vital importance in that it not only helps undo predatory jurisdiction, but it also raises the consciousness of the public indirectly in terms of how poorly they are served by those bits of bureaucracy. It is common for rights-conscious people to demand proper service from the civil services; the effective exercise of rights requires a properly functioning public administration. In the end, we need people to be lucid in their dissatisfaction – to know both specifically and correctly what it is they are or should be unhappy about. Only then does reform, both on the level of legal philosophy and public administration, stand a chance of success.

Summary

We have treated here at great length the topic of predatory jurisdiction. Pointing out the predatory and illegitimate nature of the discretionary control of the public domain as well as zoning powers, building codes, and rental controls challenges deeply engrained patterns of how people look to the state for securing social and spatial order. We are deeply habituated to thinking of public domain, zoning, building codes, and other measures as government responsibilities and powers without a downside or indispensable and mostly beneficent. It must seem strange to have to reconsider these so-called facts and discover that these powers are, in many countries, instrumental in causing disorder and chaos. Truly, they have turned into destroyers of the quality of the lives of the working-class citizens of the world. These powers are, up to a point, defensible; government action through the application of these powers can be beneficial to society. The spatial orderliness manifest in many Western countries is clearly evidence of their utility as policy instruments. Nevertheless, we must also accept that there is no power that cannot be abused. We owe it to our fellow citizens to be far more thoughtful about the application of power than we have been so far. That means we must occasionally re-examine powers that we have always taken for granted.

Chapter 7

Money and Inflation

The first panacea for a mismanaged nation is inflation of the currency; the second is war. Both bring a temporary prosperity; both bring a permanent ruin. But both are the refuge of political and economic opportunists.

—Ernest Hemingway

The operation of government and the state cost money. To cover these expenditures, governments must raise revenues. At the level of the individual income earner or the property owner, the art of raising revenues is, in the most basic sense, a process of confiscating property. However, raising revenues is such an elemental necessity to the existence of government that the lawful exercise of this authority must be tolerated. The best-known version of this power is taxation. The practice of taxation is – up to a point and subject to caveats and preconditions – defensible. Governments, however, have various other means of raising revenues; among others, they have the power to create money (or, more prosaically, to print money). In principle and in reality, governments can finance public expenditures by printing money. Historically, governments have done so time and again. Beyond a certain scale, printing money causes monetary inflation, which is called government-induced inflation. Though governments have inflated currencies for millennia, during the twentieth century, the problem acquired a force and virulence unparalleled in history. Never before had so many governments availed themselves of this tool. Never before had the exploitation of this instrument been carried out so systematically and carried to such extremes. Twentieth-century governments changed the incidence of inflation from being an intermittent experience into a chronic, pervasive concern. Hyperinflation, a historical rarity, became a problem of epidemic proportions. Prior to the twentieth century, we have only one recorded case of hyperinflation: 1795, in revolutionary France. During the twentieth century, no fewer than fifty-four cases of hyperinflation have been identified.[1] Decade after decade, one country after another was brought to their knees by government-induced inflation. Rampant inflation bleeds the life out of the economy, corrupts society, and demoralizes the people. From being mostly a non-issue before the twentieth century, managing inflation became the object of permanent, formal policymaking. Uniquely, among policy powers, the experience of inflation has resulted in a recognition that an unrestrained authority to create money poses an unwarranted hazard. Just as uniquely, this has (in many countries) resulted in a genuine attempt to restrain monetary policy powers. Nevertheless, the lessons learned are at best incomplete. The purpose, then, of this chapter is to provide an explicit and detailed exposition of the scope of predatory jurisdiction involved in money creation.

Money and Monetary Financing

In the modern world, the control of the money supply is within government jurisdiction. Expanding or contracting the money supply[2] is a political or administrative decision based on discretionary power. Government-induced inflation is never accidental and always intentional. It is the manifestation of a technical process requiring a direct and formal initiative on the part of the policymakers of the moment and conscious, organizational effort by their subordinates in various parts of the bureaucracy. The motive is the desire of policymakers to spend more than the government collects in taxes or more than it borrows. The method is printing money to cover this deficit of revenues against government expenditures. It is, in every step of its making, the result of calculated decision-making by the ruling politicians and bureaucrats. Managing the money supply (i.e., monetary policy) is an administrative responsibility – the rules and the know-how of which have been worked out in the finest detail by the science of economics. It is a special, recognized, and mature field of study. In fact, they teach this type of intervention in university in perfectly bland and value-free language. The following quote comes from a study book aptly named *Public Finance, A Contemporary Application of Theory to Policy*:[3]

> Government-induced inflation is a sustained annual increase in prices caused by expansion of the money supply to pay for government-supplied goods and services. Government authorities can simply print money to pay for costs of government-provided goods and services or take other measures to expand the money supply. The net effect of such continual increases in the money supply is, of course, sustained increases in the general level of prices – in other words, inflation. Increases in the market prices of goods and services caused by expansion of the money supply force citizens to curtail their consumption and saving, which in turn, finances the reallocation of resources to public use over the long run.

In formal terms, government-induced inflation occurs when policymakers resort to a financial stratagem called monetary financing. Monetary financing happens when the government requires the central bank to purchase debt securities issued by the state or provide it with a credit facility. These are, in effect, orders by the government to the central bank to lend money to the state. The central bank in its turn pays government for these debt obligations by printing money and thus expanding the money supply, which is precisely what the government wanted in the first place. Beyond a certain scale, monetary financing causes inflation. Every step of this process is legal, provided all procedural niceties are adhered to.[4] Rest assured that most of the proceedings were duly recorded and that there is one long paper trail including policy papers, memoranda, resolutions, minutes, decrees, written instructions, facility agreements, bookkeeping entries, registers, and (finally) the newly printed banknotes themselves. We may not be accustomed to think in these terms, but jurisdiction and policy discretion of the state in the matter of money creation makes causing inflation and destroying the value of currencies lawfully exercised authority.

Basically, monetary financing redistributes purchasing power from the existing supply of money to the newly printed money.[5] Monetary financing is, in effect, fiscal policy carried out through the expansion of the supply of money with the objective of confiscating purchasing power. Money in its various forms – cash, bank deposits, loan contracts, etc. – was meant to be a formal representation of purchasing power. Purchasing power is a claim to property or all the goods and services money can buy. Inflation impairs or destroys this claim to property. Monetary financing and government-induced inflation is, in other words, a taking of property without due process. Had government confiscated a tangible good – a piece of privately owned land or a factory or a house or an automobile – by decree and without recompense, any court in a liberal democracy would have recognized such a taking as a direct violation of property rights. However, there is not a single court on the planet that would rule on monetary financing as a taking of property without due process, which would make it a violation of property rights. At the centre of the monetary system, there is only the prerogative and impunity of the policymaker.

About the purpose of monetary financing, we can be extremely brief. There is absolutely no other point to printing money but to spend it. Monetary financing has only one use: funding overspending. Monetary financing never occurs in nations where public spending is under control, where expenditures are fully covered by the proceeds of taxation. The essence of monetary financing is the funding of spending commitments, which policymakers are unwilling to abandon but for which they could not find tax revenues and cannot borrow money. At its roots, government-induced inflation is a fiscal problem. By and large, the signs of excessive spending commitments are the same everywhere. Examples are a bloated public-sector payroll, underfunded public pension schemes, large public-sector debts, free public education and healthcare programmes, and election season spending on public works. With respect to the last item, observe that, in many countries, inflation goes up during or immediately after election season. Observe, thus, how monetary financing and government-induced inflation fit right into a wider pattern of misgovernment. The central question with inflation is always as follows: Has the state made spending commitments that it cannot meet by means of taxation and borrowing and which it is unwilling or unable to abandon? If this is the case, one must expect inflation sooner or later.

Inflation and its victims

Marxists and socialists often say that rights, especially property rights, are worthless to the poor, that the poor cannot eat formal rights. Yet what exactly do the poor and middle-class buy with wages eroded by inflation? The typical victim of government-induced inflation is the working-class or middle-class citizen living on wages and salaries. The rich usually have tangible properties of great value, stakes in enterprises, indexed contracts and, for good measure, money safely out of reach of local authorities in banks abroad; the working-class and middle-class citizens have only their bare hands and the modest wages earned with them. Inflation deprives wage earners of the fruits of their labour. We do not usually think of wages and salaries as property, but what if we did? Wages and salaries are purchasing power received in the form of cash disbursements or deposits in bank accounts. On payment day, a huge transfer of property takes place from employers to employees in the form of pure purchasing power. Almost 90 per cent of all earnings are in the form of wages. Is this not by any measure a great deal of property? The value of these earnings is the single most important property for most people and their only means to the necessities, comforts, and modest luxuries in life. In countries such as Brazil and Argentina, the elimination of inflation during the 1990s resulted in a substantial improvement of the position of the working classes and the middle class. The policy of strong, inflation-free currencies is highly valued by the poor in both of these countries. The success of the Plan Real was the *pièce de résistance* that paved the way to the presidency for its architect, the former minister of finance, Mr Fernando Henrique Cardoso. No one in Latin America has suffered more from depreciation and monetary inflation than the poor and the middle-class citizens. Phrasing the consequences of government-induced inflation in terms of how it forces "citizens to curtail their consumption and saving" makes it seem as if the theorist positing that idea has never paused to consider the full significance of that inflation – namely, that it might also refer to the process of pushing working-class people into poverty.

One classic rule according to economic theory has it that economic growth is a matter of investment, which in its turn depends upon the rate at which savings accumulate. It is the worry of every economist that inflation destroys the value of savings and, therefore, the incentive to save.

This situation destroys the basis for economic growth and development. From a monetary perspective, a country keen on economic development should therefore try to keep its rate of inflation as low as possible; ideally, it should maintain a non-inflationary currency. Historically, East Asian nations have had both lower inflation rates and higher savings rates than Latin America, and this difference shows up in economic growth rates, which have been consistently higher in the former over the past three or four decades.

The majority of people do not save for the sake of investment; rather, most people save money to secure funds for contingencies and major expenditures such as sickness, building homes, and the education of their children. However unrelated such private motives may be to investment considerations of entrepreneurs and the public sector, these are nevertheless the essential stimuli of capital formation. An inflation-free currency is, therefore, one of the most important prerequisites – though by no means the only! – for a favourable investment climate.

The following calculations provide insight into the awful burden that inflation can impose on the diligent saver. Though there are no objective standards for determining which level of inflation is acceptable, 3 per cent is frequently accepted as the benchmark of performance. The Reserve Bank of New Zealand and the European Central Bank are (by law) required to keep annual inflation below 3 per cent. An inflation rate of only 3 per cent or less may seem negligible, but it is not: at 3 per cent per year, a currency will lose 26 per cent of its value in 10 years, 45 per cent in 20 years and 69 per cent in 40 years. Such losses – which take place within the span of a person's productive life – are significant, something to keep in mind when planning for retirement. At 20 per cent per year, a currency loses 84 per cent of its value in 10 years and 99 per cent in 24 years. Twenty-four years is the time it takes to raise a child and put him or her through college. With inflation at 20 per cent per year, how must one plan and save for a child's education? For most people, saving towards such goals represents an effort of enormous discipline. Government-induced inflation casually and brutally defeats such attempts.

If we accept a 3 per cent increase in prices as the yardstick, inflation is, at this point in time, largely a developing-world problem. World Bank statistics scored 42 countries that enjoyed an average inflation rate from 1990 to 2015 of less than 3 per cent and 136 that averaged more than 3 per cent.[6] The former category of countries together had per capita incomes averaging USD 44,471, whereas per capita income averaged USD 10,833 in the latter category of countries.[7] Signally, all members of the Group of Seven (G7) sported averages below 3 per cent.[8] Furthermore, 33 countries with a combined population of 990 million – one in seven people on Earth – were categorized as suffering from average rates of inflation from 1990 to 2015 of 20 per cent or more.[9] This group includes countries such as Russia, Turkey, Venezuela, and Brazil (from which one could reasonably expect a superior performance).

One marker of poverty is a pronounced deprivation in well-being. Another defining attribute of poverty is a lack of material possessions or money. Government-induced inflation deprives wage earners of their only significant possession and source of well-being – namely the purchasing power of their earnings. When one perceives government-induced inflation as an attack on property rights, it should be no surprise that countries with a history of higher inflation on the whole tend to be poorer than countries with a history of very low rates of inflation.

Elementary economics

The confiscation of purchasing power by way of monetary financing and government-induced inflation is a form of deprivation of property. Inflation stands in opposition to the concept of property rights. This is a strange thing because the idea that a currency can be used to deprive the people of property contradicts elementary economic theory. To understand why, this section will provide readers unfamiliar with the theory of monetary economics a bare-bones primer covering a few elementary concepts needed to understand some of the functions of money.

According to economic theory, the purpose of money is to function as a medium of exchange and a store of value.[10] As a medium of exchange, it facilitates the exchange of goods. As a store of value, it is, in the words of Milton Friedman, the "temporary abode of purchasing power." The latter function is also called the asset function of money. Money as an asset is private property.

Additionally, these roles are simultaneous: to be a medium of exchange, it must also be a store of value. As soon as a currency stops being a store of value, it loses its role as a medium of exchange. In simple words, when a currency becomes worthless, it will no longer be accepted for payments. At its most extreme, this situation produces the spectacle of hyperinflation in its final throes, when people abandon the use of the currency. Apparently, in order for money to be a credible medium of exchange it must be a safe and secure store of value. The significance of this is that property rights matter. For the asset function of money to be secure, government and society must respect the concept of property rights as applying to purchasing power. After all, when purchasing power is no longer a secure property, the role of money as an honest and efficient exchange medium will have been compromised.

The point is that, if a currency can serve as an instrument for confiscating purchasing power, the enumeration of its functions must be incomplete. Besides being a medium of exchange and a store of value, it has a function as well as an instrument for reallocating resources. Accordingly, to pinpoint its potential utility as a policy instrument, let us attribute one more function to money: its use as a medium of resource reallocation. Yet, if money is meant to be a genuine store of value, its alteration into a medium of resource reallocation must be accounted for.

Power to the government

Essentially, the question is as follows: Why is it so easy for a government to inflate a currency? An answer to this question requires a proper appreciation of the fact that the type of money we are used to is only one of several kinds of money. Historically, the alteration of money into a medium of resource reallocation is the consequence of essential changes forced by government in the nature of paper currency. It is not necessary to delve at great length into the history of money; the basics are often more or less familiar to the informed layperson. It is common knowledge that, until the commencement of the Great Depression, the gold standard was the predominant monetary system around the world, and it was, for all practical purposes, abandoned thereafter. The gold standard is a monetary system based on gold of a specified weight and fineness as the unit of value.[11] There was also a silver standard or a monetary system based on silver.[12] The two most prominent adherents of the silver standard remaining at the start of the twentieth century were China and Mexico.

Gold and silver standards started as coin money standards. However, in time, as the volume and size of transactions grew, banknotes and bank transfers became the more convenient way of paying. Consequently, banknotes and account money replaced gold and silver coins as the everyday instruments of payment for most situations.[13] These banknotes were the origin of the paper currency system that we know today. In countries with a monetary metal standard, such paper currencies represented fiduciary money. Fiduciary money is money consisting of promises to pay in another medium, mostly monetary metals such as gold and silver.[14] What must be understood, however, is that there are two types of paper currency – the other type is fiat money. Fiat money is paper money made legal tender by decree of a government, and it is not based on gold or silver reserves.[15]

Fiduciary money is, in effect, a substitute for monetary metals in the form of paper notes. The banknote in this system is a promissory note – in effect, *a contract and a debt* – specifying the quantity in gold or silver to be reimbursed by the issuer upon presentation of the note. In the fiduciary money system, it is not the notes issued but the money metals that are the true store of value. The notes are, in principle, backed by a stock of gold or silver held by the issuers of the notes (i.e., banks). To put the matter differently, the supply of fiduciary money is beholden to a reserve requirement in gold or silver.

What must be understood about fiduciary money is that market forces directly regulate the paper currency supply. The issue of banknotes is strictly driven by a demand for a more convenient instrument of payment than gold or silver coins – no more and no less. The circulation of notes is directly dependent upon the amount of gold exchanged for banknotes by the public and the banks. In other words, when (on a net basis) people deposit gold, the number of notes in circulation increases. Conversely, when (on a net basis) people demand gold in exchange for their notes, the number of notes in circulation decreases. In short, the supply of fiduciary money in circulation is fixed by the supply of gold deposited within the banking system. It's the same case with silver. What is the advantage of this system? The fundamental advantage of money metal standards is that governments cannot "print" gold or silver, a reality that – since the supply of these metals is comparatively stable in the short and medium terms (and often in the long term) – protects the value of money or purchasing power from inflationary designs.[16]

Unlike fiduciary money, fiat money is not a money substitute; it is, itself, *the* standard. The creation of fiat money does not require an exchange of any "token of wealth actually produced"[17] such as gold or silver. Market forces no longer regulate the issue of banknotes, (i.e., the issue of paper currency is no longer constrained by the supply of gold or silver). For paper currencies not backed by money metals, the designation fiat money fits perfectly. *Fiat* – Latin for *let it be done* – is defined as a positive and authoritative order or decree.[18] Money is created by administrative fiat or by government orders. Qua money creation, the technical limit is the amount of paper and ink one can lay one's hands on. In this sense, fiat money is literally print-and-spend currency. An unfortunate if apt comparison is counterfeit money, which also fits the description of print-and-spend currency. The term *print-and-spend currency* may sound derogatory. Yet, to call this an offensive portrayal of fiat money would be to ignore the true nature of fiat money.

Before becoming the universal standard after the onset of the Great Depression, fiat money was usually a wartime currency. Wars are often extremely expensive affairs in which governments are often at risk of running through their gold reserves, after which they would not have a means of paying strategic imports such as arms and other war supplies.[19] To avoid this danger, governments suspend local payments in gold and requisition the stocks of gold held by banks. At the same time, governments instruct their treasury departments to issue debt notes to be used in payment of supplies. These debt notes are issued in convenient denominations of money and are not redeemable in gold or silver. Frequently, governments specify that these notes can be used for paying all taxes, dues, and liabilities to them. Also, the suspension of gold as a medium of exchange causes a shortage of money, and the public will often, out of necessity, resort to using these notes as currency in private transactions. Justice Bradley described this process by taking the example of England during the Napoleonic Wars in a ruling by the US Supreme Court:[20]

> It is well known that for over twenty years, from 1797 to 1820, the most stringent paper money system that ever existed prevailed in England, and lay at the foundation of all her elasticity and endurance. It is true that the Bank of England notes, which the bank was required to issue until they reached an amount then unprecedented, were not technically made legal tenders, except for the purpose of relieving from arrest and imprisonment for debt; but worse

than that, the bank was expressly forbidden to redeem its notes in specie, except for a certain small amount to answer the purpose of change. The people were obliged to receive them. The government had nothing else wherewith to pay its domestic creditors. The people themselves had no specie, for that was absorbed by the Bank of England, and husbanded for the uses of government in carrying on its foreign wars and paying its foreign subsidies. The country banks depended on the Bank of England for support, and of course they could not redeem their circulation in specie. The result was that the nation was perforce obliged to treat the bank notes as a legal tender or suffer inevitable bankruptcy. In such a state of things it went very hard with any man who demanded specie in fulfilment of his contracts.

Essentially, fiat money is non-interest-bearing debt paper issued by governments, originally handed to creditors in return for goods, services, and labour purchased, but which was not and will never be redeemed. Ordinary debt, if not repaid, will result in a loss to the creditor. Yet what prevents this debt paper from turning into a total loss is the fact that the original recipients have used these notes as the medium of exchange for their own purchases down the economic food chain. Thus, these bits of paper continue in circulation – primarily because there is no longer any legal alternative in the form of a metal-based currency.

In the matter of it originally being a debt instrument, this is the reason why the definition of fiat money frequently includes a reference to it being paper money issued on the general *credit* of a nation;[21] the term *credit* was originally not a mere reference to the good reputation of the government even though that is all that remains today. For readers with a financial, economic, or accounting background, observe that banknotes in circulation are inevitably presented by central banks as liabilities on their balance sheets in a notional and residual recognition of its nature.

If money is to be a store of value, one must address real and evident contradictions and contrasts. Fiduciary money and fiat money are fundamentally different types of money. In principle, fiduciary money could not function as a medium of resource reallocation given its direct dependence upon the supply and exchange of a scarce commodity. The supply of fiduciary money is subject to a reserve requirement in gold or silver. As such, fiduciary money is a paper currency – the supply of which cannot, in principle, be manipulated by the government.[22] Accordingly, fiduciary money is a safe and secure store of value. In the case of fiduciary money, every function is consistent with the other; its function as a store of value agrees fully and without contradiction with its other functions: a medium of exchange, a unit of account, and a standard of deferred payments (and vice versa).

By contrast, in fiat money we have discovered a paper currency divorced from any reserve requirement in a scarce commodity. The supply of paper currency is no longer limited by the supply of gold or silver. The supply of money is infinitely expandable. This flexibility endows fiat money with the additional function of being a medium of resource reallocation and makes it, from a monetary perspective, the perfect policy instrument. In a way, fiat money and policy discretion together represent command economics in the most literal sense of the phrase. What we have done here is identify a *differentia* qua functions between fiat money and fiduciary money.[23] For being a medium of resource reallocation, for being amenable to manipulation by the issuer to an extent that fiduciary money is not, fiat money might as well be called policy money. Thus, we have the ingredients for understanding how money can acquire the additional function of being a medium of resource reallocation.

There is one further deduction that must be made from the contrast between fiduciary money and fiat money. Historically, gold has been the most secure and stable store of value and the ultimate refuge of purchasing power. Gold, unlike banknotes, account balances, securities, and loan contracts is a monetary asset that is *no one else's liability*. As the final refuge of purchasing power, gold allows the final and most perfect application of property rights to purchasing power. As a promissory note, fiduciary money is a formal property claim redeemable in a fixed quantity of gold. Offering banknotes to its issuer for redemption in gold is, therefore, an explicit, unqualified exercise of property rights.

By contrast, the purpose of fiat money is to preclude any assertion of property rights to purchasing power; fiat money is, by definition, legal tender. Legal tender is coin or money that may be legally offered in payment of a debt, and that a creditor must accept.[24] So an unsecured, irredeemable liability, the supply of which is infinitely expandable, is made a legally binding medium of exchange. Essentially, in the case of fiat money, this means that the law (i.e., government) forces the creditor to accept in payment of a debt a currency with a value that is, as a matter of principle and practice, subject to debasement by decree. Legal tender laws mean that the creditor – a lender or seller or worker – delivers something of real value (a loan, a product, or labour) and yet must accept as payment the nominal price in depreciable, possibly worthless, paper. Creditors are, in other words, denied property rights without due process.

Legal tender legislation was, for the briefest moment in history, ruled unconstitutional by the US Supreme Court for this very reason (*Hepburn v. Griswold* in 1870), only to be reversed under great political pressure in a subsequent ruling (*Knox v. Lee* and *Parker v. Davis* in 1871). To finance the American Civil War (1861–1865) the federal government issued paper money not redeemable in specie, which eventually depreciated substantially against gold or silver money and became a source of contention. To issue this paper currency, the US Congress passed a law specifying that it was legal tender for private debt as well, including pre-existing debt. Creditors were reluctant to accept this paper currency and, thus, a number of them contested the constitutionality of these laws. In the latter ruling, the dissenting judge, Chief Justice Salmon Chase, declared the following:[25]

> The Fifth Amendment provides that no person shall be deprived of life, liberty, or property without compensation or due process of law. ... [The operation of the legal tender clause upon pre-existing debts] ... acts directly upon the relations of debtor and creditor. It violates that fundamental principle of all just legislation that the legislature shall not take the property of A. and give it to B. It says that B., who has purchased a farm of A. for a certain price, may keep the farm without paying for it, if he will only tender certain notes, which may bear some proportion to the price, or be even worthless. It seems to us that this is a manifest violation of this clause of the Constitution.

It is no accident that fiat money is, by definition, also legal tender. It *must* be made legal tender if it is to replace superior stores of value such as gold or silver (or even foreign fiat currencies with a superior track record) as a store of value. To successfully establish the fiat money system, governments have historically had to go as far as prohibiting gold ownership in addition to declaring that fiat currencies were legal tender. Without prohibition and compulsion, fiat money, because of its inflationary tendency, stands in constant danger of displacement by any monetary commodity, which is a superior store of value. Compare how this is the case even among the various fiat currencies when one or some prove to be less inflationary than others. In places, such as Eastern Europe, Africa, and Latin America, the US dollar – or, in the past, the German mark – has frequently displaced local currencies subject to inflation as the preferred medium of exchange, even though the latter was the legal tender.

The principle of expedience

From this point forwards, let us assume that the administrator of the currency has unlimited policy discretion with respect to expanding the money supply. As a matter of principle, this is the case with most contemporary currencies. The essence of unlimited policy discretion in a fiat money system is that policymakers are constantly required to consider whether to use the currency as a medium of resource reallocation or to preserve its use as a store of value. The constant in the management of policy money is its preservation as a medium of exchange; its functions as a medium of resource reallocation and a store of value both require it. If people will not use a currency, it will not be a store of value and, consequently, it becomes useless as a medium of resource reallocation. It is in fiat money that we discover a clash of functions – namely, in its use as a store of value and in its use as a medium of resource reallocation. A cruder portrayal of this conundrum is as follows: will the policymaker decide to use the currency as an instrument to confiscate purchasing power or will he or she respect the currency as a temporary abode of it? Will the policymaker respect property rights or not? The lawful authority and power of the policymaker to make this choice puts a premium on the virtue of the administrator of the currency and, at the same time, denying any appeal to property rights and, therefore, justice.

Fiat money as a credible store of value and subsequently as a medium of exchange is entirely dependent upon the objectives, virtue, and skill of the administrator of the currency. Yet virtue and skill are personal qualities. The objectives of the administrator are based on his or her personal views and temperament. Fiat money as a credible medium of exchange is entirely dependent upon personal traits, views, competencies, and desires of the administrator – plus those of all interested parties of power and influence. Obviously, this is not a problem when the administrator is a man or woman of integrity and is knowledgeable, skilled, firm, and powerful in his or her own right. But how often is that the case? To go the extra mile in driving the argument towards its logical conclusion, a fiat money standard and policy discretion legalizes the blatant pursuit of personal interests by the administrator of the currency and all those with influence on him. If it is in the *personal* interest of the incumbent politician to print more money, so that he or she can win an election, maybe that is exactly what he or she should do. There is all the more incentive to do this because it can be done with impunity because it stems from lawful authority. The ambition, the whims, and fancies of the politician replace the impersonal, impartial, solid reality of the scarcity of precious metals. In the case of fiat money, the impartial forces of the markets have been suspended, and the ruling principle has become *expedience*. If policymakers deem it politically or personally expedient to spend more than the state can tax or borrow, they can do so by printing money.

In the final analysis, fiat money is power to the government, not to the people. Fiat money does not, in the first instance, serve the convenience of public (which is the case with fiduciary money); instead, it turns the tables on the public, serving the convenience of the issuer of the currency, which is always the government, that junta of politicians. Fiat money is not subject to the discipline of market forces. That, however, should be no source of comfort because now the single source of restraint left is the mercy of the politician in public office.

The gold standard – a panacea?

Would society benefit from a return to the gold standard? The question is, as we shall see, premature. Instead, it might be more appropriate to ask two different questions: first, would a return to the gold standard result in a diminution of predatory jurisdiction? Second, would it be wise to return to the gold standard? The answer to the first question is no, not automatically. We need to clarify one crucial point with respect to the treatment in the preceding sections of the gold standard. The explanation of the gold standard in the preceding sections is based on an implicit assumption – namely, government is effectively "totally and permanently debarred from manipulating the supply of money."[26] However, there is a problem with this assumption. Strictly speaking, the gold standard as such is a monetary system; it is not a legal mechanism for regulating the powers of government. The crucial issue to grasp is that governments have, historically, always possessed unrestricted powers for determining the type of monetary system, for regulating the monetary system, and controlling the value of money. This was true as well during the era of the gold standard. Indeed, going back in history, we see that the metallic standards were frequently manipulated through various devices, none of which could be disputed in court. One instrument for abusing the metallic standards was the debasement of the currency. This involved the dilution of the gold or silver content of the coinage, often resulting in inflation. Debasement was an age-old device used for millennia by governments to fleece the people. Relatively, it is a whole lot harder to inflate a currency based on a metallic standard than one based on paper. Nevertheless, this relative difficulty should not be confused with safety from predatory government powers.

Crucially, once fiduciary money is well established, even more sophisticated measures for debasing the currency come into existence. One way of debasing fiduciary money is by lowering the statutory rate at which banknotes could be exchanged for gold or silver. With fiduciary money, one can also lower the reserve requirement that backs the notes in circulation and impose restrictions on the convertibility of the notes into gold or silver. Obviously, the ultimate form of debasement for fiduciary money is the abolition of the reserve requirement and the prohibition of the redemption of notes into gold or silver, thereby turning the currency into fiat money. The ease with which the gold standard was abolished in the United States during the Great Depression is indicative of the reign of predatory jurisdiction in monetary systems. It took a single decree by the president and two laws by Congress to confiscate all gold in the United States and turn the US dollar into fiat money.

To answer the second question: changing a monetary system is not as easy as it sounds. A move from a fiat money system to the gold standard is not a simple change with a simple outcome – namely, secure property rights over purchasing power without broader consequences for society. If we stay with the matter of introducing the gold standard, we should take note of the fact that there are various types of gold standards. Just to provide the reader with an inkling, there is the gold specie standard, the gold bullion standard, and the gold exchange standard. We would have to judge the suitability of each of these options in view of the needs of our modern economy. Also, as we already noted, it is possible to vary the supply of fiduciary money to different levels of reserve requirements and to subject the right of the public or foreign note holders to exchange notes for gold to varying levels of constraints. A pure gold standard would refer to a 100 per cent reserve requirement and full convertibility of notes against gold for all holders of notes. Gold standards allowing reserve requirements of less than 100 per cent and/or imposing restrictions on the convertibility of notes are actually hybrid money systems in a continuum between a pure gold standard and pure fiat money. In other words, returning to the gold standard requires design choices with respect to the type of gold standard, the redemption rate, the reserve requirement, and the convertibility of the notes.

More broadly, any major change of the monetary system is a wide-ranging topic on its own. Different monetary systems operate and behave differently. A change of the monetary system of this order will reshape the economics of money and, by extension, the way economies operate. These changes are profound and revolutionary in scope. Replacing one monetary system with another would transform the fundamentals of how price levels throughout the economy – in the widest sense, including the pricing of goods, services, labour, and capital –are established. It would alter the way the currency is valued against other currencies, which is a critical factor for foreign trade. It would affect the supply of credit, which is a crucial determinant of economic growth. Not least, it would change the politics of financial regulation and monetary policy. Which avenues of regulating the financial sector and methods of conducting monetary policies are opened or closed to policymakers? A careful consideration of the implications of changing monetary systems – and, no less, how such a transformation is managed – matters because the choice of monetary systems affects the welfare of whole nations. The prospects for development and economic stability are highly dependent upon the soundness of the monetary systems in question.

There is also the historical perspective. Humanity's experience with replacing monetary systems has not been very encouraging. The adoption of the fiat money system has, on balance, been a disaster that has forced generations of people across the globe to suffer the consequences of government-induced inflation. On the other hand, the return to the gold standard following the First World War is a sorry tale of bad choices, serious policy failures, and disasters ending in its abandonment during the Great Depression. Throughout history, governments have history tampered with monetary systems precisely because its legal authority to introduce or practice one form or another of debasement and manipulation was never questioned.

The advocacy of any particular monetary system, including a return to the gold standard, requires that one supply a comprehensive and balanced case to that effect. One will need to argue the case on various levels including not only questions of jurisdiction and the protection of the rights of the people, but also economic ramifications and issues involved – and not least the historical experience and the lessons to be learned from history. This makes providing a case in favour of or against the gold standard too large a task for this book. Taken together, the issues involved with changing monetary systems, and that includes the introduction of the gold standard, are so complex as to preclude further elaboration of this topic; therefore, we must refrain from making a choice here in favour of any particular monetary system.

For the purposes of this chapter, the value of discussing the gold standard is primarily educational. This chapter is no more than a primer comparing highly simplified models of two types of monetary systems. We compared the current money system (i.e., fiat money) in its most extreme form with a metallic standard, also in its purest form, (i.e., subject to the assumption that government is completely and permanently barred from manipulating the supply of money). This enabled us to grasp and thereby expose a very important form of predatory jurisdiction. From this section, it should be clear that the crucial issue is not having to make a choice between the gold standard system and the fiat money system – rather, the issue is minimizing the scope for misgovernment.

The taming of fiat money

The alternative to the reintroduction of the gold standard is to continue the system of fiat money, but restricting policy discretion to the point where its use as a medium of resource allocation is minimized. Some critics will assert that this is currently already the case in many countries. These critics are likely to point out that a number of fiat currencies are now reasonably well managed and non-inflationary. What works for one can work for another. But what is the most important distinction of fiat currencies with low levels of inflation in contrast to those with a high rate of inflation? It is precisely the extent to which policy discretion with regards to the regulation of the money supply has been limited. In other words, government has formally or informally undertaken to limit its use of paper currency as a medium of resource reallocation. The formal undertaking is often achieved by separating the administration of monetary policy from political decision-making (i.e., the creation of the "independent" central bank). An example of this is Article 7 of the protocol on the statutes of the European Central Bank (ECB):[27]

> In accordance with Article 108 of this Treaty, when exercising the powers and carrying out the tasks and duties conferred upon them by this Treaty and this Statute, neither the ECB, nor a national central bank, nor any member of their decision-making bodies shall seek or take instructions from Community institutions or bodies, from any government of a Member State or from any other body. The Community institutions and bodies and the governments of the Member States undertake to respect this principle and not to seek to influence the members of the decision-making bodies of the ECB or of the national central banks in the performance of their tasks.

The European Union also requires candidates for EU membership to enact a prohibition of monetary financing of budget deficits and sovereign debt – an extremely sensible measure in a fiat money system. The ECB protocol specifically prohibits monetary financing in Article 21 subsection 1 on operations with public entities:

> In accordance with Article 101 of this Treaty, overdrafts or any other type of credit facility with the ECB or with the national central banks in favour of Community institutions or bodies, central governments, regional,

> local or other public authorities, other bodies governed by
> public law, or public undertakings of Member States shall
> be prohibited, as shall the purchase directly from them by
> the ECB or national central banks of debt instruments.

Furthermore, the Reserve Bank of New Zealand and the European Central Bank are, by law, required to maintain price stability, which means that they must keep annual inflation below 3 per cent.

It must be understood that such setups were the result of bitter experience and disappointment of rich countries with the uses of fiat money. The fiat money standard was adopted precisely because it was believed to be better than the gold standard. The ostensible rationale of fiat money was to enable governments to conduct monetary policy with the objective of influencing economic activity – specifically, manipulating the supply of money and credit and rates of interest.[28] This, as aforementioned (constraints notwithstanding), will always remain the credo of monetary policy for as long as a fiat money system allows it. One only has to follow the news of central banks raising or lowering the discount rates with the objective of dampening or stimulating demand to recognize the practice of this doctrine.

Nevertheless, the emphasis on price stability, especially when institutionalized by procedural constraints, means that there are now limits to central bank operations. The method of price stability policies is tight control of money-supply growth as a way of squeezing and keeping inflation out of the system. But was that not the natural benefit of the metallic standards and fiduciary money? Essentially, the aforementioned procedures curtail the use of fiat money as a medium of resource reallocation (i.e., as an instrument for confiscating purchasing power). By way of procedural constraints on the expansion of the money supply, fiat money, to a degree, now mimics the core benefit of the metallic standards. Under a metallic standard there is little or no policy discretion. Under the fiat money system, it takes consciously delineated jurisdiction to limit policy discretion. In effect, the limitation of policy discretion is a partial, if unacknowledged, vindication of the virtues of a metallic standard. The institution by any country of procedural constraints on monetary policy – or, failing that, a deep commitment on the part of the political establishment to maintain a de facto separation of politics and monetary policy – is a tremendous step forward in the evolution of political systems.

Money creation is unique in that it is the only type of economic policy power for which a heightened awareness of the evils of unlimited policy discretion has become mainstream. This has resulted in a widespread recognition of the need for institutional constraints. In this respect, the development of central bank independence shows what can be achieved when the scope of government power itself becomes the object of critical review. So prudence born of bitter experience and reforms of monetary institutions have, in quite a few countries, resulted in a diminution of predatory jurisdiction. The development of central bank independence teaches us a valuable lesson: there is nothing unwarranted about revisiting and critiquing the underlying principles of long-established governmental powers and there is a lot to be gained.

Strictly taken, the choice to continue the fiat money system need not be fatal. As mentioned earlier, the crucial issue is not making a choice between the gold standard and the fiat money system; rather, the issue is to minimize the scope for misgovernment. There is one advantage to continuing an existing system over its abolishment and the introduction of a new system: it is easier to reform a familiar system than confront the public – not least the policymakers that will have to make it work – with an unfamiliar system. In terms of the existing system, we now know its shortcomings. Knowledge of its shortcomings could be seen as an opportunity to formulate solutions. Even in the case of the fiat money system, it is possible to formulate and implement effective measures to minimize the scope for misgovernment.

The fundamental step would be to separate fiscal policy and monetary policy. No less important, the organization, operation, and governance of central banks and the tenure and remuneration of its staff should be structured in such a way so as to achieve genuine central bank independence. The first task of central banks should be to protect purchasing power. The monetary financing of budget deficits and sovereign debt should be prohibited. Central banks should be relieved of all tasks unrelated to the protection of purchasing power that could well be executed by other institutions. Tasks unrelated to protecting purchasing power but inherent to the function of a central bank should also be reviewed and subjected to clear mandates so as to minimize the impact of these operations on the task of protecting purchasing power. If, on account of circumstances (namely, financial crises), the expansion of the money supply beyond the needs of a growing economy for a commensurate supply of money cannot be avoided, the monetary institution should be required to make public its policies for mitigating or easing the consequences of such action on the value of the currency in terms of purchasing power. To make it more difficult for politicians to reverse the independence of central banks, all the measures enumerated earlier should be laid down in constitutional law. Violations of the laws that govern the central bank and its relations with other branches of government should be subject to judicial review and impeachment procedures. The main purpose of judicial review and impeachment procedures is to dissuade policymakers at central banks from moving beyond their mandates and to deter the executive and legislative branches from usurping central bank powers.

Fiat money and democratic accountability

Finally, limiting the power of the state to tax the people by inflating the currency is not only a matter of safeguarding property rights, but also a matter of increasing the accountability of policymakers to the citizenry. The bottom line is that, under a fiat money system, the power to create money is a power to tax. A proper democratic process would require that citizens be notified in advance and in explicit terms of the amount for which his or her income will be taxed. Printing money undermines this process. First of all, the public has only the most limited understanding of government finances. The one part of the fiscal system that the public understands best is taxation – at least to the extent that those taxes visibly impacts its spending power. Taxation by printing money is not a transparent process, and it was never intended to be a transparent process. The whole point of monetary financing is the desire of the policymaker to avoid revealing explicitly to the taxpayer the cost of public spending. Insofar as government is allowed to enjoy unlimited power to create money, its accountability to the citizenry – especially the taxpayers – is decreased. Granting a policymaker, the authority to print money without restraint is to grant him or her power and authority for the exercise of which he will not be called to account or held responsible. This is unacceptable in a democratic society; the government and all its officers should be accountable for all their actions. The budgetary process, including the process of taxation, should be transparent. The struggle against predatory jurisdiction is, in large part, also a blow for democratic accountability.

Summary

In this chapter, we addressed one specific symptom of misgovernment: government-induced inflation. We found that this requires a specific type of monetary system using fiat money and allowing policy discretion. In the process, we identified an alternative type of monetary system, the gold standard, which cannot be used quite as easily as policy money. To be sure, the objective is not to advocate for a return to the gold standard; rather, it is to use it as a model for examining the current system in order to promote a full appreciation the dangers inherent to the fiat money system.

When one knows no alternatives to the system one lives in, it becomes extremely difficult to imagine any solution to the problems it poses. Every solution starts with a proper understanding of the nature of the problem. In human affairs, such understanding is frequently achieved easily by referring back to historical experience. The comparison with a fiduciary money system deepens our grasp of how the present fiat money standard operates. A system that is inherently flawed but accepted by its victim as inescapable or irreplaceable renders him or her impotent and forces him or her to resign himself or herself to the inevitable. But think of what that means in this instance. Its significance in the case of the fiat money standard is that the victim must resign himself or herself to abuses that, but for a deeper understanding, are avoidable.

We established that the fiat money system is naturally hazardous precisely because it is *the* prerequisite system for unlimited policy discretion. Metallic standards, by their very nature, limit the scope of policymaking; with a fiat money system, one must consciously determine and delineate the scope of jurisdiction. The two cardinal sins with regards to the institution of a fiat money system are to place a currency under direct political control and to grant unlimited discretionary power to the executive branch of government to expand or contract the supply of money. This is, at present, the case with most currencies. In many countries, the final authority with respect to printing money remains the executive branch with the Ministry of Finance as its formal locus. In the context of a fiat money system, this is the central evil. A society that wishes to escape from the ever-present danger of gross misgovernment of the monetary system must face up to the problem of predatory jurisdiction.

Chapter 8

Public Debt

We must not let our rulers load us with perpetual debt. We must make our election between economy and liberty, or profusion and servitude.

—Thomas Jefferson

With the exception of war, few events hold the potential of being so destructive to a modern economy as a debt crisis. The economic depression following the Argentinean debt crisis of 2001–2002 provides a case in point … possibly the worst ever. Argentina's descent into poverty – a nation that has always been ranked as the richest country in Latin America – has been unparalleled in peacetime history. By the middle of 2003, poverty rates had increased to the point where almost 60 per cent of the population faced severe hardship (up from one third at the start of the crisis in December of 2001). In a country that has always been one of the world's premier beef exporters, nearly a quarter of the population could no longer buy enough food to satisfy even minimum protein requirements.

The avoidance of crisis and malaise resulting from default and inflation following the monetization of the debt is as much a benefit to society as any measure for stimulating growth. The relevance of this becomes evident when we consider that a financial crisis usually results in a catastrophic contraction of the economy. The crisis following the debt default of 2001 caused Argentina's economy to shrink in GDP terms by 20 per cent. This shrinkage caused an increase in the number of poor people in Argentina by almost 100 per cent. Also, this is not Argentina's first debt crisis. Argentina already had a debt problem during the 1980s, which also mutated into hyperinflation trouble. By the end of that decade, the average per capita income was approximately 15 per cent lower than it had been 10 years earlier. Every crisis wipes out years of gains in economic growth. Also, growth and increased prosperity preceding or following crisis cannot undo the misery of the people during it. Even after debts have been restructured and the crisis resolved, investor confidence takes years to recover which means more lost growth.

One way of giving expression to the awfulness of crisis is to imagine what an economy shrinking by 20 per cent means. Think of this decrease as the average loss of income of 20 per cent for each household in Argentina. The reality is that the greater majority of households earn such modest wages that a decrease of 20 per cent represents a fatal blow to the well-being of many a family. For many households, it is the difference between being able to pay for both the rent *and* food and having to make the Hobson's choice of paying the rent *or* buying the food. In actuality, though, shrinkage of the economy by 20 per cent is never evenly distributed among the nation's households. For example, a major portion of it represents the hundreds of thousands of wage earners who have lost their jobs and have, in truth, suffered a 100 per cent loss of income. The destruction of one's livelihood in the middle of a full-blown crisis is probably one of the worst experiences that can befall a family. It is the kind of misery so hauntingly described by John Steinbeck in *The Grapes of Wrath*, a Great Depression-era novel about the migration of a dispossessed family from the Oklahoma Dust Bowl to California and their pitiful efforts at survival accompanied by shocking humiliation.

Argentina's plight is not unique. It should be understood that debt trouble is a widespread problem in the developing world. From the 1980s up to now, every Latin American country, with the exception of Colombia, has been touched by the problem. The 1980s has also been called Latin America's lost decade. Many Eastern European countries (notably, Poland during the 1980s and Russia in 1998) encountered similar difficulties. At the time, Argentina's troubles received the greatest coverage in the news, but Turkey went through a debt crisis of scarcely less harrowing proportions.

In the first chapter, we noted that the general public does not make a mental connection between economic disaster and the scope of discretionary power possessed by the state. What rights are at stake when the government has the authority to borrow money at will? This is the question to be asked by the citizens in nations that default on their debts. Yet, in the streets of Buenos Aires, the only sound was the noise of banging on pots and pans. In desperate times, ignorance finds expression in absurdity. The power of the state to borrow money at will is the germ of debt default. Though this type of awareness is alien to our sense of life, we must learn to trace the disaster of government default to lawful authority. It is high time that we examine the anatomy of this form of predatory jurisdiction. For a proper perspective, let us first address the issue of rights and its relevance to the general public.

Property rights

Ultimately, the issue of borrowing always revolves around the question of whether there is or will be a final settlement or repayment of the debt position. The essence of a loan contract is that lenders agree to advance money and borrowers agree to take money on the condition of repayment at some future date. Essentially, borrowers receive the property of lenders (i.e., *purchasing power*) on loan. In the case of government, this purchasing power is used to fund public expenditures. The condition of repayment presupposes an understanding made formal and explicit in which the lender expects to receive his property back and the borrower, the government in this instance, commits to honouring this expectation. From the perspective of the lender, the contract is a claim to property. From the perspective of the borrower, the contract represents an acknowledgement of this claim. The point of a loan agreement is that the lender and borrower agreed that the lender never ceded his claim to property or surrendered his property rights. Properly understood, non-payment – barring the condition of force majeure – would be a breach of contract resulting in a deprivation or taking of property.[1] The taking of property without due process is a violation of property rights. Therefore, non-payment of debt – again, assuming there is no case of force majeure – is, as a matter of principle, a violation of property rights. Repayment of government debt is a return of property and the obligation to repay is fundamental to the preservation of property rights.

The same line of reasoning applies in the case in which the value of the receivables is diminished through government-induced inflation. For ease of reading, the concepts of *non-payment* and *default* in this chapter will also include the use by government of monetary inflation as an instrument of diminishing the value of government debt.

In the context of this line of reasoning, there is also the obligation of good government. The obligation of good government essentially means that the public and all parties transacting with the state – and that includes creditors and foreigners – may expect a government to adhere to a standard of virtue or conduct that results in the preservation of their rights and lawful interests. Honesty, integrity, prudence, and competence are virtues required for the management of government finances in order to preserve the state's ability to repay its debts. One of the fundamentals of borrowing is that there must be an honest intention to repay. If property rights and the obligation of good government are to have any meaning at all, this principle must also apply to public borrowing.

Thus, we have, in terms of repayment of debt, formulated a theory of moral obligation and good government. When we tune into past and current debates about debt crises, however, we face a challenge to this theory: the requirement of repayment of debt in the case of highly indebted countries is portrayed as the causation of evil. The burden of debt service of these countries is frequently blamed for causing undue hardship on the population of these highly indebted countries. The charge of debt relief advocates is that current debt service requirements are so heavy that highly indebted countries are, in essence, required to pay their debts through reduced consumption and austerity or achieve adjustment through contraction. It is the obligation to repay that forces these countries to impose austerity measures that require a contraction of valued public services such as public education, healthcare, and maintenance of infrastructure. In other words, servicing high levels of public debt causes hardship and deprivation among citizens of highly indebted countries. From this point of view, the obligation of repayment is seen as injurious to the public interest.

The debt problem is often also portrayed as a clash between an embattled government representing the public interest on one hand and a creditor club consisting of commercial and multilateral banks, the selfish interest, on the other hand. Additionally, from listening to the government debt debate and the news, one gets the impression that the problem is entirely an *external* debt problem. Put another way, it is the requirement to repay foreign debt in full to a small group of foreign capitalist institutions that is the problem. The thrust of this line of reasoning is that property rights in the question of government borrowing mainly serve the interests of a relatively small group of foreign creditors. The interests of these creditors and foreigners and that of the public of those indebted countries are portrayed as being opposed and irreconcilable. In an appeal to altruist sentiment the needs of the public are advanced as taking precedence over the interests and rights of the creditors. In the context of the sovereign debt problem, the relevance of property rights to the public might therefore seem more notional than real. How must we reconcile principles such as moral obligation and good government with the charge that repayment of debt causes injury to the peoples of highly indebted countries?

There is no need to dispute the fact that, beyond a certain point, the burden of debt service can and will destroy a nation. Undoubtedly, in a number of cases, reality will require all parties to acknowledge that losses to creditors are inevitable and that debt relief or forgiveness is the only realistic course of action. This is the element in this debate that deserves recognition. Having said that, the aforementioned line of argumentation represents a fundamentally flawed understanding and biased view of the nature of a debt crisis. By making the evils of repayment the key issue, this type of discourse obscures a fundamental concern – namely, the role and nature of governments that overborrow. The failure to address this fundamental issue stands in the way of our ability to develop a deep understanding and moral view of the nature of governments that are unconstrained in their power to borrow.

What governs us?

The aforementioned proposition – that the evils of repayment as a key issue deflect attention away from the role and nature of governments that overborrow – should not be taken as a suggestion that the debt-relief movement is indifferent to the question of the causes of the debt problem. There is, in fact, an important stream within the debt-relief movement that is strongly animated by the question of responsibility. Only the primary target of their opprobrium is not the borrower ... it is the lender. This current within the debt-relief movement relentlessly promotes a version of history where the blame for the debt problem rests primarily with irresponsible lending by creditors. This line of attack shifts the onus of resolving the debt problem onto the lender rather than on the sovereign borrower.

For achieving this switch, debt relief advocates turn to standard business philosophy: the competency for managing credit risk is turned into ammunition against the lender. It is frequently argued that creditors – most of which are professional parties or institutional investors – do not require protection. Presumably, these professionals should have the skills necessary for appraising risk and managing it and, therefore, they should bear the consequences of their investment decisions. It is indeed the duty of each and every investor or creditor to satisfy his or her own mind on the quality of the credit of the counterparty (in regards to a nation's finances *and* the legal and political risks). Creditors, of course, know that, by lending out money, they bring upon themselves a default risk and, consequently, they include a risk premium into the interest charged to the borrower. This is why interest rates on loans to developing countries are so much higher than those on rich country debt: the default risk of the former is considered greater than that of the latter. Furthermore, creditors can diversify their investment portfolios to manage risk and yield. Thus, the risk premium already compensates the investor for default risk and the option of portfolio diversification allows him or her to limit his or her exposure. In many cases, when lenders or investors incurred excessive losses, they could have avoided them by doing a bit more research and by showing a bit more respect for standard risk-management practices.

In support of the line that holders of sovereign debt deserve no protection, advocates of default and debt forgiveness often refer to the Palmerston Doctrine on sovereign default by quoting from a 1934 speech by the British Foreign Secretary, Sir John Simon: "My predecessor Lord Palmerston, who is not generally regarded as having been backward in the defense of British interests, laid down the doctrine that if investors choose to buy the bonds of a foreign country carrying a high rate of interest in preference to British Government Bonds carrying a low rate of interest, they cannot claim that the British government is bound to intervene in the event of default."[2]

Strictly from a business perspective, this line of reasoning is perfectly credible and valid. In making credit decisions, lenders take risks and should live with the consequences of bad decisions. We shall call this the *argument from creditor competency*. Coming from politicians and debt relief advocates, however, this line of argumentation should be suspect. Valuable as this argument may be as an admonishment directed at bankers and investors, the argument from creditor competency does not address the true and vital concerns of *society*. The primary interest of society is good and honest government. The argument from creditor competency distracts our attention from the fact that the central character and principal villain in this play is the government (as the borrower) and not the creditor. The central issue is not whether the creditor should be made to face the consequences of lousy investment decisions, but rather what the citizens must make of governments that overborrow. To the well-being of public, it is not the virtue of the creditor that matters; rather, it is that of the government. What makes government the protagonist and villain is its high mission as a system of rule for the benefit and protection of society and its members. By overborrowing the government did not act in the best interests of society – quite the contrary. Coming to terms with why we are so ill served by our rulers is more important than raging on about creditors. For our own good, it should not be our wish to be governed by policymakers who see no wrong in overborrowing and who care so little about the consequences. Rulers, governments, and policymakers that overborrow are immoral – and not because there is some divine rule against overborrowing, but because their actions, in the long run, cause the lives of their subjects to be devastated by onerous debt-service requirements, financial crisis, and economic collapse.

Governments that first borrow too much and then default or resort to monetizing the debt are the true enemy of the people and not some dastardly group of conspiring foreigners and bankers. By defaulting or monetizing the debt, it robs people – both locally and abroad – of their savings and earnings. By borrowing too much and thereby creating onerous debt-service requirements, it jeopardizes the funding of valued public services such as education, and healthcare. A government that is prudent in its administration of its finances and one that repays its debts is a moral government. It is considerate of the interests of all. A government that is extravagant and borrows too much is considerate of the interests and rights of nobody. Any argument that portrays the interests of foreigners and bankers and those of the working-class and poor as being opposed is at best mistaken and at worst deceitful. Such an argument scapegoats foreigners and bankers for the consequences of misgovernment. If we are to protect the people from crisis and preserve their savings and earning power, we must come to terms with the need to protect property rights. We must accept property rights as a proper moral claim of universal application. In the question of government borrowing, property rights in the form of the right to receive payment are the standard of justice.

The argument from creditor competency is made by sour, rabble-rousing debtor-country politicians or anti-capitalist and anti-globalist advocates of default and debt forgiveness. The argument is propagandistic: its function is to deflect attention from the requirement to hold the real offenders (i.e., profligate debtor-country governments and their ruling elites) accountable, to sap the resolve of the creditors and creditor-country governments, and to turn the public opinion against them. The argument from creditor competency is, in a narrow sense, tightly reasoned and easily understood. This is precisely why it is such a compelling argument and effective propaganda tool for shifting the burden of the resolution of the debt problem from the debtor to the creditor. Its aim is to make us neglect the wider context of the problem and to distract us from the need to evaluate the nature of the state that governs us and hold it to the highest standards of virtue or conduct. The argument from creditor competency is disinformation by means of which we are incited to direct our attention to (and waste our anger on) the lesser, private evil: creditor incompetence (i.e., away from the greater, public evil: profligate, dishonest government). So even if we found these creditors to be fully deserving of their misfortune, would that really release governments from their obligations to act prudently and in good faith? What about the fundamental presumption underlying all borrowing and lending – namely, the honest intention of the borrower to repay? Are its wider implications – those involving citizens subjected to a dishonest and inept government – of no account? Should we be so easily distracted from taking a long and hard look at the moral nature of a state that borrows too much? We must not let their publicists waylay us with clever and facile arguments.

Private savings, public loot

Narrowing down our view of the debt problem to the doings of a mere handful of immediate creditors obscures the wider role of these creditors as intermediaries between the sovereign debtor and the public, local and foreign. Sovereign lenders are, by and large, financial institutions that take money from the public (i.e., the ordinary people like you and me) as savers and depositors, life insurance and pension policyholders, investors, etc. Very few ordinary people are conscious of the extent to which they or their equals abroad are participants in the financial markets and how that embroils them in the government debt issue. The extent of their stake in the financial markets becomes clear when we call to mind that the general public, local or foreign, has savings deposited in the banking system.[3] Savings represent a claim to property, the property being purchasing power. The saver/citizen should pause to wonder what banks – and depending upon the sophistication of the local financial systems, institutional investors such as pension funds, investment companies, and insurers – do with their money.[4] Savings are the source of funding, the raw material, used by these financial institutions to provide loans to the private and public sectors or to make investments in debt paper issued by the same sectors. When governments borrow, financial institutions are, in effect, paying out part of the savings of their clients to the government in return for a claim on future tax revenues. If future tax revenues prove insufficient to repay public debt obligations, governments will either default or start printing money. Foreign and domestic creditors are not merely putting their own capital at risk. Arguments to that effect obscure the wider role of these creditors as intermediaries between the sovereign debtor and the rest of the financial and economic system. When governments default, financial institutions might find themselves deprived of the funds necessary for returning to their clients the full value of their savings or investments. If that is the case, these institutions will eventually default on their obligations to savers, depositors, pensioners, and policyholders. This is what happened during the Russian domestic debt default of 1998. Treasury bills were an important source of investments to banks in Russia. When, on 17 August, 1998, the Kiryenko government and the central bank announced a temporary suspension of the redemption of treasury bills, many banks failed and millions of people lost their savings.

Alternatively, when governments resort to the money presses, bankers will receive payments in debased currencies and pay out this debased money to savers. Actually, governments are more likely to resort to the money presses than outright default for the simple reason that the former is easier and less messy than the latter. It is probably safe to assume that most of us will neither be so poor nor so rich as to be in the position to escape the consequences of the destruction of our financial assets should our government feel the need to rid itself of its debts or to pursue monetary finance as an alternative source of funding for its expenditures. In both instances, savers suffer a deprivation of property in the form of a loss of purchasing power. Either way, the banking system is the conveyor belt on which the purchasing power of the saver is transmitted to the borrower and when the public sector happens to be the main borrower – which it frequently is in the developing world – it is also the conduit through which government debt problems reach the public. It is not for nothing that the European Central Bank is prohibited from monetary financing. This prohibition is in recognition of the fact that, because the greater part of debt in European countries is denominated in euros, monetization is an efficient way for governments to rid themselves of their debts. The lesson of the first instance of debt crisis during the twentieth century – namely, that of Germany after the imposition of war reparations following World War I – was that its remedy, the monetization of debt, destroyed the financial assets of the middle classes. Hyperinflation following monetization of the debt permanently destroyed the earnings and capital of millions of pensioners and rentiers. The hyperinflationary experience of Latin America during the 1980s was essentially the result of having exhausted both foreign credit lines as well as domestic borrowing capacity.

Another way of clarifying the problem of government borrowing to the public is to look at banking sector statistics. Financial systems are invariably sizeable in proportion to the total economy. Even Latin America's weak financial system holds financial assets equivalent to about 90 per cent of its GDP. Combined bank funding, 80–90 per cent of it, consists mostly of the savings and deposits by the public; only a minor portion of bank funding consists of shareholders' equity. These figures indicate how much the public stands to lose in terms of property claims against the financial system. The collective savings of the public are usually the largest source of financial capital. Strictly in terms of the size of their share in a nation's basic stock of financial capital, this makes the collective body of savers – not the shareholders of banking institutions – the largest stakeholders in public debt policy. To the general public property rights contained in public debt is a serious, practical concern rather than a hypothetical issue. Because governments are *always* the biggest borrowers, every saver has a real (albeit usually indirect) interest in the performance and quality of the government as a borrower. For an easy demonstration of the degree to which savers are exposed to government borrowing, let us take the example of Brazil. Brazilian government is a bigger borrower with the domestic banking system than the entire private sector combined. Brazil's largest bank, Banco do Brasil, held at least 46 per cent of its reported assets for the reporting period that ended on 30 June, 2002, in government paper against 26 per cent for private-sector lending and leasing. The figures for lending to government versus private sector by another sizable bank,

Banespa, were respectively 39 and 21 per cent of total assets (year end of 2001). This demonstrates the degree to which Brazil's savers are exposed to government performance with respect to debt commitments. These figures are not at all uncommon in the developing world.[5]

Default on external debt is frequently advocated as preferable to the hardships of austerity programmes. It is almost as if the advocates of default strategies believe that targeting external debt isolates the consequences of default to foreign parties; the line of reasoning is that, by not paying its foreign debts, the government banishes its fiscal problems abroad. The connection between external debt trouble and domestic economic crisis is more difficult to make than in the case of domestic debt. It is nonetheless there, though, varying in its manifestations from situation to situation. Nevertheless, it is possible to discern one link: the reason for overborrowing started with chronic and structural overspending. It does not follow that, when a government can no longer borrow abroad, it will cease overspending. The public expenditure for political reasons is not easily adjusted downward to match decreased funding; trying this remedy is liable to hurt and enrage crucial constituencies dependent upon government largesse. It follows that, when it can no longer acquire funds abroad, it will shift its attention to looting a captive public. This captive public consists of the domestic savers and investors within the domestic financial system; these are the people who cannot escape the jurisdiction of the state. Therefore, when citizens sense that the government might default on its external debts, they frequently start wondering, often with past experience in mind, about the safety of their domestic financial assets. And why shouldn't they? We may not be used to thinking in such terms, but there is no reason for believing that a government that violates the trust of foreigners should be relied upon to behave with greater consideration towards its own subjects. In that respect, the crisis in Argentina in 2001 is illustrative. When the Argentinean government found that it could no longer sell its bonds to foreign investors, it "strong-armed local pension funds into buying government paper and local banks into swapping their holdings of government bonds in return for low-interest loans."[6] Basically, an overextended government cannot force foreigners to lend, but on the local scene, it has defenceless victims. By force-feeding the local pension funds and banks government paper, the Argentinean government expropriated good money in return for a claim on an overextended government. The

214

public was frightened when it perceived this, questioned the soundness of the banking system, and started a run on the banks.[7] When, as a countermeasure, the government imposed the *corralito* – a ceiling of USD 1,000 on bank withdrawals – the banking run turned into a full-fledged financial crisis. The destruction wrought on Argentina's private pension system by this government-induced crisis is summed up in the following anecdote related by The Wall Street Journal:[8]

> Perla Crivolitti, an executive secretary who is also 41, is convinced she will never see any of the money she has been socking away in a private retirement account since Argentina began allowing the funds in 1994. Her last financial statement showed her account was valued at about $2,200, down from $15,000 before Argentina spun into government debt default and currency devaluation in December. "My savings of many years have been converted into nothing," she says angrily.

The issue of property rights in the face of debt default goes further than just the destruction of the savings of the public, whether local or foreign. Debt defaults, both external and domestic, are invariably accompanied by economic collapse in the debtor country. Consider the fact that, as a consequence of large defaults, banks suffer a loss of liquidity and solvency, which causes them to suspend payments and to contract the supply of credit. The sudden credit crunch and seizure of the payments system following default is, as a rule, followed by a massive wave of bankruptcies – mainly of small- and medium-sized businesses. When the Russian government suspended the redemption of treasury bills in 1998, banks suspended payments to their clients: other banks, small- and medium-sized firms, and individual investors. The paralysis of the Russian banking system deprived thousands of small- and medium-sized businesses access to funds, rendering them insolvent – and, as a result, dramatically increased unemployment. Yet is a business not a property? The failure of businesses represents the destruction of property.

Many people care not a whit about the property rights of business owners. On the other hand, many of these same people are fanatically vigilant when it comes to the interests of the working class. Yet economic collapse – which is properly understood as nothing less than the mass destruction of business – is invariably followed by mass unemployment. A generalized destruction of property goes hand in hand with the destruction of employment. There is no point whatsoever in ignoring the interests of the financial and business communities. As with economic regulation, so with government borrowing: at the most basic level, the interests of the banker, the business person, and the working-class citizen – both as saver and as worker – correspond; there is no fundamental dichotomy or conflict of interests. As in the case of economic regulation, the problem of fiscal crisis cannot be neatly broken down along the capitalist, working-class division. The value of this approach is zero. Even in the matter of government finance, the primary concern of the working-class people, the issue of employment, leads us right back to the relevance of property rights. Violate property rights, destroy employment.

The purpose of public borrowing

Governments borrow to fund budget deficits. As a matter of fact, another name for public borrowing is deficit financing. Government borrowing has one function only, and that is to enable governments to finance spending commitments that exceed tax collection proceeds – basically, there is no other purpose to borrowing. Deficit financing is, by definition, a closing entry in public finance. Borrowing authority is a substitute for and a complement to the power of taxation. Without the power to borrow, governments would have to match all public expenditures with tax collections.[9] In contrast, the power to borrow allows the state to dispense with the year–on–year application of this procedure. Critically, once expenditures are no longer limited by the ability to collect taxes, the next limit to spending is the capacity to raise loans.[10]

Lest we forget: borrowing does not happen by chance; it is in every step of its making a deliberate and conscious act of state. It requires conscious decision-making by the government. First of all, it requires drafting and approving a budget in which expenditures exceed revenues collected. Next, it requires soliciting lenders. It requires an administrative machine for making it happen: the amount to be borrowed has to be specified by someone, and debt paper and prospectuses have to be drafted, printed, and issued, and that is human work. Just as in the case of monetary financing, there is a long paper trail attesting to the active involvement of, for example, ministers, bureaucrats, lenders, lawyers, and accountants, and this paper trail is made to comply with legal and administrative requirements that attest to the state's lawful authority to borrow.

Borrowing not only expands the capacity of the state to spend, but it also lifts the problem of managing the public finances to a higher level of complexity by introducing issues that do not exist when budgets must be balanced. In the case of balanced budgets, it is sufficient to match outlays with revenues. When government budgets do not have to be balanced, the policymaker has the additional tasks of managing the size of the budget deficit and the resultant borrowing requirement as well as servicing the public debt. This is, in the first instance, a question of virtue and skill. Prudent policymakers tax, spend, and borrow no more than society can or will bear. As with monetary policy managing, government finance is an administrative responsibility, the rules and the know-how of which have been worked out in the finest detail by economists and public administrators. It is, as much as monetary economics, a special and recognized field of study that is also called public finance. One might hope that the existence of these sciences would contribute to progress in politics. It is, however, our bad fortune that, even in the third millennium, we must still suffer policymakers who act contrary to the fundamentals of – and often sneer openly at – the sciences of economics and public finance. Such people and all their supporters deserve nothing less than our deepest contempt.

To say that managing government finance is a question of virtue and skill leads us to one explanation of the sovereign debt problem: bad politics. Indeed, fiscal policy choices are ultimately political choices. It is politicians who make spending commitments and decide taxes. All too often it is not the interest of the nation that takes precedence; rather, personal and electoral objectives (and sometimes simple stupidity) shape their decisions. Observe, for example, that deficits are frequently higher during election years. Nevertheless, such decisions – no matter how self-serving or stupid – are still covered by lawful authority. The policy and bad politics angles of the public finance problems have always been dealt with exhaustively; there is a tremendous wealth of excellent literature on every aspect of these subjects. Yet the picture will never be complete as long as we ignore the institutional or constitutional framework within which policies and politics take place.

Borrower unlimited

In hardly one country on the planet will you find tried and tested (and, therefore, unambiguously effective) restraints of any kind with respect to borrowing authority – constitutional, legislative, or judicial. Borrowing authority, as a matter of practice, coincides with the absence of a balanced budget requirement, in which case we have reason to concern ourselves with the regulation of budget deficits and deficit financing. Usually, however, there are no effective limits on the level of budget deficits and deficit financing. At the same time, there are no enforceable limits on total borrowing. There are no procedures regulating the burden of debt. Whether, how, and when a country must arrange for the conclusive settlement of the total debt position is a matter that is entirely unregulated. This, then, is the constitutional framework with respect to the scope of public borrowing authority: a classic picture of prerogative and unlimited power. The authority of the state to borrow has been with us for thousands of years. This heritage and the absence throughout history of constitutional restraints form the foundation of an unquestioned prerogative of the state to borrow at will.

The aforementioned line of arguments is borne out by the evidence of past attempts at deficit control legislation in some countries. One such attempt was the Gramm-Rudman-Hollings Act of 1985 (GRH) in the United States and its various revisions. The European Union also has such legislation in the form of pacts such as the Protocol on the Excessive Deficit Procedure of 1992 (Protocol) and The Stability and Growth Pact of 1997 (SGP). The GRH set absolute target levels with respect to budget deficits and the ultimate objective was a balanced budget. The Protocol and the SGP specified targets for its member states with respect to the proportions of the budget deficit and the national debt to the Gross National Product – at a maximum of 3 per cent in the first case and 60 per cent in the latter – with the SGP also stipulating fines for wayward members. It should be emphasized, however, that we are discussing *effective* controls on budget deficits and borrowing. Neither the GRH nor the Protocol or the SGP can be considered effective controls.

The GRH was unenforceable because it did not diminish the budgeting or borrowing powers of the administration and Congress in any way. Indeed, in accordance with its true powers, the administration and US Congress simply continued to draft, submit, and approve budgets including deficits violating targets set by GRH. For example, in spite of a target level set by the GRH at USD 100 billion, the budget deficit for 1990 hit USD 221 billion.

In a different manner, the Protocol and SGP do not appear to be effective either. The decision to impose sanctions under the SGP is a *political choice* requiring a majority vote among member states. Also, the Protocol and SGP are not law in the common sense of the word. Instead, these are treaties between sovereign nations, and there has never been a treaty that cannot be rendered inoperative by a simple declaration to that effect by the heads of state of countries party to the treaty. Correspondingly, by 2003 the government of France publicly stated that it had no intention of reducing its budget deficits in accordance with the rules of the Protocol and SGP. To quote *The Economist*:[11]

Mr. Raffarin stated that France would breach the 3 % budget-deficit limit imposed by the European Union's stability pact; France may go to 4 % in 2003, making it the worst offender in the euro zone. It could well stay in breach, added his budget minister, Alain Lambert, until 2006. The casual abandon with which Mr. Raffarin is flouting the rules is infuriating the commission. ... "My duty", the prime minister blithely told TF1, a television station, "is not to solve mathematical problems to please a particular office or country."

France, in effect, dared the other member states to impose sanctions – a challenge other member states shrunk from. Indeed, in November of 2003, France and Germany managed to persuade the council of ministers to reject the European Council's recommendation of sanctions against the pair for violating the 3 per cent maximum on budget deficits, and instead to put the entire pact into abeyance.[12] The ruling on 13 July, 2004, by the European Court of Justice that the council of ministers had exceeded its powers might be construed as a major step towards effective controls. In fact, it is nothing of the kind. To quote *The Economist*:[13]

The judgment, which had been sought by the commission, was hailed as a victory for Brussels over national governments. But that interpretation merits closer scrutiny. It has long been a truism of European politics that, when the commission gets into a fight with national governments, it is the commission that comes off worse. And, although the judges annulled the decision to put the pact in abeyance, they also said that the council's failure to adopt the commission's recommendations was not something they either could or should overrule. Thus the court's decision is unlikely actually to change French or German fiscal policy; it will remain possible for the council to ignore any new recommendations for sanctions that the commission may make.

The anatomy of debt

For a full understanding of the problem with unregulated borrowing authority, it helps to examine debt in terms of its manifestations. Earlier in this chapter, we observed that one of the fundamentals of borrowing is an honest intention to repay, a principle that also applies to public borrowing. For a full grasp of the trouble with the requirement of repayment, one must appreciate that debt exists on two levels: the contract or formal agreement on one level and the overall debt position on the other.

A contract represents one specific liability position with a set of one or more pre-specified counterparties. It also represents a formal statement of the rules of engagement – the terms and conditions – agreed upon by the parties to the contract. From the perspective of the contract, the view on the requirement of repayment is crystal clear. A contract is extinguished as soon as repayment conditions are met.

On the other hand, the overall debt position represents the sum total of all contracts outstanding at some point in time. Of the concept of the overall debt position, one should grasp that its existence does not necessarily depend upon any single contract or even the current group of contracts of which it is the sum. The settlement of one or more contracts does not necessarily signify an actual reduction or disappearance of the overall debt position; compliance with contractual obligations is not at all the same as servicing the overall debt position. The reason for this is that financial markets do not automatically require an *actual* reduction of the overall debt position; rather, they primarily require the proper settlement of contractual obligations. The option of refinancing serves to illustrate the problem: so long as lenders can be found with confidence in the credit of the state, governments can and do, as a matter of expedience, refinance their total debt by repaying expiring contracts with the proceeds from fresh borrowings. From the perspective of any given contract it does not matter whether a contract is repaid from tax revenues or from the cash proceeds of new loans. This enables government to apply the proceeds of its new borrowings marginally to fund the settlement of old contracts. This is why public debts seem everlasting.

Is it sensible to make such a fine distinction between contract and overall debt position? After all, the overall debt position exists only by grace of current contracts. Yet when examining the question of jurisdiction, it is. The abstraction of the concept of the overall debt position from its source (i.e., the underlying contracts) is clearly a fiction. Yet fictions sometimes aid in clarifying problems. Observe that though governments default *on* contractual obligations, they default *because of* the overall debt position. Paradoxically, lenders and borrowers take infinite care to negotiate and settle the details of their contracts. Yet the overall debt position of a state and its final settlement are usually not governed by any agreement between parties. Checks and balances internal to government do not specifically address the problem.[14] Properly understood, governments assume the overall debt position almost unilaterally and entirely as a matter of political discretion without any formal and binding obligation regarding its level or its settlement. Making a distinction between contract and overall debt position reveals the trouble with the requirement of repayment. With contracts, there is a clear and acknowledged requirement of repayment; with overall debt positions, such a requirement does not exist. The implications and consequences of the failure to institute a formal regulatory framework imposing clear obligations regarding the overall debt position and its settlement are truly pernicious. Let us outline some of these.

Financial markets are not very efficient when it comes to imposing restraints on public borrowing. The capacity to raise loans is a direct function of the confidence of the investor in the credit of the state. Unfortunately, the confidence of investors is not necessarily based on a rational appreciation of a government's capability to service debt.[15] Were all creditors fully rational and competent, irresponsible governments would scarcely get the opportunity to run up disastrously large debt positions. Thus, the failure to regulate the level of total public borrowing represents an opportunity for spendthrift policymakers to exploit irrational expectations and flawed assumptions on the part of lenders.

Also, creditors cannot, in advance and in a timely fashion, singly or collectively limit or restrain governments from borrowing more in order to secure their capability of servicing the existing debt stock; in short, one creditor cannot be obligated to restrain his or her lending to anyone because it serves the interest of other creditors. There is no naturally occurring market mechanism for managing or optimizing the size of the public debt for the collective benefit of creditors. Therefore, when policymakers and their creditors do not demonstrate good sense and restraint, the natural limit to borrowing usually corresponds to the imminence of a debt default. The *market failure* argument is frequently made to justify economic intervention. Yet here is one instance of market failure: the inefficiency of the financial market to deal with the level of governmental borrowing and the risks involved – that has gone unnoticed despite its monstrous impact.

In a context in which the government continually refinances its debts, the compliance with contractual obligations creates the impression that this government is respectful of its promise to repay its debts. However, this impression could well be false. It could be the case that this government has reached a point where it is merely trying to arrange a game of musical chairs in which the risk of default is continually shifted from one combination of lenders to another through the process of using the proceeds of refinancing to top up the shortfall in tax revenues and thus create an illusion of honesty and trustworthiness through formal compliance with maturing contractual obligations. In a manner, a setup in which problematic debt positions are tidied over through refinancing resembles a Ponzi scheme.[16] As a matter of practice, many highly indebted countries pay exceptionally high interest rates with the objective of luring investors into continuing lending and refinancing the debt. Frequently, even interest payments are partly or wholly financed through new borrowings. The combination of unregulated borrowing powers, unlimited discretion in the matter of whether or when to settle the debts, and the option to refinance enable governments to indulge in financial stratagems that would be, rightfully, considered fraudulent if planned and executed by private citizens.

Unlimited discretion in the matter of whether or not and when to settle the total debt combined with the option to refinance means that if they choose to postpone indefinitely the reduction or settlement of the total debt position, it is the lawful authority of the policymaker to do so. Combine this with the fact that governments borrow on behalf of the state and not in the name of the borrowing administration. The logical consequence is that this allows them to agree to maturities exceeding the term of the borrowing administration. In other words, every administration is fully authorized to pass the responsibility of redemption on to the next administration. Thus, in Argentina, the De la Rua administration inherited virtually unmanageable debt from the spendthrift Menem administration; in Brazil, the Lula administration had to try to manage debts that the Cardoso administration could not resolve and reduce (and which they had, in turn, inherited from preceding administrations) ... and we can go on and on in this manner all the way back to the 1970s. The administration that borrows and the administration that must pay no longer have to be the same. From the perspective of the administration of the moment, the link between enjoying the political benefits of borrowing and bearing the political and administrative burden of its settlement is broken. One administration can borrow and spend without restraint and leave it to some future administration to suffer the consequences. As a corollary, future administrations may not feel obligated to assume responsibility for settling problematic debt positions, the creation of which they had no part in and the resolution of which frustrates their own policy objectives and priorities. These future administrations, therefore, have an incentive to continue the refinancing game as long as this option is available (or, if not, to default when expedient). In the final analysis, one might say that governments that are not required by some regulatory framework to arrange the final settlement of the overall debt position – and to which the option to refinance is available – will, by and large, tend to avoid settlement.

The power of public borrowing is replete with paradoxes. We already noted that the issue of borrowing always revolves around the question of whether the loan will be repaid. Bona fide borrowing presupposes an honest intention to repay. At the same time, there is no market discipline in this respect. There are no constitutional checks; there are no political incentives. In the absence of any such restraints, the power to borrow puts – in terms of integrity, honesty, discipline, prudence, and skill – a premium on the virtue and wisdom of the policymaker. Be that as it may, without controls, it is also the perfect policy instrument for funding unchecked spending. To be sure, the power to borrow does not absolve policymakers of their duty to provide sound financial management. Even so, unregulated borrowing authority makes it exceptionally easy for short-sighted or mala fide or incompetent policymakers to dispense with virtue, knowledge, and good sense in the management of public finances.

The political price of unregulated borrowing authority

Society also pays a political price for unregulated borrowing authority and discretion with regard to settlement. Unchecked borrowing allows policymakers, intellectuals, *and voters* to evade reality. Unchecked borrowing cuts the mental connection that the public would have had to make between increased expenditures and the corresponding need for higher taxes if these had to be balanced within the same fiscal year. Unchecked borrowing saves policymakers and advocates of spending programmes from having to confront voters with the true cost and usefulness of their schemes and being held to account for it by these same voters. Unchecked borrowing destroys the natural awareness of the people and the policymakers of the reality of the scarcity of financial resources, of the need to husband these carefully and to debate, set, and accept priorities in view of this natural condition as well as the need for discipline and patience. It is only when people have to pay increased expenditures through higher taxes out of their own pockets that they become aware of the degree to which financial resources are finite.

Also, unchecked borrowing cuts the only link in the mind of the citizen between public expenditure and property rights. The power to tax is a necessary encroachment of property rights, but at least taxpayers get to experience that cost personally and consciously. Policymakers have to make a case for raising taxes when many people will personally experience a decrease of disposable income as a consequence. Throughout history, people have protested tax increases from time to time. Observe how careful and tactful politicians usually are when presenting tax increases.

Policymakers never have to make a case for borrowing to the general public and never do. People cannot and do not experience government borrowing in the same direct manner as taxation: when government borrows its subjects do not receive statements in their mailbox showing an overdraft. On a personal level it is extremely easy – one could say almost natural – to ignore government borrowing, to treat it as something that does not concern or affect us. Government borrowing is, no matter how you look at it, a *remote* process (i.e., one that is far removed from the daily concerns of ordinary people). In a nutshell, unchecked borrowing is anti-democratic: by cutting the link between the benefits of spending and cost of taxation to the public, it liberates the policymaker from accountability to the public (i.e., the duty of demonstrating the prudence or rightness of his or her spending policies). If some expenditure is inappropriate but happens to be funded on net by borrowing, the public may be that much less disposed to being critical for the reason that they did not directly experience having paid for it through increased taxation.

On the other hand, voters do notice and enjoy the increased government expenditures that result from public borrowing. Don't we all just love the sight and feel of fresh tarmac on the road, the smell of cheap petrol, the taste of subsidized bread, the comforts of "free" electricity and water, and the security of "free" healthcare and education? The dangers of unrestrained borrowing elude the ignorant voters while, for the time being, gladdening them with the loot. Observe how, in times of austerity, the people frequently remember former times of high spending with great fondness and no regrets. Even worse, the public often confuses high spending with good government! Essentially, the power to borrow initially reduces the cost of recklessness, ignorance, self-delusion, dishonesty, and intellectual error, even as it raises the spectre of hardship or ruination of present and future generations. Borrowing enables governments to, often literally, postpone the day of reckoning for years and often even for decades. The disaster of Argentina has been in the making for decades.[17]

Borrowing and autocracy

In the previous paragraph, we noted how unchecked borrowing reduces political and democratic accountability. In the fields of economics and political thought, there are lots of interesting theories, the reasoning of which are frequently not carried to their logical conclusions. One debate going on currently about the topic of good governance revolves around the proposition that large sources of income other than tax revenues allow governments to circumvent pressures for greater accountability. A paper written by Michael Ross in *World Politics* provides a synopsis of some of the essential concepts for understanding this hypothesis.[18] In his paper, Ross presents the results of a statistical analysis of the oil-impedes-democracy claim – a hypothesis that suggests that there is an inverse relationship between oil wealth and democratic rule. The claim purports to explain the prevalence of autocratic rule in oil producing nations. The two central concepts are the *rentier state* and the *rentier effect*. The rentier state is "one that receives substantial rents from foreign individuals, concerns or governments."[19] The rentier effect "suggests that resource-rich governments use low tax rates and patronage to relieve pressures for greater accountability."[20] In his conclusion, Ross found that the "the oil-impedes-democracy claim is both valid and statistically robust."[21]

Ross's subjects are states rich in natural resources, principally oil-exporting nations. Examples are Venezuela, Nigeria, and Saudi Arabia, states where, at various points in time, more than 50 per cent of government revenues came from sales of oil. Mineral-reliant rentier states other than oil exporters include diamond exporters, such as Botswana, and copper producers, such as Zambia and Chile. Yet the rentier state is not necessarily a mineral-reliant state. Foreign aid flows to developing nations "may also be considered a type of economic rent."[22]

The same line of reasoning is just as relevant to the effects of large-scale government borrowing. Government borrowing involves cash flows similar in magnitude to oil export revenues or development aid. The yearly budget deficits of 6–9 per cent of GDP as in the case of Argentina in the years preceding its crisis represent huge amounts of funds borrowed. As an ironic twist, after the oil shock of 1973, many oil-producing states also became large borrowers; in other words, with borrowings amplifying the rentier effect of external revenues from oil exports. Rentier states, which have overborrowed and suffered from the aftermath of debt crises, include Mexico, Venezuela, Nigeria, and Ecuador. In the same manner, foreign aid usually involves loans alongside grants. This is how sub-Saharan Africa became mired in its own variety of debt crisis.

Ross also provides a further breakdown of the rentier effect into three components, two of which are directly relevant to this account. The first component, the use of low taxes or the *taxation effect* "suggests that when governments derive sufficient revenues from the sale of oil, they are likely to tax their populations less heavily or not at all, and the public in turn will be less likely to demand accountability from—and representation in—their government. The logic of the argument is grounded in studies of the evolution of democratic institutions in early modern England and

France. Historians and political scientists have argued that the demand for representation in government arose in response to the sovereign's attempts to raise taxes. ... Another component of the rentier effect might be called the *spending effect*: oil wealth may lead to greater spending on patronage, which in turn dampens latent pressures for democratization."[23]

Observe the analogies of borrowing qua rentier effects. Public borrowing has a taxation effect: as long as governments can borrow, they are unlikely to press for higher or more efficient taxation. Argentina and Greece are cases where constant borrowing bridged inefficient tax collection and high tax evasion, and structural fiscal reform was, time after time, postponed. Borrowing also reduced the need of the government to increase taxes and pacified vital but tax-averse constituencies. The spending effect: overborrowing in the developing countries during the 1970s coincided with the heyday of dictatorial rule. Economic growth and government largesse and patronage driven by mountains of government debt enabled dictators to quiet dissent temporarily. By the same token, in Latin America at least, loss of access to capital markets and the shift from net borrowing to net debt service during the eighties also overlapped with frustration with and the decline of autocratic rule. The dilemma with unlimited borrowing authority is that, though it requires the highest degree of responsibility by policymakers, it sabotages the socio-economic processes that underpin democratic accountability.

Compare the private borrower and public borrower

There might be critics who would want to point out that private borrowers are equally unregulated in the sense that there are no legal limits to what a private party can borrow or rules governing the overall debt position assumed or the final settlement of his or her overall debt. Yet this comparison does not hold up on closer inspection. In terms of the nature of the borrower, comparing private borrowers and the sovereign state is really comparing apples and oranges. A private borrower is either an individual or a corporate body owned by individuals. These individuals possess – or should possess – rights and freedoms. Lending and borrowing is an activity within the scope of these rights and freedoms. Some borrow with the intent to finance a business. In this respect, the freedom to borrow furthers the cause of the right to pursue a lawful occupation. Others borrow with the objective of acquiring goods and services, which may serve to increase one's enjoyment of life. In this sense, the freedom to borrow facilitates the right to the pursuit of happiness.

The state, on the other hand, is not an individual or any type or form of creature in its own right. Unlike human individuals, states do not exist for their own sake, as an end in and of themselves. A state does not or should not produce or consume goods and services for its own sake and glory. To follow the republican ideal, the state is an entity instituted by the citizenry to serve the people; its only purpose is to serve the public interest. The state cannot be the beneficiary of "rights." To serve the public, it must have powers, but every power granted to the state should be the consequence of its purpose – no more and no less. Human individuals enjoy rights and freedoms by virtue of their nature; states are granted powers to fulfil mandates – these are not the same things. Unlimited authority obviously does not serve the public interest; that is, instead, a carte blanche for doing harm. If and when a state is granted a power or jurisdiction, its rationale must be clear and the scope of discretion should fit the bill. Granting a state powers without valid purpose is inviting mischief and eventually disaster, and the frequency of public debt crises proves this point. This is one good reason why we should be more concerned with the scope of the state's borrowing authority.

The sovereign borrower

The distinction between private and public borrowers is revealing in another sense: the enforcement of loan contracts with the state through adjudication presents, on account of the nature of the state, special problems that do not exist in the instance of loans between private parties. The state is a type of debtor unlike any other: the state is an entity with sovereign powers. Accordingly, a default by a state is not a bankruptcy in any normal sense. In the case of a private debtor default, the usual instruments for collecting debt in the event of non-payment are receivership, bankruptcy, liquidation, or attachment. In the case of government default, these instruments are not available or effective; that sovereign states cannot and should not be subjected to the usual adjudication procedures is a requirement of sovereignty.

Consider why forcing a sovereign state into receivership or bankruptcy is not a valid course of action. Observe that receivership and bankruptcy procedures essentially require the treatment of non-payers as subjects of authority. The term *subject,* as used in this context, should be defined as follows: "One who is under the governing power of another, as of a ruler or government."[24] To treat a state like an ordinary debtor is tantamount to making the state in question a subject. Yet, of which or what higher authority is the defaulting state when placed in receivership supposed to become the subject? Is not the state already the supreme authority? To put a sovereign state into receivership would inevitably involve an encroachment on its sovereignty. The only way to set up the institutional mechanism for putting a state into receivership is to rely on other states to apply or threaten force in order to ensure its enforcement.

During the nineteenth century, Western imperial powers frequently imposed receivership through international commissions charged with assuming control of the finances of insolvent nations. An example of this was the establishment in 1881 of the Ottoman Public Debt Commission in the Ottoman Empire, an institution that, according to the historian Alan Palmer, "became virtually a separate and parallel Ministry of Finance, under an international directorate (French, Dutch, British, Italian, German, Austro-Hungarian, Ottoman) and employing some 100 foreign experts."[25] The institution of the Ottoman Public Debt Commission came under the threat of force. Egypt's descent into colonial rule started with the establishment and imposition (in 1876 by France and England) of the Caisse de la Dette Publique (Commission of the Public Debt) for the service of the Egyptian debt.[26] Refusal to submit to such arrangements frequently meant being at the receiving end of gunboat diplomacy. This was the experience of Venezuela during the rule of Cipriano Castro, a particularly murderous, quarrelsome dictator given to extravagant living. "When he refused to make payments on foreign debts, British, German, and Italian ships set up a blockade in 1902 to force payment. The issue was eventually resolved through arbitration."[27] If Venezuela escaped the worse fate of Egypt, it is by virtue of the existence of the Monroe Doctrine.[28]

I am not in the least sympathetic to spendthrift dictators and dissolute, incompetent despots. It is not easy to make a case in defence of incompetent oppressors, which is frankly why such regimes were also such easy victims of imperialism. Yet the case is often not quite so cut and dried. Think of the dilemma of a sovereign democracy. Democracy is not possible without a sovereign parliament.[29] One of the powers of a sovereign parliament is its supremacy over the nation's tax-and-spend powers. How would one justify the application of receivership if the defaulting government happened to be democratically elected as in the case of Argentina or Greece? How does one in such instances reconcile the power of international commissions to tax, which is what receivership in the case of states boils down to – with the sovereign powers of the subject nation's parliament. The power of such an international commission would override the supreme authority of parliament in the matter of taxation. Also, if a sovereign parliament embodies the right of the citizenry to representation, does not the overlordship of the international commission encroach upon that right?

Also, there is the practical issue of asymmetrical power, (i.e., the dilemmas caused by some countries being more powerful than others). Some of the largest sovereign borrowers, such as America, France, England, and Russia, also happen to be way too powerful to reduce to receivership. Some significant creditor nations such as Singapore, Hong Kong, and Kuwait, on the other hand, are not powerful enough to impose receivership on other nations. Also, the idea of a nation such as Russia with a rather nasty and recent tradition of imperialism applying receivership against some of its former possessions in the Baltic, the Caucasus, and Central Asia is positively horrifying. Here, it should suffice to say that there is no agreed-upon mechanism for dealing with sovereign debt default through receivership that is perceived, even remotely, as being impartial, just, appropriate and workable.

Applying bankruptcy and liquidation procedures against states makes even less sense. The best way to demonstrate why is to take the issue literally and to pursue it to its logical conclusion. Literally taken, a bankruptcy and liquidation would mean the dissolution of the state. We can understand the rationale for dissolving a bankrupt company, but what is the precise significance of dissolving a state? How does one arrange the liquidation of a state? How should a society formally represent itself without a state or government? Does liquidation include cessation of the vital services such as the police, the judiciary, and the military? For example, literally taken, a liquidation of a state would mean that the judge presiding over the liquidation would be, effectively, firing himself. Finally, do we expect these institutions – especially the military arm of the government – to take this lying down? The very idea of subjecting the state to these procedures is so preposterous as to warrant no further consideration.

There is the alternative of attachment. In cases of non-payment by a private party, simple attachment – seizure of property – is the regular, most common procedure everywhere; the court usually orders seizure of the assets of the defaulter in order to satisfy valid creditor claims without resorting to bankruptcy procedures. To the extent that creditors feel themselves forced to resort to litigation, attachment does, to some extent, represent a real option in the case of a government debt default. States have – at home and abroad – property, including bank accounts and tangible assets, which could be seized in theory.

In the matter of attachment, it is necessary to distinguish between secured and unsecured debt. Collateralized government debt does exist. Governments can and have provided collateral to lenders, such as mortgages, pledges, and assignments of government properties including land, securities, gold, and concessions. Secured government debt is one specific category of public debt in which common collection procedures are, at least in principle, effective in that there is a specific property that can be identified and seized by the court and sold off to satisfy the outstanding claim.

Yet the problem is precisely that most government debt is unsecured. To that effect, when addressing problems with government borrowing and sovereign debt default, one is generally referring to unsecured debt. In the absence of a provision of collateral by the sovereign borrower, the situation becomes quite problematic. One is faced with the question of which government properties are suitable for seizure and which should be off limits. It is hardly sensible to argue in favour of the power of the courts to seize at will – that would be a carte blanche for the seizure of military hardware, exchequer accounts, embassy property, and national treasures, for example.[30] Seizures of such properties strike at the heart of legitimate and, in many cases, vital government functions, which must be continued in spite of default. The state has a number of functions that are vital to its proper functioning, and the resources for this must of necessity remain beyond the reach of any adjudication process – even in the event of a sovereign default. In the matter of sovereign default, adjudication is just not an effective or desirable course of action.

Can't pay or won't pay?

As we have already noted, collection procedures are, by and large, useless in the case of sovereign borrowers. To pursue the issue to its logical conclusion, because legal coercion is no longer an option, the willingness of government to pay becomes the central issue. In the question of borrowing, the ability to pay and the willingness to pay are essentially distinct issues. One can conceive of debtors who are perfectly capable of paying and yet unwilling to pay. The question is: Can they get away with refusing to pay? In developed countries, a demonstrable ability or capacity of private borrowers to pay makes the issue of willingness a near irrelevancy; the judiciary – the state – usually enforces the contract. By contrast, policymakers, the state itself being immune from the usual sanctions, can look upon the act of non-payment as a policy option, even when the state might still be capable of paying. Public borrowers can therefore give free rein to a range of considerations that affect their willingness to pay, which private borrowers cannot. The grounds for doing so are by no means restricted to bona fide reasons. To pay or not to pay, that is the question, and the pull of expediency vies with principle.

The rule of expediency is the antithesis of property rights. Under the rule of expediency, the moral obligation to repay is ignored; instead, repayment is made contingent upon the advantage or disadvantage of doing so to policymakers. In practice, this means "the trigger for default isn't the arrival of an interest bill when there is no money in the bank, but the realization that to pay it would require a politically unsustainable level of domestic austerity."[31] In other words, policymakers may value their political interests – mostly their popularity with the public – above moral obligations. It should be safe to assume that many people would intuitively recoil from and reject any explicit argument in favour of a purely calculating attitude by policymakers. It cannot be in the interest of the public to be ruled by a government run by policymakers whose view on their obligations is mainly based on considerations of expediency. Nevertheless, unrestrained, unregulated borrowing authority combined with the virtual immunity of the state conspires to create conditions favourable to the eventual practice of the rule of expediency.

Toxic mixes

The problem of creditor security with the nature of the borrower as a sovereign entity, however, is not limited to considerations of sovereignty. The functions of government pose further challenges. Observe the function of the sovereign borrower as the issuer of the currency as well as its role as legislator. The power to create money provides governments desiring to rid themselves of debt – especially in the case of debt denominated in its own currency – with an alternative to outright default, namely, inducing inflation or monetizing the debt. By inducing inflation, the government erodes the value of its debts in purchasing power terms, thereby reducing the real cost of repayment. By monetizing the debt, the government repays its debts by printing money.

This power is, in almost all cases, backed by legal tender laws, one example of the power of the sovereign borrower as legislator. In the case of debt denominated in the domestic currency, this means that the creditor is legally obligated to accept as payment the nominal value of the principle and interest in a depreciated, possibly worthless, currency. Under these conditions, the act of repayment loses its substance – the return of purchasing power lent and borrowed – and thereby reduces the loan contract to an empty promise and the act of repayment to a meaningless formality.

If a private individual were a known counterfeiter, it is quite unlikely that any moneylender would be prepared to grant him or her a loan and for obvious and valid reasons. Yet none of us seem to perceive the slightest conflict of interest when a government is authorized to enact legal tender laws, to borrow in its own currency, and, at the same time, possess the power to create money. Concurrently, no lender would sign a contract including a clause granting a private borrower the power to change the terms and conditions unilaterally and without notice. Yet does not the power to legislate in effect supersede the terms of a contract? The power of one and the same entity to borrow, print money, and legislate is one poisonous mix of conflicting interests.

Summary

When private individuals or companies fail to pay their debts, creditors can usually resort to action in court, the latter being capable of forcing the debtor to restructure its business and marshalling its assets in order to satisfy valid creditor claims. Even though bankruptcy procedures frequently involve the acceptance by claimants of permanent losses, the least one can say is that the principle of property rights has been asserted and enforced with real consequence. The creditor and private debtor are, in principle, equals in court; with a bit of luck, each enjoys or can be made to enjoy reasonably clear rights and a comparable measure of legal protection. In other words, the creditor and private debtor are – in court at least – comparable powers (i.e., both are subjects of authority). On the other hand, the private creditor and the sovereign debtor can never be equal powers.

We have every reason to be concerned with the nature of the sovereign borrower and the scope of its powers. The very nature of a borrower as a sovereign entity has severe implications for the degree to which lenders can exercise their rights. In the event of non-payment of debt against the general credit of the state, the lender to the state – quite unlike the creditor to private parties, at least in principle – is usually left without effective legal recourse. Without recourse to legal protection, there can be no due process. For this reason, sovereign debt default automatically implies a taking of property without due process and, therefore, a violation of property rights.

As a matter of fact, the debt default issue is broader than the immediate violation of property rights resulting from non-payment. Beyond the issue of the taking of property without due process, one must include destruction of property resulting from bankruptcies of companies during crisis and the accompanying unemployment problem. There is no way in which limited processes such as adjudication or debt negotiations can address these broader processes of destruction. And yet, do not owners of business properties and their employees also deserve protection from the consequences of government default?

The purpose of this chapter is not to champion the state or to elevate it beyond the reach of law and morality. Instead, the point is that, when the terms of sovereignty are such that immunity of the state is, for reasons discussed above, an imperative, the possession by the state of unlimited borrowing authority becomes utterly unacceptable. It is not and cannot be right that the state should, at the same time, enjoy virtual immunity in the case of default and unregulated borrowing powers.

It is not in the interests of society to permit the continuation of a state of affairs that is conducive to such violations of rights or, in a wider context of economic crisis, the destruction of business property and employment. Even when contracts – in this instance, with the government – cannot be directly enforced, there is still a moral obligation to provide some form of protection of rights and interests. Without effective recourse to adjudication for protection, it is up to society to find alternative ways of making the state, government, and its agents demonstrate their positive commitment to property rights. What cannot be achieved in one way must be done in another. In the absence of recourse to legal protection, we must consider some form of legal or constitutional restraint against borrowing authority as the substitute for the process of adjudication.

Chapter 9

Balancing the Budget

The budget should be balanced, the Treasury should be refilled, public debt should be reduced, the arrogance of officialdom should be tempered and controlled, and the assistance to foreign lands should be curtailed lest Rome become bankrupt.

—Marcus Tullius Cicero

The idea that borrowing authority must be restricted and regulated in order to protect the public and the economy against the state would probably sound peculiar to many people. It is one of those articles of faith of our age that government borrowing represents an appropriate, useful, and valuable policy instrument for economic management and development; it is one of those elemental teachings absorbed by most people with some form of economic or financial education.[1] Yet the hypothetically beneficial uses of a power as a policy instrument should never be the sole consideration for its legitimacy as a lawful authority. As we already noted in the previous chapter, the study of government finance, including the budgeting process and the management of public debt, belongs to the field of study called public finance. The promotion of a field of study and research is usually done on the basis of its perceived usefulness to society. The attribution of such value requires one to presume that wisdom gathered in that field of study will eventually be put to good use. In the case of public finance, this means that one must presume that policymakers would be interested in improvement of the management of government finances and, for this reason, willing to take note of and apply the wisdom of public finance theory. This also requires one to assume that policymakers will more often than not be men and women of high calibre working for the greater good and prosperity of the nations under their rule. Unfortunately, these assumptions do not accord with reality. It appears that, over the period of 1800 to 2012, there have been at least 268 instances of sovereign default and debt restructuring.[2] Of these, 137 occurred after World War II, when public finance had already come into its own as a mature science. A number of these instances are no doubt cases of force majeure, caused by wars, revolutions, and national catastrophes. Still, the most common reason was the peacetime mismanagement of public finances. Note that this history of sovereign default should be understood as one of those instances of people refusing to learn from past mistakes. In fact, quite a few countries are serial defaulters. Two nations, Venezuela and Ecuador, set the record with eleven defaults each. The failure in this instance of people refusing to learn from history is not so strange. Unregulated borrowing authority fosters conditions ideal for ignoring science, wisdom, and history. As we already noted in the previous chapter, unregulated borrowing authority makes it easy and advantageous for short-sighted or mala fide or incompetent policymakers to dispense with virtue, knowledge, and good sense in the management of public finances. Unregulated borrowing authority is a perverse incentive that provides irresponsible policymakers with a competitive advantage in politics at the expense of responsible policymakers. Unregulated borrowing powers debase the process by which people elect their rulers. Political party spending pledges are the common currency in democratic politics. Extravagant spending pledges provide irresponsible politicians with the means to outbid responsible politicians. Indeed, this is the reason why so many countries must suffer the rule of legislators who are unfazed by spending commitments that will eventually bankrupt the nation. Therefore, we have every cause to impose constraints upon the powers of our policymakers to engage in sovereign borrowing.

The solution

Governments that do not borrow cannot default. This may be a tautology; it is also perfectly true. The most comprehensive measure against overborrowing would be to ban deficit financing. Alternatively, this could be structured in the form of a balanced-budget provision to the constitution of a country or otherwise through the abolition of the borrowing authority of government. Of the latter, there are no examples at present. Of the former, we have the case of the United States. Forty-nine out of fifty states in America have implemented balanced-budget provisions in their constitutions, and at the federal level, there is, of varying intensity, an ongoing debate about the desirability of introducing a balanced-budget amendment to the constitution. An effective balanced-budget provision bars the government from spending more than it collects in taxes within the fiscal year. In principle, this means that any increase in expenditure must result in higher taxes immediately, and any decrease in revenues must be compensated by reductions in public spending.

One purpose of a bona fide constitution is to enumerate the rights of the individual that the state must protect. Presumably, these are then protected by providing the individual with some form of recourse to judicial review. Yet, sometimes, citizens cannot derive adequate protection through the enumeration of rights. This is clearly the case with government borrowing. Observe that the act of borrowing itself does not result in a clear and direct violation of any individual right – or even an imminent danger to that effect in the same way that detention without trial does with respect to the right to a fair trial, which is a corollary of the right to liberty. The act of borrowing does not automatically or instantaneously produce victims; on the effective day of borrowing, we cannot point at clearly wronged or visibly injured parties. This observation also finds its expression in the issue of *standing*: courts will normally admit cases only when plaintiffs can demonstrate direct, specific, and personal injury. From the incidence of any given budget deficit – even in those instances where there is a public consensus regarding its excessiveness – it is usually not possible to demonstrate standing at a personal level. Also, it requires more than a few budget deficits to ruin a country. Actually, some portion of the borrowings may even have been put to good use.

Nevertheless, this does not mean that there is no case against unrestrained borrowing authority; as a thinking species, humans have the gift of conceptualizing danger on an abstract level and the ability to learn from history. Thus, prior to actual default or monetization, identifying the danger in government borrowing (or, more precisely, of unregulated borrowing authority) to the public interest is really an effort of abstract thinking and long-term planning and precaution, and it is one supported by historical evidence much of which is recent. In that case, we cannot secure the interests of the public through the enumeration of rights and the provision of recourse to judicial review; rather, only through the constitutional procedure of restricting or abolishing borrowing authority itself can we achieve these aims. It is our ability to grasp the danger of unrestrained power that justifies this precautionary measure.

A bona fide constitution is a social contract specifying controls against the abusive power of government, one expression of which is the enumeration of rights, the other of which is the delineation of public powers. In the case of government borrowing, only its formal restriction or abolition will provide proper jurisdiction for judicial review, thereby rendering the protection of property rights effective. A balanced-budget clause, it must be understood, is not a direct, instrumental remedy against the violation of property rights. Instead, the protection provided is a derivative – a by-product as it were – of the contestability of the legality of a public power (namely, borrowing authority). For example, it does not in any way diminish the power to tax, which in itself represents an infringement of property rights, albeit one that is necessary and inevitable if we want effective government. But to the extent that it shields the financial system from fiscal policy through its restriction, it is an advance in securing property rights through greater economic stability. The Argentinean public should wish that they had this protection.

The political dividends of statutory discipline

A balanced-budget provision would also reinforce democratic accountability and political responsibility by forcing advocates of additional expenditure to own up fully to its current cost and to defend spending proposals in terms of why they merit higher taxes. The obligation to balance the budget substantially raises the cost of many, if not all, political, ideological, technocratic, or even personal standpoints that translate into public spending. It eliminates many easy opportunities for self-delusion and opportunism on the part of the voters, quackery by advocates of spending programmes, and guile on the part of the policymakers that the power to borrow makes possible. It confronts the voter year after year with the true cost of spending proposals, and it makes it a little bit easier to judge the quality and character of their advocates inside and outside of government (i.e., their honesty, integrity, wisdom, and prudence in these matters). How much room there is for manoeuvring in the instance of fiscal policy has a real impact on whether issues will, to whatever degree possible, be discussed responsibly and what quality of politician will profit from such a system. Unrestrained spending and borrowing authority rewards those politicians with the least scruples, those who, without batting an eye, would destroy the finances of their nation to gain or hold on to power. In the year 2000, the share of public spending in GDP in Argentina stood at 30 per cent while it collected around 21 per cent of GDP. A significant portion of this deficit was the consequence of President Menem trying to buy political support for an unconstitutional third term. Power corrupts and, one might as well add, uninhibited borrowing corrupts absolutely.

There are also social and economic benefits to balanced budgets. Countries that do not borrow have no debt service obligations. This is not a benefit to be sneezed at. Many countries, both poor and rich, commit as much as 10–30 per cent of their budgetary outlays on debt service, mostly interest payments. That is money equally lost to discretionary spending and reduced taxes. Public funds spent on interest payments and retirement of debt is lost to education, healthcare, infrastructure, and proper wages for civil servants. This 10–30 per cent is the equivalent of a steady loss of blood draining poor nations, year after year, of the resources necessary to develop. People should wish their countries had never borrowed in the first place. Yet even countries that are already in debt can limit further losses by desisting, on a net basis, from borrowing more money. By stopping the growth of the public debt, the share of the government budget dedicated to servicing the debt should eventually fall on account of the budget growing in conjunction with the economy. As the share of debt service in the budget decreases, room for discretionary spending and/or reduced taxes should – all else being equal – increase.

It must be understood that there are limits to the benefits of a balanced-budget provision. Though it shields the financial sector from overborrowing it does not shield the taxpayer from excessive taxation. Though it forces policymakers and, by extension, voters to prioritize or to be more conscious of the choices to be made, it cannot force them to do so wisely; policymakers and their constituents could, for example, still choose to waste tax money on subsidizing consumption – think of the bread and petrol subsidies – over funding the advancement of education or the building of roads. These are not issues that are so easily dealt with through constitutional procedure and will still require the vigilance of voters. A balanced-budget provision is only meant to lighten the burden of controlling the inclinations of policymakers and voters (and thus keeping in check some of the worst fiscal excesses).

The complexities of the balanced-budget provision

A balanced-budget requirement, though it may sound like an easy or simple solution, is actually a difficult and complex issue. The pursuit of a balanced-budget provision raises a great many practical questions, and it could not be otherwise given the complexity of government finances as well as how it affects the powers and standing of the three branches of government. What follows is an overview of some of the issues that must be dealt with. Which parts of the government finances should be subject to the requirements of the balanced-budget provision? The balanced-budget provision could be made to apply to the total budget or only a part of it. American states, for example, typically balance only their operating budgets, which fund only current expenditures, including wages and public pension programmes but not capital budgets, which fund long-term investments such as infrastructure projects. The second scenario allows scope for funding public investments with borrowing; the first scenario does not. This is probably the easiest issue to deal with – from here on, the matter becomes increasingly complicated.

How stringent should the provision be? The provision could be made to apply to the submission and enactment of the budget (i.e., proposed and approved expenditures and revenues to be collected). Alternatively, the provision could be made to apply to the balance of actual expenditure and revenues collected. The first scenario allows actual expenditures to exceed taxes collected; the second does not. In other words, accidental deficits would be legal under the first scenario but unconstitutional under the second.

Should the balanced-budget amendment be binding or not? This is probably the hardest issue to deal with. The issue here is whether the requirement should be enforceable and how it should be enforced. A non-binding provision would have moral force but lack enforceability. Essentially, that would leave the current situation of unlimited borrowing authority unchanged. If governments should choose to ignore this requirement, a balanced-budget provision would amount to a dead letter. The point of a balanced-budget provision is to provide a means or source of statutory discipline in the absence of, or as a reinforcement of, the practicable will of policymakers and legislators. Yet a binding provision would require some form of enforcement mechanism when the government fails to enact a balanced budget. This raises even more questions. Which of the branches of government would be charged with compelling compliance with the provision? The executive? The legislature? The judiciary? Which instruments of enforcement are valid?

Finally, there is the matter of the exception to the rule. No constitutional provision should be so rigid that no exceptions are possible. The point of a balanced-budget provision should not be to make government borrowing impossible; rather, it should be the object of the greatest possible restraint and exception. Some circumstances are so extraordinary that the need to borrow must be acknowledged. Wartime borrowing is one such instance. Even where no objectively exceptional circumstances, such as a state of war, can be determined, just enough flexibility should be allowed in the constitution to make borrowing possible. This is a question of human nature; in politics, one should always leave – however little – some room for action. The danger of not allowing any wiggle room is that, without it, politicians will, under pressure, use extraordinary conditions to damage or destroy a proper constitutional framework. Balanced-budget provisions should therefore include a clause allowing government borrowing if some pre-specified supermajority – for example, 60 per cent or two-thirds – could be found in parliament. All such eventualities and circumstances must be provided for in any balanced budget provision.

Opposition to the balanced-budget provision

The issues above were not raised merely to portray their complexity; instead, they were raised because these (and others not mentioned here) are the issues that the inevitable opponents of this proposal will raise. A search on the Internet for *balanced-budget amendment* will generate thousands of hits – a great many advising against this solution. Internet surfers will discover that the debate about the balanced-budget amendment is almost entirely an American debate right now. The United States is probably the only country where balanced-budget amendments are a recurrent and high-profile political issue. The majority of the issues raised by the opponents of the balanced-budget provision deserve serious consideration. The reader will find many of these criticisms, taken at face value, to be credible. Yet, in the end, it is usually not the objective of the opponents of balanced-budget provisions to enlighten us about the complications but to discredit the proposition. To accept their objections at face value is to lose view of the context as well as of the limited purpose of these arguments (namely, the discrediting of the proposal). Most of these issues are soluble one way or another.

For demonstration take the issue of enforcement. One tactic is to raise a *straw man*, which is a sham argument set up for demolition. In the question of enforcement, opponents will usually propose only the following "solution" (typically never suggesting and exploring any alternative): granting the executive or judiciary the power to cut expenditures or raise taxes when parliament fails to enact a balanced budget and then demonstrate its flaws. Indeed, this so-called solution cannot, from the vantage point of a proper balance of powers between the branches of government, hold up under scrutiny. To grant the head of state the power to determine budgets in the case of a failure by parliament to enact balanced budgets is to introduce rule by decree – one of those hallmarks of tyranny. The same powers in the hand of the judiciary are even worse: it is downright undemocratic; judges are appointed officials, not the elected representatives of the people. A true democrat has no alternative but to reject this so-called solution. Nevertheless, there are solutions that do not necessarily entail granting the executive or judiciary powers to rule without parliamentary fiat.

One solution would be to institute a rule that the submission of unbalanced budgets would automatically trigger a requirement of supermajority support in a legislature. A supermajority represents a majority greater than a simple majority (e.g., for example a pre-specified majority of two-thirds or three-fifths). The purpose of a supermajority requirement is to make the process of adopting a certain type of legislation – for example, a change to a constitution – more difficult. Some states in the United States impose supermajority requirements for tax increases. The requirement of a supermajority could conceivably make the process of adopting unbalanced budgets more difficult, thus serving as an incentive for a government to stick with balanced-budget proposals for which it could rely on simple majorities. It should be noted that the effectiveness of such a voting procedure depends in part on the type of government and the political culture of a country.[3]

There is also the matter of defining the legal framework for the budget submission process. The failure to comply with a constitutional requirement represents a form of lawbreaking – hence, the institution of some form of legal sanction should be perfectly logical. The preparation and submission of a government budget is normally the responsibility of the executive branch of government. Therefore, one could consider making the submission by the executive of an unbalanced budget a violation of the constitution and an impeachable offense, a lapse for which parliament could dismiss the head of state and/or the cabinet. Conversely, a parliament that enacts an unbalanced budget could be made subject to automatic dissolution followed by the call of an election.[4] Additionally, a recall election process could be instituted by which citizens would have the right to remove the executive from office or dissolve parliament before its term ended.[5]

Are such measures excessive? Not at all. Such an objection would be spurious; elected officials are already subject to formal measures of greater severity than mere dismissal from office or the dissolution of their congress. In most nations, high-level public officials are, at least formally, impeachable for crimes or misdemeanours in office. Submitting or enacting an unbalanced budget is certainly not a criminal offense, but it should at least be deemed a violation of a proper constitutional order.

Finally, one could conceive of giving citizens or groups of citizens or substantial parties (such as individual legislators, registered political parties, the general auditor, etc.) the right to submit unbalanced-budget proposals for judicial review. There is the question of standing in court. If no one could claim standing, the citizen's right would prove unenforceable. Yet, even here, there is a solution: one could provide standing to the plaintiff on the grounds of the public interest. That is not as farfetched as it sounds: in the Netherlands, every citizen can, by law, challenge an auditor's opinion[6] in court without the need to demonstrate direct, personal interest – the explicit legal basis for standing being the public interest. As for who should be the plaintiff, this is a matter of how a specific society or constitutional order functions. To some societies the idea of a private citizen gaining standing would seem bizarre or excessive. If that is the case, there is still the possibility of granting standing to substantial parties such as individual legislators, registered political parties, or the general auditor, for example.

With the example of the analysis of the enforcement problem, we have demonstrated that, usually, there is a solution. It is to be hoped that these alternatives to the straw man proposition are in their turn not taken as being the enumeration of all available solutions or that it should be seen as so adequate that it would preclude the need for further thought on their elaboration or even a need for supplementary measures; we should believe nothing of the kind. Though we have examined only one issue here, it should be obvious that the range of measures needed to make the balanced-budget provision work is a study all by itself. Yet a comprehensive blueprint is not forthcoming here because it does not serve our mission, which is to examine misgovernment in its various forms from its origin in government jurisdiction. It should suffice that we have received a taste of the political and technical issues involved. Still, beyond the question of how to structure and make effective balanced-budget provisions, there are a few critical points made by its opponents that also deserve rebuttal.

The balanced budget and economic policy

A serious challenge to the balanced-budget provision is the argument that banning deficit financing will intensify the effects of recessions and weak growth. The reasoning is that budget deficits can serve as anticyclical stabilizers. Because tax revenues tend to drop during recessions, the main burden of budget cuts would fall precisely on recession years and thus potentially hurt the economy during its weaker moments. The idea of the budget deficit as anti-cyclical stabilizer is to maintain or increase the level of government spending while tax revenues lag, thus counteracting recession and stabilizing the economy. It is ironic, however, that this argument should be made in opposition to the balanced-budget provision while failing to draw attention to its full theoretical context. The basic formula underlying this instrument is to run budget deficits during recessions in order to support national consumption through public expenditure and to run surpluses in years of high growth to pay down the national debt accumulated during preceding recessions. The second half of the prescription serves the first half by securing fiscal health, thereby ensuring government access to financial markets at all times. In other words, as a policy prescription, automatic stabilization is premised on fiscal prudence over the long term. In practice, policymakers seldom comply with this formula and, in many countries, recession years *and* boom years see budget deficits in an endless ratcheting up of the national debt; accumulated debt is simply not paid down.

Governments that overborrow will eventually deprive themselves of the blessings of this policy instrument and suffer precisely those circumstances that the opponents of the balanced-budget provision profess to fear. In time, they will no longer be able to borrow money and discover that – barring inflationary spending – they will not be able to spend more than current tax receipts, which amounts to balanced budgets and austerity by *default*. One tell-tale sign of this situation in countries going through a debt crisis is the common occurrence of public sector workers, public pensions, and suppliers going unpaid for months on end (and the coincident decay of much of the public infrastructure). Also, observe how, in the run-up to and in the aftermath of the Argentinean debt crisis, the government found itself – with creditors shrinking from lending more and the IMF pressing for increased austerity measures – hacking away at its budget in the middle of a protracted recession.

Deficit financing, as an automatic stabilizer, requires discretionary borrowing authority. For budgets to be effective as stabilizers, governments must have the discretion to allow deficits to rise any level deemed necessary. Limits on the size of deficits are therefore out of the question. Thus, the question to be put to the opponents of the balanced-budget provision is as follows: How do they propose to restrict deficit financing to its proper uses, which includes anti-cyclical stabilization? In other words, how do they propose to prevent government deficit financing authority from degenerating into an opportunity for chronic fiscal irresponsibility?

We could amend this theory as follows: If using deficit financing as an anti-cyclical stabilizer is such a critical necessity, why not run surpluses during the good years to create a surplus fund to be used for supporting spending levels during a recession? In the framework of the budgeting process, disbursements from this surplus fund for covering shortfalls of tax revenues against public expenditures could be accounted for as government income or "negative expenditure." From a theory of anti-cyclical stabilizers, it does not matter whether you maintain spending levels during recession by means of deficit financing or from a surplus fund. In both cases, the government draws down on national savings.[7] In other words, the balanced-budget provision and government spending as an anti-cyclical stabilizer are not even mutually exclusive propositions. Nevertheless, one should not be overly serious in making this proposal because it is no doubt as difficult for policymakers to muster the fortitude and self-possession to run surpluses to build up a surplus fund as it is to pay down the national debt.

Somehow, when all is said and done, this argument about the aggravated risk of recession, without debating the correctness of the reasoning as such, is rather unsatisfactory. Why should we be so much more concerned with the lesser injuries caused by austerity during recession than with the larger destruction caused by overborrowing followed by a sovereign debt crisis? If one is honestly concerned with the welfare of the people, one must look at the matter in context: most governments are so bad at managing their finances (thereby repeatedly provoking grave fiscal and monetary crises) that, on net and over time, the relative benefits of statutory discipline may well outweigh the availability of deficit financing as an anti-cyclical stabilizer. Recessions hurt people for a few years, but the drama of debt crisis can last up to a decade or longer – vide the Latin American crisis of the eighties. In the case of Argentina, debt crises occurred twice within two decades. In the case of Russia, debt crises occurred twice within one decade, 1994 and 1998. If a choice must be made, which is preferable?

Simpletons in budget-land

The one unforgivably stupid argument of opponents of the balanced-budget provision is that the people need only elect representatives with the will to balance the budget. This argument is either disingenuous or naive. It wilfully ignores a near-perfect record of recurring deficits in too many countries for too long, showing that we cannot rely on popular or voter vigilance. The relentless increase of state debt around the globe strikes no fear in the hearts of the average voter because the funding side of the budget process, especially the borrowing part of it, is such a remote experience and arcane subject to him or her. At the same time, the same public is profoundly affected by and devoted to public expenditure and turns its ears to the siren song of politicians promising more of it. Budget cuts and austerity programmes, on the other hand, no matter how salutary and restorative to the health of the government finances, are mostly unpopular. Because of its appetite, ignorance, and gullibility, the public is no match for the unscrupulous politician.

Also, the media is as dull-witted and destructive a channel as one could fathom. It swings from an immovable indifference to the dangers of persistent deficits to full blast panic mongering when it is already too late. In between, it invariably reports increased expenditure as good news. On the other hand, it is often sensationalist on the subject of budget cuts and austerity and an eager mouthpiece for hostile opinion. The notion of popular vigilance as the check on unregulated borrowing authority is so pathetic, such a fantastic claim that it should have been too embarrassing to advocate. Let us stop using bromides and show a bit more regard for the dreadful experience of history.

This is not to say that the cause of probity in government finance is a lost cause. Rather, the point is that it is not a popular preoccupation. Prudence in public finance is an elite or technocratic issue. Wherever you find sound government finances, you will discover that widespread support for such a policy *within the political classes* has managed to overcome the populist urges of sections within these same classes. Furthermore, all cases of austerity and retrenchment are the achievement of a few statesmen pushing through policies to that effect on the basis of their own views on the matter and who, on the strength of their character, have proven willing to brave public opinion and hostility.

Debt relief advocacy reviewed

The preceding sections have looked mostly at the debt problem as a consequence of misgovernment. In this respect, we are concerned primarily with understanding underlying structures and causes in terms of predatory jurisdiction (i.e., the scope of discretionary power, the nature of the state, and its functions). This approach does not deal with the question of what to do about existing debt problems.

It should be stressed that, up to this point, the goal in studying the issue of government debt has been to make a case for the prevention of a form of misgovernment, which is a different issue altogether from addressing existing debt problems. In this respect, debt trouble is a bit like an unwanted pregnancy. One could, for example, consider unregulated borrowing authority as the equivalent of reproductive capacity and its exercise as comparable to unprotected sex. You can avoid pregnancy through the proper use of contraceptives or by abstaining from sex. On the other hand, once pregnant, the use of contraceptives or abstention are no longer the immediate issue, and a whole range of different concerns make their entrance: the choice of abortion or carrying to term, angry parents or an upset partner, the vanishing lover, the embarrassment of gloating neighbours, the money to raise the child, etc. A balanced-budget provision is thus prophylactic in the same way that a contraceptive is. The protection of the financial system and economy afforded by balanced budgets and the various dividends are comparable to the practice of safe sex.

The current debate about debt trouble, on the other hand, is hardly about causes or prevention. We have, instead, a debate narrowly focused on one issue: the purported unfairness of denying debt relief to highly indebted countries and requiring them to service their debts in accordance with contractual requirements. The charge of debt relief advocates is that contractual debt service requirements are so heavy that highly indebted countries are basically required to pay their debts through reduced consumption and austerity, which is also called adjustment through contraction. In other words, servicing high levels of public debt results in deprivation and misery for large sections of the local population. A number of countries may have reached this point. Taken at face value, this argument all but implies that debt relief would contribute to improved economic conditions in beneficiary debtor countries. There is no need to dispute the fact that, beyond a certain point, the burden of debt service can and will destroy a nation. Undoubtedly, in more than a few cases, reality will require all parties to acknowledge that losses are inevitable and debt relief or forgiveness is the only realistic course of action. This is the one element in this debate that deserves recognition.

Yet the exclusive focus of this debate on the problem caused by debt service must be put in perspective. There is a general awareness and consensus among debaters and publicists on the history of the origins of debt trouble.[8] Yet, strangely enough, the participants in this debate never seem to detect a moral to the story about the proper role of the government. You cannot find much genuine thought or any broadly supported and articulate debate on whether it was right of the government to borrow so much, on the impunity with which this destructive borrowing is carried out – in other words, on the legitimacy of unrestrained borrowing authority. Observe that the advocates of debt relief generally seem coldly indifferent and often even openly hostile to the creditor whose money was taken. More than a few advocates go so far as to smear creditors (properly understood, victims that stand to lose money) in vile terms. To the last person, debt relief advocates seem unencumbered by the matter of contract, the moral obligation to repay. When advocates reserve *all* their indignation for the consequences of debt service and show not the slightest concern for destructive behaviour by the state, their moral standing should be considered suspect. A person who does not care for property rights, a man who is silent about bad behaviour by the state while denouncing those claiming what is rightfully theirs is at best ignorant – but if not ignorant, immoral. Debt relief advocacy is not a proper moral cause; in fact, it is much closer to being a morally suspect cause.

That said, debt relief advocacy is generally viewed as a humanitarian mission. Underlying this mission is the assumption that debt relief will somehow benefit the poor. This premise, however, is fundamentally flawed for one plain yet generally overlooked reason: the payback accruing from debt relief first goes to the state and not to the poor. From there on, the question of who benefits from this payback is decided by those in charge of government, the ruling politicians, and not the public, the humanitarians, or anybody else. History teaches us that the agendas of rulers do not necessarily correspond with those of the poor or the public or with the ideas of the humanitarians. Bear in mind that the payback of debt relief – as is the case with all public funds – can be used in ways that are not necessarily beneficial to the society in question. It is as easy to use the payback for schemes that primarily benefit the people in power and their constituents, as it is to apply it to programmes of genuine benefit to the public. From the perspective of the people in power, debt relief advocacy is frequently nothing more than a propaganda instrument in a bait-and-switch strategy: first promote relief as a measure for the benefit of the poor, and then capture its payback for resuming the same profligate and dysfunctional ways of yesterday. Under such circumstances, debt relief would merely shore up or perpetuate a dysfunctional government system instead of contributing to a meaningful and sustained improvement of social and economic conditions in debtor countries. For this reason, debt relief can never be a standalone measure; it must be part of a greater project – namely, the structural reform and redirection of government finance and, ultimately, the institution of good government.

For debtor country governments, desiring to escape the cost of past wastefulness and seeking to diminish the pressure to reform, the call for debt relief is a valuable propaganda tool. When continued debt service is portrayed as the primary cause of poverty and debt relief is presented as the silver bullet, deeper reform suddenly becomes a lesser issue. The idea of debt relief as a measure of direct benefit to the people becomes the perfect bait for gaining the support of the domestic public and foreign advocates, as long as they believe (without applying critical thought to the correctness of this assumption) that the payback will be used accordingly. The politics of debt relief advocacy, therefore, is one where the domestic public plays the part of the sucker whereas the foreign advocates act the part of stooges.

As a matter of practice, many debtor governments do not negotiate debt restructurings in good faith, and there is a reason for this: restructuring often destroys the very raison d'être of these governments. These governments are often rooted in political structures that are energized by patronage, cronyism, corruption, populist programmes, socialist ideologies, and lots of borrowing. These governments and their constituencies thrive on wasteful and overstaffed bureaucracies; inefficient, corrupt revenue services; consumer and producer subsidies; and hostility to privatization, for example. Rational people consider it self-evident that such ailments should be addressed. To this type of political elite and its natural constituency, trimming bureaucracy, expanding the tax base, cutting subsidies, and opening parts of the public sector to private investment are fundamental threats. This is one of the main reasons why negotiations are usually such long, drawn-out processes.

That demand for reform must often come from abroad is not a very good sign when many of these reforms are necessary anyway for domestic reasons. In fact, debtor-country political systems are frequently quite reactionary; in many countries, achieving debt relief with an absolute minimum of reform has become a source of prestige. Many politicians thrive on and build careers on being seen as resistant to the demands of foreign creditors and especially the hated IMF, assuming a public finance variety of the "Defender of the Nation" role. Every concession by creditor negotiators to these types vindicates their falsehoods, bolsters the careers of cynical and opportunistic people or ideological dinosaurs, and generally entrenches dysfunctional politics for another round of misgovernment.

As in a vicious circle, the failure to reform also reduces the ability to repay. Indeed, could it be that the accusations of debt relief advocates and debtor-country politicians concerning the height of the debt service requirements reflect low expectations with regard to reform or even a lack of interest in its necessity? If one does not expect or desire reform and the resulting higher growth, one must, unsurprisingly, be pessimistic about the future ability of these countries to repay their debts. If one does not insist on reform, one obviously has no alternative but to accept debt relief as the only route to closure in the matter of debt trouble. This is one very good reason why creditors, the IMF, and the Paris Club must insist on reform – if only to increase prospects for recovering outstanding claims.

In the end, what counts is what the rehabilitated debtor country or country seeking rehabilitation will do with its restored fiscal health. Here, the supreme irony of the matter is that the parties involved – the IMF, the US Treasury, the Paris Club, debt relief advocates, local policymakers, and others – all appear to share at least one objective: to rehabilitate the debtor country in question in the capital markets (i.e., restructure or forgive in order to restore that country's ability to resume borrowing). It is amazing to see how the resumption of borrowing by a formerly truant debtor nation is taken as a sign of health. The first successful bond issue after restructuring is invariably applauded in the press and plugged by the issuing government to the domestic public and the world as the end of its fiscal problems. Yet should it not be seen as a sign of ongoing addiction? Is it not the equivalent of encouraging a reformed alcoholic to celebrate his recovery by downing a shot of bourbon? It seems as if, in such cases, neither the public of the debtor country, the intelligentsia, nor their government have learned any lessons from the brutal experience of crisis. Indeed, many troubled debtor nations have a long history of recurring cycles of defaults, hyperinflation, and restructurings.

So what good is debt relief without the institution of good government? Recall that debt repayment is a moral obligation and non-payment by government is a taking of property without due process. Repayment in full is also a requirement of honest government and, in fact, it is the ultimate proof that it is not engaged in deception and fraud. Correspondingly, it is not right to endorse a course of action such as debt relief unless it is accompanied by genuine institutional reform by the debtor government. To do so would represent a sacrifice of the creditor (i.e., the taking of rightful property without, at the very least, the corresponding comfort that his or her loss served a just cause – the promotion of good government). Obviously, no debtor nation can be forced to reform, yet what is gained by granting absolution to unrepentant sinners? In this respect, creditors and creditor governments, even in those cases where the prospect of a loss is sure and acknowledgement of this the only realistic course of action, they would do well to hold out and insist on real reform.

Debt relief on its own is not a solution, let alone a panacea. Its advocacy is not a moral cause. If it is to be contemplated at all, it must be from a broader view on the problem of borrowing and the true interests of the debtor-country society than is now the norm. The current debate and many of its participants treat the requirement of debt service as being the central evil instead of it being a symptom of a deeper problem originating in misgovernment. This is pure range-of-the-moment thinking in which proper reasoning about cause and effect is neglected. It agitates everybody, serves to distract from serious thinking, and solves nothing in the end. In sum, one can never entirely rule out the need for debt relief; nevertheless, its advocacy should be countered with a great many caveats.

Summary

What is stranger than a highly sophisticated field of study such as public finance of which the mechanics have been unravelled in the minutest detail by scholars and administrators only to find one aspect (i.e., the fundamental nature of borrowing authority) practically unexamined? One of government's unquestioned powers and policy instruments turns out to be one of the most aberrant forms of authority. In the absence of a constitutional framework constraining or delineating borrowing authority, the requirements of sovereignty, the functions of government, including its legislative powers and the power to create money, all conspire to foster conditions maximally favourable to sloppy and opportunistic government finance. Such a nexus of prerogative and power makes government a type of borrower so dangerous both to the rights and interests of the creditor to the financial system and to the economy in general that the very legitimacy of its power to borrow must be questioned. The theoretical benefits of government borrowing as a source of investment finance and deficit financing as an instrument of economic stabilization pale once the hazards of policy discretion inherent in uninhibited authority and the historical outcome of its practice are taken into account. We must wake up from the view that borrowing authority is a natural, normal, or regular power of government. It is not. This sense of its naturalness is nothing but a form of restricted awareness resulting from the fact that this power is so widespread among the states of our world and from being such an ancient prerogative. This obliviousness to the predatory power inherent in unrestrained borrowing authority prevented us from setting explicit standards of justice and good government. We now have the conceptual tools to do so.

Chapter 10

The Dynamics of Predatory Jurisdiction

Quis custodiet ipsos custodes?
(Who guards the guardian?)

—Juvenal, Roman satirist

In the previous chapters, we have taken a number of practical concerns such as inflation, sovereign debt default, and the size of the informal sector and demonstrated how one can work out the scope of predatory jurisdiction on the basis of how the rights of individuals are affected. Now we must lift our examination of predatory jurisdiction as a cause of misgovernment to a more abstract level.

The essence of predatory jurisdiction is authority that is lawful yet insufficiently restrained. Unrestrained authority is dangerous and easily used for evil purposes. However, in our day and age, the blatant pursuit and use of government power for unmistakably evil purposes – oppression, exploitation, arbitrary rule, and ruler's glory – is no longer considered acceptable or permissible. Yet unrestrained authority (and its dangers and potential for evil uses) did not wither away with the discredit of despotic, colonial, autocratic, or totalitarian government. Instead, over the course of the twentieth century, it gained a new lease on life as an adjunct to the currently dominant democratic ideal. This adjunct propagates a belief that a democratic government should possess all the means necessary to regulate the economy. In an increasingly democratized world, this belief or ideal has almost imperceptibly become the residual basis for justifying predatory jurisdiction.

The object of criticism will, therefore, be this ideal that the state should possess all the means necessary to regulate the economy. This ideal is based on the belief that government power can and should be made to work for the benefit of society. This belief, in and of itself and in the most general sense, is perfectly reasonable: it underlies the quest for good government. Yet good government does not require unlimited authority. However, as we already noted at the start of chapter 2, the ideal that the state should possess all the means necessary to regulate the economy is also a profession in favour of unrestrained authority – whether so intended or not. For all intents and purposes, the ideal that a state should possess all the means necessary to regulate the economy attempts to reconcile the idea of good government with unrestrained authority (i.e., unrestrained power as the handmaiden of benevolent government). The objective of this chapter is to show the untenability of this position. The proposition will be that unrestrained authority is inherently inimical to the public interest.

As in previous chapters, we are concerned exclusively with policies and other acts of government that are entirely within the legal authority of the state (i.e., the consequence of valid jurisdiction). We will examine in great detail and in the most realistic terms possible the dynamics of authority and policymaking in the case of predatory jurisdiction. The discussion of predatory jurisdiction will be framed in terms of its manifestation as unrestrained authority. This allows us to expose the brutal fundamentals of authority in a relatively uncomplicated manner. Factually, this is neither unreasonable nor unrealistic because this is, in many situations, precisely the case. (Note the generally uninhibited character of borrowing power or entry regulation.)

To understand why unrestricted authority cannot be thought of rationally as beneficial, we will, in the most realistic terms possible, make explicit what it means to unleash unrestrained authority on the lives of people. Probably the best way to demonstrate the impact of unrestrained authority on the lives of people – and thereby to show its incompatibility with just and beneficial authority – is to push the analysis of unrestrained but lawful authority to its logical extreme. In doing so, we also include a detailed analysis of the impact of unrestrained but valid authority on the legal position of the individual and the consequences for his or her rights and legitimate interests.

A primer on jurisdiction

Before proceeding with exploring the dynamics of predatory jurisdiction, let us digress briefly and present a primer on how jurisdiction relates to policymaking. In the first chapter, we defined jurisdiction as the lawful right to exercise authority. The key concept in this definition is *lawful right*. The basic source of jurisdiction is law (i.e., law creates jurisdiction). The concept of jurisdiction is consistent with the general principle that the state and its agents may do nothing but that which is authorized by law.[1] The concept of jurisdiction works two ways. On the one hand, it sanctions the exercise of power over something and how it may be used; on the other hand, it defines the bounds and limits within which government action is legal. Jurisdiction is an expression used for substantiating valid authority for government policy or action. All types of law at every level or branch of government create jurisdiction. That includes constitutional law, statutory law, jurisprudence, decrees, and regulations. Laws of any kind – in terms of the function of government – ultimately entail either a mandate to act or the authority to enforce. For a proper understanding of the concept of jurisdiction, we need to realize that the *existence* of jurisdiction is not the same as its *exercise*. It is, as the definition of the concept tells us, a lawful right. In other words, jurisdiction is latent power; it is dormant if it is not exercised. Whether or not it is exercised is a matter of choice and judgement, frequently referred to as the practice of *discretion*, a concept that we will elaborate on in the next section.

In a proper constitutional order, the existence of jurisdiction provides the legal basis for policymaking. Policymaking, in other words, is the application of jurisdiction by government. The authority to engage in policymaking is commonly described as policymaking power. For the purposes of this chapter, the terms *policymaking power* and *jurisdiction* will be used interchangeably. Obviously, the point of policymaking is to make policies. A policy is a plan of action of a government for the administration of the society over which it rules or on behalf of it. The creation of laws, regulations, and standards for government action falls within the scope of policymaking. For example, drafting and passing labour legislation is policymaking (labour policy!). Formulating a plan of action or standards of conduct with respect to foreign affairs is called a foreign policy. Governments have policies for virtually all the functions, which they exercise. In other words, governments have monetary policies, fiscal policies, economic policies, law enforcement policies, education policies, healthcare policies, and many others. It is the scope of policymaking powers that determines whether or not we are dealing with predatory jurisdiction.

As an aside, where there is policymaking, there are policymakers. Note that the term *policymakers* refers to those politicians who have captured government power and their immediate helpers, such as policy advisors and top-ranking bureaucrats, such as central bank presidents. The term *policymaker* has the advantage over the concept of *politician* for being more precise: it includes only those politicians who can actually make or genuinely influence policy *and* those people who may have some form of policymaking power or influence on the process without necessarily being politicians themselves (including, for example, top-ranking bureaucrats, central bank presidents, and attorneys general).

Whereas jurisdiction provides a legal basis for policymaking and government action, the question of whether governments should have jurisdiction or how governments should apply jurisdiction is typically less of a legal issue and more a matter of political choice. Policy objectives – or, more fundamentally, the pursuit of policymaking powers – may originate in election campaign pledges, ideological convictions, promises to pressure groups, treaties, and events necessitating government action, for example. These various sources together constitute the mandate for policymaking powers and policy options. Policies and policymaking powers tend to derive their legitimacy from two sources: jurisdiction and political mandate. Observe, by the way, that, in many instances, there is no definite hierarchical order between policymaking and jurisdiction in that the former follows from the latter. Jurisdiction provides a legal basis for policymaking, yet policymaking can also translate into laws and regulations that create jurisdiction. The highest expression of the process where political mandates precede the creation of jurisdiction is the constitution. Constitutional law, the ultimate legal source of jurisdiction, is the end result of a political process in which widely shared and deeply held views on the organization of society and the state collectively embody a political mandate for its adoption.

Lawmaking and the creation of jurisdiction is always a political process. If lawmaking becomes the source of predatory jurisdiction, we should recognize that there might be a problem with the political process. The occurrence of predatory jurisdiction signifies that the process of lawmaking is not balanced by the protection of rights. The relevance of the political process lies in the fact that both the political classes and the voters might not perceive a problem with a lawmaking process that violates the rights and interests of people. This is not mere theorizing. Without an awareness of and acceptance of certain rights as inviolable, a free citizenry can use a perfectly proper legislative process to enact unjust laws. Some of the most appalling legal regimes were promulgated by nations with deep and strong democratic and constitutional traditions. Apartheid in South Africa consisted of a systematic and comprehensive legislative project including almost sixty laws implementing or bolstering racial segregation and white supremacy.[2] Apartheid advocates used a proper legislative process to institutionalize racial discrimination. Much the same occurred with the enactment between 1876 and 1965 of racial segregation laws in the United States (the Jim Crow laws) at the state and local level. Let there be no misunderstanding that the racial segregation laws in South Africa and the United States were enacted by properly constituted and democratically elected legislative bodies based on venerable constitutional traditions. Only a long and hard struggle using the right to equality as the standard of justice overcame entrenched law and racial prejudice. Today, many people around the world accept racial equality as the natural order of things. Yet, not even one hundred years ago, it was racial inequality that was the standard. In the same manner, it is, even now the standard that governments should, as a matter of jurisdiction, have the powers to implement policies that result in overregulation, hyperinflation, overtaxation, runaway budget deficits, excessive borrowing, corruption, and, ultimately, the perpetuation of poverty. Here, again, the basis for the perpetuation of misgovernment resulting from predatory jurisdiction is a lack of awareness of fundamental rights and the failure to define and apply a bona fide standard of justice to the policies and actions of government.

Discretionary power

In our examination of the dynamics of predatory jurisdiction, there is one specific term of art that needs to be elaborated upon: *discretion* (or *discretionary power*). Discretionary power is a key concept for grasping the difference between benign forms of jurisdiction and predatory jurisdiction. One definition of discretion is the power or right to make official decisions using reason and judgement to choose from acceptable alternatives.[3] Governments have the authority to formulate and decide on a range of different policies or actions. Discretion is a type of freedom of choice or "latitude" allowed to policymakers in pursuing their objectives. These objectives may originate in election campaign pledges, ideological convictions, promises to pressure groups, or events necessitating government action. For example, policymakers can choose from various economic schools to shape their monetary and fiscal policies, between, for instance, monetarism and Keynesian economics – or even some mix of prescriptions by such schools. As noted in the previous section, the question of whether and how governments should apply jurisdiction is not typically a legal issue but more a question of political choice.

The broader the latitude or scope of discretionary power, the greater the variety of choices that can be made within the scope of a specific type of jurisdiction. For the public, the latitude for discretion in policymaking becomes visible by the range of options discussed in policy debates. The range of policy options – political choices, in practical fact – that a specific type of jurisdiction is capable of accommodating is indicative of the scope of discretionary power. The larger the scope of discretionary power, the greater the range of policy options will be. An example of this is a debate on fiscal policy wherein politicians, policymakers, pundits, and interest groups find themselves debating different fiscal strategies (e.g., expansionary fiscal policy versus neutral fiscal policy).

In traditions of good governance originating in the West, it is generally the rule that discretionary power "must be used reasonably, impartially and avoiding oppression or unnecessary injury."[4] Also note that the definition of *discretion* provided earlier requires decision-making on the basis of acceptable alternatives. Still, discretionary power or the scope for policymaking is what can give jurisdiction its predatory quality. The scope for policymaking allowed by jurisdiction determines whether jurisdiction restricts government to benign policies or sanctions imprudent and harmful policies. It is at this point, again, that it becomes clear why a standard of justice based on the rights of the individual is necessary. Without a standard of justice, how do we define the range of acceptable alternatives? And how do we avoid oppression or unnecessary injury? The question, therefore, is what happens to society when there are almost no limits to the political choices that can be made?

Sometimes, the simple grant of jurisdiction is itself sufficient to cause predatory jurisdiction. An example of this is the power of government to borrow. The power to borrow is difficult to control through any restriction. Here, the crucial question may be whether or not governments should possess this power. More often, predatory jurisdiction arises through the latitude for policy choices allowed in a specific type of jurisdiction. The expansion of the scope of discretionary power beyond a certain point causes predatory jurisdiction. An example of this is the power to create money by administrative fiat. Central bank mandates define the latitude for the ease or difficulty with which a government can pursue inflationary policies. Is monetary financing prohibited or allowed? Is a mandate focused mainly on safeguarding purchasing power, or does it include conflicting instructions such as promoting the goal of maximum employment? These questions show that gradations are possible in policymaking powers. The scope of discretionary power in a specific type of jurisdiction is directly relevant in those cases where government jurisdiction is natural or indispensable. When it is necessary to grant government certain powers, the question of latitude becomes critical. Without a standard of justice based on the rights of the individual or a conception of predatory jurisdiction, we are in danger of being defenceless against arguments from necessary evil – that because governments must possess certain powers, one must meekly resign oneself to predatory levels of discretionary power. On the other hand, a familiarity with the concept of discretionary power enables us to pursue the question of predatory jurisdiction at the appropriate level, thereby foiling arguments from necessary evil.

The citizen and his or her relationship to sovereign authority

How do you even begin to expose the brutal fundamentals of sovereign authority in a relatively uncomplicated manner? To fully appreciate the dynamics of predatory jurisdiction, it would be helpful to explain the position of the individual member of society within the scheme of sovereign authority. This explanation is essential because, ultimately, all exercise of authority affects the welfare or interests of this individual. It is the individual citizen who experiences, in its ultimate consequences – whether positive or negative, and however direct or indirect – the impact of government action. It is the individual citizen who benefits or gets hurt. To understand why jurisdiction and policymaking are so deeply relevant to the citizen, let us look at one dimension of the relationship between the government and the individual.[5]

The relevant dimension of this relationship is the instance where government represents the jurisdiction exercised over the people and where jurisdiction, in its turn, is defined as the lawful right to exercise authority. Additionally, we define authority as the right to command and to enforce obedience.[6] In this scheme of government authority, the role of the individual is that of subject: a being under the power of another, owing or yielding obedience to sovereign authority.[7] Looked at in terms of the exercise of authority over people, one basic function of government is to compel its subjects to fulfil the will of government. Within a state possessing effective authority, all people are effectively subjects owing obedience to that state. These subjects are, of course, you, me, and just about everybody else living on this planet. Within a state wielding effective authority, the condition of being a subject is inescapable. Being the subjects of sovereign authority is one core element of our relationship with the state or government. The condition of the individual being a subject of sovereign authority applies in every instance where jurisdiction exists – whether beneficial or predatory, just or unjust. Predatory jurisdiction being lawful authority, even when its exercise leads to misgovernment, commands obedience.

At its core, the basis of effective authority (and, by extension, jurisdiction) is obedience. The requirement of obedience to authority serves an inherently legitimate purpose. Sovereign authority is exercised generally through law or on the basis of it. In essence, laws are rules that govern behaviour. The behaviour of the citizen is often formally regulated through prohibitions, directives, and procedures. Laws prohibit theft, trespass, and violence, and they provide for directives through traffic rules or specify procedures for litigation. At a higher level, constitutional law also regulates behaviour but, in this case, that of government. In the final analysis, the law is only effective if it can be enforced. (Enforcement may require coercion.)

The modus operandi of effective authority is not to rely exclusively on the readiness of subjects to comply with commands on the basis of their own free will. The basis of sovereign authority is the duty to obey. This means that, if obedience cannot be achieved on the basis of the free will of the subjects, it must be exacted through coercion. Sovereign authority is conclusively effective only to the degree that obedience can be coerced. Coercion, however, requires power. Most humans instinctively understand power and coercion. However, let us be precise about its meaning by borrowing from the insights available in the theory of warfare. In his famous book, *On War*, Carl von Clausewitz defines war as an act of violence intended to compel our opponent to fulfil our will.[8] Using the analogy of the Clausewitzian definition of war, the concept of power could be paraphrased as the capacity for violence sufficient to compel our opponent to fulfil our will. One could almost say that the authority of the state is based on the ability of the state to wage war on anyone who poses a challenge to its authority. This capacity for violence is available to uphold all forms of jurisdiction, including those forms that are predatory.

The military, the police, and the courts are the instruments of the government that allow it to assert its authority (i.e., commanding and enforcing obedience). The fight against crime by the police is an example of public power; the suppression of riots and rebellions by the military is another. To kill is not only the ultimate form of violence, but also of suppression. However remote and latent, the ghost of law and authority and the fear of police or military action is sufficient to render most people quiet and obedient. The citizen as subject is the object of coercive power. The authority of the state – to collect taxes; make and impose laws, rules, regulations, directives; and conscript and adjudicate – ultimately rests on its willingness and ability to use force. Public authority and power also operate directly in the economy as evidenced by such forces as licensing power; rulemaking power (such as building codes and town and country planning); and the power to set prices, prohibit or monopolize commercial activities, grant monopolies, set quotas, confiscate, nationalize, protect industries, grant concessions, and much more. It is not only *just* authority that employs these instruments; rather, all these instruments are equally available to uphold the exercise of predatory jurisdiction and to suppress disobedience against it. To resist is to risk prosecution, police action, humiliation, trauma, or even death. Violence is potentially a hazard to the well-being of the subject, meaning power and authority are potentially hazardous. Placing the individual under the authority of the state is placing his or her well-being to the mercy of violent power.

The condition of being a subject, of owing obedience, is deeply relevant to the position in life of every living person – and, more broadly, society. The first question should be as follows: Why is this condition of owing obedience so deeply relevant to this subject? The answer to this question is as follows: the subject is not a soulless, lifeless puppet without material interests and volition. He or she, the subject, is a living being engaged in the frequently difficult task of self-sustaining action (i.e., a creature engaged in the task of taking all the actions required by the nature of a rational being for the preservation of his or her life). For good or ill, any requirement imposing a duty to obey represents an intervention by authority in the endeavour by this living being of self-sustaining action. By imposing a duty to obey, we are intervening in the personal choices that the individual needs to make to sustain and/or preserve his or her life. This intervention may add value to the endeavour of self-sustaining action, but it can also cause harm. Criminal law and the protections of the police and the courts can ease the burden of self-sustaining action. Overregulation makes self-sustaining action much harder. When authorities start imposing a duty to obey, those authorities have a moral obligation to think through the consequences of such interventions in the lives of people.

We have rendered explicit and visible a specific dimension of the relationship between the individual and the state. Let us call this specific type of relationship a subject–authority relationship. In terms of predatory jurisdiction, what is the fundamental meaning of this subject – authority relationship? For the citizen, the assertion or exercise of predatory jurisdiction empowers the government to issue commands that are injurious to his or her legitimate interests and imposes a duty on the citizen as subject to obey harmful commands. At this stage, it should be obvious that authority – and, more importantly, unlimited authority – is a formidable creature in its own right, and it is not simply a handmaiden automatically or exclusively dedicated to benevolent government.

Jurisdiction: the absurd and the evil

Why is it fundamentally irrational to think of unrestricted authority as beneficial? What happens to society when there are almost no limits to the political choices that can be made? What does the exercise of predatory jurisdiction signify for the subjects of sovereign authority? The sanction of jurisdiction in practice has real and serious consequences. Depending upon its reach and errors in its premises, it may open the door for bad policymaking. Policies that are flawed are harmful not just because they can be inappropriate or inadequate for the task at hand and because they can be evil by design (created by self-serving politicians and their supporters). They are, above all, harmful because jurisdiction allows government to use power to assert its right to command and exact obedience for its implementation; it can prescribe, proscribe, prosecute, incarcerate, convict, assault, and kill in the attempt to force through its policy objectives – even, or possibly especially, when these are unsound, irrational, or malicious. Policy objectives that are unsound, irrational, or malicious must, in time, cause harm to men and women, and when they notice this and identify the policies in question, they will eventually protest or challenge the will of government. This point must not be passed over lightly because when the government and the victims disagree – that the policies in question are harmful indeed and need to be retracted or compensated, but that government decides that it is in the right or refuses to admit wrong – the government will still have the sanction of jurisdiction and might of public power on its side; under these circumstances, it can, of law and at will, ignore victims. Obviously, public power is a non-issue when government policy is always in agreement with the objectives, interests, and actions of the citizen. It is when political choices collide with the interests, objectives, or actions of the private citizen that authority becomes an issue. This is the logic of authority *and* predatory jurisdiction: power is the instrument of authority intended for compelling the subject to fulfil its will in case of and in spite of disagreement. Power is what makes jurisdiction exercisable at the same time that jurisdiction makes the exercise of power lawful. Power makes the consequences of policies, intended or unintended, for better or for worse, inescapable. If there is anything wrong with the goals of government, God help us when it has the power to pursue them. The modus operandi of all policies, including disastrous ones, is always the same: ideals or ad hoc ideas determine jurisdiction and policy objectives and authority and public power are the tools that make the consequences inescapable for the victims. If we want government to work for our benefit, we had better examine what that means – the wrong answer means that policymakers will be vested with the legal authority to wreak havoc on society and with impunity (i.e., with no legal obligation to heed the cries of victims). The issue here is that government action can, under certain circumstances, be at once lawful and injurious. The most powerful party is government within any society. As the most powerful party, one with moral, legal, and territorial monopoly on force, and the arms to uphold its will, it can impose its decisions in every corner of its territory on any individual or group (i.e., on all citizens, corporations, trades and industries, schools, unions, and associations). The implication is simple: no human agency can do as much damage to society as government.

Therefore, again, the following question arises: where is the harm? A state that has been granted all the means necessary to regulate the economy is one with unlimited discretionary power in this respect. The greater the discretionary power of policymakers, the greater will be the scope for policymaking. By extension, the greater the discretionary power of policymakers, the greater the scope for conceiving and implementing flawed policy objectives and exacting obedience to the dictates that flow from these policies. This is unavoidable because errors will be made; it is in human nature to do so. Actually, any analysis of jurisdiction and the scope of policymaking power and discretionary power must also include the potential for irrational and even evil decisions (and the disaster these can bring). It should be brutally clear by now that discretionary power, unrestrained, in essence and in practice means that policymakers can legally make any number of decisions that are wrong, counterproductive, crackpot, rash, heartless, ruinous, bizarre, self-serving, predatory, unjust, extortionist, pointless, or evil. Whomever sees the unrestrained authority of, for example, Russian or Egyptian or Indian government as anything less awful than this must either reject reality or approve of its actions. Indian government, for instance, uses its regulatory power to prohibit companies from closing unprofitable factories, even when they are already demonstrably bankrupt, which is about as crackpot as you can get. In practice, the owners often abandoned the factories. The jurisdiction of the ministry of defence, the mining office, social affairs ministry, and the antiquities department, with respect to issuing desert land to citizens in Egypt, represent equally bizarre and half-baked ideas. There is clearly nothing in the constitution of these countries to check and stop the government from making any of these rules and liberally sprinkling about these powers throughout the body of public administration. The consequences have been disastrous for the societies in question. It is vital to understand that these bizarre and extreme powers are perfectly legal, vested acts of authority; it is a crime to act contrary to this authority. Therefore, the highest duty of the subject–citizen is obedience, even to incompetent or unreasonable rulers! If this kind of logic goes against the grain, if the mind rebels against such statements, know that this is an understandable reaction – the irrational and bizarre are hard to fathom. But this reaction is quite similar to what real victims feel when things actually start happening to them, which is why victims say to themselves, *This is insane. This must be a nightmare. This can't be happening to me. They can't demand that from me. Why are they doing this to me?* And yet the victim must submit or obey. The citizen pays twice for the state having this authority: first as a taxpayer and then again as a victim. And the worst part of it is to be a victim of authority and yet to receive no recognition for being a victim because that authority is lawful. The line of argumentation so far should already be sufficient to free us of the belief that unlimited authority can be reconciled with the cause of good government.

Unlimited regulatory powers as lawful authority means that the government can legally coerce citizens to submit to laws and regulations that are contrary to their interests. What does it mean to coerce a citizen to do what is contrary to his or her interests? It is to sacrifice that individual or a whole group of them because policymakers have motives or identified interests that ignore the welfare of these victims. The seventy-seven procedures required to acquire and develop desert land in Egypt can also be understood as at least seventy-seven policy objectives that are deemed more important than the private needs, interests, ambitions, or dreams of the citizens. And in case you forgot: extralegals *are* citizens. The thirty-one government offices involved can also be understood as representing no fewer than thirty-one interests that are deemed more important than the happiness of the citizens. Government possessing all the means necessary to regulate the economy makes public power in practical terms a hostile force, a constant menace, to the private initiatives and ambitions of citizens because discretionary power implicit to unlimited authority makes political choices contrary to private interests legal, possible, and probable. The most fitting and passionate denunciation of government on these accounts was made by Pierre Proudhon, and it still rings true:

> To be governed is to be watched, inspected, spied on, regulated, indoctrinated, preached at, controlled, ruled, censored, by persons who have neither wisdom nor virtue. It is every action and transaction to be registered, stamped, taxed, patented, licensed, assessed, measured, reprimanded, corrected, frustrated. Under the pretext of the public good it is to be exploited, monopolized, embezzled, robbed and then at the least protest or word of complaint, to be fined, harassed, vilified, beaten up, bludgeoned, disarmed, judged, condemned, imprisoned,

shot, garrotted, deported, sold, betrayed, swindled, deceived, outraged, dishonoured. That's government, that's its justice, that's its morality! And imagine that among us there are democrats who believe government to be good, socialists who in the name of liberty, equality and fraternity support this ignominy, proletarians who offer themselves candidates for President of the Republic![9]

The scorn he heaps on it should be recognizable to every subject, rich and poor, of all-powerful governments in the developing world. Nevertheless, I have no desire to live in a world without government. Proudhon's dream of no government is, in reality, the nightmare of a failed state; life in Liberia and Somalia is not my cup of tea. Rather, let us be more modest or subtle in our analysis and take this quotation, use the concept of *unrestrained regulatory power* as a substitute for the word *government,* and observe how well this replacement fits.

In politicians we trust

As we have already mentioned, any analysis of jurisdiction and discretionary power should always include the potential for erroneous, irrational, and even evil policymaking. If not, our way of thinking about political power and authority becomes positively Panglossian. In practical life and workaday politics, we usually do not make an explicit and comprehensive case for unlimited authority. Yet, strictly for the sake of argument, there is no reason why we could not. The case in favour of unlimited discretion in policymaking is that government can be trusted to make power work for the greater good and prosperity of humankind; unlimited authority is a force for good, and that a government with unlimited authority can be benevolent.[10]

With these fine intentions in mind, what else must we assume? In practical terms, one must assume that the overwhelming majority of politicians will be men and women of high moral standards, mostly unselfish and largely free from temptation, impartial where it counts, and equipped with the strength and will to resist special interests – incorruptible – clearly worthy of our trust, especially with such unlimited discretion. One must assume that these policymakers are genuinely filled with love for the nation and imbued with an honest desire to serve the people. One must assume that there will be virtually no evil design on the part of policymakers. One must assume that our politicians will be so judicious that they will practice forbearance in applying this discretionary power to policymaking. One must assume that fatal incompetence, on balance to be reasonable, is most unlikely. We should count on the security of faith and the solemn say-so of those who are to be trusted with this limitless power – without protection, escape, fallback positions, or safeguards – that those unlimited powers will not be abused. We must trust people whom we are not personally acquainted with and whose character is unknown to us with unlimited power. And should one not believe in the superior intellect and high virtue of politicians and still insist that this government with unlimited authority will, at the end of the day, still be a force for benevolence, one must believe in miracles and mysteries. We must accept evil designs as the price of achieving an even greater good – and in any case, great causes excuse sacrifice (i.e., causing harm and making victims). Thus, we bid farewell to the evidence of history, abandon good sense, and repress our fear of power. Therefore, governments in India, Russia, Egypt, Brazil, and a majority of countries, by doing their utmost to practice this unrestrained authority, deserve our admiration. The red tape and overbearing bureaucracy with its endless regulations and directives from which "permission must be obtained to work out the least details of personal, family and professional life,"[11] and the accompanying corruption and exclusion so abundant in these countries, ample evidence of discretionary power being practiced with great eagerness, are the price of a greater good that is about to be achieved. As they say, one can't make an omelette without breaking a few eggs.

Good and bad policy

It is probably inevitable that this way of analysing discretionary policymaking powers might be criticized for ignoring the reason or objective, the method or wisdom of economic policies. We might be accused of passing over without mention a vast body of economic know-how in regards to policymaking and the good to which this know-how may be applied. One could argue that the greater our know-how about economics, the greater the experience with economic policymaking, the greater the opportunity for improved and more effective policymaking. Does that not, at least to some extent, justify discretionary policymaking power? Also, the needs and circumstances of countries change with time, sometimes radically. Is not the whole point of discretionary policymaking power to enable governments to choose, craft, and tailor economic policies appropriate to the needs of the country and its circumstances? Taking all these issues together, are we therefore not being overly simplistic in criticizing discretionary policymaking power?

There are two assumptions involved here. One is that more know-how and experience will in time translate into better policymaking. The other is that the very range of policy options on offer along with the diversity of circumstances validates freedom of choice for policymakers (i.e., discretionary power). More know-how and experience can, of course, translate into better policymaking and, from time to time, that actually happens. The problem, however, with this assertion is that there is no causal relation between increasing know-how and improved policymaking. The very fact that there are still so many poor countries is proof to the contrary. In country after country, policymakers not only ignore the most rational policy options available, but also persist in adopting policies even when all leading economists advise against them and the business community and the financial markets protest. As for the range of policy options on offer, in the case of unlimited policy discretion, that includes every imaginable flawed policy option (including all policy options that have already been tried and proven disastrous). To make matters worse, bad policy options are quite often based upon or supported by economic theories. Typically, such theories have been proven wrong or flawed, but that fact seems to escape their adherents and fails to stop such theories from gaining new devotees. As for the circumstances of the countries, it is often the governments that created these circumstances by applying bad policies in the first place.

We can instead distil a universal truth from this: the case against discretionary policymaking powers is precisely that the availability of good policy options has never stopped governments from adopting bad policy prescriptions. The point of discretionary authority is that the good comes with the bad. In Argentina, for example, good policy in one area, sound monetary policies – one of the prime achievements of the Menem government – were ultimately undone by bad policy in another area: fiscal weakness and a failure by the same government. In the end, the stage was set for economic collapse by the end of 2001.[12] Fascinatingly, during this calamity, Mr Domingo Cavallo, celebrated policymaker, destroyed his own accomplishments precisely because he had the authority to fiddle with them. At the start of the 1990s, Mr Cavallo had been the principle architect of an independent central banking system and a sound money system (by setting up a currency board under which the peso was fixed by law at par to the dollar, and a money supply restricted to the level of hard-currency reserves) and a healthy banking system. Yet, ten years later, in a desperate attempt to turn around a depressed economy, he destroyed his own creation by tampering with its fundamentals, stripped the central bank of its independence, eased reserve requirements for banks, and forced the banks and pension funds to swallow government debt at unfavourable terms. The outcome was a banking crisis, rioting, and political implosion. The simple truth about discretionary policymaking power is that it is dangerous; it makes the quality of policymaking variable and unpredictable. The choice among policy options is the prerogative of political minds; an abundance of excellent policy options will not stop the fool or the knave from making a dismal choice. Once we start thinking about the purpose of unlimited discretionary powers and the uses to which these can be, have been, and will be put, an analysis of policies on their technical merits becomes a digression. It is for this reason that we will not investigate interventionist policies in regard to their effectiveness; doing so adds no value in view of the central problem presented by unlimited authority.

Nevertheless, this is not to suggest that economic theory is of no consequence. Actually, it is extremely relevant! There are piles of studies by economists wherein economic policies and regulations are taken apart. A significant portion of economic research at universities in the West, by no means hotbeds of laissez-faire sentiment, is directed at uncovering the harmful effects of economic regulation, including protectionist measures, environmental controls, labour legislation, industrial codes, and health and safety measures. The economists doing this type of research are not so much in disagreement with the policy objectives – who could possibly find fault with the goal of a prosperous society of happy, healthy people safe at work in a clean environment – as they are interested in the economic distortions that misconceived regulations cause, outcome efficiencies of regulations, the regulatory burden and rent-seeking. By now, they have uncovered massive evidence of distortion, rent seeking, and waste, which is the consequence of such interventionism. A look at this mounting body of findings should put a chill on our eagerness for interventionist government; if anything, the evidence of academic research is more a cautionary tale against policy discretion than an endorsement.

But even sensible economic policy points away from unrestrained interventionism. The best policies, more often than not, require less instead of more political control of and interference with the economy. Freeing markets is usually sold as a *policy* to the public; it is also, to one degree or another, a retreat from interventionist government. Sound money is a policy; it is also eschewing the policy of redistribution, meaning less political interference with the economy. Thus, ironically, good *policy* often entails less government intervention. But that, by implication, destroys the case for unlimited discretionary power in economic policymaking: if such and such economic policy demonstrably injures the interests of the citizen, why must we allow government the discretion to adopt, implement, continue, repeat this policy?

We can say this much about economic policy: one way or another, interventionist policies often conflict with the legitimate objectives of citizens. We are all aware that interventionism is essentially well intentioned. This picture of good intentions is, however, a big problem – it distracts the attention of the uninformed from the question of feasibility and the consequences.

The rights and the sufferings of the individual

We now have made explicit what it means to claim that the state should possess all the necessary means to regulate the economy. In the remainder of this chapter, we will use the concept of the right to life (as in Locke's right to life, liberty, and property) as a tool for our continued examination of the logic of predatory jurisdiction. If the citizen is ever going to become anything more than the subject of authority – earlier defined as a being under the power of another, owing or yielding obedience to sovereign authority – we better start thinking of this "subject" as an autonomous agent, one with private interests and legitimate objectives that must not be violated. By resorting to natural rights, we avail ourselves of the ultimate expression of a view on the welfare of the people. The theory of natural rights is the best-developed reply, and, in fact, the *only* opposite point of view to the publicists of absolute power. The idea of natural rights is the perfect antithesis of absolute power; it is a theory of *individual* rights and the word *individual* says it all: in the most general terms, each and every person is acknowledged as an autonomous agent with interests and objectives that are inviolable. Thus, natural rights allow us to examine the issue of power by its contrast, which is the concept of rights. Natural rights enable us to set a standard of justice and thereby define the criteria for just authority. Let us take the right to life as the yardstick for the continuation of this chapter.

In chapter 3, we defined the concepts of production and trade in accordance with Rand's philosophy. Now let us elaborate on this: the basic unit of economic activity *and* the subject of the right to life is the individual. If the individual is to enjoy the right to life, it follows that he or she should have the freedom to produce and trade, which is a human's mode of self-sustaining action. This, then, is the meaning of private interests of the individual; the individual embodies the private interest. He or she sets the objectives or the course of action to be taken to meet his or her needs by creating wealth, be it building homes, providing a service, or developing a business – actions that are essential to his or her life. A different way of saying that these actions are essential to his or her life is to note that these actions are right and necessary. This is why actions such as building homes, starting a business, and providing a service are legitimate objectives. Production and trade should have been the derivative rights of (or corollaries to) one's right to his or her own life. A human's objectives, his or her dreams and ambitions in terms of productive effort and trade are legitimate because they are necessary for sustaining his life. And let us again repeat the question: can humanity survive without production and trade? In a word: no.

The crucial test of the significance of the right to life is to reverse the argument. Suppose that there is no such thing as the right to produce and trade despite the fact that it is necessary and right. The consequence is that the individual would no longer *by right* engage in self-sustaining action but he or she would have to do so by *permission*. To say the individual has no right to produce or trade is to say that the individual lives on permission or at least at the sufferance of some authority and must accept refusal of permission and, therefore, in the worst case, maybe even embrace death as the ultimate expression of his submission to authority. The critical insight gained from this analysis is that the denial of rights expands the scope of authority.

The point is basically this: within the context of the economy, the citizen has interests and objectives that are right and necessary and, therefore, inviolable (i.e., where he or she is not or should not be a subject of authority). There must be some irreducible point beyond which nothing can excuse the interference by government if he or she is to be anything more than a subject of authority. Why do we accept that a man or woman should be the master of his or her own voice (free speech) but not of his or her hands? When you need a dozen permits to set up a business, you are nothing but a grovelling subject beholden to, possibly, that same number of masters. This is the purpose of a theory of rights: to examine what is rightly the preserve of each and every individual, where his or her interests and objectives are accepted upfront, at face value, without suspicion or alarm. A million promises of forbearance and prudence from our rulers will not provide the citizen any security or the dignity of citizenship as long as the principle of unlimited authority is not abandoned.

Without its corollaries – the right to produce and the right to trade – the whole concept of the right to life becomes meaningless. Note that, until now, there has never been a fully explicit declaration of the inalienable right of the individual to produce and trade. The closest we come to this definition of rights are the ideals of free enterprise, free trade, and free markets. These, however, are outcomes, resultants, of rights to produce and trade. Observe how most people seem to embrace the concepts of free enterprise, trade, and markets without any explicit and prior definition of the rights that are required to make these outcomes possible. The issue at stake is that, in the long run, freedoms are very hard to protect effectively without the declaration of rights. Is it any wonder that government interference is so unrestrained in the economy, that governments take the liberty of proscribing and prescribing at the slightest whim? In the context of economics, policymaking power, for better or worse, means government asserting authority over basic life processes. In this context, unlimited authority means exactly this: the state may subordinate essentially legitimate objectives of private individuals to political choices or decision making, to compel the citizen to fulfil the will of government even when no harm was intended by this citizen and such government action is contrary to his or her interests. The keyword here is the *interest* of the citizen. This is not some dirty word; in fundamental terms, the interest of any citizen is his or her right to life, liberty, and the pursuit of happiness. Therefore, the principle that the state should possess all the means to regulate the economy at the bottom conflicts with this right.

A government with an unrestricted mandate to regulate the economy is a government that has been granted jurisdiction over private decision-making (i.e., broad discretionary powers to interfere with the personal choices that the individual needs to make to create wealth necessary for sustaining and/or preserving his or her life). An individual wishing to create wealth by his or her own effort (i.e., by producing and trading) finds that these actions, which are both necessary and right for his or her existence, are subject to the requirement of permission, prohibitions, restrictions, and instructions. And such is life for most people.

Let us make no mistake: we are *not* discussing thieves, robbers, highwaymen, swindlers, fraudsters, muggers, or looters; we are discussing ordinary men and women who can be counted upon to mind their own business and who need to produce and trade – pursuits that seemed both positively innocent and necessary when we analysed the meaning of economic activity. Whether we are conscious of the fact or not, we have granted the final authority in the land, the power to investigate, proscribe, issue directives, prosecute, incarcerate, convict, assault, and kill men and women who are engaged, strictly speaking, in nothing less peaceful and more necessary than productive effort and voluntary exchange. This is not even theoretical; rather, it is real, practical authority ... even if it sounds as grindingly dull and ordinary to the average man or woman as does licensing power, import trade restrictions, foreign currency controls, rent control laws, country and town planning, price controls, and other types of restrictions. Yet open and declared defiance of any of these powers of the state is perilous – it may well be met with state violence.

These are the facts about power: unlimited authority will, regardless of the original motives, always mean that government may, as a matter of policy choice, block or restrict the objectives of or undo the actions of the citizen, which are necessary and right and beneficial to him or her; it can stop the individual from building homes, starting businesses, and providing services. The analysis is by no means extreme – it is basically the experience of the extralegal: exclusion means that people are prevented by the legal system from achieving such basic goals within the formal sector. When the process of policymaking goes wrong and policymakers finds reason to become hostile or indifferent to our objectives, we citizens are in trouble. The legal system and its accompanying bureaucracy are turned into an obstacle course. Gaining fiat, keeping in line with the rules can suddenly become a stark struggle for survival, a source of pain, anguish, and loss precisely because our objectives are essential to our well-being. In this respect, it is crucial that we understand that it does not matter whether this outcome is by design or whether it is unintentional. What matters is the reach of this power, the will of those in power to exercise it, and the disastrous consequences. This is what untrammelled public authority means to bona fide private interests when the object of public authority becomes the essentially legitimate objective of private individuals.

Jurisdiction, immunity, and impunity

This leaves us with one final question about public authority and power: can a legal system where the state possesses all the means necessary to regulate the economy offer anything at all in terms of protection to private interests against the lawful exercise of discretionary power or the consequences? The answer is: no. The orderly and non-violent conduct of human relationships in society and the security of individuals in that society necessitates a final or supreme authority acting as the ultimate arbiter in the affairs of people. This authority should not be open to challenge and represents public power that must not be resisted by citizens (which is one very good reason why governments must hold a legal monopoly on the use of physical force). In matters of public policy, government is this supreme authority; policymaking is the rightful affair of government because it is intrinsic to the art of governance and legislation. Provided that government stays within the limits of its jurisdiction and discretionary powers, policymaking power carries its own insurance of immunity: government, its representatives, agencies, and officers cannot be held liable for the consequences of their decisions. It is a principle of public law that recourse to legal protection does not extend to dissent against public policy. To extend recourse to legal protection to dissent against public policy as a matter of principle would defeat the principle of final authority and the provision of jurisdiction and discretionary power. In other words, public policies adopted and implemented within the discretionary power of government cannot and should not, in principle, be challenged in any court. If you have ever wondered why misgovernment does not appear to carry any penalties for government and its agents, this is one very important reason.

This issue cannot be solved. There are two reasons for this: first, the need for a final authority is fundamental to the organization of society and the state, including government, is the supreme organization in society;

second, the representatives of final authority are human, and to err is part of human nature. Understanding the problem of misgovernment requires us to grasp the full consequence of jurisdiction and discretionary power. The greater our faith in and appetite for government action, the broader the latitude for policymaking and public authority required. At the same rate, the scope of legal security and recourse to legal protection shrinks. At this point, the pieces of the puzzle start to fall in place. The discretionary power of government is a hazard to the economy and the citizen. It is an absence of restraints in making political choices or a void at the centre of the legal system where government can decide, impose, and enforce at will. Discretionary power originating in proper jurisdiction – and that includes the predatory variety as well – is public authority exercised lawfully and with impunity. Within its limits, the legitimacy of a citizen's objectives, appropriateness of private interests, or rights lose their power to protect; legally, there is nothing that can stop the state and its agents.

This much must be repeated about the concept of legal protection or safeguards. Legal safeguards normally protect only against the government overreaching its authority and not against actions – lawmaking, regulatory, and administrative measures – that are deemed lawful. To put it simply: you cannot protect yourself against unlimited authority. There is, therefore, no recourse to legal protection against the harm caused by the exercise of predatory jurisdiction. This should not be dismissed as mere theorizing; after all, try filing a suit against the government for causing inflation. In law, what is theoretically possible is sooner or later practical authority.

Predatory jurisdiction versus the principle of limited government

Unrestrained authority is inherently inimical to the public interest. Unrestrained power is no handmaiden of benevolent government. Good government cannot be achieved by means of predatory jurisdiction. Observe, however, that even at a conceptual level, the reality of predatory jurisdiction as such poses a profound problem: it is the product of a conception of lawful authority that contradicts the rationale of limited government. Limited government is a familiar principle in political philosophy, and for this reason, we will not explore this broad and complicated subject in its totality. It denotes a form of government whose powers exist only within predefined limits prescribed in a constitutional framework. The relevant fact here is that the principle of limited government represents the antithesis of the practice of arbitrary, unlimited, or unconditional power.

A proper grasp of predatory jurisdiction requires that we take note of a fundamental contradiction in this concept. This contradiction becomes evident by looking at the concept of jurisdiction as applied in the context of the principle of limited government. In this context, we discover that it was not intended to denote unlimited political power and authority. We have already defined jurisdiction as the lawful right to exercise authority, with the key concept in this definition being *lawful right*. We also noted that the basic source of jurisdiction is law (i.e., law creates jurisdiction). The concept of jurisdiction is of special relevance to one of the building blocks of limited government: the rule of law. *Rule of law* is the idea that the power of government is subject to and limited by law. Conceptually, jurisdiction is consistent with one of the principles underlying the rule of law (i.e., the state may do nothing but that which is authorized by law). This, in a broader context, is consistent with the concept of limited government (i.e., a conception of a government whose powers exist only within predefined limits prescribed in a constitutional framework). The rule of law is part of a broader tradition of checks on government power. The purpose of the rule of law is to protect the people against the power of the state by subjecting the actions of rulers to explicit and formal rules. The question of jurisdiction makes sense only to the extent that government action has been subjected to formal and explicit rules and laws. It is an expression used for substantiating valid authority for government policy or action. As an expression on valid authority, the term *jurisdiction* denotes not only the powers that may be exercised, but also the bounds and limits within which government action is legal. Jurisprudence on the validity of government jurisdiction gives rather elegant expression to this principle by qualifying government actions as *intra vires* or *ultra vires*. These Latin expressions may be respectively translated as follows: *within the powers* and *beyond the powers*. To quote Wikipedia on its usage in the legal world: "If an act requires legal authority and it is done with such authority, it is characterised in law as intra vires .... If it is done without such authority, it is ultra vires."[13] In this context, the concept of jurisdiction is part of a tradition presuming checks on government power.

The modern idea of rule of law developed in opposition to absolute monarchy or absolutism. *Absolutism* is a form of monarchical rule not limited by laws and constitutions and unconstrained by other institutions (i.e., absolute power). Absolutism as a practice is as old as history. From ancient times, rulers have, as a norm, either acted unrestrained by laws and constitutions, indulging in the arbitrary exercise of power, or sought the power to do so. In Europe, absolutism as an ideology developed during the seventeenth century: the objective was to raise the ruler above law and to make him or her accountable to no one.[14] The logical consequence of this objective was that it provided evil rulers with an ideological basis for justifying the practice of tyranny. It allowed the ruler to use government power for his or her own pleasure, with no consideration for the welfare of the ruled. It is the "right" or prerogative of the ruler to oppress and exploit the people with only his or her whim as the guiding principle of government while having no judge above his person. Absolute power gave King Louis XIV of France bragging rights to the presumption that he could run his country as he saw fit: "It is legal because I wish it."

The purpose of rule of law is to end or thwart the practice of absolute power and arbitrary rule and to promote legal security and equality before the law. The concept "implies that every citizen is subject to the law, including law makers themselves. It stands in contrast to the idea that the ruler is above the law."[15] On a different level, the purpose of rule of law is to promote good government, one that is respectful of the interests of and beneficial to the citizenry, not to serve the pleasure of the ruler. The law was to be the instrument of delineating the powers of the rulers (i.e., to grant jurisdiction). In this context, the law was seen as the means to protect and promote the interests of the citizenry. In the words of John Locke, the people were to be governed "by promulgated established laws" that were to be "designed for no other end ultimately, but the good of the people."[16] This, then, is the historical context of the concept of jurisdiction. From a historical perspective, jurisdiction is indicative of limits on government powers. It is fundamentally contrary to the idea that government should have unlimited powers or the authority to practice ill government. As we can now see, predatory jurisdiction contradicts the true spirit of the concept of jurisdiction. In a sense, the concept of jurisdiction was not meant to denote unrestrained authority.

Predatory jurisdiction: perverting the concept of jurisdiction

We need to be clear in our understanding that predatory jurisdiction is also based on the general principle that the state may do nothing but that which is authorized by law. The basic source of predatory jurisdiction is law. Predatory jurisdiction in a formal sense conforms to the principle that the actions of the rulers are subject to explicit and formal rules. Predatory jurisdiction is valid authority for government policy or action. Also, in the way that laws are invariably adopted and promoted as being for the benefit of the people, so predatory jurisdiction is justified as the grant of authority for the benefit of society. Yet predatory jurisdiction, though definitely law, does not conform to a basic principle of the rule of law, namely that laws should be "just ... and protect fundamental rights, including the security of persons and property."[17] From a perspective of limited government, the problem with predatory jurisdiction is that the basic function of jurisdiction has been subverted: where the grant of jurisdiction was intended to limit government, now it is a carte blanche to exercise unrestrained power. The point of jurisdiction is to protect us; predatory jurisdiction removes all protection. Law was meant to restrain government; instead, law is used to unleash almighty government upon us *and* to grant this perversion the sanction of legality. The purpose of defining jurisdiction was originally intended to make the actions of government predictable and accountable; under predatory jurisdiction, the actions of government are no longer predicable and, because it is valid authority, it carries its own insurance of immunity. Thus, to the extent that predatory jurisdiction exists, the idea of limited government is rendered meaningless. Under predatory jurisdiction, the scope of government authority is now so broad that policymakers no longer have to violate a law (i.e., exceed their authority) in order to cause harm. The power to injure the public interest is not *ultra vires*. The formal qualification of government power and actions as *intra vires* no longer represents meaningful or material proof of just authority.

The ethical status of unlimited authority

At this point, we arrive at an ethical question: is a legal system in which the authority of the state is unrestrained, unstoppable, and immune still just? The answer must be *no* if the standard of justice is the rights of the individual and the deprivation of rights constitutes injustice. The idea of just authority stands for the insight that it is not sufficient that authority should conform to a standard of legality, but that it should also live up to a standard of justice. We must now conclude that, to evaluate the rightness of government action, it is not sufficient to find jurisdiction. We should also evaluate whether a certain kind or scope of jurisdiction is good or evil. In earlier chapters, we found that, in the case of predatory jurisdiction, lawful acts of government infringe upon the rights and interests of the people. Looking at predatory jurisdiction from an ethical perspective forces us to appreciate the difference between legality and morality. As noted earlier, the basic source of jurisdiction is law (i.e., law creates jurisdiction). The tension between what is moral and what is lawful is well known in the field of ethics: two Latin phrases reveal the underlying difference: *ius quia iustum*, which means *the law is that which is just* and its opposite, *ius quia iussum*, which means *the law is that which is commanded.* With authority deriving its sanction from law, predatory jurisdiction relies excessively on the principle of *ius quia iussum*.[18] Law and morality can and often do mesh. On the other hand, law can be used to create and sanction unrestrained, unstoppable, and immune authority (i.e., predatory jurisdiction). A moral view on the mission of government based on a standard of justice derived from natural right militates against unlimited authority. Properly understood, rights are moral principles, and the ultimate purpose of these is the protection of human life and dignity. By extension, justice is a moral principle for the protection of such natural rights. Unlimited authority – in this case, through predatory jurisdiction – turns law into the enemy of morality. To make unjust laws, one must first render such moral principles as rights and justice inoperative and impotent. Unlimited authority or predatory jurisdiction requires subjects that are obedient not only to just laws but also to laws that violate moral principles. A regulatory system based on the presumption of unlimited authority is fundamentally unjust.

In discussing the concept of the right to life, we found we could apply it to economic activity. We found that, essentially, people do not engage in self-sustaining action by permission but by right. When the state possesses all the means necessary to regulate the economy, self-sustaining action by the individual is not practiced by right, but only by permission from and at the sufferance of the state. In other words, the right to life – or more specifically, the corollary rights to produce and trade – is now repealed and has no protective power (and the interests of the individual can be thwarted with impunity). Unlimited discretionary power means that there is a hole at the centre of the legal system, and by extension, government and politics, where there is no justice. And to make matters worse: injustice can be committed with impunity by ruling politicians and their bureaucrats within the scope of a moral void. As a matter of principle, this denial of rights is a fundamental necessity to the exercise of unrestrained discretionary power. Rights, by their very nature, shrink the scope of discretionary power available to policymakers; we discovered that the relationship between rights and discretion is inverted: the relationship between authority and individual rights is very intimate *and* very negative. Thus, we have an answer to our question of what happens to society when there are no limits to political choices, as is the case when the state possesses all the necessary means to regulate the economy. Any political system that allows so much scope for injustice is both, in principle and in practice, immoral. Misgovernment to any extent made possible by unlimited authority is an injustice perpetrated against the people. Misgovernment based on predatory jurisdiction is a system of policymaking power that flouts the idea of just authority. How can one persist in believing that unlimited authority is reconcilable with beneficial authority once one realizes that the former means the negation of moral principles for the protection of human life whereas the latter ultimately requires its affirmation? In summary, this is what people everywhere must understand if they would like to do something about misgovernment: the denial of rights is the problem at the centre of economic mismanagement, exclusion, corruption, extralegality, overborrowing, government-induced inflation, and many other problems.

The remains of discretionary power

The question arises of whether discretionary power can at all be legitimate or acceptable in any manner. Let us note that the thesis is not that the grant of discretionary power to government can never be right. Essentially, what we must guard against is unexamined unlimited power and authority, the idea that government should possess by default and without critical review all the powers necessary to regulate the economy. The measure of the right and wrong of discretionary power is whether its scope clearly and damagingly violates the rights and interests of the individual. In other words, there is scope for discretionary power to the extent that it does not violate this or that standard of justice. Government should have certain regulatory powers for the reason that the exercise of rights or the pursuit of one's private interests does not include being a nuisance or a menace to your fellow citizens. Chapter 3 includes the case of market failures. In the case of pollution, for example, there is no single solution that solves the whole problem. For this reason, some leeway in terms of discretionary policymaking power is necessary. On the other hand, even then this room for policy discretion may not be used as some kind of a backdoor for hollowing out the inviolability of rights. The objective is to propagate an awareness of predatory jurisdiction, not to destroy effective government. At this time, the worry that an emphasis on diminishing the scope of discretionary policymaking power should reduce the effectiveness of government is totally laughable. Such a stance is only possible by ignoring both the evidence of history and ongoing drama of current policymaking. Governments with the lawful authority to practice without restraint any or all forms of misgovernment can hardly be considered effective, at least not from the perspective of the common good. Any suggestion to the contrary is either mendacious or reveals a lack of good sense.

The charge of legalism

It is possible that this book, by looking at the question of misgovernment only from the perspective of the formal jurisdictional powers of government and the rights of the individual, might be critiqued for being excessively and narrowly legalistic or formalistic and therefore too shallow in its approach to the problems of non-advanced economies. Surely there is more to misgovernment than just the matter of the formal powers of government and their scope. In fact, it is noteworthy that though governments in many rich and poor countries have the same sort and scope of powers the latter are much worse governed. From this observation, one could hypothesize that there is more going on than formal structure alone. Also, the powers of government are not reformed in some kind of vacuum; there are broader political and social processes that must be accounted for. These include, for example, how people perceive the role of government in society or what the public and various special interests expect from government, and not least how people – especially those in or near power – view the uses of state authority, public power, etc. The essence of this criticism is that it is the attitudes and behaviour of people, their values and views, that determines whether or not a country is well governed.

There is no denying that there is truth in this line of reasoning. These are, indeed, hardly investigated in this book. The answer to the charge above is that that this book was never meant to answer all questions about misgovernment. For example, acts beyond the legal power or authority of the government are categorically excluded from the scope of this book. That is excluding a lot. Much of what goes by the name of misgovernment in poor countries is about unconcealed abuse of power, the clear illegality and illegitimacy of how a country is ruled. The way President Robert Mugabe systematically destroyed Zimbabwe is typical of a situation where, in the short term, the question of predatory jurisdiction as such becomes virtually irrelevant; Zimbabwe's first and highest priority is the difficult task of getting rid of outright tyranny, not predatory jurisdiction. Many countries may first have to work at changing their political culture or structures simply to make democratic processes and the rule of law feasible.

Also, no matter how one structures the formal jurisdictional powers of government there are always going to be issues about competence, honesty and integrity, policy design, the strength and effectiveness of institutions, the management and efficiency of bureaucracies, and other matters. In other words, one must consider issues of virtue, structure, and performance. Thus, solving the problem of misgovernment is more than just specifying and fixing the limits and boundaries of government authority and enumerating the rights of the individual. It is also about putting in place the right sorts of institutions, improving the management of the public administration, and ensuring rule of law, for example. In the first chapter, we noted that we are used to applying standards of virtue to the problems of misgovernment. Doing so is indubitably necessary and yet insufficient. The point of a theory of predatory jurisdiction is to expand our understanding of the problem of misgovernment beyond questions of virtue, structure, and performance, not dwelling exclusively on them.

Nevertheless, the analytical framework presented so far has broad significance: attitudes, values and views of people, and even their behaviour are, to a significant extent, also influenced by what people know and do not know and, in fact, also by what they know others know or do not know. What people know about how a state operates and how that affects their lives and about their rights can affect their views and attitudes about what is right and wrong about how they are governed. What you gain in knowledge about the nature of government and your rights changes your expectations and therefore your attitudes, values, and views. So a government of a society, where the influential portion of the public has become rights-conscious and aware of the concept of predatory jurisdiction and its consequences, will eventually behave differently from one that governs people who are oblivious of such concepts and ideas. A government that can exercise its borrowing powers without questions from the public is likely to have a fundamentally different attitude towards the importance of fiscal prudence than one that must face a public well aware of how public borrowing could endanger property rights. When you know that a public power such as government borrowing can eventually destroy the value of your savings and pension fund and bring on a crisis that will bankrupt your business or the company you work for, you are liable to look at the scope of government authority with new eyes. When a significant portion of the public or some influential section of society becomes similarly conscious and worried that changes the arithmetic of voting behaviour and eventually the mathematics of campaign promises. The challenge, then, is to change those attitudes, values, and views, rather than to study them by providing the public a new framework for understanding the causes of misgovernment.

In many ways, misgovernment is inevitably a formalistic or legalistic topic. In discussing the problems of misgovernment it is often impossible to avoid the issue of the legal powers of government or the scope of its authority. Misgovernment is, strange as it may sound, a species of *government* (i.e., the exercise of formal power and authority or jurisdiction, and not merely its outcome). Modern government exercises its powers through legal and administrative systems. Misgovernment, then, is intimately tied to how legal and administrative systems work. Take the example of free speech versus censorship. If you value free speech and abhor its restraint you must eventually discuss the legal powers of government; you must sooner or later come to the question of whether government should have formal censorship powers or not. In fact, the very willingness of a government to formally surrender its censorship powers is by now often enough accepted as one test of its legitimacy. Also, when those censorship powers have been abolished and the right of free speech has been enumerated in positive law, we have the issue of government compliance. When a government continues to persecute journalists and dissident politicians, we often define these actions in terms of a violation of the law. We do not scoff at people for being excessively legalistic for calling the persecution of journalists a violation of the law of a deprivation of a right. The question of whether a government should have some power is a more profound, even radical, statement than saying that it should use it wisely. A proposition that censorship powers are not the problem, but rather the wisdom with which it is applied will simply not wash with the free press or the political opposition. Any such proposition is generally perceived as insincere, the clever line of reasoning one would expect from the enemy of liberty and their stooges.

Finally, the charge of legalism cuts both ways. When a government of a developing country, like that of Peru for example, issues more than one hundred laws and regulations each working day regarding how people produce and distribute wealth, is that not evidence of excessive legalism on the part of legislators and policymakers? Another somewhat perverse if nonetheless real example of excessive legalism is the corrupt bureaucrat who uses burdensome regulations against foreign investors as a means of extortion. The point of the concept of predatory jurisdiction and the use of natural rights as a standard of justice is to offer the public an instrument against such legalistic immoderation.

Summary

The concept of predatory jurisdiction is a critical factor in understanding the problem of misgovernment. Understanding predatory jurisdiction is really very easy: it is about realizing that, when government power and authority knows no restraint, the adoption of bad policies is both unavoidable and inevitable, and the cost to society will, over time, overwhelm any good that can be achieved by it. It is also a matter of grasping that, in many cases, destructive policies could have been avoided or at least mitigated had the powers of government been more restricted. To the extent that misgovernment is the result of predatory jurisdiction it is also an injustice perpetrated by government against the people under the cover of lawful authority. Chronic, systemic misgovernment, in other words, points to an unjust system of government power, law, and administration. If the citizens of developing countries wish to see the prevalence of misgovernment diminished they will have to start articulating their rights and place limits on certain powers of government. Most people in the developing world lost faith in the virtue of their governments long ago; they are fully aware of the dysfunction of their governments. Is it not high time for the people of the developing world to draw some positive and practical lessons from their experiences with the way they are governed and to translate this into a practical programme for reducing the capacity for mischief by their governments?

Chapter 11

The Constitution

Those who seek power need power. Those who need power ought not be entrusted with it.

—Chinese proverb

How do you reduce the capacity of governments to rule in ways that are injurious to the interests of the citizenry? The answer in the most general sense is to bring limited government to economic policy. In the general affairs of politics and governance, we no longer disparage the notion of limited government. We have come to accept the need for constitutionalism, the rule of law, division of powers, checks and balances, the separation of state and church, democracy and representative government, habeas corpus, human rights, etc. These concepts, principles, and practices – in one way or another – represent explicit and conscious limits on the authority of our rulers. In these matters, jurisdiction has been predefined and delineated or divided and parcelled out among the various branches and levels of government. We have become used to perceiving any violation of these limits as a threat against freedom or the safety and security of the public from oppression. We are habituated to the idea that such limitations should be expressed in one way or another in a constitutional framework.

As clear as we usually are about civil and political rights so vague, fragmentary and awkward is our conception about the need to limit government in the sphere of economics. Observe that we have not made the least effort to put in place a constitutional framework to protect our

287

economic well-being against arbitrary authority. The relevance of this observation becomes clear as soon as we contrast the idea of a state possessing all the power necessary to regulate the economy with the idea of limited government. Once we become familiar with the concept of predatory jurisdiction and revisit the notion of limited government we should admit that we rarely think about economic freedom in constitutional terms. Most governments are, as a matter of practice, constitutionally endowed with the authority to inflate and debase the currency, overborrow and bankrupt the country, regulate business activity to a standstill, cause chronic high unemployment, and keep billions of citizens suspended in the informal sector. The proposition is that limited government must not only protect civil and political rights but also secure economic freedom and contribute towards economic stability by constitutionally regulating the policymaking powers of government – meaning a proper application of the concept of jurisdiction. In short, the economy must be deemed the subject of a bona fide constitutional order. Bringing limited government to economic policy, consciously regulating and structuring policymaking powers, and judiciously defining jurisdiction would yield real and lasting benefits (i.e., increased economic stability and the protection of legitimate economic interests).

The constitution and economic freedom

How do you use or structure a constitutional framework to limit predatory jurisdiction qua economic policy powers? There is, at this stage, no generally accepted body of thought available to answer this question. This does not mean that there are no instances where such limits exist. One of the oldest constraints is due compensation of expropriated property (featured in the US Constitution). In view of the history of Apartheid, the South African constitution specifically includes a provision for the right of every citizen to choose his or her trade, occupation, or profession freely. Inflation targeting by an independent central bank is a constraint on predatory jurisdiction. However, taken together, these are limited, ad hoc, isolated instances rather than a product of a comprehensive system of thought on the issue of predatory jurisdiction in economic policy powers. Nowhere on the planet can we find a constitution that effectively restrains government from overborrowing and bankrupting the country and overregulating business activity. Even the clauses that do exist rarely provide comprehensive (let alone coherent) protection. Due compensation of expropriated property clauses provide no protection against confiscatory practices such as rental controls or government-induced inflation. The right to choose one's trade, occupation, or profession freely does not protect against excessive entry regulation.

What is necessary is a far more rigorous body of thought on how to bring limited government to economic policymaking. To secure economic freedom a coherent and comprehensive body of inalienable rights must be defined and established that include not just civil and political rights but also cover the actions and interests of the individual in the economic sphere. Economic freedom essentially means a formal recognition that, on a fundamental level, the act of engaging in self-sustaining action cannot be the object of a requirement to act by permission from anybody or any authority. The recognition of this principle must be made explicit meaning, among other things, that we must formulate and enumerate a number of principles, rights, and freedoms to be included in a constitutional framework. The outcome, in a broad sense, should be free markets, free enterprise, free trade, and free soil.

A proper constitution should include an overarching provision that prohibits the state from depriving any person of life, liberty, or property without due process of law (i.e., a due process clause).[1] The value of such a due process clause is to formulate, at the most abstract level, the range of rights that must be safeguarded. What are generally missing in the constitutions are the definitions of the terms *life, liberty,* and *property.* One of the regrettable consequences of this is that the protective scopes of these concepts have been elaborated far more generously for civil and political rights than for economic freedoms. One reason for this is that a due process clause tends to protect rights enumerated in a constitution much better than unenumerated rights. Typically, civil and political rights are enumerated comprehensively, whereas economic liberties tend to be dealt with sparingly. One remedy for this would be to incorporate definitions into a constitution for these concepts that would more effectively cover the economic and the non-economic actions and interests of the individual citizen. In this respect, the writings of Leonard Peikoff and Ayn Rand provide fine examples of such definitions. The right to life, for example, could be defined as "the right to take all the actions required by the nature of a rational being for the preservation of his life."[2] The right to liberty could be defined as the right "to act in accordance with one's judgment."[3]

The right to property could be defined as "the right to gain, to keep, to use and to dispose of material values."[4] Observe that such broad but explicit definitions will make it much harder to ignore the economic actions and interests of individual citizens.

Another remedy would be to enumerate rights that safeguard economic freedoms. A proper constitution that includes protections against unrestrained economic policymaking powers should no doubt include the right to produce, the right to trade, and such corollaries as the right of free entry and the right to occupy unappropriated land. The best remedy would be to both incorporate definitions of the concepts of life, liberty, and property into a constitution and to enumerate rights that safeguard economic freedoms. The point should be to introduce principles, concepts, and ideals into the legal system, and the practice of government and legislation that will serve as an expanded and more comprehensive set of standards of what is right and what is wrong in the rule and administration of society. It should be noted that the use of a constitutional framework to safeguard economic freedoms is in large part predicated on the presumption that a robust process of judicial review has been put into place.

The problem of police powers

Establishing inalienable economic freedoms cannot mean destroying the regulatory powers of government. Establishing an inalienable right to produce does not create an inalienable right to pollute. Securing an inalienable right to trade does not create an inalienable right to defraud. The government should have the powers to act against pollution and other ills that may accompany fundamentally legitimate economic activity. The duty of government is not just to secure and protect freedoms, but also to promote and maintain order, safety, public morals, and health on behalf of the public. In the United States, the powers to make laws and regulations that promote and maintain order, safety, morals, and health are called police powers. There is, in a sense, a balance of interests that must be maintained between the rights of the individual and the protection of the general welfare.

However, in many countries, there is not even a shadow of such a balance; the power to regulate is usually unlimited and extreme overregulation is rife. To understand this statement better, let us examine the general perspective on police powers in the US law. In America, it is a fundamental rule that if "a law enacted pursuant to the police power does not promote the health, safety, or welfare of the community, it is likely to be an unconstitutional deprivation of life, liberty, or property."[5] In other words, the presumption is that police powers (i.e., the power to make laws and regulations) should not be uninhibited but still subject to constitutional restraints – in effect, some standard of justice. The United States – and many other advanced countries – has traditions of good governance that are deeply rooted and highly regarded. In the instance of advanced economies traditions of good governance do matter in an incremental sense to the protection of economic liberties and interests. In these countries, these traditions serve – however incompletely and imperfectly – to impose at least a real process of deliberation on and review of the legislative process. In these countries, this process has often enough resulted in the forestalling or annulment of instances of violations of economic rights. In the absence of such well-established traditions – generally compounded by the total absence of a consequential framework of rights that protect economic liberties and interests – the situation in non-advanced economies is, as a matter of practice, out of control.

Note that police powers are fundamentally predicated on the principle that individual liberties may be restricted in order to protect the general welfare. This principle, however, does not imply that such powers may cause the cancellation of the rights of the individual – there must be some kind of "core" within the rights that are abridged that should be inviolable. On the matter of police power, legal thinkers generally agree that, presently, there are few clear restrictions on the use police power. In the words of Justice Shaw: "It is much easier to perceive and realize the existence and sources of this power, than to mark its boundaries, or prescribe limits to its exercise."[6] This is understandable: it is not possible to determine in advance all instances where the general welfare is threatened or injured (meaning the precise scope of police powers cannot be fixed beforehand). Nevertheless, the courts in the United States clearly recognize, on principle, this inviolable core of rights. In every case where the constitutionality of a law enacted pursuant to the police power is challenged, US courts consistently refer to and take into consideration the rights of the plaintiffs. The function or method used in US jurisprudence, the standard of reasonability, is to reveal this inviolable core. This, then, is the practice in US law.

Yet the US legal tradition is also demonstrative of the weaknesses in the US constitutional framework – one that is actually quite instructive. It is apparently not robust enough to prevent bad legislation, including wage and price controls, rent regulation, and pervasive trade and industry regulation. Note that these types of bad legislation typically interfere with property rights as well as free markets and free enterprise. One important reason for this in a fundamental sense is that the US Constitution does not clearly and explicitly enumerate rights that safeguard economic freedoms to the same extent that it does civil and political rights. This should not be taken to imply that the US legal tradition has always shown deference or debility in the face of government interference with economic liberties. In fact, during the nineteenth century and early twentieth century, the courts created a substantial body of constitutional jurisprudence protecting economic liberties, largely based on the illumination of unenumerated rights (i.e., rights not explicitly coded in the Constitution or any written statute). However, the elucidation by the courts of unenumerated rights to protect economic liberties proved deeply controversial. Critics of this process argue that the courts are, in effect, usurping legislative powers, displacing the democratic process of determining policy and morality, and reading views into the Constitution that are unsupported by the contents of the document or the views of its drafters. The rise of legal realism in the courts, combined with the Great Depression, rising hostility to market economics, and New Deal liberalism extinguished a large part of this body of constitutional jurisprudence.

Though this may be speculative, a constitution providing a greater range of enumerated rights for the safeguarding of economic freedoms might have provided a better defence against bad legislation of the kind mentioned earlier. The reasons for this are the general and deep reverence of the American population for the Constitution. Also, the American public loves the idea of the individual citizen defending his or her constitutional rights in court. Governments routinely enact bad laws while making lofty claims to do so in the interest of the general welfare. When such a claim cannot be contested in court it usually means that the argument by government will not be refuted in the public arena. It is different when an individual citizen has the right to come forward and dispute such a claim in court in defence of his or her constitutional rights. It is much harder for the public to perceive the harm in the law enacted when a lofty claim to act in the interest of the general welfare stands unrefuted than when a real life individual with a grievance claims the contrary in court.

The lesson should be that to protect an inviolable core within a right against encroachment by police power one must first formulate a right (and, if at all possible, see it enumerated in a constitution). Police powers tend to be less invasive when rights are enumerated than in the case when they are not. The situation in advanced countries, though clearly imperfect, is also demonstrably less problematic than what we see in non-advanced countries precisely because of a greater (even if still incomplete) awareness of rights. Police power is extraordinarily convenient for creating predatory jurisdiction precisely because the scope of police powers cannot be fixed beforehand. In the absence of clearly articulated rights this is causing an intolerable situation for people in non-advanced economies. Clearly or explicitly defining and enumerating rights will, in a number of cases, contribute in meaningful ways towards limiting the excessive scope of police powers. An example of this would be the right to free entry, which would abolish the ability of authorities to use entry regulation as an instrument of police power.

Constitutions and economic stability

The economic interests of the public can also be protected by promoting economic stability through constitutional limits on the application of certain powers of the state. As mentioned in chapter 9, sometimes citizens cannot derive adequate protection through the enumeration of rights. This is the case with certain policy powers that, though potentially hazardous, are not, as a matter of cause and effect, harmful, and given prudent usage, they are conceivably beneficial. When used prudently, the exercise of this type of policy power is unlikely to produce victims that are able to demonstrate direct, specific, and personal injury. Yet, even if used imprudently, the harmful effects may be indeterminate for a long time. The consequences of imprudent use by one administration may be mitigated by resort to corrective measures by a later administration, resulting in an instance where the imprudent use may never cause demonstrable harm. Also, the harmful effects, once these become manifest, are frequently not attributable to specifiable moments of imprudent use. The problem, therefore, is that it is extremely difficult to define the terms under which standing in court should be established. And yet history has abundantly demonstrated the frequency with which the use of such policy powers have been ruinous to many nations.

Nevertheless, this does not mean that there is no remedy against unrestrained policy powers: as a thinking species, humans have the gift of conceptualizing danger on an abstract level and the ability to learn from history. Let us look at the cases of overborrowing and government-induced inflation. The rights under threat from these powers are property rights. As we have previously argued, promoting economic stability through balanced budgets and sound money can help protect this right. By protecting the public from the consequences of debt crisis and inflation, public trust is secured, and that is good for economic growth.

The one and only instance of genuine constitutional reform that seems to have caught on across the globe seems to be the idea of the independent central bank. The point of an independent central bank is to diminish direct political control over the power to create money; the executive branch of government retreats from the administration of monetary policy leaving that to the governors of the central bank. In this respect, the independent central bank is a fine example of practical application of the idea of limited government. It is also an example of imperfect reform. Only rarely is the principle of the independent central bank as the guardian of purchasing power enshrined in the constitution. Also, its mandate to safeguard purchasing power is rarely unambiguous.

The desire for balanced budgets is another fashion that seems to have spread around the world. However, this fashion does not seem to be accompanied by a corresponding desire for diminishing the power of governments to borrow. As a moral cause the advocacy of balanced budgets relies entirely on appeals to policymakers to exercise virtue in fiscal policy (i.e., prudence, skill, integrity, for example). At this point in time, the idea of a balanced-budget provision as a constitutional constraint on the powers of government is a topic alien to political discourse in most of the world. The United States is practically the only country where balanced-budget provisions are a recurrent political theme. As noted in chapter 9, most states in America have implemented some form of a balanced-budget provision in their constitutions, and there is (of varying intensity) an ongoing debate about introducing a balanced-budget amendment to the US Constitution. This is the kind of debate that would be salutary for many countries in the developing world and beyond.

Predatory constitutions

For the most part of the nineteenth century, constitutions were meant to be charters of liberty and limited government. The essence of these constitutions was that the people delegated specific powers to the state, all others being reserved to the people, and that the state protected the liberties of the people, which included, as a matter of practice, economic liberty. For most of the twentieth century, however, the purpose of a constitution was to codify and sanction unlimited powers for the state to intervene in the economy or to accommodate the expansion of government powers to control the economy.

Currently, collectivist, statist, or anti-capitalist ideologues and proponents of economic interventionism appear to be the only people who are actively preoccupied with the topic of the economy as the subject of the constitutional order. Their concern, however, is not for limited government, but to secure the legality and legitimacy of discretionary policymaking powers by enshrining these in the constitutions of their nations. This becomes clear when one reads the texts of the various constitutions. Let us take the example of the Indian constitution.

In its preamble, the constitution of India states that India is to be constituted "into a sovereign *socialist* secular democratic republic." The objective, then, of Indian government is to promote, among other things, socialism. If anything, socialism means full political control of the economy and the extinction of economic liberty. It should be noted that Indian government and politics has long been inching away from rather than advancing towards socialism, but before the 1990s, Indian government unmistakably pursued an agenda of socializing the economy for decades.[7] The preamble expressed the will and intent of its writers: they were socialists and dead serious about promoting socialism. Visions and ideals like these are expressed in many constitutions around the world. One way to give an idea of the depth and relevance of the meaning of such preambles is to imagine the difference of vision that would have been projected by a preamble stating that India is to be constituted "into a sovereign *liberal* secular democratic republic" – *liberal,* here, referring to classic liberalism. The relevance of the preamble of the Indian constitution is that it demonstrates that its writers had a vision of a government for India with unlimited discretionary policy powers in economic matters.

Indeed, the Indian constitution is quite consistent in this respect. It is so written that one can never, on the basis of it, lay claim to any inviolable economic rights. To understand the concept better, one should read Part III, Article 19, clauses 1g and 6. In clause 1g, one is first told that "all citizens shall have the right … to practise any profession, or to carry on any occupation, trade or business." After uplifting our spirits by solemnly spelling out this excellent principle, it then dashes all hope for proud and inviolable freedom as one reads clause 6, which tells us the following:

> Nothing in sub-clause (g) … shall … prevent the State from making any law imposing … restrictions on the exercise of the right conferred by the said sub-clause, and, in particular, nothing in the said sub-clause shall … prevent the State from making any law relating to … the professional or technical qualifications necessary for practising any profession or carrying on any occupation, trade or business, or … the carrying on by the State, or by a corporation owned or controlled by the State, of any trade, business, industry or service, whether to the exclusion, complete or partial, of citizens or otherwise.

Consider the significance of clause 6: it represents a foil with which the citizen is deprived of recourse to legal protection against the predations of the state against his or her rights. Thus, the constitution of India unmistakably enshrines predatory jurisdiction. Note that the Indian constitution states that such power is to be used "in the interests of the general public" and that restrictions on the exercise of the right conferred by clause 1g of article 19 should be "reasonable." We must wonder, then, what should be regarded as reasonable or in the interests of the general public. These addenda were apparently not meant to stop the government from regulating the economy to a standstill. If the objective of Indian government was to lift the population out of poverty, then its practice after independence should be considered overwhelmingly unreasonable and clearly not in the interests of the general public.

Indian public administration is the prototype of predatory jurisdiction. After independence, the government expanded its administrative powers into what came to be called the loathed Licence Raj. In Wikipedia, the Licence Raj is described as follows:

> Licence Raj refers to the elaborate licences, regulations and the accompanying red tape that were required to set up business in India between 1947–1990. The Licence Raj was a result of India's decision to have a planned economy, where all aspects of the economy are controlled by the state and licences were given to a select few. ... The architect of the system of Licence Raj was Jawaharlal Nehru, India's first Prime Minister. Inspired by the economy in the Soviet Union, he was determined to implement the model in India. Nehru was also an admirer of Stalin, and initiated steps for converting India into a socialistic pattern of society. ... The key characteristic of the Licence Raj is a Planning Commission that centrally administers the economy of the country.

In the end, the Licence Raj operated as a vast, corrupt and bureaucratic protection racket and was brought to heel only by a balance of payments crisis at the start of the 1990s that forced the government to retrench it. For India's fiftieth independence anniversary, *The Financial Times*[8] reported the extent of the License Raj's power:

> The range and intensity of government interference in industry defies belief. The government:

- Told businesses what to produce, how, where and in what quantities
- Prevented them from laying off labor or closing unprofitable factories
- Placed obstacles against expansion by big private business, both domestic and foreign
- Limited the entry of competitors
- Provided subsidized credit to favored users
- Controlled prices, notably of steel, fertilizers and petroleum products
- Controlled imports and inward investment
- Created monopoly importers of raw materials

- Nationalized banks and insurance companies and owned a substantial number of industrial enterprises
- Monopolized provision of infrastructure.

Many proponents justified these policies as helping the poor. But … 'Almost all government interventions in industry have […] reduced the demand for labor. At the same time, almost all controls have channeled the benefits of growth […] to a minority of the population.'

The result of the License Raj was four decades of a Hindu rate of growth, while the population doubled to a billion souls. Of India's population, almost one half is still illiterate and a similar number live in poverty. India now has more people continuously going hungry (more than a quarter of a billion) than it had voters upon achieving independence (the initial voter roll was 175 million). Let no one claim that constitutions are no more than bits of paper. India's government practices what its constitution preaches.

The advocates of economic freedom have been surprisingly passive and negligent in the matter of the economy as the subject of the constitutional order. The concept of predatory jurisdiction and the corresponding standards of justice should prompt reformers and social activists to start thinking about the problem of predatory constitutions and how to reform these. The primary purpose of a just and effective constitution should be to protect basic rights, not to endorse as lawful authority government powers that in truth violate these rights. We have long passed the point beyond which we would accept as legitimate the use of constitutional law to grant government the authority to practice censorship. In the same manner we should now fight endorsements included in constitutions of predatory powers over the economy as illegitimate.

Constitutional reform and institutional reform: two sides of the same coin

It should be obvious that constitutional reform by itself will not suffice. Adding a balanced-budget amendment to the constitution or securing central bank independence is almost meaningless if government does not or cannot organize an effective system of collecting taxes and, yes, show to the extent necessary a willingness to collect higher taxes. Government borrowing and government-induced inflation are in many instances practiced precisely because of fiscal weakness. If such fiscal weakness is not resolved, the constitutional framework itself cannot survive. The destruction of the independent central banking system in the run-up to the Argentinean debt crisis of 2001 proves the point. For constitutional reform to work, the organs of government, the state institutions, or the various bureaucracies must be reformed. The effective exercise of rights requires a properly functioning public administration. Many critical and legitimate government functions have been neglected, demoralized, and corrupted. The effective implementation of a constitutional framework for securing the rights of the citizens requires properly functioning courts and law enforcement agencies as well as an honest, competent civil service. This will require a competent and ready supply of judges, jurists, law enforcement officers, and civil servants who will understand the intricacies of legal and administrative systems. To organize effective government institutions will require substantial investments of financial, technical, and human resources, and this is most certainly just as difficult as the struggle against predatory jurisdiction. Yet the advocacy of constitutionally protected rights is of vital importance in that it raises the consciousness of the public that they have one further fundamental right: to be properly, prudently, and honestly governed and to be served and protected in a just, clean, and competent manner by the state. Lest we forget: the protection of rights is, from a managerial or organizational perspective, a service, in this instance provided by the state! Rights- conscious people are far more likely to demand proper service from the state than people who lack rights-consciousness. People should have an instrument with which to mobilize against dysfunctional governments. Properly drafted constitutions can, in effect, serve as rallying instruments of political and legal confrontation with dysfunctional governments.

Summary

Throughout this chapter, we have explored the reasons for advocating the reform of constitutions. Yet this is not merely a matter of rewriting documents. Of greater importance is the degree to which aspiring political reformers, social activists, and human rights advocates realize that these are living principles, standards of justice by which one can measure the actions of government and the consequences for the people. It is the unceasing work of a non-governmental organization such as Amnesty International that has made the right not to be tortured a living principle around the globe. The same should be done for economic rights, and it can be done. Once upon a time, people in nineteenth-century United States such as George Evans laboured to promote the idea of free soil as a right and actually succeeded. The implementation of such rights will be the source of a great many controversies. Many of the laws, rules, and regulations that should fail the test of these rights have their champions, and they will oppose and fight the idea of economic freedom based on inalienable rights. The fight for economic freedom is fraught with difficulty, but it is a worthwhile and viable cause. In a most general sense, a constitution ought to represent an expression of some sort of vision of a particular form of governance. Defining a constitutional framework is, in a sense, translating this vision into a set of principles and rules that govern the operation of a state. It seems reasonable to expect that such a vision would be based on some idea of what constitutes good government. In defining a constitutional framework for safeguarding the economic well-being of the citizenry, we seek to establish a system of lawmaking that is less likely to generate or perpetuate predatory jurisdiction. The outcome of such a constitutional framework should be a decrease in the scope for misgovernment.

Chapter 12

The Embarrassment of Democracy

Democracy must be something more than two wolves and a sheep voting on what to have for dinner.

—James Bovard[1]

At the end of the twentieth century, we witnessed a quantum leap in the advance of democracy. At the turn of the millennium, for the first time in history, a majority of the global population lives under some semblance of democratic rule. Yet, in spite of this good news, we are already witnessing a countertrend of disillusion with democracy in many new democracies. Some of this disillusion is understandable as euphoria wears off and unrealistic expectations are brought down to earth. Yet there is also a deeper, more worrying disillusion of the kind where people respond to the perception of how corrupt, dishonest, and incompetent government persists in spite of the introduction of democracy. Let us grant that the political and civil rights available to citizens in democracies work to prevent certain forms of abuse and misery. Often, the press is no longer systematically muzzled, political dissidents are no longer routinely and summarily jailed or executed, people are free to form political parties, and non-governmental organizations flourish. Yet these are improvements that, in the most immediate sense, benefit or affect only a relatively minor portion of the population (i.e., the journalists, students, intellectuals, politicians, and social activists – actually, often people from a privileged or elite or middle-class background or professionally involved in politics). After the introduction of democracy the majority of the people, the working class, the informals, the poor, for example (i.e., mostly those to whom the practice of politics is a remote process) discover that their situation is little changed. Governments still misgovern, and bureaucracies are manned by the same people who served the old regime and as difficult to deal with as before. Economies tend to be just as weak and crisis is hardly less frequent. When these conditions persist it often leads to political instability with the outcome being the destruction of democracy in some countries. Latin America for example has gone through various cycles of this process. The latest examples are the Russia of Vladimir Putin and the Venezuela of Hugo Chavez. If we are to secure democracy in the developing world and formerly communist countries, it is imperative to understand the processes that destabilize them. Predatory jurisdiction is one source of instability because it sets the stage for misgovernment.

Revisiting the democratic process

The line of argumentation in this chapter relies on a usage and conception of the term *democracy* as generally used in current mainstream political discourse (i.e., elective representative democracy).[2] This usage typically refers to democracy as a political system for choosing and replacing the government through free and fair elections. Within the scope of mainstream understanding, the purpose of democracy is to allow the citizenry to participate in the political decision-making process. Note that the purpose of allowing the citizenry to participate in the political decision-making process incorporates a potential for achieving good government. This potentiality accounts, to a large degree, for the belief or expectation that the establishment of democratic rule will or should result in the institution of good government. Yet this expectation also points to confusion in our understanding of democracy. We are, in effect, confusing potential and process. Democracy is first and foremost a specific process serving specific objectives. The process is free and fair elections. The specific objectives are securing the representation of citizens in government and ensuring an orderly transmission of government power from one set of rulers to another. Democracy does a specific job; it is not the total sum of government activity. Basically, in showing disenchantment with democracy, people might be blaming a process – unfairly, one might say – for failing to deal with problems, which it did not create in the first place and is not designed to solve. The quality of a society depends not only on how a government is selected but also on how it is governed. Properly understood, the concept of democracy and the processes involved do not prescribe or include principles or rules on how to govern. In other words, the democratic process itself does not include in any causal sense prescriptions on how to translate a potential for achieving good government into practice. It does not, as a matter of cause and effect, bring about competent and just rule. To realize the potential of representative government one must set one's sights *beyond* the process of selecting government to the process of how governments operate, its rules, principles, and practices. At this stage, we are invariably confronted by a long-standing legacy of dysfunctional and predatory governance practices.

Legacies of predatory power

New democracies do not start in a legal or administrative void. From the autocrats, dictators and colonial authorities new democracies inherit – usually virtually wholesale and intact – legal and administrative systems, bureaucracies, and other institutions. The successful establishment of a working democracy and the reform of the legal and economic systems in developing countries is, to a large extent, contingent upon our ability – and willingness – to understand the history and basic premises of those legacy systems and their reflexes. Most nations do not have a long-standing democratic tradition (if any), but they have plenty of experience with unrestrained authority. It is upon this heritage that the currently prevailing idea of democracy, including the notion of a state possessing all the necessary means to regulate the economy, is being grafted without critical appraisal of the implications. The point is that these states *already* operate under the assumption – but here springing from the far older and more fearsome tradition of autocracy and dictatorship – that the state possesses all the necessary means to regulate the economy! What is democracy expected to contribute in this respect? When democracy is transplanted to a developing country or formerly communist countries it will leave untouched predatory jurisdiction. What is this democracy that is being built? How does democracy reconcile the notion of the voter as a proud and free citizen with the economic subject as a cringing supplicant, sacrificial lamb, and puppet? Obviously, the institutional legacy has not been dealt with.

Strictly speaking, in the matter of misgovernment, the ideal of liberal democracy holds no new lessons for the developing countries or formerly communist countries. The scope of formal or de jure discretionary power in policymaking in twentieth-century liberal democracy is in many respects, on a prima facie level, almost impossible to tell apart from the autocratic tradition. This is dismaying for a very simple reason: the practical experience of rich industrial nations with liberal democracy as a heritage of political culture and tradition is special, unique, and very different from the autocratic tradition; it is one intangible that cannot be transplanted to countries such as Russia or Peru. The essential legal powers such as to confiscate, nationalize, control, inspect, impose license requirements, and prescribe detailed rules and restrictive regulations are not less absolute in the Netherlands or Great Britain than in Russia or Peru. The crucial difference is the cultural and historical context, the actual and customary practice, which is immeasurably less hazardous and more stable in the first two countries. But this is a matter of degree in the exercise of public power – the extent to which power is exercised – and the *quality* of the experience of freedom rather than a formal legal framework.

To introduce democracy to developing nations and formerly communist states without any fundamental break in the assumption that the state should possess all the means necessary to regulate the economy is tantamount to informing the political class, often insiders to the ancien régime and themselves unused to the experience of the West, that in matters concerning the economy, democratic reform is business as usual minus the Gosplan and plus a token recognition of property rights. There is a major problem with this: collectivist economics represents a fundamentally politicized economy; every economic decision is a political or administrative decision. A democratic ideal that does not challenge the assumption that the state should possess all the means necessary to regulate the economy represents no move away from the experience that every economic decision requires a political or administrative decision (i.e., no retreat from unlimited authority). Concurrently, the whole administrative apparatus and all the laws and regulations remain in place barring a bit of surgery to scrap economic planning, liberate prices, and implant an alien body of commercial code. This is exactly what has happened.

The darker and ancient experience with the untrammelled exercise of unlimited power, still fresh, recent, and part of the political reflexes of this political class can now be pursued on a subtler level in the economic arena but still through the same administrative means. Thus, there is not even the option of ignoring politics. The survival of the administrative apparatus and the greater part of the original body of law and regulations, which was hostile to any degree of private ambition and capitalist enterprise to start with, presents such a messy challenge to doing business and pursuing one's private interests that the business-minded are forced to resort to seeking political assistance in clearing the bureaucratic obstacles to their objectives.

This is the precise experience of Russian "capitalism," where politicians and tycoons work in shifting rival alliances with casualties whenever there is a change of power in the president's office and exclusion for those without political leverage. *The Economist,* in a survey of Russia, mentions that "authoritarian habits left over from Soviet and tsarist days are so deeply rooted that they could be sprouting again of their own accord."[3] But it isn't just a matter of habits; it is a whole legal system and bureaucracy that was never reconstituted – *reform* is too weak a term for what is necessary in many of these countries – or even in parts abolished and replaced. It is therefore unsurprising that the same survey informs us that Russia's institutions are resistant to reform, "not much good at administration, but adept at extortion," unaccountable, and heavy-handed.[4] There is only one possible and correct conclusion: communism as a doctrine may have been cast aside, but the idea of authority, as unlimited discretionary power in policymaking, remains unchallenged as a political and administrative principle. This is the bane of Russia's legacy and the clue to its troubles – one that has never been examined or acknowledged.

In short, textbook democracy does not break the bonds of serfdom in the economic sphere; the patterns of humiliation, exclusion, and corruption that silence and disempower the poor are left in place. Its internal contradictions are flagrantly visible for all who care to notice in that it combines representative government with an illiberal economic policy framework: it is an unconvincing institutional set up. The textbook framework of liberal democracy tells politicians and bureaucrats that their power over the economy is undiminished, meaning they can still borrow without restraint, print money with abandon, use the administrative machinery to practice cronyism, and exclude the masses from the public domain. Indeed, people soon notice that the introduction of democracy has left their private circumstances unchanged. Their personal dealings with bureaucracy and dishonest politics are unimproved, and disillusion with democracy sets in. Accordingly, an opinion poll taken by Latinobarometro and published by *The Economist* found the number of people agreeing with the statement that "democracy is preferable to any other kind of government" had been drifting down in virtually every Latin American country since 1995.[5]

Rational ignorance

It is a common view that the democratic system and popular representation make government more accountable for its policies and actions to a voting citizenry. This has the potential to improve policymaking. This is certainly true to the extent that there are groups of concerned citizens showing deep and lasting interest in and knowledge of certain issues or causes *and* that have managed to organize themselves in effective pressure groups. It is a fact that established democracies tend to be relatively better governed than dictatorships. Western nations are, in comparison to developing countries, well governed (among other things) for this reason. In the meantime, the spectacular growth of NGOs in the developing world, mostly in newly democratic countries, shows the potential for increasingly accountable government in these countries. Yet, to the same degree, one must realize that democracy does not result in perfect accountability – nor is accountability the automatic or even its invariably beneficial outcome. Although democracy offers the citizen a vote and forces the politicians to compete and campaign for the favour of the public, there are countervailing forces that undermine government accountability. One of these forces is the problem of the "rational ignorance" of the citizen. In the words of Mancur Olson:[6]

> The typical voter is, accordingly, "rationally ignorant" about what choices would best serve the interest of the electorate or any majority in it. This point is most dramatically evident in national elections. The gain to a voter from studying issues and candidates until it is clear what vote is truly in his or her interest is given by the difference between the value to the individual only (rather than the society) of the "right" and the "wrong" election outcomes, multiplied by the probability that the change in the individual's vote will alter the outcome of the election. Since the probability that a typical voter will change the outcome of the election is vanishingly small, the typical

citizen, whether he or she is a physician or a taxi driver, is usually rationally ignorant about public affairs. ... The rational ignorance of electorates, and thus of majorities, means that majorities will often fail to see their true interests. They can be the victims of predations that they do not notice. They can be persuaded by superficially plausible arguments that a given policy is in the interest of the majority or of the society as a whole, when it really only serves some special interest.

In other words, the average person on the street does not seek to be knowledgeable on policy issues since he or she does not believe the effort to be worthwhile. Examples of how voters fail to see their "true interests" and how they can become "victims of predation that they do not notice" are often amazingly extreme. In many developing countries, unscrupulous politicians perpetuate their own hold on office by relying on their victims (i.e., poor, illiterate voters). An article in *The Economist* about elections in the Philippines, appropriately called *"Middle-class rage,"* gives a distressing example of how this process works:

Before anyone went to the poll, Tony knew that the incumbent mayor would cheat, would win easily and would bolster Mr. Estrada's Senate candidates in the process. While trying to fight back, he learned how much local power bosses rely on poor, illiterate voters, often living in decrepit squatter communities. Although their elected leaders systematically rob the country, those voters will happily return them to office every three years in exchange for a bit of their money back. "I never saw it before, but I realize now that they want us to remain [a country of] squatters," Tony says of the local bosses.
Mrs. Arroyo's other supporters have echoed those sentiments. The class propaganda churned out by Mr. Estrada's loyalists, they say, overlooks the twisted relations between poor voters and fat-cat politicians who take their votes and do little with them, to the fury of middle-class voters, who see nothing being done to rein in corruption, tackle congestion, or promote a sounder economy.

Understandably, it is easier for the illiterate voter to understand the value of a sweetener than to judge a candidate on his position on the evils of deficit financing. Full-fledged democracy and illiteracy are clearly a volatile mix. Fortunately, Mr Estrada's ouster and imprisonment on corruption charges point to greater accountability in Filipino politics.

Still, there may be a limit to the degree to which the majority of voters are willing to study in-depth issues and candidates. Middle-class voters in the Philippines are, by and large, no more likely to study in detail a candidate's exact position on deficit financing than the illiterate squatter. Let us follow this line of argument to its logical conclusion. The problem with social and economic policy matters is that these issues are more often than not exceedingly complex, and a proper grasp of the ramifications and consequences of such matters may require a great deal of learning. Voters suffer from a restricted awareness because political economy and the process of policymaking and public administration is not part of their collective understanding. This prevents the majority of the voters from seeing the full context of the politician's performance in office. It stops the voter from getting the full picture of the consequences, intended and unintended, administrative and economic, of the political programmes of electoral candidates. In fact, the average voter is so ignorant about vital economic theory, the technical issues involved in policymaking of government, and how these interface that politicians are almost never called to account for their performance qua administrator. It is hard to imagine any majority of voters consciously and scientifically examining the degree to which protectionism is a rent-seeking ploy by interest groups resulting in a socially inefficient outcome (economic-speak for harm to the *overall* electorate's own interests) and discharging any politician accordingly. The average voter, therefore, is no guardian of the prudence of the policymaker. In the final analysis, the politician qua administrator has power for the exercise of which he or she may never be called to account or held responsible. In a manner of speaking, the politician qua administrator is accountable only to God, his own conscience, and his power-broking peers. Rational ignorance and unlimited authority combined undermine the practice of responsible government. The voters' grasp of such matters is the hole at the heart of any democratic government without limits on public authority. Additionally, the ignorance of the electorate turns the discovery of effective statesmen, stateswomen, and reformers among the clamour of the myriad of politicians into a hit-and-miss process; if one does not truly understand the significance of a politician's campaign, the voter's choice is unlikely to better the outcome of throwing dice. The average voter is, of course, quite keen on protecting his or her own well-being. But he or she lacks the intellectual tools to make an accurate and detailed picture of what is bringing the citizens to their knees. So long as the public authority is unlimited, he or she is at the mercy of the political classes on account of his or her ignorance, and the democratic vote does not fundamentally alter this situation.

Carte blanche

As much as it is naturally right that there should be democratic popular representation, this right is proof neither of the people's virtue nor of their wisdom. If the contrary were true, the public would, before long, have voted for a more responsible and professional class of politicians. As to the virtue of the people: too often they have proven gullible, greedy, obsessively receptive, or addicted to debauched political programmes and stubbornly ornery against sound economic policies. Politicians, on the other hand, seldom convey the full significance of their programmes to the electorate, not to mention their personal agendas and ulterior motives. An ignorant, credulous, covetous, superstitious, and prejudiced public is easily misled. The issue, then, is as follows: What is the advantage to the voter of granting carte blanche in policymaking to politicians and bureaucrats when the subject matter is so hard for them to understand and so difficult to explain to them? Frankly, none whatsoever.

When a public is unable to make a proper evaluation of the cost or benefit of this or that economic policy, the only measure of its merit is the final outcome, the end result, the ultimate consequence of a policy (i.e., boom, stagnation, bust, low inflation, high inflation, hyperinflation, high credit ratings, low credit ratings, debt default, low unemployment, high unemployment, massive unemployment, increasing prosperity, impoverishment, starvation, a strong banking system, or frozen savings, for example). In other words, in the case of bad policies, the voter must suspend judgement until calamity strikes and then render judgement in retrospect, when it is too late to forestall the injury. This is a form of accountability, of course, but is it not too crude? But even the timing of accountability is off: note for example that debt crises are usually decades in the making because debts mount slowly and are forever being rolled over. And then, after creditors finally lose faith, it seems to take one or two decades to sort out a debt crisis. The generations that should have judged the policies of their rulers and the ones that suffer the consequences may not be the same. So much for accountability.

But even the voters' retrospective judgement is of questionable value. Observe how the Argentinean crisis of 2001 did not result in better government. Often enough, the public learns nothing from a crisis. It is not as if the Argentinean public, after suffering the consequences of debt default and the destruction of the currency board system, is now clamouring for constitutional measures against government borrowing and for the effective protection of the currency and the financial sector. Instead, President Kirchner was quite popular for lambasting foreign creditors and investors and for measures – such as maintaining price controls on gas, telephony, and electricity – that will, in the long run, harm the public.

The impact of rational ignorance cannot be fully understood until one makes explicit its effects in the context of a democratic system where the state has all the means necessary to regulate the economy. Looking at the problem of economic mismanagement from this angle, the question is as follows: Can an omnipotent government be accountable? This would require a sizeable – and sufficiently influential! – section of the public to be deeply knowledgeable about political economy and public administration … and fully tuned into the policymaking process. Yet this is almost like calling for a republic of economists.

An economically illiterate people would benefit from the acknowledgement of a few principles setting irreducible and inviolable standards for safeguarding their interests. Inalienable, individual rights and constitutional procedures can serve as such safeguards. The previous chapters contain a few examples, hopefully the most urgent ones, of such rights and procedures. With regard to fiat money, a constitutionally independent central bank reinforced by a constitutional ban on monetary financing could be an example of a procedure to the same effect. A balanced-budget provision is another such procedure. The recognition of property rights, the right to occupy land, and the right to pursue a lawful occupation or enterprise as a restraint on licensing power are more instances of individual rights at work. Of course, these examples and the way we have dealt with them represent only the briefest sketch of what are evidently rather complicated issues. The point is that individual rights matter as much in economic as in political affairs, that the design of legal and constitutional systems and provisions, the powers, jurisdictions, and discretion are fully relevant to the economic interests of the people and that some form of legal protection is both necessary and possible. Frankly, when one looks at the rational ignorance of the voter, the case for democracy – at a deeper level – actually becomes a case for constitutionalism.

Earlier in this chapter, we noted that a democratic ideal that does not challenge the assumption that the state should possess all the means necessary to regulate the economy represents no move away from the experience that every economic decision requires a political or administrative decision. We also noted that, on the whole, a legacy administrative apparatus and the corresponding legal system would remain untouched. The corollary in the political market place is that special interest groups will continue to draw strength from this system. This places the new democracy at a disadvantage. It is forced to start out with a built-in capacity for frustrating good government: a dysfunctional legal and administrative system which every first reflex is to get in the way of new business, incumbent pressure groups with every interest in frustrating change, and policymakers with the power to cater to the interests of these same incumbents. This is one reason why enthusiasm for democracy frequently tends to fade almost as soon as it is established. This is most unfortunate because democracy is, by implication, blamed for problems that it did not create and was never designed to solve.

Democracy versus dictatorship

There is a risk that this chapter might leave an impression of scepticism about the value of introducing democracy to developing countries. It should be stressed, however, that this is not the case. The *overall* record of non-democratic rule has been so horrible that one should wonder how that contrasts positively with the *overall* record of democratic rule. In most instances, non-democratic rule has meant and still means outright dictatorship. A dictatorship is a state under the rule of a dictator.[8] A dictator is a person having absolute powers of government.[9] Going by the logic underlying the concept of predatory jurisdiction, one should certainly oppose dictatorship. Dictatorship is, after a fashion, the ultimate form of predatory authority: dictatorship is about unrestrained power, and the same caveats apply as in the case of predatory jurisdiction.

It has long been fashionable to theorize that non-democratic government would or could be more conducive to the economic development of poor countries than democratic government. This case is frequently made on the basis of the experience of countries such as China or Chile in contrast to that of India and Russia. The Pinochet Model is probably the best-known example of this kind of thinking. Noteworthy as these individual cases are, they fail to inspire confidence as soon as you set off these few successes against the usual performance of most other non-democracies. For every authoritarian ruler that has successfully managed to promote and nurture development, dozens have, by their deeds, ruined their countries. The total count of countries owing durable and ongoing development to non-democratic rule is frankly disappointing: all of six countries including South Korea, Taiwan, Chile, Hong Kong, and (more recently) China and Vietnam – or eight when including such heavily authoritarian democracies such as Singapore and Malaysia. Against these are ranged more than a hundred poor countries that know or, until recently, knew dictatorship and have nothing to show for it but a long history of oppression, decay, and impoverishment. The reality of the average African tyrant certainly does not conform to the archetype of the enlightened despot; instead, in Africa, dictatorship and kleptocracy are virtually synonyms, and decades of this situation has resulted in systematic failure and impoverishment in virtually every African country. The Middle East is mostly in thrall to ruthless tyrants or obscurantist rulers whose economic policies have largely been statist and ruinous – or entirely reliant on the fortunes of oil. In fact, the only genuinely dynamic economy and society in the Middle East is a democracy: Israel. But for oil, not one country in the Middle East can compare favourably with South Korea or Singapore. In Latin America, dictators have alternated between populist rule and thuggery and usually caused their own discredit by messing up their countries' public finances and economies. Their exit from power corresponded with the biggest debt crisis ever (i.e., that of the 1980s, the result of their reckless borrowing). Even today, many of the sorriest countries are dictatorships as one can see in the cases of North Korea, Burma, Sudan, and Zimbabwe – and, as far as we can see, not one democracy is behaving quite so atrociously towards its citizens.

Also, the few examples seemingly favourable to authoritarian rule are not quite so straightforward as they appear. Many autocracies' standing model started out as full-blown nightmares. The same communist party that now presides over China's booming economy first destroyed it several times over, initially by provoking civil war, and then through its collectivization of the economy, followed by the Great Leap Forward, and finally by setting off the Cultural Revolution. The case of Taiwan is just as dubious. The Kuomintang (Nationalist) government, which is usually credited for setting Taiwan on its way to development, was originally China's monumentally dishonest, corrupt, and incompetent government. It was the Kuomintang government that first failed to defend the country against the Japanese and then lost the mainland to the communists. Vietnam's rulers are now lauded for getting their country's development going, yet this is the same government that first ruined the country through war and collectivization; Vietnam's government also deliberately destroyed the south's emergent capitalist economy.

Typically, and perhaps uniquely, the authoritarian models mentioned above were instrumental in fostering durable growth only to the extent that they not only minimized violence against their own subjects and provided a modicum of law and order, but also allowed their subjects some degree of economic and social freedom, all of which has historically been contrary to the natural reflexes of most autocratic systems. For example, China's emergence as the world's fastest growing economy is – no matter how you look at it – the result of an ongoing process of demolishing and relaxing numerous state and party controls over the economy and, more broadly, society (i.e., the opposite of the unrestrained practice of power, once so stridently propagated by its totalitarian ideologues). The Pinochet Model is all about deliberately dismantling political and bureaucratic control over the economy with the object of creating a semblance of a free-market economy.

In any case, to those who wish to ignore the overall historical record and persist in believing that economic development has a better chance under authoritarian government should note the following contradiction: this belief implies that choosing dictatorship over democracy can, at the level of the nation as a whole, be a matter of rational self-interest. Yet the fact of the matter is that authoritarian government, by definition, means that we the people are not in control of our very lives. Is it truly rational self-interest of a whole nation to submit to dictatorship or what is, in effect, a choice based on delusion followed by slavery? Look at the dismal side of modern history: when people become disgusted with democracy and cried for a strong man to take over, they usually ended up with an even worse situation than the democracy that was so easily scorned and abandoned. The Germans who voted for Hitler and the Zimbabweans who voted for Mugabe ended up in desperate conditions. When we surrender our freedom we become slaves to the whims of men who, by dint of their role as dictators, are under no obligation to us. It is up to the autocrat to decide whether he or she is going to be so gracious as to rule in our interests or to despoil us. The degree to which these models are atypical of how autocracies usually operate and perform bodes ill for the frequency with which we can expect these to be repeated. It is therefore probably wiser for developing countries to pursue democracy and then seek a measure of sense in economic policy.[10]

Summary

The purpose of this chapter is to show that predatory jurisdiction is one very important reason why the introduction of democracy to developing countries is so fraught with difficulty. Since the fall of the Berlin Wall, command over these unreformed jurisdictions are increasingly being taken over by democratic governments. In other words, democratic governments are assuming unlimited powers sanctioned by jurisdiction defined by prior regimes over society. Though the advance of the democratic spirit is, in itself, a positive development, the idea that democracy is being grafted onto unreconstructed legal and administrative power structures is deeply worrying. Electoral democracy is essentially about the accumulation and use of power. There is nothing in the concept of democracy itself that is fundamentally corrective with respect to the application of public power. In other words, predatory jurisdiction gets a new lease on life. Predatory jurisdiction is essentially an opportunity for irresponsible behaviour. The greater the opportunity for elected officials to behave irresponsibly, the more of a sham democracy may come to seem in the eyes of the general public. It is not just the viability of democracy that must be thought through, but also what powers elected officials should or should not have. It is bad enough that, until recently, we almost routinely had to suffer dictators that arrogated to themselves all kinds of predatory powers. Must we now grant democratically elected officials these same predatory powers?

Chapter 13

From Misgovernment to Freedom and Dignity

Had I been present at the creation, I would have given some useful hints
for the better ordering of the universe.

—Alfonso X, thirteenth century king
of Castile and Leon

The point of good government is freedom and dignity. In freedom
and dignity lies the seed of economic development and prosperity.
Dealing with the causes of misgovernment requires political reform.
The objective of political reform based on a theory of predatory
jurisdiction is to acknowledge the inalienable rights of the individual
and, following that, to set clear limits to the scope of government power.
People should be able to pursue their legitimate objectives by right and
not by permission from the state. To make their property rights more
secure certain inherently destructive state policymaking powers should
be abolished or restricted. People should be able to pursue their objectives
with a sense of dignity that cannot be injured by the state under the
pretence of lawful authority. Examining misgovernment in terms of
predatory jurisdiction and how the rights of the individual are affected
focuses and structures our understanding of the areas where such reform
is necessary. If you know the causes of misgovernment, you also know
what must be reformed.

There is also a dire need for a type of reform that would give poor countries that one powerful thrust needed for escaping the seemingly unchanging mess of bad government and economic underdevelopment. This type of reform should be easy to conceptualize, easy to execute on relatively short notice, and require minimal resources. The essence of being a poor country is that it is short of resources, both in terms of financial means and human capital. Logically, its reform objectives should match resources. Nevertheless, many of the reforms, programmes, and projects so urgently promoted and advocated, often as first order priorities, are in fact complex, expensive, and long-term endeavours. Examples of such reforms are the expansion of public education and healthcare across a country or the reform of dysfunctional institutions such as a corrupt judiciary or police force. The general rule is that reforms requiring a great deal of institutional infrastructure or involving many organizations tend to be complex, expensive and prone to failure. Furthermore, though unmistakably and absolutely vital, these difficult reforms usually fail to provide, in the short term, the immediate boost coupled with an enduring payoff that is also necessary to break out of the vicious circle that is underdevelopment. Finally, it should be the sturdy foundation on which a variety of further reforms can be grafted.

The abolitionist revolution

What would reform based on a theory of predatory jurisdiction look like? From the preceding chapters the reader may already have derived an idea of what reform based on a theory of predatory jurisdiction would look like. Another way of providing an impression of what this kind reform would look like would be to work out one example and try to imagine what it would look like and what results to expect.

So let us imagine that a reformist movement had managed to gain control of government and parliament in a country notorious for monumentally dysfunctional and corrupt politics and bureaucracy and a bad poverty problem. Let us assume that these reformers have taken note of our theory of predatory jurisdiction and grasped the problem of predatory jurisdiction. In that case, the single most profitable starting shot that such a reformist government could make would be to begin with abolishing the entire body of entry regulation pressing down on the economy.

Abolition of entry regulation, though politically sensitive, is quite easy to execute once the decision to do so has been taken. It is a process that a new administration can complete within months of gaining power. It does not require elaborate institution building; it requires abolishing, suspending, or amending laws and regulations. It does not require the input or cooperation of reluctant and scheming bureaucrats; many of them will, in fact, become redundant. Reformers can do the planning and execution of the abolition efforts using outsiders; all that is necessary is parliamentary control and a team of jurists, accountants, managers, and a select number of senior civil servants (plus fresh support staff). Planning and executing abolition is vastly cheaper and immeasurably easier than trying to improve and to streamline the quality of the bits of the government bureaucracy responsible for entry regulation.

The payoff will be immediate. Abolition of entry regulation should noticeably boost economic growth. It is the kind of reform that could easily help boost annual growth rates to 7 per cent or more. This is the kind of growth rate that will initiate real, durable economic growth and development and which carried countries like Singapore, South Korea, Hong Kong, and Taiwan to general prosperity and developed status. It can also help enlarge the formal sector and thereby increase the tax base. Increased budgetary resources and economic growth are some of the ingredients of popular government, and reformers can use all the popularity they can get. Abolition of entry regulation is an example of a relatively painless reform for society as a whole.[1] It is not a seriously painful measure comparable to budget cuts and inflation fighting. It seems as if people in general have come to expect substantial reform as something that must necessarily be painful. Frankly, it does not always have to be that way.

Abolition of entry regulation would be transformational experience for societies such as India, Indonesia, and Nigeria, which are mired in some of the worst corruption conceivable. Imagine how the very experience of doing business in India, probably the very look of economic and even social life itself in that country would change for the millions of people engaged in businesses, large and small, local and foreign, formal and extralegal. Think of how a society of millions of entrepreneurs, workers, managers, and self-employed people habituated to grovelling before or wheedling with extortionist bureaucrats and politicians could be transformed into a brave, new world of free men and women fearlessly doing business free from corruption. The formal process of starting and operating a business would no longer be a tour de force reserved for the rich and the powerful, insiders, sly folks, and those thriving on corruption. Just with this reform only, doing business in India could – both for locals and foreigners – start looking like a passably honest game, a genuinely agreeable experience. That would be revolutionary! Doing business without having to resort to corruption is a normal, natural experience in many rich countries; abolition of entry regulation would be a major step towards introducing a wholesome sense of normality to doing business in India. People in the developing world have the right to experience the same kind of dignity that people living in rich countries take for granted. It cannot be good for the soul of people to be forced to belong to a society where, for every action in one's life, one is dependent upon permission from a state thoroughly corroded by corruption. In this respect, abolition of entry regulation is a moral act, an act of cleansing the business of government, and allowing people to live clean lives, of morally rehabilitating government, and morally uplifting society. This would be good for the soul of a nation such as India so deeply habituated to corruption in government and business.

The catalysts of reform

Abolition of entry regulation also has the major advantage that it represents the type of basic reform that can be turbocharged by other reform measures. These include among other things tax reform, labour law reform, bankruptcy law reform, judicial reform, privatization of public enterprises, and land ownership law reform. Onerous taxation regimes and labour laws are causes of informal activity of the same order of importance as entry regulation. The difficulty of obtaining permission to fire staff, high severance payments, high payroll taxes, and social security contributions are important causes why small businesses prefer extralegality and why formal businesses tend to outsource work to informal businesses. Consequently, abolition of entry regulation alone will not cause all or even most informal businesses to register. Yet it is most likely easier to boost formalization of extralegal businesses – by reforming or relaxing labour laws and tax codes – *after* abolition of entry regulation than the other way around. Imagine that a country would reform its tax code and labour laws and yet fail to abolish or reform a particularly obstructive entry regulation regime. It is likely that a large part of its informal sector would still not be able to join the formal sector, thereby robbing tax and labour law reform of much of their potency. Tax code, labour law reform, and privatization are, by the way, also reforms that are – at least technically – relatively easy to execute.[2]

We should also combine the abolition of entry regulation with the institution of land ownership and public land policies founded on the recognition of the right to occupy land. Abolition of entry regulation and the right to occupy land would together form the basis for an absolute and enduring expansion of individual freedom. In doing so, billions of informals could at last join the formal sector on reasonable terms. This would allow society to tap into a vast reservoir of repressed entrepreneurship and capital locked up in extralegal real estate holdings. As noted in chapter 5, credit is the way to the Land of Opportunity. Properly titled real estate is the single most important source of credit. In the United States, two-thirds of all business start-up capital is raised through mortgages. Imagine how a rights-based land policy together with abolition of entry regulation would release Nigeria from its near-exclusive dependence on investment capital in the oil industry, probably the only type of investor resourceful and hardy enough to brave the worst bureaucracy and corruption. With over one hundred million inhabitants, Nigeria cannot even remotely hope to base its prosperity of such a large population on oil export revenues alone. The reform of land ownership and public land policies is more of an effort that spans the medium term. Land policy reform requires much more effort to work than abolition of entry regulation or tax and labour law reform. It is, to a large extent, dependent upon serious structural or institutional reform of land registries and the court system, for example. Also, without the establishment of the rule of law and efficient courts and land registries, the benefits of land ownership and public land policy reform are going to be largely hypothetical.

Abolition of entry regulation could also significantly complement government development plans. Governments of poor countries are usually short of financial resources. The private sector unencumbered by entry regulation could quickly move to fill in needs for all kinds of services that are usually deemed to be public services. This includes building or

319

expanding vital infrastructure such as harbours, airports, airlines, ferry services, highways, bridges, railroad, schools, universities, clinics, hospitals, power plants, power distribution grids, waterworks, and telecom services. The government could boost this activity by privatizing many of these same services. Minimizing government action where the private sector is capable of profitably supplying these services would release scarce public resources for taking care of those parts of the infrastructure that cannot be made profitable by the private sector but which would nevertheless result in substantial social and economic benefits to society. These would include expanding or improving the quality of the public road grid in cities and towns or irrigation systems in the countryside; highway projects that are unprofitable for private companies; funding the expansion of the court system, police forces, company registries, and land registries; increasing pay for civil servants; immunization programmes, extermination programmes for disease-carrying pests; providing schools and scholarships to those too poor to pay for the education of their children. Imagine ramshackle infrastructures in developing countries being upgraded to world-class levels. Try visualizing Kolkata or Lagos enjoying utilities and harbour and airport facilities on a level of quality equivalent to that found in the Rotterdam, Tokyo, or Singapore. The point is that it is not at all impossible; in fact, it is perfectly achievable on a medium term of five to ten years.

There is another reason for giving priority to abolition of entry regulation and implementing land rights reform above other reforms. There is a chance that the bare fact of increasing the numbers of people and businesses included in the formal sector might also increase the demand for rule of law. As we already noted in chapter 2, people in the informal sector do not seek the protection of the law; for them, dealing with the law is fraught with risk instead of a source of protection – the law is their enemy. Getting people into the formal sector is the first step towards normalizing the relationship of the great informal masses with their government and with the law. Getting informals to enter the formal sector changes people from objects and victims of legal persecution to bona fide citizens with clearly lawful interests or customers and voters free to demand better service from the state. Large numbers of people who were never before concerned with the quality of the legal system would suddenly have a stake in its improvement.

The reforming party should try to get the constitution amended to secure abolition of entry regulation. Yet, if it failed to secure constitutional amendment, that would not be the end of the world. One could, as the reforming party, make a clear, publicized statement of principle rejecting entry regulation as an administrative instrument and implementing this policy line by repealing the entire body of entry regulations and/or suspending its application. Whether or not constitutional reform is possible, reforming parties should use the resources of the state to propagate rights-consciousness in this respect among the general public. In chapter 10, we noted that what people know about their rights might well affect their views and attitudes about what is right and wrong about how they are governed. By fostering this rights-consciousness among the public the reforming administration would foster among the public a degree of intolerance of predatory jurisdiction that is currently entirely lacking. The point of this is to make it harder for anti-liberal forces to reverse these achievements. In taking a clear, public position on the matter, it would force other parties to come to terms with the issue.

In summary, abolition of entry regulation followed up or complemented by various other reforms would fundamentally reshape the legal, economic, and social environment for the better. It would quickly engender the kind of durable growth that is the way out of deep and widespread poverty. It would, by eliminating government monopolies on the provision of utilities, infrastructure, education, and health services in the medium term, substantially improve both the business environment and the quality of life for huge numbers of people. It would also represent an important step in the moral rehabilitation of government and society. This is merely a peek of how a theory of predatory jurisdiction could shape or structure priorities and approaches to reform, using the example of only one type, abolition of entry regulation. There are various other reforms falling within the scope of such a theory of misgovernment, including the reform of the budgetary powers and the monetary powers, establishing freedom of contract, instituting rule of law, and so on. Not all reforms fall within the scope of a theory of misgovernment founded on the concept of predatory jurisdiction. Improving the quality of the civil service is an example of a reform that does not fall within the scope of such a theory of misgovernment. Nevertheless, it is ultimately essential not only for being

321

valuable in and of itself, but also because good government requires an honest and competent civil service.

The new reformers

After considering the things discussed so far, we should ask ourselves what kind of people would we need to bring about the reforms that will redeem the developing world and formerly communist countries and set them on the road to good government and sustained development. The developing world will need a thousand reformers. We must wish that these reformers will have but one ambition: a consuming desire to be the heroes and saviours of their nations. Yet, this time, the way to eternal fame and glory must be different from that of the past. Up to now, the heroes of the developing world have been warriors, such as the great liberator, Simón Bolívar, or great souls such as Mahatma Gandhi. Their cause was the struggle to liberate their nations and peoples from foreign oppression and, in this goal, they succeeded spectacularly. Yet, without good government, the cause of liberation is unfinished business. One promise in national liberation was the promise that self-government would benefit the native people. Frankly, in many countries, the benefits of liberation were never brought to fruition because of misgovernment. Ideally, the next great wave of heroes should be lawmakers and administrators. Remember that America's greatest heroes are the writers of its constitution, the famed Founding Fathers. Indeed, as Machiavelli noted, "Nothing brings a man greater honour than the new laws and new institutions he establishes. When these are soundly based and bear the mark of greatness, they make him revered and admired."[3] Now, in the poor countries of the world, there is no lack of work in this respect. And, among the people, there is a constant hankering after leaders who will show them the way out of hardship and injustice and to freedom and dignity. Mostly, the enemy from without has been vanquished; now it is the enemy from within that needs to be overcome. And of all the enemies within, the greatest are the people themselves in their own unthinking surrender to unregulated powers of the state and the failure to conceive of inalienable rights. We must learn to question the legitimacy of the unregulated powers of the state and to love our rights with passion. In the first chapter, we asked the following question: Is it right that government should have such broad powers that it can legally harm the interests of the people? We now have practical conceptual tools for answering this question.

The politics of reform

Reform movements have constituencies because misgovernment makes victims. People eventually demand political reform when they become increasingly aware of how the dysfunction and abuses of the system harms them. Clearly, incompetent, dishonest, predatory politics and wasteful, hostile, obstructive bureaucracy enrage people across the globe. In the most general sense, all political reformers set themselves the task of battling those evils and bringing virtue to the business of government and justice to the governed. In essence, the political reformer is a leader to and avenger of the victims of misgovernment. The mission of the reformer is to bring relief to those victims and address their grievances by improving the business of government and by making its operation more just.

The twentieth century was not short of aspiring reformers; it was short of successful reformers. This is evident when we note how, during the twentieth century, only a handful of non-European countries – South Korea, Taiwan, Singapore, and Hong Kong – managed to join the rich, developed world. The fact of the matter is that, even with the best of intentions, it is extremely hard to implement reform successfully. This is seen in the frequency with which reform and protest movements, after unseating incompetent, oppressive, corrupt governments and assuming power, run into trouble quite quickly. With his radical programme, the reformer is often perceived as a profound challenge to the existing order. It is generally acknowledged that resistance to change and innovation, which is what political reform is about, by those who benefit from the existing order, causes much trouble. Machiavelli already warned against this last point as cause of trouble to the reformer:[4]

> It should be borne in mind that there is nothing more difficult to handle, more doubtful of success, and more dangerous to carry through than initiating changes in a state's constitution. The innovator makes enemies of all those who prospered under the old order, and only lukewarm support is forthcoming from those who would prosper under the new. Their support is lukewarm partly from fear of their adversaries, who have existing laws on their side, and partly because men are generally

incredulous, never really trusting new things unless
they have tested them by experience. In consequence,
whenever those who oppose the changes can do so, they
attack vigorously, and the defense made by others is only
lukewarm. So both the innovator and his friends come
to grief.

Yet this is not the whole story of the trouble with managing reform.
The gist of our theory of predatory jurisdiction is that reformers also
run into trouble precisely because they leave far more of the old system
unchallenged and unchanged than is good for the cause of reform.
Dysfunctional systems persist not only because it suits some old order and
because of the vigour of their resistance, but also because the victims and
their leaders, the political reformers, fail to fully grasp one central feature of
the existing system of governance: predatory jurisdiction. Instead, suffering
the same cluelessness of most people, the reformer – for the greater part
instinctively or without thinking – accepts this scope of unlimited power
to be perfectly normal and natural to the art and exercise of government,
never doubting the legitimacy of the scope of this power. The question
is as follows: What are the odds of a reformer successfully improving the
business of government if he or she is oblivious to predatory authority?
As a matter of fact, without a clear conception of predatory jurisdiction,
much of the existing legal and administrative system, as inherited from
the old order, would remain virtually untouched and its destructiveness
undiminished.

When reformers manage to come to power, they assume command
over a vast array of legal and administrative systems. The reformer will
grasp that he or she is acquiring vast powers and, it was most likely a
conscious desire to gain control of these powers, believing them to be
useful to his or her programmes. Yet here lies a paradox. The reformer
without a grasp of predatory jurisdiction is not becoming a slayer of an
evil system; contrary to his or her best intentions, he or she risks becoming
its prisoner and instrument. Let there be no mistake here: the reformer
needs to grasp that he or she is seeking and assuming a central position
in a system rendered evil and dysfunctional by predatory jurisdiction.
By assuming public office, he or she will become responsible for the
management of this evil system. If it is not changed or reformed, this system
will soon require its new master to exercise this predatory jurisdiction

in the same manner as his or her predecessors. Predatory jurisdiction makes people completely dependent upon the state. As long as nothing changes, people must try to pursue their interests through this system of predatory jurisdiction. If people cannot do business freely, then, driven by sheer necessity or irrepressible ambition, they will eventually corrupt the business of government.[5] This is imperative and inevitable: when the system stays the same, people, driven by necessity and ambition, have no other way out. Government, even in the hands of the so-called reformer, remains the focal point of the needs, expectations, ambitions, obsessions, frustrations, fears, and anger of the whole of society – its body politic and all economic interests. This pressure is so great that it could distract the reformer from his or her original mission and if he cannot or does not change the system, it may well change him or her for the worse. Thus, when the reformer fails to deal effectively with the problem of predatory jurisdiction, its symptoms – overregulation inaccessible bureaucracy, for example – will inexorably result in pressure to dispense patronage, condone dishonest and corrupt practices, and become himself or herself the object of inducements to participate in such activities. You could almost say that, without a grasp of predatory jurisdiction and a corresponding standard of justice, the reformer risks becoming an agent of the oppressive status quo and a traitor to the cause of justice and the people. This is the sorry spectacle of anti-corruption crusaders and wannabe reformers ending up as figureheads of failing and corrupt administrations. They did not arrange the roll back of the predatory powers of the state and enable their citizens to pursue their lives free from constant interference by the state. This is why, after gaining power, reformers find themselves first being feared and despised by the old order, and then becoming embarrassed due to failure. After failure, he or she becomes a bitter disappointment to the voters who supported him or her and who now conclude that he or she is no better than the previous bunch.

There is a bit of a contradiction in terms to calling someone a political reformer when he or she leaves basic flaws in the system unchanged. He or she may be an angry, young person or, on a higher plane, a crusader (for example, as in the case where he or she campaigns for the eradication of corruption) but not a reformer until he or she grasps that predatory jurisdiction is an important root cause. Obliviousness of predatory jurisdiction is a kind of primitiveness: as an illiterate cannot read a book, so a so-called reformer without a grasp of predatory authority cannot fully understand government. Properly understood, aspiring reformers without a theory of predatory jurisdiction are mostly way out of their league. True reform starts with understanding, getting the facts and reasoning right. So far, there is not one reformer in this world who has made conscious work of the predatory jurisdiction as a way of dealing with the problems of economic weakness and corruption. Reformers – Fernando Henrique Cardoso and P.V. Narasimha Rao – come and go, and they never raise the issue of predatory jurisdiction by this or any other name. Therefore, in the end, the scope of power never changes. Once you realize how much misgovernment is rooted in predatory jurisdiction, and how little is done about that, you start to grasp the inadequacy of current and past reform attempts in so many countries. It is my fondest hope that our theory of predatory jurisdiction will equip future reformers with the conceptual tools to better understand the pitfalls ahead when assuming public office.

The intelligentsia

The people who should be doing this thinking about predatory jurisdiction will have to be the intelligentsia – especially those of the developing nations. For better or worse the intelligentsia is better placed to influence politics than the great masses. The truth is that the masses have never originated any idea worthy of note. It is the intellectuals who determine the intellectual environment both for the politicians and for the humbler masses. Ideas are usually created or propagated by intellectuals. The awareness of things among this class is usually the first condition for any climate favourable to change. It was John Maynard Keynes who said, "The ideas of economists and political philosophers [...] are more powerful than is commonly understood. Indeed, the world is ruled by little else. Madmen in authority, who hear voices in the air, are distilling their frenzy from some academic scribbler of a few years back."[6]

Observe that intellectuals as a class of people usually belong to professions close to the business of modern government and national politics. These are also professions where ideas tend to be the stock in trade: civil servants, lawyers, judges, economists, journalists, editors, publishers, teachers, academics, business people, consultants, human rights activists, development workers, social advocates, etc. Typically, people from these professions are acutely aware of the role of their profession in the development of their societies. In developing nations, much more than in rich ones, the intellectual professions have a mission: to uplift their nation from oppression, poverty, and ignorance to freedom, prosperity, and knowledge. Teachers and academics believed that spreading education would raise the level of the whole nation. Economists thought that their ideas would enable government intervention to work miracles. Doctors and nurses believed that bringing healthcare to the nation would invigorate the people. The intervening decades, however, have, in the greater majority of developing countries, brought failure, defeat, and disillusionment. Today, these ideals as such are not yet dead, but now they are subdued and weighted down by frustration, bafflement, and loss of heart. Looking back over those decades, it is evident that misgovernment and flawed ideas about the role of government in society have contributed greatly to this sense of disappointment. A major problem for each profession exists in the fact that they had expected – and mostly, even now, devoutly do – to be able to ride to victory on the back of government intervention. In not one profession, except, to a degree, the branch of economics, did people grasp the paradox of government intervention and its requirement of discretionary policy power. This was and still is possible only because cluelessness about predatory jurisdiction pervades all disciplines vital to the art of government.

Let us consider the failures of intellect in some professions. Observe how economists think all the time about how flawed government policies distort, weaken, and destroy economies. Yet rarely do they think about why flawed government policies are at all possible. Human rights activists work very hard at advocating the human rights. They speak up for and campaign to save a thousand victims of persecution and torture. These same advocates of human rights are entirely unconscious of how, all over the globe, predatory governments and bureaucracies trample the right to life of billions of people on the most elementary level, criminalizing and humiliating up to 60–80 per cent of the economically active population for failing to secure permission to make a living and to seek shelter. Journalists passionately oppose the idea that their activities should be subject to permission from government. Most journalists fail to recognize that this immunity so dear to them might also apply to the most basic economic interests of the people. Dissidents have struggled against tyranny and fought for freedom and democracy. Yet, when the tyrant has fled, the first election is past and the dissidents have assumed office, the voters find that the tyrant's laws, bureaucrats, and police officers are still in place, and their corrupt and obstructive ways remain unchanged. Once in power, the former dissident is time and again stumped as to how to make democratic government work for the benefit of the people.

Social advocacy and activism

The intelligentsia also includes an exceptional category of people whose role deserves special mention: the social activist or advocate. Ideally, a new branch of social advocacy or activism would evolve from our theory of predatory jurisdiction. One of the goals of social advocacy and activism is to educate the public or a portion of it and to raise their awareness of certain issues, to organize specific groups of people to whom these issues are relevant, and to influence government policy, for example. Our theory is the perfect tool for naming a problem, establishing its cause, identifying the culprit and the victim, and establishing and applying a standard of justice. The concept of predatory jurisdiction provides a special and practical focus to the job of analysing and dealing with misgovernment. Together, these steps will provide the basic ingredients for an advocacy programme. One can, for example, name weak economic growth combined with an excessively large informal sector as a problem, establish burdensome entry regulation as an important cause for both, identify business owners (formal and informal) as the victims, diagnose the ideal of government possessing all the powers necessary to regulate the economy as the culprit and promote, as the standard of justice, the inalienable rights to produce and trade (and, thus, to establish a business without the requirement to do so by permission). The basic ingredients for an advocacy programme are a cause, the rights of the informals, a target, the legal system and bureaucracy, a potential popular constituency, the extralegal business owner, and maybe even his or her employees. One could, for example, imagine an NGO specializing in organizing informals into an effective pressure group unified by a shared awareness of their interests, rights, and grievances. For NGOs, this type of advocacy has huge potential. There are, by any calculation, vast dormant constituencies left unexploited. To pursue the example of the extralegal economic activity, approximately 10–30 per cent of the population of any given country is self-employed or the owner of a business. In the case of informal land and home ownership, the percentages are even higher: 50–90 per cent of the population in many countries. Imagine the power that would accrue to those NGOs that succeeded in organizing any significant portion of these groups of people into a viable social movement or pressure group or bloc of calculating, rights-conscious voters. It doesn't have to be an illusion. The Free Soil movement of nineteenth century in the United States is proof of that.

We have, with a few broad strokes, outlined the potential of our theory to the discerning advocate. Our theory is precisely the right tool for conceptualizing, articulating, or formulating a whole new range of advocacy platforms. To recapitulate, we have essentially crafted an analytical methodology that enables social activists and aspiring politicians to gain a deeper understanding of how misgovernment works, to do the detective work for establishing the link between certain social problems and policy powers, and to craft a language of rights suitable to the problem. Social advocacy and activism is essentially about making a moral case or, more aptly, a moral cause. The calling of the social activist or advocate is to do battle against injustice. To win this battle, he or she must seek to capture the moral high ground. Our theory provides the ammunition for capturing that high ground, the conceptual instruments for crafting a standard around which one can rally the forces. It is the mission of the true social activist or advocate to shine the light of freedom into corners of societies that have not yet seen it.

Retailers of ideas

There is one more class of people crucial in the struggle against predatory jurisdiction: the journalist and editor. One could think of journalists and editors as the packagers and retailers of ideas. Presupposing a reasonably independent press, the journalist and editor, together more or less, determine the content of the public media. Under these conditions, these two professions wield immense influence over whether or how the problems of their society are formulated to the general public. But, by the same token, they also influence the political classes. Let us recall that it was a journalist and editor, George Henry Evans, who first propagated the idea of free soil – first through his own newspaper, and then through a network of hundreds of newspapers throughout America – before it was taken up by politics and ultimately translated into the Homestead Act. Without this journalist-editor, founder of the Homestead movement, America would have been a different country.

What is unknown cannot be told. Having no conception of predatory jurisdiction, the press itself suffers from the same restricted awareness as the public. If people so central to the workings of the media have no idea of predatory jurisdiction and have no corresponding standard of justice by which to measure the performance of government, how are they ever going to communicate anything sensible to the public about the problem of misgovernment? It is nowadays often an article of faith that the free press – as the voice of political dissent – acts as a check against governmental power. Yet how much of a check against governmental power is the free press when it has no theory of misgovernment?

It is frequently noted that the press is often quite weak in the developing world and many formerly communist countries. Could there be a relationship between this weakness and the press lacking a theory of misgovernment? Without a theory of misgovernment, it is difficult to inform the people in a structured and meaningful way about how government power can injure their interests and trample their rights. Thus, precisely because the public does not regularly get to experience the press as a source of information plainly and deeply relevant to their vital interests, (i.e., information that can be used to judge the impact of government action on their personal, clearly legitimate interests), it cannot develop a perception of a free press as a meaningful protection against the abusive power of government.

In saying this, it must seem as if we might be overlooking the role of the press in promoting ideas of great value such as political and civil rights and democracy. In fact, we are not. Yet, to put it a bit crudely, it is not sufficient to tell people that they should be free to speak their minds and vote. To understand why, we must grasp that the perspective of people on rights depends upon their position in life. Put differently, all rights are of equal importance to all people, yet there is also the issue of perception to deal with. The degree to which one experiences or perceives the immediate relevance of a specific right frequently depends upon one's position in life. To people close to the business of government, politics, the media, or academia – the opposition politician, the union leader, the political philosopher, the social activist, the academic economist – the right of free speech is a direct practical necessity and therefore clearly relevant. These people cannot do their job if they cannot speechify, broadcast, promote, or publish their views, ideas, opinions, concerns, and arguments. A small, extralegal furniture producer, on the other hand, is probably more of a mind to avoid publicity and would, at the same time, yearn for clear freedom or at least trouble-free permission to produce and trade and have unambiguous property rights to his workshop and home. This man would therefore feel better served by a medium that would give voice to his concerns as to his rights and freedoms in the question of labour, production, and trade than one that tells him that he has voting rights without giving him a clue about which politician will serve his interests, which one is useless to his cause, and which one threatens to make his life even more difficult. The kind of news he could use is this: Does this or that politician care about my troubles with bureaucracy? What are they going to do about it, and will that benefit me or make matters worse? Do these politicians understand and care about my desire for clear title to what I believe to be my property? Observe that such news would also change the terms of debate in politics and force politicians to answer for their positions and omissions in new ways. Only then – when the paper educates him or her about his or her rights, when the paper clarifies which politician is his friend and which his enemy – will free speech and voting rights become valuable to the masses.

A press that cannot inform the people about matters immediately relevant to their situation is, to those people, no more than an entertainment medium or a scandal sheet or a political pamphlet full of seemingly irrelevant bromides. Obviously, then, a great part of the public will not necessarily perceive measures against the free press by government as an attack against their own interests. If journalists and editors genuinely care about their independence and seriously wish to serve as the voice of political dissent – if their goal is to expose to the public the causes of their situation – it would suit them to take note of our theory of predatory jurisdiction. Without it, they will not be able to make a full and practical identification of their clients' true interests. It must be clear that we are not belittling the value of political and civil rights or democracy; rather, we are exhorting the media to broaden the scope of their mission and, in so doing, expand the public that will see a free press as relevant to their interests. Currently, there is so much abuse built into the system that having a proper theory of misgovernment to navigate by should open up a brave, new, exciting world of investigative journalism and editorializing.

Summary

People across the globe yearn for clean, honest, civilized, well-organized, and competent governments that will let them enjoy freedom, security, dignity, and prosperity. This is the real meaning of good government, and one might even claim *moral* government. To achieve this, the practice of government in most developing countries and formerly communist countries must undergo far-reaching reform. Essentially, a key objective of reform is the moral rehabilitation of government (i.e., a system of government perceived by the people as just and worthy of trust).

The mission of the reformer should be to improve the business of government and to make its operation more just. This will require reformers capable of understanding the causes of misgovernment. Dysfunctional systems and misgovernment persist not only because vested interests succeed in resisting and sabotaging reform, but also because victims and reformers fail to fully grasp one central feature of the existing system of governance: predatory jurisdiction. The reformer, without a grasp of predatory jurisdiction, is an unlikely candidate for successfully reforming an evil system and, contrary to his or her best intentions, risks becoming its prisoner and instrument. When he or she fails to deal effectively with the problem of predatory jurisdiction the reformer risks becoming an agent of the oppressive status quo and traitor to his or her own cause and the people.

True reform starts with awareness and understanding and getting the facts and reasoning right. Resolving the causes of misgovernment resulting from predatory jurisdiction will require a deep reassessment of government systems, practices, principles, and doctrines. To prepare the ground for reform, however, we need the intelligentsia – in other words, men and women who will engage in critical study, thought, and reflection about the reality of misgovernment, men and women who will propose solutions for the problem of predatory jurisdiction, men and women who will, by such discourse in the public sphere, achieve support for such solutions. Ideally a new branch of social advocacy or activism should evolve from these endeavours. We need a free press that is proficient at turning the reality of predatory jurisdiction into news. We have essentially crafted an analytical methodology that enables the intelligentsia, social activists, journalists, and aspiring reformers to gain a deeper understanding of how misgovernment works, to establish the link between certain social problems and government practices and, finally, to craft solutions suitable to the problem. This then is the vision on the basis of which we must proceed.

Conclusion

A nation of sheep will beget a government of wolves.

—Edward R. Murrow

Misgovernment in its many forms is the reason why it is so difficult for developing countries to escape their miserable condition. This book is meant to serve as a challenge to this strange failure of the people around the globe – high and low, rich and poor, educated and illiterate, politically involved or not – to conceive of and understand misgovernment and economic crisis as the logical outcome of deliberate political and administrative processes made possible by government jurisdiction. How unquestioning they are of a system of government powers that, as a matter of jurisdiction, readily allows the routine and unchecked exercise of powers that result in overregulation, wasteful bureaucracy, inflation, overtaxation, runaway deficits, and excessive borrowing. Because of all of this, the system also perpetuates poverty, exclusion, corruption, and humiliation. What is needed is the recognition of some basic truths: that people should be allowed to produce, trade, invest, and make use of land by right and not by permission. We do not need governments that seize our earnings by printing money at will and borrowing money they do not intend to repay. Omnipotent government is not the road to a glorious future; instead, it is the enemy of justice, morality, and reason. Predatory jurisdiction and our lack of rights-consciousness makes a tiny group of men masters and the rest of us beggars to be abused by the former.

Ultimately, the essence of this book is to remind people of that great republican ideal: that the state is an entity instituted by the citizenry to serve the people. We must also discover or recover the ideal of citizenship. A citizen is more than a subject – a being under the power of authority, owing or yielding obedience to sovereign authority; he or she is also a person by nature endowed with inalienable rights that no state may encroach upon. We can only be saved and recover our lawful state when we cease being the unthinking subjects of authority that knows no restraint and reclaim the rights, freedoms, and immunities to which we the citizens are naturally entitled. It is the right and duty of the citizenry to claim back the state as the servant of society. This, then, is the single most important project for each and every nation.

Afterword

Authority that is deemed lawful or accepted as normal and natural can itself provide the foundations for misgovernment. This book aims to describe how that happens. Lawful authority is often called jurisdiction (i.e., the lawful right to exercise authority). One bit of government jurisdiction that people everywhere on Earth accept as natural and lawful is licensing power. Licensing power, a type of administrative law, represents the power to grant or refuse, to renew, and to revoke licenses or permits that may be required by statute for the pursuit of such professions as law and medicine and the conduct of certain forms of business. The power to license was the first type of administrative law or government power that I became aware of during my childhood, and it intrigued me to no end. It is also the first type of government power that I came to associate with the problem of misgovernment.

I grew up in the 1960s and 1970s on the island of Curaçao in the Caribbean where I saw how a class of politicians stopped economic growth.[1] Their ideology was militant unionism and hostility to and suspicion of foreign enterprise, foreign workers, and entrepreneurship. Their means were law and bureaucracy. For most of its history, Curaçao has had a classic capitalistic economy based on free trade. At the end of the sixties, this era came to an end. After the Revolution of 1969, this new class of politicians came to power determined to set right the injustices of history – racism and exploitation – against the working-class majority. These new politicians personally and directly used the existing administrative machinery of the civil service and public law as an instrument for keeping out foreign investors, foreign workers, and, for all practical purposes, they imposed a nationwide ban on firing employees. The surprising part about this is that this new class of politicians did not change this administrative machine in any way; they merely used the system as they found it. The tools for keeping out foreign investors, foreign workers, and imposing the blanket stop on all firings – a system of licenses and permits granted or withheld – were already in place. The result was a stagnant economy, an ossifying business sector, massive unemployment, a steady loss of population, and a brain drain due to emigration.

In the mid-1980s, after finishing college, I moved to Saint Martin, another island in the Caribbean, and I was deeply surprised to find a boomtown economy. Politicians on this island were deeply and personally involved in fostering the growth of the tourist sector, and they accomplished this feat with astounding success. Why was this so remarkable? My point is that Saint Martin and Curaçao had the exact same legal and administrative system: both islands were, at that time still part of the same country, the Netherlands Antilles, a Dutch dependency. This same system did not seem to interfere with foreign investment and the entry of foreign workers and business people. Again, these politicians had done nothing to change this system; they had not improved it or made it work better. Here, we had a dynamic business sector, high growth, zero unemployment, and a growing population – mainly due to inbound labour migration. The system was exactly the same as the one in Curaçao, but the results could not be more different.

My ethnic background also afforded me another angle on the issue. I was born in 1961 in Suriname, a South American country that was, in those days, also a Dutch dependency. My father, a Surinamer, had, because of hard times in Suriname, migrated with his family to Curaçao and settled on the island in search of work. In spite of different levels of economic development and cultural differences, both countries were, in certain important ways, very similar. Both countries had Dutch-derived legal and administrative systems. From their former colonial masters, the Dutch, both countries had inherited a comparatively well developed and, at least originally, a corruption-free system of public administration and rule of law. Compared with most other colonies around the world, both countries also had good educational systems, fostering relatively high levels of literacy.

And yet there was, and there still is, this real, substantial difference in the level of economic development between the Antilles and Suriname. The Antilles had, in those days, a standard of living equivalent to that of a rich, developed country. Suriname, by contrast, had a standard of

338

living closer to that of a developing country. One salient feature of the Surinamese economy is that it had seemed to suffer, practically over the entire length of the twentieth century, decade after decade of weakness, decline, crises, stagnation, and depression. During that same age, several of the islands of the Netherlands Antilles have known real, prosperity-generating growth. The economic policies of Suriname and the Antilles also show a few significant differences. The monetary and currency regime is one such fundamental difference. For most of the twentieth century, the Antilles had virtually unregulated currency markets. Suriname, on the other hand, had a non-convertible currency regime. The critical point in time at which I became aware of this was when the Antillean government decided to impose limits on foreign currency sales to the public. I was sceptical about the sense of such a measure and told my father so. Having travelled a lot, my father told me that such controls were in fact quite common around the world. After the Second World War, the idea was that it was right and proper that government should have control over foreign exchange flows, and it should have the power to use the resulting reserves to direct economic activity and development. The Antillean government was, by this logic, failing in its duties and allowing a valuable resource, foreign exchange, to go to waste. My father, and many of his acquaintances belonging to the Surinamese community on the island, were prone to chronicle and lament the frequency with which business projects or plans of acquaintances back in the old country would come to nothing due to the difficulty involved in procuring a license to buy foreign currencies.[2] It occurred to me that, in the Antilles, one's dreams did not fail because one could not procure foreign exchange. It was then that I made the mental note that Suriname was also much poorer than Curaçao, leading me to wonder whether the poverty of Suriname was the result of the excessive interference of government with business activity. It was thinking through this topic that I had my first doubts about interventionist government. From that perspective, Suriname suddenly came across to me as a sad place full of broken dreams.

By the time I could pose such questions, it was also clear to us that Curaçao itself was in decline. Many people, including myself, were deeply disturbed by the manner in which the government in Curaçao systematically obstructed foreign investment, and dismayed by the steep decline in the work ethic and service standards that resulted from labour protection. By now, the question had become relevant to the case of the island of Curaçao itself. At that time, it was my gut feeling about these matters that made me pose such questions. But in those days, my father and I did not have the frame of reference to formulate closely reasoned and carefully articulated answers to such questions.

Later, I became deeply aware of and interested in the legal and administrative system of the islands on account of a course in public and administrative law during college. This course had provided me with the grasp of how much business activity depends upon the legal and administrative system and how policymakers apply that system to economic activity. Among other things, I studied the laws, the rules, and the regulations that controlled business activity. To put it differently, on account of this course, it occurred to me that, through legal and administrative systems, policymakers – mostly politicians – could, consciously or unwittingly, for better or worse, wield effective control over economic activities. I do not believe that this course was really intended to provide me with such understanding. The objective was to train us in law. The broader impact of the law on the economic health of the nation was never a topic of discussion during any of the lectures. I was not a law student; I was studying business administration. I took this course, which was an optional course for the business administration curriculum, out of personal interest in politics and the workings of government. The course was instrumental in providing me with a deeper and more systematic grasp of the legal and administrative issues involved – knowledge that helped me articulate my views better. Armed with this new vocabulary, I set off to Saint Martin and found that island in the happy situation described above.

As I became familiar with business in Saint Martin, it became clear to me that the single most important ingredient fuelling the economy of Saint Martin was easy business licenses. I soon noted that the people living in Saint Martin or coming to the island saw acquiring business licenses as a pure formality, certainly the easiest part of doing business! The logic of the licensing process – that it could not only be granted, but also denied, did not seem to be operating in any noticeable manner. I had become acutely aware of this logic precisely because of the frequency with which foreign investors in Curaçao had been seen off. How do you interpret such a situation? My understanding of it was that, in Saint Martin, the government was processing bits of paper and not exercising its regulatory powers. A system formally endowed with interventionist powers – for example, licensing power – operated in actual practice along non-interventionist, laissez-faire lines. Let us note that there is a logic to licensing: the point of licensing is to deter undesirable business operators (e.g., producers and sellers of inferior or illegal goods and businesses that cause nuisance and pollution). Yet the business community in Saint Martin, where licenses were easy to get, did not seem to have a greater share of undesirable operators than Curaçao, where licenses were hard to get. With these experiences in mind, I started questioning the benefit to society of licensing. On one hand, it seemed harmful in the hands of politicians and bureaucrats keen to use this power; on the other, it seemed like a procedure government could dispense with almost no harm to society. The experience of boomtown Saint Martin in the 1980s left an indelible impression on me and became the template I took with me to Europe when I moved to the Netherlands.

It is one of those typical things about being human that one can sense and see things and yet fail to articulate them clearly or grasp the full context of what one has found. This was the case with how I perceived the problem with the system of licensing and permits in the Antilles and Suriname. I had developed a clear and conscious grasp that these systems were problematic. Yet I did not grasp that my observations had relevance beyond that microcosm of those tiny islands in the Caribbean and that small, isolated society on the fringes of the vast emptiness of the Amazon. Also, I was stumped for an answer about the solution. I turned that corner when I read the book *The Other Path,* by Hernando de Soto.[3] This book provided a vindication of my observations, but on a scale I had not imagined. This book is, in fact, a research report on the degree to which government bureaucracy stifles the economies of developing countries. In my own words, I would say that the point of this book is that the problem with governments in developing countries is not that they are primitive, but rather oversized administrative machines that interfere with the economy by overregulating it. I had wondered before reading that book about the seeming inability of developing countries to escape their predicament, but I had not expected my personal observations to be, in a basic sense, applicable to such a span of societies. It could not be otherwise because I am not an academician involved in researching such matters. Nevertheless, such books help provide a proper context for one's personal observations. Conversely, it is also easier to grasp the meaning and relevance of such literature when one has seen such matters first-hand.

As I developed these non-interventionist views and started to express them, I was soon confronted with the disbelief and scepticism of the majority of the people I talked with. This incredulity seemed to be about the inability of most people to be at peace with the idea that people should be able to start and operate a business or to transact with other people – or to allow people to come into a country to work, or to allow businesses to hire and fire employees at will without a requirement to act by permission of some public authority. I fully and explicitly grasped this state of mind only after a business acquaintance of mine – a US lawyer – had expressed his disagreement with me, arguing that operating a business should be considered a privilege granted to its operator by society through the agency of government. And this was a former lawyer quoting current American legal doctrine. What a vision of the Land of the Free! It was this conception of doing business as a privilege handed down by some authority that made me realize that most people, including most highly educated people, have no conception of freedom as a *natural* right, or that such a natural right could apply to normal business activities. This realization brought me to the conclusion that the subject deserved more research. It was also the point at which the idea of writing a book about this type of topic started to germinate. My research was mostly a matter of reading up on any type of literature, much of it philosophy and economics, that touched on the matter. This phase of research was an extremely happy and satisfying period in my life. It was with great joy that I wrote this book. It is my hope that some of this joy will shine from the pages and enlighten the souls of its readers.

By any measure, I am a small islander. My frame of reference is, to an important degree, the microcosm of the Dutch world, that minute world of six little islands and two tiny countries on opposite sides of the Atlantic.[4] From this frame of reference and my readings, I have presumed to draft a theory about some the difficulties of that enormous expanse of the developing world and some of the formerly communist countries. I am aware of the fact that I have no formal education matching the level of this topic. I am just a bookkeeper by profession with an amateur's love for reading history, philosophy, economics, and politics. I would have preferred to buy this book readymade. I wrote this book in part because I could not find it on the bookshelves of any bookstore or library. I have done my best to write it in the manner in which I would have liked to find it. I have written it with the knowledge that there are men or women more qualified or knowledgeable than I am (and who might have been able to write it better). To my mind, it is the kind of book that should have been written by an academician. I think that it should have been an economist with a penchant for legal philosophy and administrative law or a legal philosopher moonlighting in the fields of economics and economic policy. Nevertheless, it seems that there were none that took up the topic of this book in the manner that I did. Why did experts, legal philosophers, economists, political scientists, and social or human rights activists fail to take note of this topic? I wonder, but I do not know ... and maybe it is of no importance. If readers find that this book is of any worth and has any significance, it will have served its purpose.

Appendix

Hong Kong

If government half a century ago had provided us with all our dinners and breakfasts, it would be the practice of our orators today to assume the impossibility of our providing for ourselves.

—Auberon Herbert

A theory of predatory jurisdiction will raise the question of whether economic development is possible without the full range of interventionist powers. The elimination of predatory jurisdiction will result in a decreased scope for government intervention. We must therefore try to conceive of development without the full panoply of interventionist powers to which societies around the world are nowadays habituated. Consider the scenario where economic development is simply not possible without wide-ranging powers of intervention; in that case, a theory of predatory jurisdiction becomes irrelevant; in that case, predatory jurisdiction is the price a society inevitably or necessarily pays to achieve development when development is the highest goal. Indeed, if the only choice available is between predatory jurisdiction and development and minimal intervention and no development, the choice is clear. And this is precisely the case that policymakers and industrial-policy advocates make constantly: development is not possible without some measure of protectionism to foster infant industries, monetary financing, public sector borrowing, and many other interventionist policies. But what if there were one country that could provide a real contrast to their case; one that has, by and large, managed to achieve prosperity with minimal intervention; one that proves that people are not so helpless that it takes far-reaching government interference to abolish poverty, prevent severe unemployment, raise the standard of living of the nation, and bring about rapid social development? To most people, a government that is not directly responsible for these functions is inconceivable. The inability, however, to conceive of prosperity not the result of economic intervention is a case of a failure to do proper research – or worse, evasion. Any proposition to be validated requires that one examine the world, our environment, the universe, and other nations for clues to the contrary. If we pose that interventionism and welfarism are necessary, we must look for clues to the contrary and examine the evidence of such an instance. Failure to do so is an indication of intellectual sloppiness, mediocrity, a provincial mind, and (in the worst case) dishonesty.

Improbable statistics

The achievement by Hong Kong of a sophisticated economy and a high level of prosperity is the result of a calculated economic policy of *positive non-intervention*. The term portrays a free economy with low levels of taxation and no import tariffs. Government interventionism, while minimal, is practiced to create a regulatory and physical infrastructure for promoting entrepreneurship. The result is the world's eighth largest trading economy, with exports estimated at USD 499 billion for the year 2015.[1] Today, Hong Kong is a prosperous society ranking eighteenth in terms of purchasing power parity (PPP) per capita (2015: USD 56,700), a level of prosperity that fully matches that of the United States, which is ranked nineteenth (2015: USD 55,800).[2]

Hong Kong is a society relatively low on welfare benefits. Budgeted social welfare spending for 2014–2015 amounted to 3.8 per cent of GDP.[3] By comparison the OECD average for 2014 amounted to 21.6 percent of GDP.[4] Yet, for a society low on welfare benefits, Hong Kong's statistics are shockingly comparable to those of rich welfare states in Europe. Life expectancy at birth for the total population in Hong Kong is 82.86 years, and the infant mortality rate is 2.73 deaths per 1,000 live births (2015 estimate).[5] For comparison, life expectancy in Denmark for the total population is 79.25 years, and the infant mortality rate is 4.05 deaths per 1,000 live births (2015 estimate).[6] Danish social expenditure amounted to 30.1 per cent of GDP.[7]

Note that this near-laissez-faire regime achieved this in the face of an inauspicious start; a barren rock on the edge of a hostile continent, Hong Kong had been devastated and traumatized by Japanese occupation. Soon thereafter, in 1951, because of the Korean War, its entrepôt trade with mainland China was strangled by a United Nations embargo. Moreover, it had a refugee problem of a size (2–3 million) that is nowadays considered to be an unmanageable problem. By these measures, Hong Kong should have been a basket case.

This is the story of one developing territory that has outperformed advanced nations without any of the hallmarks of interventionism such as economic planning, industrial policy, business subsidies, infant industry protection, domestic or international trade restrictions, domestic or foreign investment restrictions, complicated regulatory and licensing regimes for business formation, capital flow controls, foreign currency controls, cheap credit policies, or restrictive labour laws and regulations. When it does regulate, it tends to do so with a comparatively light hand. For comparison, we have the observation from Milton Friedman that "indirect government spending via regulations and mandates is negligible in Hong Kong but accounts for around 10 per cent of national income in the United States."[8]

The monetary system

The Hong Kong Monetary Authority (HKMA) operates a currency board system under which the Hong Kong dollar is officially linked to the US dollar at the rate of 7.8 Hong Kong dollars to one US dollar.[9] Under this linked exchange rate system, the Hong Kong government undertakes to back the entire monetary base[10] of Hong Kong with US dollars. In other words, the currency board system ensures that the monetary base in Hong Kong is fully backed by foreign currency reserves. This system is also prescribed in plain language by Hong Kong's constitution, the Basic Law, Article 111:

> The Hong Kong dollar, as the legal tender in the Hong Kong Special Administrative Region, shall continue to circulate. The authority to issue Hong Kong currency shall be vested in the Government of the Hong Kong Special Administrative Region. The issue of Hong Kong currency must be backed by a 100 per cent reserve fund.

The system regarding the issue of Hong Kong currency
and the reserve fund system shall be prescribed by law.

Under the monetary rule that governs the currency board system, any change in the monetary base – whether an increase or a decrease – must be matched by corresponding changes in foreign reserves. In other words, the Hong Kong government has renounced both exchange-rate policy and monetary policy because the money supply is not determined by political or administrative considerations but by changes in the foreign reserves, which in turn result from capital inflows and outflows. By taking policy discretion, that great incalculable, out of the equation, citizens and investors get a system described by the HKMA as being simple, predictable, and transparent. In short, under this system the government cannot cause inflation by printing money. In this sense, the currency board system resembles fiduciary money. (The difference, of course, is that the reserve currency, in this instance the US dollar, is fiat money.)[11] The inflation rate for 2015 was estimated to be around 2.5 per cent.[12] At the end of 2015, the value of the Fund stood at USD 439 billion (HK$ 3,423 billion), which makes it one of the largest official reserves in the world. USD 204 billion (HK$ 1,593 billion) would have been sufficient for covering the monetary base.[13] Unusually among monetary systems, and a mark of solid conservatism, the Hong Kong government allows several local banks to issue their own banknotes (against reserve accounts kept with the HKMA).[14]

The fiscal system

The Hong Kong tax system is not complicated; the territory has achieved economic growth without resorting to special fiscal incentives such as tax holidays or special concessions. While mostly keeping its budgets balanced, its maximum individual income tax rate is 15 per cent, and the corporate income tax is 16.5 per cent. There are no custom duties or capital gains taxes. Yet, the government is able to forecast fiscal reserves of about 34 per cent of GDP (March 2015 estimate) and equivalent to 22 months of government expenditure (March 2015 estimate).[15] Note that fiscal reserves represent funds accumulated over the years as government revenues have consistently exceeded public expenditures. Imagine what degree of moral fibre and managerial competence Hong Kong's policymakers must possess to achieve such an excellent fiscal position. Indeed, from 1999 to 2015, budgetary surpluses in Hong Kong averaged 1.25 per cent of GDP.[16] By contrast, budget deficits in the Netherlands, the fiscal paragon of Europe, averaged 2.01 per cent of GDP over the same period.[17]

Yet, more than its current fiscal fortunes, it is Hong Kong's fiscal history that is inspiring. Hong Kong's rise to advanced-economy status took place from the 1950s to the 1980s. For its 2000 budget, the Hong Kong's financial secretary stated that the territory had no operating deficit prior to 1998 for the preceding fifty years.[18] This basically means that Hong Kong, a poor country in those days, developed its economy without resorting to government borrowing. Still, around the world, for all practical purposes, it is an article of faith that poor nations must borrow to develop their economies. Fifty years of balanced budgets and no public debts in view of low taxation rates is *never* a question of good fortune; it is deliberate, long-term, consistent, prudent, down-to-earth policymaking. Enviably, the Hong Kong Chief Executive, when visiting Germany during a trade mission in 1998, was able to tell his hosts that "there is no government debt."[19] In the face of the virtues of prudence, frugality, and discipline exhibited by Hong Kong government, I defy Argentina to name the cause of its crisis.

The management of public-sector debts is first and last a matter of fiscal policy. Failure in this respect is government failure – no more, no less. Public-sector debts are not deposited on the doorstep of some poor and unfortunate country. Argentina's public sector debt of USD 155 billion at the time of its crisis in 2001 was not a devious neo-liberal conspiracy; a government and society without fiscal discipline assumed it. In fact, to the extent that these loans were granted by commercial bankers, these so-called capitalists now stand exposed for being fools that were easily separated from their money. Unmanageable sovereign debts are the closing balance of all government action prior to default. Every action of government requires resources. If there is anything wrong with government policy, it will, in the long run, translate into a waste of financial resources, and that tends to translate into public-sector debt. The essence of interventionist policy is that its implementation requires bureaucracy, which must be paid for, subsidies that have to be paid for, restrictions on the business sector that result in reduced growth, and, by extension, a shortfall on tax receipts that has to be made up for. But in any case, buried under the debris of flawed government policies, is the citizen who was either powerless to oppose government policies that were not in his or her interest or who was clueless. Most probably, the average Argentinean cannot imagine their minister of finance publishing a budget statement including a declaration that, "There is no government debt." It is beyond his or her conception of reality. The crime here is that a system that can produce such a statement gets no press. Is there any chief editor down there in Buenos Aires smart enough to make headline news of this statement?

Most countries have national debts; Hong Kong has surplus funds above and beyond its national debt. As of March 2015, Hong Kong government had net financial assets in excess of USD 71 billion (HKD 554 billion).[20] This represents the government's accumulated fiscal reserves resulting from budgetary surpluses over the years. Thanks to long-standing frugal finances, this near-laissez-faire polity is in a perfect position to practice Keynesian counter-cyclic fiscal policies – that eternal infatuation of the interventionist – to the extent that it does not have to increase tax rates or reduce its spending immediately because of budgetary deficits in the aftermath of the East Asia crisis of 1997 (and later, the financial crisis of 2007–2009). Increasing tax rates in a recession or depression only weakens consumer spending while accelerating decreasing business profits and, thus, aggravating the downturn. This was one of Argentina's misfortunes during the crisis of 2001. The government had such a large budgetary deficit and public-sector debt that it had to cut its budget and raise taxes in the middle of a grinding recession, which exacerbated the deflation that came from its recession.

Microeconomics

There is also something quite remarkable about Hong Kong's prosperity: Hong Kong has achieved an advanced-nation standard of living while being less productive than rich countries such as the United States. Milton Friedman noted this fact by comparing the resources applied to generating income by the United States with that by Hong Kong. This is what Milton has to say about America:[21]

> We are more productive than Hong Kong. But we have chosen, or been led by the vagaries of politics, to devote roughly half of our resources to activities to which Hong

Kong devotes 15 or 20 percent. Our higher productivity means that we can produce with 50 percent of our resources the same per capita income as Hong Kong can produce with 80 to 85 percent of its resources.

Let us follow this idea to its logical conclusion. If Hong Kong had to accept the full extent of active government that Americans take for granted, it would have been that much poorer. The reasons for this are provided here. Productivity is a factor that cannot be changed except over the long term. In other words, at a lower rate of resource utilization, its productivity could not have been greater and more likely less. At the American rate of resource utilization of 50 per cent, Hong Kong's income per capita (PPP) would have been approximately USD 35,000[22] or almost 40 per cent lower than it is now. In practice, no such linear extrapolation is possible; Hong Kong, in all likelihood, would have been even poorer for the reason that the impediments of active government would have slowed its rate of growth. One shudders at the thought of how much lower Hong Kong's income per capita would have been at European rates of resource utilization. The beauty of capitalism as practiced in Hong Kong is that it allowed a less productive people to marshal its resources so effectively that it could still enjoy the highest standard of living possible to them.

With an income per capita (PPP) of USD 35,000, Hong Kong would have ranked in the same league as Spain (2015: USD 34,800).[23] Note that Spain has, for decades, suffered from a double-digit unemployment in excess of 15 per cent, whereas Hong Kong's unemployment figure has mostly remained below 5 per cent.[24] So much for the charge that unregulated capitalism destroys job security. What is it that makes interventionist governments impervious to the charge of incompetence and laissez-faire economics invisible in its success? Our leaders, the presidents, the representatives in parliament, the labour union leaders, the government bureaucrats – none of these people in charge of wise and well-directed government action have made the least effort to awaken us to the example of and virtues of so much freedom and administrative efficiency as exists in Hong Kong. Are these people in high places really ignorant of these facts? If they are, these people are not the cosmopolitans we expect statesmen and stateswomen to be; rather, they seem like ignorant provincials. What is a statesman if he or she is not properly informed? If, on the other hand, he or she is knowledgeable, then he or she must be so filled with aversion to or hatred against what is clearly the closest thing to a laissez-faire system – one that also works extremely well – that he or she cannot bring himself or herself to come clean about its accomplishments. The first case would be our misfortune, but the latter attitude would be pathological and treasonous.

Sir John Cowperthwaite

This policy of minimal government intervention was not accidental nor a question of neglect. Instead, it was a deliberate policy that should be credited to a disciple of Adam Smith, Britain's post-war administrator in Hong Kong, Sir John Cowperthwaite (financial secretary from 1961 to 1971). In the debate over the 1966–1967 budget, Cowperthwaite clearly articulated his views on government which he, true to his convictions, practiced:[25]

> I largely agree with those that hold that Government should not in general interfere with the course of the economy merely on the strength of its own commercial judgment. If we cannot rely on the judgment of individual businessmen, taking their own risks, we have no future anyway. And, even if I could claim I was right against all other opinion in recent years, and I do not make so categorical a claim, I think I would have been wrong to press my opinions to the point of restrictive action. For I still believe that, in the long run, the aggregate of the decisions of individual businessmen, exercising individual judgment in a free economy, even if often mistaken, is likely to do less harm than the centralized decisions of a Government; and certainly the harm is likely to be counteracted faster.

His suspicion of government intervention ran very deep. He was convinced that, if his staff did gather economic data, they would succumb to an irresistible temptation to use it for economic planning. Sir John Cowperthwaite refused for many years to gather much economic data. He backed up this refusal by asserting that "we are in the happy position where the leverage exercised by the government on the economy is so small that it is not necessary, nor even of any particular value, to have these figures available for the formulation of policy."[26] The result of this calculated and far-reaching non-intervention was a community reputed for being nimble. During the 1980s, Hong Kong transformed itself from a centre of low-cost manufacturing to a financial services centre providing a gateway to China, a meeting point where Western and Hong Kong capital could meet prospective mainland entrepreneurs. In the process, Hong Kong transferred the equivalent of two million manufacturing jobs to the mainland without raising the figure for unemployment in any given year much above 3 per cent, without the safety net of a social security system, and virtually no labour unrest – a feat beyond the grasp of people habituated to interventionism. Sir John's budget address in 1961 stands vindicated.

A final word on Hong Kong

We have our answer. People are not helpless at all and can achieve prosperity without far-reaching government intervention. Hong Kong is a case where, thanks to liberty – that is freedom of action for the individual, open society, free markets, free enterprise, and free trade – private initiative (not economic interventionism) abolished poverty, prevented severe unemployment, raised the standard of living of the nation, and contributed to rapid social development. To most people outside Hong Kong, a government not directly responsible for these functions is beyond belief. In Hong Kong, people consciously rely on their own efforts, and they have been doing so almost continuously for over fifty years.

Government in Hong Kong had a role in this: it created the conditions in which freedom of action is effective. Its objective is to consciously minimize the regulatory burden and bureaucracy, to keep down the fiscal burden, and to uphold the rule of law. In this sense, the government in Hong Kong was extremely active; whereas, in most countries – in some instances, even in rich countries – these are glaring weaknesses. To take the example of the fiscal burden: Hong Kong is lightly taxed, it has a well-paid civil service and no sovereign debt. This, by any standard, is top-quality management. It contributes directly to the welfare of the people in general by making Hong Kong a safe place for savings, capital accumulation, and investments. Note how debt crises in Argentina, Russia, Mexico, and elsewhere have frequently destroyed the investment climate of these countries; in these countries people with money are afraid to keep their savings in the country and invest there. What a shame, what a waste. In Hong Kong, the reverse is the case: people trust their own polity and save and invest in their own territory as well as abroad. The rule of law is the same story. Hong Kong has the whole elaborate structure of law and corresponding institutions, one that can compete on equal terms with those of the United States, England, and the Netherlands. Not for Hong Kong the embarrassment experienced by Thailand where creditors calling in their loans discovered, during the financial crisis of 1997, that bankruptcy courts did not even exist.

Notes

Chapter 1

[1] *The New Encyclopedia Britannica,* page 303, Volume 26, Fifteenth Edition, 1997.

[2] The figure – 40 countries out of 190 – is an approximation of the number of countries that have been categorized as advanced economies by the IMF. In 2015, the IMF categorized 37 economies as "advanced economies." See Table B. Advanced Economies by Subgroup, page 150; International Monetary Fund. 2015. *World Economic Outlook: Uneven Growth—Short- and Long-Term Factors.* Washington (April). The categorization by the IMF can be used as an approximate measure of rich, developed country status. This statistic is also the basis for the earlier breakdown by *developed* and *developing* countries of around one-seventh to six-sevenths of the world's population.

[3] People do not normally associate a functioning government with public ills. A government that regularly inflicts public ills upon society is often deemed dysfunctional. Yet this common view is not quite accurate. As we noted earlier, a functioning government is a government able to perform its regular function. Because most people desire good government, this definition might cause most people to conflate the idea of a functioning government with good government. However, what is to be understood as being the regular function of a government or the state is actually a matter of perspective. This is best illustrated by using an extreme example, (e.g., by contrasting the perspectives of the tyrant and his or her victims). The perspective of a tyrant on what constitutes the regular function of government – in terms of the purpose of government rule – is fundamentally different from that of his or her victims. From the perspective of a tyrant,

oppression and exploitation is the regular or right or proper function of the state. From the perspective of the oppressed, a functioning government is not only the opposite of good government, but it is also its enemy. Yet the extent to which the oppressed believe resistance to be futile and yield obedience to the tyrant is a tribute of sorts to a "functioning" government.

4   *The Funk & Wagnalls Standard Desk Dictionary.*

5   *The Funk & Wagnalls Standard Desk Dictionary.*

6   *The Virtue of Selfishness: Man's Rights,* Ayn Rand. Signet, 1964. Page 93.

7   Park Chun Hee was president of South Korea from 1963 to 1979. Kwoh-ting Li was Minister of Economic Affairs of Taiwan from 1965 to 1969 and Minister of Finance from 1969 to 1976 before becoming a minister without a portfolio with responsibility for science and technology development in 1976. Premier Yun-suan Sun was Minister of Communication from 1967 to 1969 and Minister of Economic Affairs from 1969 to 1978, before becoming premier in 1978 (until his retirement in 1984). Lee Kuan Yew was the prime minister of Singapore from 1959 to 1990. Sir John Cowperthwaite was financial secretary in Hong Kong from 1961 to 1971.

8   It is with good reason that Lee Kuan Yew can boast the following in his memoir: "The foundations for our financial center were the rule of law, an independent judiciary, and stable, competent, and honest government that pursued sound macroeconomic policies, with budget surpluses almost every year." As such, Singapore's administration bears a closer resemblance to (near) laissez-faire Hong Kong, which makes practically the same boast, than to interventionist India. Indeed, Singapore has a world-class financial center.

9   *Two Treatises of Government,* John Locke; Everyman, reprint 1994; Chapter 14 Of Prerogative, pages 200–201, paragraph 166.

10 Up until the start of the financial crisis of 2007–2009, Spain, Greece, and Ireland owed much of their development and prosperity to their accession to the European Union. Accession and membership in the European Union and its predecessors has many benefits. The most obvious is free trade (i.e., access to a vast and prosperous market). Additionally, new members often receive huge subsidies to finance structural change. A less obvious (but nevertheless most important) benefit is that candidate-members must meet certain political, legal,

and administrative standards before accession is granted. Accession requirements strongly emphasize democracy, rule of law, human rights, and a liberal market economy. Note that the requirement of rule of law goes a long way to securing property rights and the enforceability of contracts. The crises in these countries, however, are to a large extent caused precisely by misgovernment stemming from predatory jurisdiction.

Israel is, to a significant degree, a European settler nation in the likeness of Canada, America, or Australia; the dominant political, economic, intellectual, cultural, and social class is Ashkenazi. Hong Kong and Singapore were free ports administered on laissez-faire principles with entrepôt economies. As such, these colonies were very different from the usual exploitation colonies such as Indonesia, Vietnam, Belgian Congo, Brazil, or Mexico, which knew colonial rule based on mercantilist principles.

[11] This quote was found in *Open Society and Its Enemies: Volume 2, Hegel & Marx*, K.R Popper, Page 54.

Chapter 2

[1] *The New Encyclopedia Britannica,* page 701, Volume 16, Fifteenth Edition, 1997.

[2] This statement is not concerned with whether the ideal was meant to be understood in these terms. We are primarily concerned with the logical consequence of an argument.

[3] *Informality, Firm Size and Economic Growth: Testing the de Soto Hypothesis,* Lennart Erickson; Brown University, Preliminary Draft: October 8, 2002.

[4] Paragraphs detailing Mr De Soto's personal history and how ILD came into existence represent material borrowed from the history page on ILD's website: www.ild.org.pe: The ILD's History: The Origins of the ILD. The statistical results of research work and conclusions by the ILD mentioned in these same paragraphs were also published in *The Other Path: The invisible revolution in the third world,* Hernando de Soto, 1989, I.B. Tauris & Co Ltd, London.

[5] *The Economics of the Informal Sector: A Simple Model and Some Empirical Evidence from Latin America,* Norman A. Loayza; Policy Research Working Paper no. 1727; The World Bank, Policy Research

Department, Macroeconomics and Growth Division, February 1997, page 4.

6   *The Other Path: The invisible revolution in the third world,* Hernando de Soto, 1989, I.B. Tauris & Co Ltd, London, pages 133–134.

7   The total of USD 3.35 times 173.33 hours per month times 31. From 1 January 1981 up to 1 April 1990 the Federal minimum hourly wage was USD 3.35. Source: History of Federal Minimum Wage Rates Under the Fair Labor Standards Act, 1938–2009 History of Federal Minimum Wage Rates Under the Fair Labor Standards Act, 1938–2009, United States Department of Labor, Wage and Hour Division, copy dd. 10 July 2016.

8   *The Other Path: The invisible revolution in the third world,* Hernando de Soto, 1989, I.B. Tauris & Co Ltd, London, page 148.

9   *The Economics of the Informal Sector: A Simple Model and Some Empirical Evidence from Latin America, Summary Findings,* Norman A. Loayza; Policy Research Working Paper no. 1727; The World Bank, Policy Research Department, Macroeconomics and Growth Division, February 1997.

10 World Bank Group – Labour Markets website; Workers in the Informal Economy:
    http://wbln0018.worldbank.org/HDNet/HDdocs.nsf/2d5135ecbf351 de6852566a90069b8b6/3d876a6c6f40389d85256a7100589c85? OpenDocument&ExpandSection=1.

11 *Informal Sector – A Billion Dollar Lifebelt,* Pilar Franco; Latin America Committee website: Latin America report; Mexico: 23 May 1999; Website: http://www.converge.org.nz/lac/articles/news990523a.htm.

12 From abstract of Formal and Informal Labor Force Market Survey 1994 Labor Force Survey by National Statistical Office Thailand (NSO).

13 *The Economics of the Informal Sector,* Loayza, page 26.

14 The calculation of the correlation coefficient was performed by the author by means of the CORREL function wizard in Microsoft Excel.

15 *The Economics of the Informal Sector,* Loayza, page 1.

16 *The Economics of the Informal Sector,* Loayza, pages 7–8.

17 *The Other Path: The invisible revolution in the third world,* Hernando de Soto, 1989, I.B. Tauris & Co Ltd, London, page 153.

18 From abstract of Formal and Informal Labor Force Market Survey 1994 Labor Force Survey by National Statistical Office Thailand (NSO).

19 *The Other Path: The invisible revolution in the third world,* by Hernando de Soto, 1989, I.B. Tauris & Co Ltd, London, page 154.

20 *The Economics of the Informal Sector,* Loayza, page 1.

21 *Power and Prosperity,* Mancur Olson, page 186.

22 *Power and Prosperity,* Mancur Olson, page 180.

23 *The Economics of the Informal Sector,* Loayza, page 9.

24 *The Other Path: The invisible revolution in the third world,* Hernando de Soto, 1989, I.B. Tauris & Co Ltd, London, page 154.

25 *Barriers to Participation: The Informal Sector in Developing and Transition Countries,* Catherine Kuchta-Helbling, The Center for International Private Enterprise, Washington. Data used was found in Table 2 (Informal Sector Employment in non-agricultural employment, by sex 1994/2000) on page 8 and Table 5 (Contribution of informal sector to GDP in selected developing countries) on page 11. These two tables have 11 countries in common, including Algeria, Benin, Chad, Colombia, India, Indonesia, Kenya, Mexico, Morocco, Philippines, and Tunisia.

26 *The Mystery of Capital; Why Capitalism Triumphs in the West and Fails Everywhere Else,* Hernando de Soto, Basic Books, page 252.

27 *The Mystery of Capital; Why Capitalism Triumphs in the West and Fails Everywhere Else,* Hernando de Soto, Basic Books, page 20.

28 *The Other Path: The invisible revolution in the third world,* Hernando de Soto, 1989, I.B. Tauris & Co Ltd, London, pages 24–25.

Chapter 3

1 Wikipedia: Mohamed Bouazizi, http://en.wikipedia.org/wiki/Mohamed_Bouazizi, copy 19-01-2014.

2 *Peddler's martyrdom launched Tunisia's revolution,* Lin Noueihed, Reuters, Wed Jan 19, 2011 11:16 p.m. GMT.

3 *Sakharov Prize for Freedom of Thought 2011, Sakharov prize laureates grateful for Europe's support to Arab Spring,* European Parliament website, http://www.europarl.europa.eu/news/en/news-room/content/20111014FCS29297/1/html/Three-finalists-for-Sakharov-Prize-2011-honouring-human-rights-activists.

4 My use of the term *entry regulation* and its definition was inspired by the following working paper:

The Regulation of Entry, Simeon Djankov, Rafael La Porta, Florencio Lopez de Silanes, and Andrei Shleifer; Working Paper No. 1; Visions of Governance in the 21ˢᵗ Century Project, Kennedy School of Government, Harvard University.

5 Objectivism: The Philosophy of Ayn Rand, Leonard Peikoff, 1991, Dutton, page 351.

6 Police power, in US constitutional law, the permissible scope of federal or state legislation insofar as it may affect the rights of an individual when those rights conflict with the promotion and maintenance of the health, safety, morals, and general welfare of the public. Source: The New Encyclopedia Britannica, page 559, Volume 9, Fifteenth Edition, 1997.

7 The Virtue of Selfishness: Man's Rights, Ayn Rand. Signet, 1964. Pages 93–94.

8 Objectivism: The Philosophy of Ayn Rand, Leonard Peikoff, 1991, Dutton, page 352.

9 Note that, in accordance with this definition, any transaction is a trade, which would also include services such as finance, investments, education, and medical care.

10 Let us not quibble over such alternatives as the hunter-gatherer mode of life. Even in the most primitive form of this mode of life, there is a significant and, in fact, indispensable element of productive effort and trade. The other alternatives – social welfare and charity for the unemployed, elderly, sick, and disabled – are no proof to the contrary either. At some point, the means to their sustenance will have to be produced. Humans, therefore, are first and foremost producers and traders. To reverse the argument: the producers can survive without the economically inactive, but the latter cannot survive without the former.

11 This assertion must necessarily be expressed as a potentiality rather than as an imperative for the reason that, before advocating government intervention, one must first consider the possibility that intervention might exacerbate matters rather than improve them.

12 The Funk & Wagnalls Standard Desk Dictionary.

13 The Funk & Wagnalls Standard Desk Dictionary.

14 The Funk & Wagnalls Standard Desk Dictionary.

15 The Regulation of Entry, Simeon Djankov, Rafael La Porta, Florencio Lopez de Silanes, and Andrei Shleifer; Working Paper No. 1; Visions

of Governance in the 21ˢᵗ Century Project, Kennedy School of Government, Harvard University.

16   *The Regulation of Entry,* page 3.

17   *The Regulation of Entry,* page 2.

18   To make dates for the countries comparable, the work group established what they called a standardized firm. To quote from the working paper: 'Regulations of start-up companies vary across regions within a country, across industries, and across firm sizes. For concreteness, we focus on a "standardized" firm that an entrepreneur may want to set up. It has the following characteristics: it operates in the capital city, it is exempt from industry-specific requirements (including environmental ones), it does not participate in foreign trade and does not trade in goods that are subject to excise taxes (e.g., liquor, tobacco, gas), it is a domestically-owned limited liability company, its capital is subscribed in cash (not in-kind contributions), it rents (i.e., does not own) land and business premises, and it does not qualify for investment incentives. Although different legal forms might be used in different countries to set up the simplest firm, to evaluate how regulators address the same problem in different countries, we need to look at the same form.' *The Regulation of Entry,* pages 7–8.

19   *The Regulation of Entry,* page 3.

20   *The Regulation of Entry,* page 6.

21   Table I: List of Procedures for Starting-up a Company; *The Regulation of Entry,* pages 24–25.

22   *The Regulation of Entry,* page 24.

23   *The Regulation of Entry,* page 11.

24   *The Regulation of Entry,* pages 15 and 19.

25   *The Regulation of Entry,* page 21.

26   *The Regulation of Entry,* pages 3–4.

27   Quote found in *The Regulation of Entry,* page 4, Re: page 10, World Bank, 1999, "Administrative Barriers to Investment in Africa: The Red Tape Analysis," FIAS, Washington, D.C.

28   Arthur Cecil Pigou (1877–1959) was one of the most eminent British economists of the twentieth century, noted for his study of welfare economics. Alfred Marshall's concept of "external economies and diseconomies" was developed by Pigou into a far-reaching distinction between private costs and social costs, thus laying the basis of welfare theory as a separate field of economic enquiry. Pigou's most significant

and influential work was *The Economics of Welfare* (1920), in which he sought to explore the effects of economic activity upon the total welfare of society and its various groups and classes. Together with his mentor Marshall, Pigou laid the theoretical foundations for what became known as the Cambridge school of Economics. Source: *The New Encyclopedia Britannica,* Fifteenth Edition, 1997, page 438, Volume 9 and page 345, Volume 27.

NB: Public choice theorists have since assaulted Pigouvian theory for its naive "benevolent despot" assumption (i.e., the implicit assumption, held by Keynesians and others, that government effectively corrects market failures). Public choice theory asserts that policymakers should recognize that there are government failures as well as market failures. Finally, Ronald H. Coase demonstrated its irrelevance when property rights are properly assigned. Sources: http://cepa.newschool.edu/het/profiles/pigou.htm and http://www.econlib.org/library/Enc/PublicChoiceTheory.html.

[29] *The Economics of Welfare,* Arthur C. Pigou; 4th edition, Reprint 1950, London: Macmillan and Co; pages 331–332.

[30] *The Economics of Welfare,* page 333.

[31] *The Economics of Welfare,* page 333.

[32] Member states that acceded to the European Union up to and including the year 1995 are Austria, Belgium, Denmark, Finland, France, Greece, Germany, Ireland, Italy, Luxembourg, Netherlands, Portugal, Spain, Sweden, and the United Kingdom.

[33] Romance languages are French, Italian, Spanish, and Portuguese. Germanic languages include English, Dutch (including Flemish), German, Danish, and Swedish. There are two languages unrelated to these groupings: Greek and Finnish. I have nevertheless classified Finland as a Germanic country on account of its close cultural ties to other Scandinavian nations. Greece is classified as a Romance nation on account of the Mediterranean heritage it shares with the Romance nations.

[34] Each of these countries was, by 2012, mired in a sovereign debt and banking crisis caused by governments borrowing more than they could pay back or, in other words, by predatory jurisdiction. At this time, this situation threatens to reverse the gains in prosperity since joining the EU. Also note that financial markets and debt negotiators have frequently expressed their concerns about the overregulation of these countries.

35 On the 2001 Corruption Perceptions Index, Transparency International, Sweden ranks sixth, whereas Greece ranks forty-second. By 2012, Sweden's rank had risen to fourth, whereas Greece's ranking had slipped to ninety-fourth, the same rank as India and Colombia.

36 Hoover Digest, 1998, No. 3, *The Hong Kong Experiment*, Milton Friedman.

37 This statement is entirely conditional, which is why I use the qualification "up to a point." The reason for this is that it is always possible to adopt entry regulations, which are unaffordable to the great majority of people. One example is the minimum capital paid-up requirement for establishing credit institutions in the European Union, which is set at EUR 5 million. That, along with the requirement that directors should have at least three years' experience managing a bank, effectively stops all but the tiniest minority of people from setting up a bank.

38 Gross domestic product per capita in current US dollars in 1997; Source: *The Regulation of Entry,* page 26.

39 Re: Table III, Panel B: Means by Quartiles of GDP per Capita in 1997, *The Regulation of Entry,* page 30.

40 Refer to Note 37 for the example of establishing credit institutions in the European Union.

41 The 2002 Index of Economic Freedom: *Chapter 5 Explaining the Factors of the Index of Economic Freedom,* William W. Beach and Gerald P. O'Driscoll, Jr., page 74.

42 Obviously, the other strand is political, legal, and administrative reform. The nineteenth century saw a large-scale effort in Western nations to reform and abolish. Outside the Anglo-Saxon community of nations, there is, to my knowledge, practically no tradition of judicial activism.

43 Elizabeth I (1533–1603), queen of England from 1558 to 1603; last Tudor sovereign royal.

44 *The New Encyclopedia Britannica,* page 52, Volume 29, Fifteenth Edition, 1997.

45 *The New Encyclopedia Britannica,* page 52, Volume 29, Fifteenth Edition, 1997. This page provides a particularly fine synopsis of the process by which the power of the Commons expanded: "Imperceptibly, the House of Commons was becoming the instrument through which the will of the landed classes could be heard and not an obliging organ

of royal control. In Tudor political theory this was a distortion of the proper function of Parliament, which was meant to beseech and petition, never to command or initiate. Three things, however, forced theory to make way for reality. First was the government's financial dependence on the Commons, for the organ that paid the royal piper eventually demanded that it also call the governmental tune. Second, under the Tudors, Parliament had been summoned so often and forced to legislate on such crucial matters of church and state – legitimizing and bastardizing monarchs, breaking with Rome, proclaiming the supreme headship (governorship under Elizabeth), establishing the royal succession, and legislating in areas that no Parliament had ever dared enter before – that the Commons got into the habit of being consulted. Inevitably a different constitutional question emerged: if Parliament is asked to give authority to the crown, can it also take away that authority? ... Should the crown's leadership falter, there existed by the end of the century an organization that was quite capable of seizing the political initiative, for as one disgruntled contemporary noted: 'the foot taketh upon him the part of the head and commons is become king.'"

46 *The New Encyclopedia Britannica,* page 53, Volume 29, Fifteenth Edition, 1997.

47 *Mercantilism,* Eli F. Heckscher, 1931, translated by Mendel Shapiro (1935), revised edition, E.F. Söderlund (1955), 2 volumes, London: George Allen & Unwin Ltd, page 290.

48 *Mercantilism as a Rent-Seeking Society: Economic Regulation in Historical Perspective,* Robert B. Ekelund, Jr. and Robert D. Tollison, Texas A&M University Press, 1981, page 66.

49 *Mercantilism,* Eli F. Heckscher, 1931, translated by Mendel Shapiro (1935), revised edition, E.F. Söderlund (1955), 2 volumes, London: George Allen & Unwin Ltd, page 288.

50 *Darcy v Allen*; Case of Monopolies, 11 Coke Report 84b, 77 English Reports 1260; Report date: 1602.

51 *Mercantilism,* Eli F. Heckscher, 1931, translated by Mendel Shapiro (1935), revised edition, E.F. Söderlund (1955), 2 volumes, London: George Allen & Unwin Ltd, page 274. In the middle ages, the concept of liberty did not have modern, laissez-faire connotations; it was a concept encompassing "primarily guaranteed privileges for certain estates, groups or corporations" (quoting Heckscher, page 274).

52   I am calling the argument plausible for the reason that I am not implying here or anywhere in this book that the argument – that rich countries are none the worse for imposing entry regulation – is in any way valid. This is on one hand an economic question and on the other hand an ethical issue. The ethical dimension has already been dealt with earlier in this chapter.

53   *The Common Law Right to Earn a Living*, Timothy Sandefur, The Independent Review, v. VII, n.1, Summer 2002, ISSN 1086-1653, Copyright © 2002, pages 69–90. At the time of its publication, Timothy Sandefur was a third-year student at Chapman University School of Law. The Independent Review is a journal of political economy.

54   *Adams v. Tanner*, 244 US 590 (1917); text adopted as quoted in *The Common Law Right to Earn a Living.*

55   Judicial review is the power exerted by the courts of a country to examine the actions of the legislative, executive, and administrative arms of the government – and to ensure that such actions conform to the provisions of the constitution. Actions that do not conform are unconstitutional and, therefore, are null and void. *The New Encyclopedia Britannica,* page 641, Volume 6, Fifteenth Edition, 1997.

56   The New Deal was the domestic programme of the administration of US President Franklin Roosevelt between 1933 and 1939, which took action to bring about immediate economic relief as well as reforms in industry, agriculture, finance, water power, labour, and housing – vastly increasing the scope of the federal government's activities. Source: *The New Encyclopedia Britannica,* page 633, Volume 8, Fifteenth Edition, 1997.

57   US Supreme Court ruling in *Whitney v People of State of California,* 274 US 357 (1927); Summary of sentence: Miss Whitney was convicted of the felony of assisting in organizing, in the year 1919, the Communist Labor Party of California, of being a member of it, and of assembling with it. Opinion: The constitutional right of freedom of speech and of assembly and association is not infringed by a statute providing punishment for one who knowingly becomes a member of, or assists in organizing, an association to advocate, teach, or aid and abet the commission of crimes or unlawful acts of force, violence, or terrorism as a means of accomplishing industrial or political changes. Commentary: The Whitney case is most noted for Justice Louis D.

Brandeis's concurrence, which many scholars have lauded as perhaps the greatest defense of freedom of speech ever written by a member of the high court. He and Justice Holmes concurred in the result because of certain technical issues, but there is no question that the sentiments are a distinct dissent from the views of the prevailing majority.

58   Compendium van het staatsrecht, door Mr T. Koopmans, Derde druk, Kluwer – Deventer – 1982, page 48.

59   Let us not forget that, in many cases, perpetrators of fraud frequently passed as highly reputable members of society.

60   There is the question of whether legally required qualifications, protected titles and diplomas, and professional organization-administered registration and state-enforced numerus clausus or fixus as restrictions to access to education amount to regulation of entry. I believe it does. These are, after all, legal requirements without which one cannot pursue affected professions and occupations.

61   The reason why it is not possible to make this case, even in heavily polluting industries, is that it is possible to prescribe anti-pollution remedies. Alternatively, given such regulations, it is possible to shut down violators or force them to sell the facilities to responsible operators.

62   Of course, small-scale activity can collectively pose a serious environmental problem. But in many instances, these problems are the result of government failure too. Think of the failure of governments to provide adequate sewers and sewage treatment facilities or specify, supply, and enforce proper industrial zones.

63   *The Regulation of Entry,* pages 10–11.

64   *The Funk & Wagnalls Standard Desk Dictionary*: one who favors the ideology or program of a particular group without being a member. During the Cold War era, the term was used frequently to label sympathizers of Communism who were not official members of a communist party. Communist movements often used the names and prestige of fellow travellers to enhance the image of communist front organizations.

65   *The Oxford Companion to Philosophy,* edited by Ted Honderich. Oxford University Press, 1995; Liberalism, page 483.

66   Other means besides entry regulation are government procurements and supplies, jobs, and preferential access to government services, such as subsidies, education, and healthcare.

67   Dutch sectarianism has its origin in the Reformation of the sixteenth century and sectarian Protestantism. The major (and still-existing) confessional divisions were the Dutch Reformed Church, the Calvinists and the Roman Catholics. The nineteenth and twentieth centuries saw the rise of what is called pillarization, (i.e., each confession organized its own political movement – a pillar). The advent of political ideology in these centuries resulted in two additional secular pillars for the liberals and the socialists. Dutch political, social, religious, ideological – and to some degree, even economic life – took place entirely within these pillars. From the 1960s, further secularization and individualization led to depillarization, the disappearance of the pillars as dominant socio-political phenomena.

Chapter 4

1   *The Other Path: The invisible revolution in the third world,* Hernando de Soto, 1989, I.B. Tauris & Co Ltd, London, page 154.

2   Article 22 of the 1996 Constitution of South Africa: "Every citizen has the right to choose their trade, occupation or profession freely. The practice of a trade, occupation or profession may be regulated by law."

3   On the other hand, abolition would make it somewhat easier for those with the courage to proceed because at least the prejudices of public officials would no longer matter.

4   Internationale Samenwerking, Februari 2002; Overleven in de stad: Arm zijn kost handenvol geld, page 12.

5   This was precisely the case with economic substantive due process in the United States and the controversy concerning the question of whether the unenumerated rights fell within the scope of judicial jurisdiction certainly contributed to its demise.

6   Observe that it is not possible to go further than to speak of cancellation, suspension, and scaling down with respect to import restrictions. Import restrictions, as such, do not directly constitute entry regulation. It is difficult, therefore, to argue that substantive tests must necessarily result in outright abolition of such restrictions. For example, import tariffs are perfectly acceptable as a taxation measure, even if not as a measure for banning imports. As long as an importer has a reasonable shot at making a living by importing (i.e., the tariff does not in the course of the ordinary conduct of business

present a barrier that can never be profitably taken), there can be no objection by way of the freedom of entry doctrine to the tariff in question.

7   *Private education: the poor's best chance?* By James Tooley, professor of Education Policy, University of Newcastle (United Kingdom). Article published in the UNESCO Courier; November 2000 – Education: The Last Frontier for Profit.

8   *Private Schools for the Poor: India.* E.G. West Centre, School of Education, University of Newcastle Upon Tyne, England.

9   *Private education: the poor's best chance?* By James Tooley.

10 *Private education: the poor's best chance?* By James Tooley.

11 *Private education: the poor's best chance?* By James Tooley.

12 "The abyss of public schooling," in *Writing On The Wall, a* column by Ashok V Desai Business Standard, February 12, 2002 (also citing Kingdon, Geeta (1996). *The Quality and Efficiency of Private and Public Education: A Case Study of Urban India.* Oxford Bulletin of Economics and Statistics 58.1.

13 "The abyss of public schooling," by Ashok V Desai Business Standard, Desai citing Kingdon (1996).

14 *Private Education for the Poor?* Claudia Hepburn, Fraser Forum. Claudia R. Hepburn is Director of Education Policy at The Fraser Institute and a former teacher. She has a B.Ed. and an M.A. from the University of Toronto. She works in Toronto. Claudia cites James Tooley and Geeta Kingdon.

15 *Why India's Poor Pay for Private Schools* (international edition), *Businessweek Online* – April 17, 2000, Issue (International Letter).

16 *Private education: the poor's best chance?* James Tooley, also citing the Indian government-sponsored Public Report on Basic Education in India (PROBE), Oxford, Oxford University Press, 1999.

17 *Why India's Poor Pay for Private Schools* (international edition), *Businessweek Online* – April 17, 2000, Issue (International Letter).

18 *Private education: the poor's best chance?* James Tooley.

19 "The abyss of public schooling," Ashok V Desai citing the PROBE (1999) report.

20 *Private Education for the Poor?* Claudia Hepburn.

Chapter 5

[1] *The Mystery of Capital; Why Capitalism Triumphs in the West and Fails Everywhere Else,* Hernando de Soto, Basic Books, page 256.

[2] *The Mystery of Capital,* Hernando de Soto, page 35.

[3] *The Mystery of Capital,* Hernando de Soto, page 20.

[4] *The Mystery of Capital,* Hernando de Soto, page 21.

[5] *The Mystery of Capital,* Hernando de Soto, pages 20–21.

[6] *The Economist;* "How to make Africa smile: A survey of sub-Saharan Africa," 17 January, 2004, "Breathing life into dead capital; Why secure property rights matter," page 8.

[7] *The Mystery of Capital,* Hernando de Soto, pages 6–7.

[8] *The Other Path: The invisible revolution in the third world,* Hernando de Soto, 1989, I.B. Tauris & Co Ltd, London, pages 24–25.

[9] We must stress that supply of credit and supply of valid property titles is just one – and never the only explanation – of chronic poverty.

[10] For the sake of argument, we assume that inflation is not a concern.

[11] There is also an opportunity here for some creative academic economist to create a model of supply of credit based on the supply of property title.

[12] *The Mystery of Capital,* Hernando de Soto, page 35.

[13] *The Mystery of Capital,* Hernando de Soto, page 251.

[14] *The Mystery of Capital,* Hernando de Soto, page 252.

[15] This is a rough estimate of my own on the basis of de Soto's statistics. De Soto estimated that 85 per cent of urban parcels were informal. Approximately 2 billion people live in urban areas. These estimates are based on figures from Table 2.1, page 36 of *The Mystery of Capital; Why Capitalism Triumphs in the West and Fails Everywhere Else,* Hernando de Soto, Basic Books.

[16] "Chapter Five: The Missing Lessons of US History," *The Mystery of Capital,* de Soto. This chapter served as the source of inspiration for this section.

[17] "Chapter Five: The Missing Lessons of US History," *The Mystery of Capital,* de Soto, pages 105–151.

[18] The Mystery of Capital, de Soto, page 113.

[19] *The New Encyclopedia Britannica,* page 674, Volume 9, Fifteenth Edition, 1997.

[20] *Two Treatises of Government,* John Locke, Everyman, reprint 1994, "Chapter 5 Of Property," page 128, paragraph 27.

21 *Two Treatises,* Locke, "Chapter 5 Of Property," page 130, paragraph 30.

22 *Two Treatises,* Locke, "Chapter 5 Of Property," page 131, paragraph 34.

23 *The New Encyclopedia Britannica,* page 26, Volume 6, Fifteenth Edition, 1997.

24 *The New Encyclopedia Britannica,* page 26, Volume 6, Fifteenth Edition, 1997.

25 "The Free-Soil Movement," essay by Wendy McElroy, published in Freedom Daily, May & June 2001, from The Future of Freedom Foundation.

26 *The New Encyclopedia Britannica,* page 615, Volume 4, Fifteenth Edition, 1997; founding year of the National Reform Association borrowed from "The Free-Soil Movement," an essay by Wendy McElroy.

27 *The New Encyclopedia Britannica,* page 964, Volume 4, Fifteenth Edition, 1997.

28 *The New Encyclopedia Britannica,* page 964, Volume 4, Fifteenth Edition, 1997.

29 *The New Encyclopedia Britannica,* page 26, Volume 6, Fifteenth Edition, 1997.

30 These estimates are based on figures from Table 2.1, page 36, *The Mystery of Capital,* Hernando de Soto. The reference to these figures is not meant to suggest that all this real estate is the result of not complying with requirements for access to land. De Soto mentions four causes of informality; the other three are, one, building in violation of express laws; two, formal properties that became informal; and three, construction by the government without complying with legal requirements.

31 A social category of men in medieval England not in slavery or serfdom.

32 Magna Carta, Clause 39: No free man shall be seized or imprisoned, or stripped of his rights or possessions, or outlawed or exiled, or deprived of his standing in any way, nor will we proceed with force against him, or send others to do so, except by the lawful judgment of his equals or by the law of the land.

Clause 40: To no one will we sell, to no one deny or delay right or justice.

Chapter 6

[1] In all fairness it must be admitted that anti-capitalists never make the claim that the collective body of the people should, in one manner or another, have done anything at all to earn or deserve collective ownership.

[2] In saying so, it must be understood that I am not pushing for an invalidation of the idea of state property! A public domain including state properties such as public roads, parks, sidewalks, squares, reservoirs, government buildings, and many other public amenities deserves to exist for the good of the public.

[3] It is conceivable that externalities could arise on account of the use of land with result in damages to members of the public. But these are nuisance issues that also exist in the case of the use and exploitation of properties under long-standing use. There is no reason why externalities arising from the occupation and use of unappropriated land and undeveloped resources need to be singled out as being a greater evil than those resulting from existing properties.

[4] *Two Treatises,* Locke, "Chapter 5 Of Property," page 135, paragraph 40.

[5] *Two Treatises,* Locke, "Chapter 5 Of Property," page 128, paragraph 27.

[6] This reference to males only is not meant to ignore the notable contributions of the occasional alpha female to the political process. I merely wish to economize on words in the interest of readability.

[7] In day-to-day government, ideals translate into legal doctrines, laws, rules, regulations, protocols, and a variety of administrative instruments and controls.

[8] Donald Stewart, Jr (Brazilian property-development specialist), "Brazil's Favelas: Clinton Just Didn't Get It," *Wall Street Journal,* December 5, 1997.

[9] *The Mystery of Capital,* Hernando de Soto, page 258.

[10] *The Mystery of Capital,* Hernando de Soto, page 254.

[11] Definition found in Wikipedia on 26, August 2007.

[12] *The Other Path: The invisible revolution in the third world,* by Hernando de Soto, 1989, I.B. Tauris & Co Ltd, London, page 10.

[13] The tiger in front: A survey of India and China, 5 March, 2005, *The Economist,* page 10.

[14] It should, therefore, not surprise us that the rescinding of rent controls usually results in stratospheric rent increases. Unfortunately, this consequence is often seen as a vindication of the belief that free-market

policies in housing must inevitably hurt the poor. Such reasoning, however, is out of context: as long as the supply of free and legal land and free-sector rental housing – a primary market in real estate properties, as it were – is not expanded, there is a managed market where large increases in property and rental prices are no more than the violent response to the release of pent-up demand. It is regrettable that, over and over again, we must be treated to the same knee-jerk reactions that blame such market developments on speculators and greedy landlords instead of searching for more fundamental causes, and that includes taking a hard look at government policies.

[15]   *The Mystery of Capital,* Hernando de Soto, page 31.

[16]   Translation: "What do the victims matter if it's a fine gesture?" This quote was found in *The Proud Tower: A portrait of the world before the war, 1890-1914,* Barbara W. Tuchman, Page 91. Laurent Tailhade used this repartee to make light of the bomb attack on 9 December, 1893, by an impoverished and desperate anarchist August Vaillant on the Chambre des Deputes in which several deputies were wounded by a spray of shrapnel.

Chapter 7

[1]   *World Hyperinflations,* Steve H. Hanke and Nicholas Krus, Cato Working Paper, August 15, 2012.

[2]   The money supply is expanded or contracted by changing the rate at which notes and coins are printed and minted and issued, government securities are issued or repurchased in open market operations or by raising or lowering the reserves that banks are required to maintain, and the discount rate at which they can borrow from the central bank. Most developing nations have such primitive or inadequate financial systems that the only realistic option for expanding the money supply is printing money.

[3]   *Public Finance: A Contemporary Application of Theory to Policy,* by David N. Hyman; Fourth Edition, The Dryden Press. Page 364.

[4]   In practice, it is as likely as not that policymakers dispense with even the procedures and shortcuts may have been taken (i.e., procedures may have been ignored) in the process. My basic argument, however, is that, even if they did not dispense with procedures, the effective power to induce inflation would be undiminished.

5   As a matter of practice, monetary financing is redistributive politics. Printing money does not increase a nation's stock of wealth; it does not increase production. The proof in the pudding is its causation of inflation: if monetary financing resulted in a matching increase in productive effort, inflation would not be possible. Monetary financing funnels purchasing power, as part of its general spending, to those interest groups in society that live on the subsidies of government. Consequently, when one does not or cannot benefit from the extra public spending made possible by monetary financing, one suffers a loss of purchasing power.

6   The World Bank, World DataBank, World Development Indicators, Series: Inflation, consumer prices (annual %), Time: 1990–2015, Last updated: 10 August 2016. Retrieved: 28 August 2016.

7   Data source: my own calculations based on The World Factbook, Central Intelligence Agency, Country Comparison, GDP Per Capita (PPP), data retrieved, 15 August 2016, Country Comparison, Population, data retrieved, 26 August 2016; The World Bank, World DataBank, World Development Indicators, Series: Inflation, consumer prices (annual %), Time: 1990–2015, Last updated: 10 August 2016. Retrieved: 28 August 2016

8   The World Bank, World DataBank, World Development Indicators, Series: Inflation, consumer prices (annual %), Time: 1990-2015, Last updated: 10 August 2016. Retrieved: 28 August 2016.

9   Data source: my own calculations based on The World Factbook, Central Intelligence Agency, Country Comparison, Population, data retrieved, 26 August 2016; The World Bank, World DataBank, World Development Indicators, Series: Inflation, consumer prices (annual %), Time: 1990–2015, Last updated: 10 August 2016. Retrieved: 28 August 2016.

10   In this section, I discuss only two functions, but money serves four major functions: medium of exchange, store of value, unit of account, and source of deferred payment. As unit of account, it is a common unit for measuring the value of every good or service. As a source of deferred payment, money serves as an agreed unit of measure that enables people to contract for future payments and receipts.

11   *The Funk & Wagnalls Standard Desk Dictionary.*

12   *The Funk & Wagnalls Standard Desk Dictionary.*

13   Account money represents credit balances of clients on account with banks. Bank deposits are also part of the money supply. Commercial bank demand deposits, for example, are considered to be the full monetary equivalents of banknotes and coins in circulation. In this chapter, no more mention will be made of account money than strictly necessary because the theory of money applies to it in the same manner that it applies to notes and coins in circulation. One reason for concentrating on banknotes is that, in developing countries with underdeveloped financial sectors, cash holdings are substantially more important than in rich countries with their highly sophisticated financial systems.

14   *The New Encyclopedia Britannica,* page 252, Volume 8, Fifteenth Edition, 1997.

15   *The Funk & Wagnalls Standard Desk Dictionary.*

16   Government-induced inflation is actually a subspecies of monetary inflation. Monetary inflation is not impossible under a monetary metal regime and has, in fact, occurred from time to time. Historically, the Spanish conquests of the Inca and Aztec empires in the sixteenth century, and spectacular gold and silver strikes in Brazil, Mexico, the United States, and South Africa in the eighteenth and nineteenth centuries have fuelled a degree of money inflation. All the same, the effects of monetary inflation as a consequence of increased gold and silver supplies have been rare and relatively mild – they certainly never had the virulence of hyperinflation – in comparison to government-induced inflation. Also, gold and silver coin standards can be subjected to debasement, which is the case when the mints decrease the precious metal content in the coins. Nevertheless, debasement of metal currency as a means of government-induced inflation cannot compete with the convenience, efficiency and efficacy of a fiat money standard as a means of reallocating resources to public use.

17   "Egalitarianism and Inflation – Chapter 12" in *Philosophy: Who Needs It,* Ayn Rand, New American Library, 1982; page 127.

18   *The Funk & Wagnalls Standard Desk Dictionary.*

19   Countries fighting a major war often had no credit abroad. In these cases, foreign suppliers often required payment of gold in order to avoid any credit or currency risk.

20   US Supreme Court: Legal Tender Cases 79 US 457 (1870); *Knox v. Lee & Parker v. Davis,* page [79 US 457, 568].

21 *The New Encyclopedia Britannica*, page 252, Volume 8, Fifteenth Edition, 1997.

22 Observe that, as soon as government starts tampering with the fundamental mechanism of the reserve requirement, the currency stops being "pure" fiduciary money and starts turning into fiat money.

23 A differentia is a specific difference or a characteristic attribute distinguishing a species from others of the same genus. It is a conceptual means used in philosophy, epistemology, and logic for defining the identity of entities. The genus in this instance is the concept of money of which the concepts of fiat money and fiduciary money are two species with the medium of resource reallocation being the attribute distinguishing the two.

24 *The Funk & Wagnalls Standard Desk Dictionary.*

25 US Supreme Court Legal Tender Cases 79 US 457 (1870), *Knox v. Lee & Parker v. Davis*, December Term, 1870 [79 US 457, 580].

26 *Money, Sound and Unsound,* Joseph T. Salerno, 2nd printing 2010, the Ludwig von Mises Institute. Page 355.

27 Protocol on the Statute of the European System of Central Banks and of the European Central Bank.

28 *The New Encyclopedia Britannica*, page 252, Volume 8, Fifteenth Edition, 1997.

Chapter 8

1 Obviously, a default on debt in and of itself does not automatically constitute a violation of property rights: force majeure – circumstances beyond one's control, such as a war or a natural catastrophe resulting in general economic distress, or personal misfortunes, such as illness or the loss of a job – can destroy the ability of a debtor to repay debts. In the case of government, force majeure can include war or a nationwide natural catastrophe. In this chapter, however, our argumentation leaves out of consideration the occurrence of force majeure, strictly assuming peacetime circumstances and the absence of natural catastrophes with budget-busting consequences such as have occurred in Nicaragua and Honduras via hurricanes.

2 Quote found in B. Eichengreen & R. Portes, "After the deluge: Default, negotiation and readjustment during the interwar years," in

The International Debt Crisis in Historical Perspectives, B. Eichengreen & P. Lindert, 1989, Cambridge, MA, MIT Press, page 19.

3   I am limiting this analysis to savings deposited within the banking system. This is a simplification of reality. In highly developed nations, the financial system is often much larger and more complicated than the banking system, and the general public's involvement with the financial system is correspondingly much more complex. This simplification, however, is justified because, in developing nations with simpler financial systems, the banking sector component is frequently predominant. Also, the essentials of this analysis apply to other parts of the financial system.

4   The concept of savings includes all moneys deposited in some form with financial intermediaries. Therefore, it includes deposits with banks, but it also includes premiums paid by policyholders to insurance companies and pension funds and purchases of shares or units in investment funds.

5   Nor, for that matter, in developed countries. In developed countries, however, the main investors on behalf of the public in government paper are institutional investors such as pension funds, insurers, and investment funds rather than credit institutions.

6   *The Economist*, "Special report, Argentina's collapse: A decline without parallel," 2 March, 2002, pages 27–29.

7   The other actions included destroying the independence of the central bank and tampering with the currency board system. Source: *The Economist,* "Special report, Argentina's collapse: A decline without parallel," 2 March 2002, pages 27–29.

8   South America Offers a Lesson in Privatizing Pension Systems, Pamela Druckerman, *Wall Street Journal,* July 30, 2002

9   For the sake of argument, we assume that government cannot and will not resort to printing money for funding expenditures.

10   The ultimate limit to spending is hyperinflation, when government has printed all the money it can up to the point of destroying the function of the official currency as a medium of exchange.

11   *The Economist*, "Ambitious, France's prime minister," 13 September, 2003, pages 28–30.

12   *The Economist,* "Stability and instability, The European Union's troubles," 17 July, 2004, page 25.

13 *The Economist,* "Stability and instability, The European Union's troubles," 17 July, 2004, page 25.

14 In parliamentary democracies, government budgets are adopted subject to the approval by parliament. Strictly as such, the executive branch of government cannot adopt budgets without ratification by parliament. Nevertheless, that by itself has been no source of financial discipline.

15 During the 1970s, for example, it was universally presumed that the power of the nation-state to tax secured the highest level of creditworthiness. This notion lost its naturalness during the Latin American debt crisis during the 1980s. The fact of the matter is that projected cash flow combined with the willingness to pay is the only true measure of creditworthiness. Likewise, lenders had, from the interventions by the IMF and the US Treasury during virtually every financial crisis during the 1990s, inferred that these institutions would continue to intervene – an assumption that proved mistaken as evidenced by the hands-off approach to the Argentinean crisis of 2001. The truth is that neither the IMF nor the US Treasury ever made firm commitments of any kind to that effect.

16 A Ponzi scheme is a type of investment fraud scam where the returns paid out to the initial investors – which are, as a rule, extraordinarily high – are serviced by the contributions of a rising number of new investors. A fine explanation of the Ponzi scheme is provided in a piece of writing found in *Internet, Bubble and Ponzi Schemes Used in Investment Fraud Scams,* Mark Fleming, Consumer Protection Lawyer – Seattle 05/02, http://www.crimes-of-persuasion.com/Crimes/InPerson/MajorPerson/ponzi.htm. To quote the website: "Named after Carl Ponzi, who collected $9.8 million from 10,550 people (including ¾ of the Boston Police Force) and then paid out $7.8 million in just 8 months in 1920 Boston by offering profits of 50% every 45 days.

A swindle of this nature, referred to as a "bubble" for the hundreds of years it has existed and now referred to as a "Ponzi scheme" is basically an investment fraud where investors are enticed with the promise of extremely high returns or dividends over a very short period of time. This shorter period between payouts and high rate of return is required to create the impetus for the frenzy that is to follow as word leaks out, and is soon verified, by numerous sources. The truly experienced con will balance these two factors (payout period and promised rate of return) against the expected duration of the operation so as to maximize his take while still maintaining some semblance of credibility.

In the true sense of borrowing from Peter to pay Paul, Ponzi schemes are a simple fraud whereby initial investors are paid exceptional dividends as interest cheques from the deposits of a growing number of new investors.

"Profits" to investors are not created by the success of the underlying business venture but instead are derived fraudulently from the capital contributions of other investors.

A few people invest in the scheme, then as news of the offer spreads, more investors are drawn in. Usually there is no actual investment involved, contrary to your understanding, just money being shipped in from new investors to the earlier ones.

Ponzi schemes eventually collapse because the underlying asset upon which the investment was based either never existed, or was grossly overvalued. And unlike pyramid schemes, where one's potential gain is measured by the active and conscious practice of participant recruitment, Ponzi schemes attribute their moneymaking abilities on some elaborate and inventive investment or business process, with the influx of new depositors the result of word-of-mouth only."

17 For readers from the rich countries, there should be no comfort in despising Argentina – the ageing of the populations of rich countries is set to create massive fiscal problems in the next 50 years if nothing is done to reform their public pension systems. Japan and Italy are the first countries expected to run into trouble because each of these countries has already has public-sector debts currently standing at 140 and 110 per cent of GDP. Within fifteen years, these debt ratios will rise to 200 per cent or more if no measures are taken now.

18 *Does Oil Hinder Democracy?*, Michael L. Ross, World Politics 53 (April 2001), 325–61.

19 Michael L. Ross, World Politics 53 (April 2001), 329.

20 Michael L. Ross, World Politics 53 (April 2001), 327–328.

21 Michael L. Ross, World Politics 53 (April 2001), 356.

22 Michael L. Ross, World Politics 53 (April 2001), 329.

23 Michael L. Ross, World Politics 53 (April 2001), 332–334, Re: Moore's claim footnote 28, Barrington Moore, *Social Origins of Dictatorship*

and Democracy (Boston: Beacon Press, 1966). Ross also refers to a third component that "might be called a group formation effect. It implies that when oil revenues provide a government with enough money, the government will use its largesse to prevent the formation of social groups that are independent from the state and hence that may be inclined to demand political rights. One version of this argument is rooted in Moore's claim that the formation of an independent bourgeoisie helped bring about democracy in England and France." It is indeed typical of developing-world rentier countries that they frequently have large state sectors that absorb the greater part of the middle classes.

24   *The Funk & Wagnalls Standard Desk Dictionary.*

25   *The Decline and Fall of the Ottoman Empire,* by Alan Palmer, paperback edition 1993, by John Murray (Publishers) Ltd., page 162.

26   *The New Encyclopedia Britannica*, page 138, Volume 18, Fifteenth Edition, 1997.

27   *The New Encyclopedia Britannica*, page 940, Volume 2, Fifteenth Edition, 1997.

28   Cornerstone of US foreign policy enunciated by James Monroe, fifth president of the United States (1817–1825), declaring that, among other things, the western hemisphere was closed to further colonization by Old World powers beyond existing possessions and dependencies, and that any attempt by a European power to oppress or control any nation in the western hemisphere would be viewed as a hostile act against the United States. Source: *The New Encyclopedia Britannica*, page 269, Volume 8, Fifteenth Edition, 1997.

29   Apparent exceptions, such as the democracy in dependencies of Great Britain, Netherlands, and France do not diminish the truth-value of this statement when one considers that these dependencies enjoy the right of auto-determination, which is one of the preconditions for sovereignty.

30   This is not speculation as proven by the Nessim Gaon Case. Compagnie Noga d'Importation et d'Exportation SA, a Swiss company owned by a colourful entrepreneur, Nessim Gaon, had trade receivables outstanding in the amount of USD 1.5 billion against the Russian state, on which the latter defaulted. In the course of attempts to collect by attachment, Noga has tried to seize Central Bank assets, embassy property, Russian art treasures, President Putin's personal aircraft, the

Russian tall ships Sedov, Mir, and Kruzenshtern, one Su-30 fighter and one MiG-AT fighter trainer at the Le Bourget air show in France, and even shipments of nuclear warheads to the United States for reprocessing. It is worth noting that, in spite of their failure, these efforts caused the Russian state and the various host states tremendous legal and diplomatic problems.

Source: *Reputations and Sovereign Debt*, by Mark L. J. Wright, Department of Economics, Stanford University, First draft: July, 2001, this version: September, 2002, pages 35–37, Appendix A Legal Remedies in Sovereign Defaults: A Case Study.

[31] *How to default: a primer*, Norman Strong. The following article appeared in Left Business Observer #99, February of 2002. According to LBO, Norman Strong is a pen name.

Chapter 9

[1] According to standard curriculum, government borrowing is a policy instrument for funding public investment, thereby fostering economic development. In the form of deficit financing, it can also serve as a policy instrument acting as a countercyclical stabilizer in the event of a recession.

[2] List of sovereign debt crises, Wikipedia, http://en.wikipedia.org/wiki/List_of_sovereign_defaults, copy 20-04-2014.

[3] There is a risk involved with supermajorities. In certain political cultures, supermajority requirements could backfire by energizing favour-trading behaviour by legislators.

[4] It is conceivable that the election committee could be charged with the task of monitoring violations of the constitution by the parliament and implementing measures to dissolve a parliament responsible for such violations.

[5] Recall elections exist as a procedure in countries such as America, Canada, and Switzerland.

[6] An auditor's opinion is a public statement by a certified public accountant about whether the financial statements of a company provide a true and fair view of the financial position of that company in accordance with accepted accounting principles and in compliance with legal requirements for financial statements. In the Netherlands, the purpose of an auditor's opinion is to inform the general public – not

merely the shareholders – about the financial position of audited companies.

7   The instrumental difference of deficit finance through borrowing is that the function of saving is left to the public; whereas, in the case of the surplus fund, it is the government that does the saving.

8   Stripped to its essentials, the story is that, during the 1970s, developing countries and bankers respectively borrowed and lent heavily in anticipation of rising primary commodity prices and revenues. The ostensible purpose of state borrowing was to fuel and accelerate economic development. Conditions for borrowing were especially encouraging as bankers, flush with petrodollars subsequent to the oil shock of 1973, went on the lending spree of the century. The oil shock of 1979 then caused a recession in the rich countries, resulting in a slump of demand for primary commodity imports. At that point, many developing countries, finding themselves short on export revenues and locked into high expenditure patterns, continued borrowing to maintain public spending and consumption levels. Eventually, when it became clear that there was not going to be a quick revival of the commodity trade, the debtor countries and their bankers found themselves facing insolvency and default. Writers on the subject generally admit to the fact that much borrowing was squandered on imprudent investment and consumption subsidies to buy popular acquiescence. Also, a significant portion of amounts borrowed was siphoned off through corruption. This story has been repeated in an endless variety of publications on the subject of debt trouble and, by and large, it is correct.

Chapter 10

1   *Entick v Carrington* [1765] EWHC KB J98.

2   Wikipedia: Apartheid legislation in South Africa, http://en.wikipedia. org/wiki/Apartheid_legislation_in_South_Africa, copy 19-01-2014.

3   *The Free Dictionary,* Farlex, Discretion in Decision Making, http://legal-dictionary.thefreedictionary.com/Discretion+in+Decision+Making, copy 16-08-2015.

4   US Legal, Inc., Discretionary powers, http://administrativelaw.uslegal. com/administrative-agencies/discretionary-powers/, copy 16-08-2015.

5   The exercise of sovereign authority is only one aspect of the relationship between the individual and government. The relationship between

the government and the individual is obviously more complex and variegated than this aspect alone.

[6] *The Funk & Wagnalls Standard Desk Dictionary.*

[7] *The Funk & Wagnalls Standard Desk Dictionary.*

[8] *On War,* Carl von Clausewitz, 1968, Pelican Books, page 101.

[9] *The Proud Tower: A portrait of the world before the war, 1890–1914,* Barbara W. Tuchman, page 65.

[10] This is essentially a fundamental premise of collectivist and totalitarian ideologies such as communism, fascism, and socialism, but it also holds true for populism and economic interventionism.

[11] *Foreign Affairs: Is Pinochet the Model,* Angelo Codevilla, November–December of 1993.

[12] *The Economist,* "Special report, Argentina's collapse: A decline without parallel," 2 March. 2002, pages 28–29.

[13] Wikipedia, Rule of law, http://en.wikipedia.org/wiki/Rule_of_law, copy 25-01-2014.

[14] The ideal of raising the ruler above law and making him or her accountable to nobody is not unique to Europe or the seventeenth century. Many civilizations in earlier times and in other parts of the world had similar ideologies. The uniqueness of the seventeenth-century experience in Europe with the rise of absolutism is how it interacted with the concept of the rule of law.

[15] Wikipedia, Rule of law.

[16] Section 142, Chapter XI, Of the extent of the legislative power, *Two Treatises of Government,* John Locke.

[17] *The World Justice Project: What is the Rule of Law?* http://worldjusticeproject.org/what-rule-law, copy 25-01-2014.

[18] There is a caveat that needs to be made with respect to the assertion that predatory jurisdiction relies excessively on the principle of *ius quia iussum.* Not every law based on the principle of *ius quia iussum* is automatically unjust or a case of predatory jurisdiction. To clarify this point, let us propose that government should abstain from making laws based on the principle of *ius quia iussum.* It should be clear, however, that this is neither practical nor desirable for the reason that a great deal of lawmaking does not involve questions of justice (i.e., of right or wrong). Consider the many laws that advance the common good without necessarily advancing justice. An example of this is a law that imposes right- or left-side driving. To pursue this example: there is no

intrinsic right or wrong in choosing right- over left-side driving or vice versa. In this instance, the purpose of the law is to promote prudent behavior for the sake of the common good, not justice. Laws on weights and measures, taxation, and product standardization, for example, are mainly based on the principle of *ius quia iussum,* and yet they are necessary or desirable for promoting or safeguarding the common good. The application in lawmaking of the principle of *ius quia iussum* must be retained. Of course, that does mean that this principle will also remain to some extent available for incorrect, imprudent, or evil uses.

Chapter 11

1   The US Constitution provides two articles to that effect – namely, the Fifth and Fourteenth Amendments.

2   *Objectivism: The Philosophy of Ayn Rand,* Leonard Peikoff, 1991, Dutton, page 352.

3   *Objectivism: The Philosophy of Ayn Rand,* Leonard Peikoff, 1991, Dutton, page 352.

4   *Man's Rights, The Virtue of Selfishness,* page 94.

5   Police power, http://legal-dictionary.thefreedictionary.com/Police+Power, quote dd. 24-11-2015.

6   *Commonwealth vs Cyrus Alger,* 7 Cush. 53, 61 Mass. 53, March, 1851.

7   When I say *inching away,* I mean that almost literally. In spite of its current lack of enthusiasm for socialist economics, it has not dismantled the gargantuan bureaucracy that grew up over the decades from its past efforts to socialize the economy, much of the economic regulations are still in place, and the state is still predominant in various important economic sectors, for example. Socialism may be dead; its rotting corpse is still lying on top of the Indian economy.

8   "Perils of 'licence raj,'" Friday, 11 July, 1997, *Financial Times Limited,* Performance, 1997.

Chapter 12

1   *Lost Rights: The Destruction of American Liberty,* James Bovard (St. Martin's Press: New York, 1994), p. 333.

2   It should be noted that elective representative democracy is, from a historical perspective, only one form out of various types of democracy.

In our day and age, it is the dominant type – almost, if not entirely to, the exclusion of any other type. Given the topic at hand, it should be clear that an analysis of the concept of democracy as such is beyond the scope of this book.

3   *The Economist,* "A Survey of Russia," 21 July, 2001, page 8.

4   *The Economist,* "A Survey of Russia," 21 July, 2001, pages 9–13.

5   *The Economist,* "The Latinobarometro poll: An alarm call for Latin America's democrats," July 28st 2001, page 49.

6   Power and Prosperity: Outgrowing communist and capitalist dictatorships, Mancur Olson, 2000, Basic Books, page 93–94.

7   *The Economist,* 19 May, 2001, "Middle-class rage: The Philippines' elections," page 64.

8   *The Funk & Wagnalls Standard Desk Dictionary.*

9   *The Funk & Wagnalls Standard Desk Dictionary.*

10   I am aware that this last piece of advice is or will often be countered by the assertion that not all countries are ready for democracy. There is often truth in such counterpoints. It is true, for example, that democracy cannot function when societies are deeply and violently divided on certain issues, such as race, religion, or ethnicity. Also, when politicians and soldiers see seizure of office by force of arms as an acceptable means to power, democracy rarely stands a chance. But this is a different level of problems than those discussed in this book.

Chapter 13

1   In saying that abolition of entry regulation is, by and large, painless, I am not ignoring the degree to which special interests would deem it to be a threat to their interests. It should be noted however that such special interests usually consist of small minorities.

2   I am aware that labour law reform tends to be an extremely contentious issue. Labour unions tend to have disproportionate power and influence in view of the relatively small share that organized labour represents on the whole of the economically active population of most developing nations. The challenge for a reforming administration is to neutralize the unions so as to enable them to implement labour law reform. This is not exactly easy, but it is often quite doable. One could, for example, offer those categories of workers, especially unionized employees, who are actually enjoying employment

protection transitional provisions securing the continuation of their employment protection. Acquiescence and silence of many labour leaders and relevant opposition leaders could be bought by securing significant personal advantages for them. These are but two examples, but I am sure that most politicians (and that should include reformers) are both more knowledgeable and resourceful in this respect than I am as a layperson.

3   *The Prince,* Niccolo Machiavelli, "Chapter XXVI, Exhortation to liberate Italy from the barbarians."

4   *The Prince,* Niccolo Machiavelli, "Chapter VI, New principalities acquired by one's own arms and prowess."

5   The alternative is to opt for extralegality.

6   Quote found in an obituary of Arthur Seldon in *The Economist,* 22 October, 2005, page 90.

Afterword

1   Curaçao is one of six Dutch dependencies in the Caribbean. It is the largest island of the Dutch Leeward Antilles and of the Dutch dependencies. Its area is 171 square miles (444 square kilometres) and it is situated some 37 miles (60 kilometres) north of the coast of Venezuela.

2   The business plans frequently involved the importation of foreign equipment or products. These could only be bought from abroad if one could procure enough foreign money. For this, one needed permission to buy foreign currencies.

3   *The Other Path: The invisible revolution in the third world,* Hernando de Soto, 1989, I.B. Tauris & Co Ltd, London. Hernando de Soto (2 June, 1941) is a Peruvian economist known for his work on the informal economy and championing the importance of property rights. He is the president of Peru's Institute for Liberty and Democracy (ILD), located in Lima. In *The Other Path,* de Soto outlines the consequences of excessive regulation and lack of a strong rule of law. In three distinct industries (housing, trade, and transportation) de Soto shows how productivity and wealth generation are hampered by poor laws and law enforcement. This book is essential for anyone interested in the microeconomics of development.

4   Aruba, Bonaire, Curaçao, Sint Maarten, Saba, Sint Eustatius, Suriname, and the Netherlands. With the exception of Sint Eustatius, I have lived, worked, or at least visited all these places. Most of the people in my life come from these places, and that includes Sint Eustatius and quite a few islanders from the West Indies.

Appendix: Hong Kong

1   *The World Factbook*, Central Intelligence Agency, Hong Kong, page last updated, July 28, 2016.

2   *The World Factbook*, Central Intelligence Agency, Country Comparison, GDP Per Capita (PPP), data retrieved, 15 August 2016.

3   The share of budgeted social welfare spending 2014/2015 (18.5 per cent) of taxes and other revenues (20.7 per cent of GDP). Source of data regarding social welfare: *The 2014–2015 Budget, Speech by the Financial Secretary, the Hon John C Tsang moving the Second Reading of the Appropriation Bill 2014*, Wednesday, 26 February 2014. Source of data regarding taxes and other revenues: *The World Factbook*, Central Intelligence Agency, Hong Kong, 2016.

4   OECD.Stat export, Dataset: Social Expenditure – Aggregated data.

5   *The World Factbook*, Central Intelligence Agency, Hong Kong, 2016.

6   *The World Factbook*, Central Intelligence Agency, Denmark, page last updated, July 29, 2016.

7   OECD.Stat export, Dataset: Social Expenditure - Aggregated data.

8   *Hoover Digest 1998,* No. 3, "The Hong Kong Experiment," Milton Friedman.

9   The details on Hong Kong's monetary policy in this chapter, is derived from the Hong Kong Monetary Authority's website: http://www.hkma.gov.hk/eng/key-functions/monetary-stability/linked-exchange-rate-system.shtml, last revision date: 26 August 2011.

10   In Hong Kong, the monetary base consists of one, the Certificate of Indebtedness (which backs the banknotes issued by the three note-issuing banks and coins in circulation exactly); two, the balances of the clearing accounts of banks kept with the HKMA (known as the Aggregate Balance); and three, the Exchange Fund Bills and Notes, which are issued by the HKMA on behalf of the government. Source of information: http://www.hkma.gov.hk/eng/key-functions/

monetary-stability/linked-exchange-rate-system.shtml, last revision date: 26 August 2011.

[11] This means that, if the originator of the reserve currency mismanages its monetary policy, the currency board system will partake in the consequences of such maladministration, including inflation, deflation, or high interest rates. In fact, Hong Kong has, at various times, suffered such blows, including the sudden and dramatic devaluations of the pound sterling in 1949 and 1967, the flotation in 1972 of the same currency, and the weakening of the US dollar during 1974 – all of which were disruptive to Hong Kong's financial system. Source of information: http://www.info.gov.hk/hkma/.

[12] *Annual Report 2015*, Hong Kong Monetary Authority.

[13] *Annual Report 2015*, Hong Kong Monetary Authority.

[14] Three note-issuing banks now issue currency notes in Hong Kong: The Hongkong and Shanghai Banking Corporation Ltd, the Standard Chartered Bank and the Bank of China. All Hong Kong banknotes issued are fully backed by US dollar reserves held in the Exchange Fund.

[15] *The 2014-2015 Budget* (Hong Kong Government).

[16] Hong Kong Government Budget 1999–2015, Trading Economics, New York, www.tradingeconomics.com, search date, 21 August 2016.

[17] Netherlands Government Budget 1999–2016, Trading Economics, New York, www.tradingeconomics.com, search date, 21 August 2016.

[18] *The 2000-2001 Budget*, Scaling New Heights, Speech by the Financial Secretary, moving the Second Reading of the Appropriation Bill 2000, Wednesday, 8 March 2000.

[19] Cited from Speech by the HKSAR Chief Executive, Mr Tung Chee Hwa, at the Hong Kong Trade Development Council luncheon in Frankfurt, Germany Wednesday, March 11, 1998.

[20] Accrual-based Consolidated Financial Statements for the year ended 31 March 2015, page 39.

[21] *Hoover Digest 1998*, No. 3, "The Hong Kong Experiment," Milton Friedman.

[22] Calculation: USD 56,700 GDP (PPP) per capita (2005 est.) times 50 per cent divided by 80 per cent subject to the assumptions that the United States produces its per capita income with 50 per cent of its resources and Hong Kong with 80 per cent of its resources, Hong

Kong has a per capita income of USD 56,700, and linear extrapolation is possible.

23 *The World Factbook*, Central Intelligence Agency, Country Comparison, GDP Per Capita (PPP), 2016.

24 Spain Unemployment Rate 1976-2016 and Hong Kong Unemployment Rate 1981-2016, Trading Economics, New York, www.tradingeconomics.com, search date, 21 August 2016.

25 Hong Kong Legislative Council, Official Report of Proceedings, Meetings of 24th and 25th March 1966, Report of the Select Committee on the Estimates for 1966-67, pages 215–216.

26 *Statistics: A Vehicle for Collectivist Mischief,* John T. Wenders, The Independent Institute, Posted: Monday 1 June, 1998. http://www.independent.org/newsroom/article.asp?id=186.